Anxiety in Preschool Children

Anxiety in Preschool Children provides a comprehensive, integrated, and scientifically current resource for both clinicians and researchers who work with or encounter anxiety in preschool-aged children. With a focus on organizing and consolidating the most current research, this informative new volume offers an assortment of practical interventions and evidence-based strategies for assessment, treatment, and prevention that are tailored to preschool-aged children. This groundbreaking volume will prove to be an invaluable resource for anyone working with this unique patient population, from parents to practitioners.

Brian Fisak is an Associate Professor at the University of Central Florida and a licensed psychologist. His primary research and clinical interests are in the areas of anxiety disorders, prevention, and evidence-based interventions. He has an active research program in these areas and is the author of over 25 peer-reviewed publications.

Paula Barrett is internationally recognized as a prominent scholar and groundbreaking researcher in the field of child psychology. Paula has a distinguished international reputation as a keynote presenter, and has been published widely in the area of prevention and treatment of anxiety and depression, and the promotion of resilience through the evidence-based FRIENDS programs.

Anxiety in Preschool Children

Assessment, Treatment, and Prevention

Edited by
Brian Fisak and Paula Barrett

Routledge
Taylor & Francis Group

NEW YORK AND LONDON

First published 2019
by Routledge
52 Vanderbilt Avenue, New York, NY 10017

and by Routledge
2 Park Square, Milton Park, Abingdon, Oxon OX14 4RN

Routledge is an imprint of the Taylor & Francis Group, an informa business

© 2019 Taylor & Francis

Library of Congress Cataloging-in-Publication Data
A catalog record for this title has been requested

ISBN: 9780415789691 (hbk)
ISBN: 9780415789707 (pbk)
ISBN: 9781315213828 (ebk)

Typeset in Goudy
by Taylor & Francis Books

Contents

Illustrations

Author affiliations

Chelsey S. Barrios, M.S.
Department of Psychology
University of Maryland, College Park

Paula Barrett, Ph.D.
FRIENDS Resilience, Pty. Ltd., and
School of Arts and Humanities
Edith Cowan University

R. Lindsey Bergman, Ph.D.
Department of Psychiatry and Biobehavioral Sciences
University of California, Los Angeles

Shana Celi, M.Sc.
Department of Psychosomatics and Psychiatry,
University Children's Hospital Zurich, Switzerland

Lea R. Dougherty, Ph.D.
Department of Psychology
University of Maryland, College Park

Brian Fisak, Ph.D.
Department of Psychology
University of Central Florida

Natalie Games, B.Sc (Hons)., D. Psych (clinical)
Alliance Counselling, Singapore

Araceli Gonzalez, Ph.D.
Department of Psychology
California State University, Long Beach

Sarah A. O. Gray, Ph.D.
Department of Psychology
Tulane University

Dr. Julia Gallegos
Professor, School of Psychology
University of Monterrey, México

Ann-Christin Haag, M.Sc.
Department of Psychosomatics and Psychiatry
University Children's Hospital Zurich, Switzerland

Marina Iniesta-Sepúlveda, Ph.D.
Department of Psychology and Education
Catholic University of Murcia, Spain

Markus A. Landolt, Ph.D.
Department of Psychosomatics and Psychiatry
University Children's Hospital Zurich, Switzerland
Division of Child and Adolescent Health Psychology
Department of Psychology, University of Zurich, Switzerland

Katherine A. Leppert, M.S.
Department of Psychology
University of Maryland, College Park

Anuja Mehta, M.D.
Department of Clinical Sciences
University of Central Florida College of Medicine

Nicholas D. Mian, Ph.D.
Department of Life Sciences
University of New Hampshire

Peter Muris, Ph.D.
Department of Clinical Psychological Science
Faculty of Psychology and Neuroscience
Maastricht University, the Netherlands

Lauren Persad, B.S.
Department of Psychology
University of Central Florida

Lauren Phillips, B.Sc Psych.
FRIENDS Resilience, Pty. Ltd., and
School of Arts and Humanities
Edith Cowan University

Jasmine Reyes, M.A.
Department of Psychology
University of Central Florida

Jennifer A. Scheurich, M.S.
Department of Psychology
University of Central Florida

Susan H. Spence, Ph.D.
Australian Institute for Suicide Research and Prevention, and
School of Applied Psychology,
Griffith University, Brisbane, Australia

Paul Stallard, Ph.D.
Department for Health
University of Bath, U.K.

Eric A. Storch, Ph.D.
Menninger Department of Psychiatry & Behavioral Sciences
Baylor College of Medicine, Texas

Introduction

A number of advances in the area of preschool anxiety have led to increased interest in this topic among researchers and clinicians. These developments include the recognition, based on large-scale epidemiological studies, that anxiety and related difficulties are surprisingly common in preschool-aged children – possibly the most common category of psychiatric disorders in this age group. Related to this point, there is research to suggest that these difficulties often persist and worsen over time. Further, a number of exciting advancements have occurred in regards to the treatment and prevention of anxiety in preschool-aged, including development and empirical evaluation of protocols specifically tailored to this age group. In addition, advances have occurred in regards to the assessment and accurate identification of anxiety in preschool-aged children, including reliable and valid parent-report measures and observational measures. It is also noteworthy that advancements have occurred in the area of posttraumatic stress disorder (PTSD) in preschool children. In particular, specific criteria for posttraumatic stress disorder (PTSD) in preschool-aged children have been recognized and added to the DSM-5, and the recognition of preschool anxiety has led to the development of evidence-based treatment protocols for this population.

Moreover, practitioners and researchers need to empower and include parents and teachers in treatment protocols, interventions in schools, and group work with preschool-aged children. At this early developmental stage children heavily rely on their parents and teachers, for learning positive coping skills. Empowering parents and teachers, by learning the same skills we are teaching the children, provides a systemic "language" of positive, coping strategies, which can be used when challenging situations occur. The modeling of positive skills from caregivers and educators is paramount for this early age group.

In response to the recognition that preschool-anxiety is a growing area of interest, we set out to create the first known book to focus exclusively on anxiety in preschool-aged children. Our vision for this edited book was to organize, integrate, and consolidate the current research in the area of preschool anxiety, with a particular focus on evidence-based strategies for assessment, treatment, and prevention. Further, we hoped to develop a book that may facilitate new research directions by bridging gaps in the literature and highlighting potential directions for future investigation. Consistent with this goal, coauthorship and collaboration were emphasized, and the end result was a book with contributing authors living in six different countries across three continents.

We anticipate that this book will also be of interest to researchers, as the book is written with a strong scientific and theoretical foundation. At the same time, we sought to develop chapters that are practical and accessible to clinicians, educators, and policy makers. More specifically, we believe that practitioners will appreciate evidence-based treatment and assessment recommendations provided in the book, along with efforts to bridge science and practice and the resource lists. Finally, we anticipate that many sections of the book may be of interest to parents of anxious preschool-aged children who may have concerns about emerging signs of anxiety in their children

Overall, we believe that we have successfully developed the first, comprehensive resource, focused exclusively on anxiety in preschool-aged children, and we hope you enjoy reading this book as much as we enjoyed developing it.

Brian Fisak & Paula Barrett

1 Epidemiology and Nosology of Preschool Anxiety Disorders

Chelsey S. Barrios, Katherine A. Leppert, and Lea R. Dougherty

Overview

Anxiety disorders are highly prevalent, associated with negative clinical and functional outcomes across the lifespan, including lower educational attainment, employment, and physical health problems, and incur substantial societal and economic burden (Kessler, Aguilar-Gaxiola, et al., 2009a; Kessler, Ruscio, Shear & Wittchen, 2009; Lépine, 2002). Most anxiety disorders emerge in childhood, and childhood anxiety disorders predict later psychopathology and functional impairment in adulthood (Copeland, Angold, Shanahan, & Costello, 2014; Copeland, Shanahan, Costello, & Angold, 2009; Copeland, Wolke, Shanahan, & Costello, 2015). Increased scientific and clinical attention has focused on identifying anxiety disorders during early childhood (Angold & Egger, 2007; Insel & Fenton, 2005). The preschool period represents an ideal time to identify child psychopathology and intervene due to greater behavioral and neurodevelopmental plasticity (Belsky & de Haan, 2011). Recent research has documented that preschool anxiety disorders occur at similar rates to those observed in school-age children, demonstrate stability over time, and are associated with significant impairment, warranting clinical attention (Bufferd, Dougherty, Carlson, & Klein, 2011; Bufferd, Dougherty, Carlson, Rose, & Klein, 2012; Copeland et al., 2014, 2015; Lavigne et al., 1998, 2001; Wichstrøm et al., 2012). Given the public health significance of anxiety disorders across the lifespan, it is essential to understand the early emergence of anxiety disorders in preschool-age children. This chapter will review the nosology and epidemiology of preschool anxiety disorders.

Phenomenology of Anxiety Disorders

Anxiety disorders are characterized by an over-activation of the adaptive fear response, negative affect and hyperarousal, and perceptions of potential threat, uncontrollability, and unpredictability (Barlow, 2002; Barlow, Allen, & Choate, 2004; Bender, Reinholdt-Dunne, Esbjorn, & Pons, 2012). It has been proposed that anxiety disorders include primary features which underlie all anxiety disorders, and secondary features which distinguish specific anxiety disorders (van der Heiden et al., 2010; Watson 1999, 2005; Weems, 2008). Primary features include activation of physiological (e.g., sympathetic nervous system activation), cognitive (e.g., cognitive distortions, difficulty concentrating, rumination), and behavioral (e.g., avoidance/withdrawal, freezing behaviors) response systems (Barlow, 2002).

Secondary features differentiate the specific anxiety disorders proposed in the *Diagnostic and Statistical Manual of Mental Disorders, Fifth Edition* (*DSM-5*; American Psychiatric Association, 2013). The seven anxiety disorders in the *DSM-5* consist of separation anxiety disorder, social anxiety disorder, generalized anxiety disorder (GAD), specific phobia, selective mutism, panic disorder, and agoraphobia. Several changes were implemented in *DSM-5* that impacted the classification of DSM anxiety disorders: obsessive-compulsive disorder (OCD) and post-traumatic stress disorder (PTSD) were removed from the anxiety disorders section, and separation anxiety and selective mutism were reclassified as anxiety disorders rather than "Disorders Usually First Diagnosed in Infancy, Childhood, or Adolescence." In addition, separation anxiety is no longer limited to childhood, and agoraphobia and panic disorder are now recognized as separate anxiety disorders.

According to the *DSM-5* (American Psychiatric Association, 2013), *separation anxiety disorder* is characterized by distress upon separation or anticipated separation from a caregiver. *Social anxiety disorder* is defined by fears of social evaluation. Individuals with GAD experience various recurrent, future-focused worries, which are difficult to control. *Specific phobia* reflects a developmentally inappropriate fear of specific objects or situations, such as spiders or heights. The defining feature of *selective mutism* is the refusal to speak in certain settings, with certain individuals, and/or under certain conditions. *Panic disorder* is characterized by panic attacks occurring seemingly "out of the blue," as well as fear of developing future panic attacks. *Agoraphobia* is characterized by fear and avoidance of situations or places where an individual feels trapped and unable to escape. Although OCD and PTSD were removed from the anxiety disorders section in the *DSM-5* and added to the "Obsessive-Compulsive and Related Disorders" and "Trauma- and Stressor-Related Disorders" sections, respectively, they are considered anxiety-related disorders and will be discussed in this chapter. OCD is characterized by uncontrollable, recurrent thoughts and unnecessarily repeated behaviors, and *PTSD* is a mental health condition triggered by a terrifying or traumatic event that is associated with symptoms such as flashbacks, nightmares, and severe anxiety.

Despite the classification of anxiety disorders according to their secondary features in the *DSM-5*, a consensus on the factor structure of preschool anxiety disorders has yet to be reached. Some findings support that anxiety symptoms in early childhood conform to the current nosology in a manner similar to those in older children (Angold & Egger, 2004; Edwards, Rapee, Kennedy, & Spence, 2010b; Egger & Angold, 2004; Mian, Godoy, Briggs-Gowan, & Carter, 2012; Sterba, Egger, & Angold, 2007), whereas other findings identify variations in the factor structure of preschool anxiety disorders that do not map directly onto the DSM disorders (e.g., Benga, Tincas, & Visu-Petra, 2010; Eley et al., 2003). Some researchers have also suggested that primary features of anxiety may first manifest very early in development as an underlying vulnerability factor, while secondary features become more prominent across development and coincide with normative changes in fear expression across developmental periods, such as fear of separation in early childhood, fear of death in middle childhood, and fear of social evaluation in adolescence (Costello et al., 2005; Weems & Costa, 2005). Furthermore, research has demonstrated high comorbidity (Bufferd et al., 2012; Costello, Egger, & Angold, 2005) and similar treatment outcomes (Hirshfeld-Becker et al., 2010) among the various anxiety disorders in preschool-age children, further questioning the validity and clinical utility of these secondary features. Taken together, these findings demonstrate that the factor structure and classification of preschool anxiety warrants further investigation, and requires consideration of the developmental context.

Assessment of Preschool Anxiety

At the foundation of research in epidemiology and nosology is the quality of our assessment measures; thus, it is critical to evaluate the reliability and validity of our assessment tools for early childhood anxiety disorders in order to provide a context for our review on the current state of epidemiological and nosological research. For a comprehensive review of the assessment of preschool anxiety, we refer the reader to Philips, Games, Barrett, & Fisak (Chapter 3, this volume) and Spence (Chapter 4, this volume). The assessment of psychiatric disorders in preschool-age children has dramatically improved over the last decade (Bufferd, Dyson, et al., 2016). Historically, preschool anxiety disorders were primarily assessed using parent- and teacher-report questionnaires, such as the Preschool Anxiety Scale (Edwards, Rapee, Kennedy, & Spence, 2010b) and the Child Behavior Checklist (CBCL; Achenbach & Rescorla, 2001) (for a complete list, see Silverman & Ollendick, 2008). Informant report questionnaires are most commonly used to assess children's symptom severity and treatment response (e.g., Barrett, Fisak, & Cooper, 2015; Donovan & March, 2014; Kennedy, Rapee, & Edwards, 2009). Informant report measures of preschool anxiety symptoms demonstrate adequate internal consistency, test-retest reliability, and construct validity (Achenbach & Rescorla, 2001; Edwards et al., 2010b; Goodman, 1997; Sprafkin, Volpe, Gadow, Nolan, & Kelly, 2002). In addition, parent and co-parent reports show adequate cross-informant agreement (Achenbach & Rescorla, 2001), though cross-informant corre-lation between parent- and teacher-report of anxiety symptoms is low (Achenbach & Rescorla, 2001). This may reflect differences in behaviors across settings (e.g., Cai, Kaiser, & Hancock, 2004; for a review, see Dirks, De Los Reyes, Briggs-Gowan, Cella, & Wakschlag, 2012) and underscores the importance of assessing clinically relevant anxiety symp-toms in multiple settings, particularly given that teachers have a unique perspective on how the child's symptoms compare to those of his or her peers in a school setting. Despite the clinical utility of questionnaires for preschool anxiety symptoms, they have key diagnostic limitations: they provide limited information about the onset, frequency, intensity, and duration of each behavior, which is necessary to make a diagnosis, and they depend entirely on the informant's (parent or teacher) observations and interpretations of the child's behavior as either normative or abnormal (Bufferd, Dyson, et al., 2016; Campbell, 1995; DelCarmen-Wiggins & Carter, 2004; Wakschlag & Danis, 2009).

More recently, structured and semi-structured diagnostic interviews with parents have been developed for preschool-age children. Clinical interviews assess the onset, duration, intensity, and frequency of beha-viors. Semi-structured interviews also allow the interviewer to probe with additional questions to verify that the symptoms reported by the parent meet the diagnostic guidelines. Interviews developed specifically to assess psychopathology in preschoolers include the Preschool Age Psychiatric Assessment (PAPA: Egger, Ascher, & Angold, 1999), Diagnostic Infant and Preschool Assessment (DIPA; Scheeringa & Haslett, 2010), and Diagnostic Interview of Children and Adolescents for Parents of Preschool and Young Children (DICA-PPY; Ezpeleta, de la Osa, Granero, Domenech, & Reich, 2011) (for a full list, see Spence, Chapter 4, this volume; Silverman & Ollendick, 2008; Philips, Games, Barrett, & Fisak, Chapter 3, this volume). Although not originally designed for use with preschool-age children, other interviews, such as the Anxiety Disorders Interview Schedule (ADIS; Silverman, Saavedra, & Pina, 2001) and the Kiddie Schedule for Affective Disorders and Schizophrenia (K-SADS; Kaufman et al., 1997), have been used to assess preschool psychopathol-ogy, including anxiety disorders (e.g., Birmaher et al., 2009; Kennedy et al., 2009). The most frequently employed interviews for diagnosing preschool anxiety disorders are the ADIS (e.g., Donovan & March, 2014; Rapee, Kennedy, Ingram, Edwards, & Sweeney, 2005), the K-SADS (e.g., Hirsh-feld-Becker et al., 2008, 2010) and the PAPA (e.g., Bufferd et al., 2011, 2012; Egger, Erkanli, et al., 2006; Egger & Angold, 2006; Mian et al., 2015). Previous studies have also examined the recurrence of preschool anxiety disorders using the PAPA (Bufferd, Dougherty, et al., 2016) and established sensitivity to treatment response using the ADIS (e.g., Barrett, Fisak, & Cooper, 2015; Donovan & March, 2014; Fox et al., 2012; Kennedy et al., 2009; Pincus et al., 2008; Rapee et al., 2005), the K-SADS (Hirshfeld-Becker et al., 2010), the PAPA (Chronis-Tuscano et al., 2015), and the Diagnostic Interview Schedule for Children – Parent Scale – Young Child Version (DISC-YC; Lavigne, LeBailly, Hopkins, Gouze, & Binns, 2009).

Preschool anxiety diagnoses and symptoms assessed via clinical interviews evidence fair to excellent inter-rater reliability (ICCs = .80–1.00 and Kappas = .37–1.00; Bufferd et al., 2011, 2012; Kennedy et al., 2009; Mian et al., 2015; Rapee et al., 2005) and acceptable test-retest reliability over an 11-day follow up (Kappas = .36–.60; Egger, Erkanli, et al., 2006). In addition, multiple studies have demonstrated convergent validity of the PAPA (Bufferd, Dougherty et al., 2016; Dougherty et al., 2013; Dyson, Klein, Olino, Dougherty, & Durbin, 2011), the DICA-PPYC (Ezpeleta et al., 2011), and the DIPA (Scheeringa & Haslett, 2010) by highlighting their associations with laboratory observations and informant report questionnaires of child anxiety symptoms. However, clinical interviews are not without limitations. Notably, no large study to date has examined how various interviews compare to one another in the assessment of preschool anxiety disorders in the same sample. A preliminary study interviewed 14 parents of preschool-age children with both the KSADS and the PAPA, and the interviews were generally comparable; however, of the 14 children, only one child was diagnosed with an anxiety disorder (social phobia) on the KSADS, but this child had no social anxiety symptoms on the PAPA (Birmaher et al., 2009). Thus, information pertaining to the comparability of these clinical interviews is sorely needed. Furthermore, many anxiety behaviors are relatively common during early childhood (e.g., social fear, separation anxiety). However, none of these clinical interviews have empirically-derived guidelines as to what is normative vs. nonnormative in this age range; thus, whether these interviews are capturing clinically significant diagnoses of anxiety or a broader phenotype is unknown and requires further investigation (discussed below in *Challenges in the Assessment of Preschool Anxiety* section).

Given the importance of using a multi-method, multi-informant assessment approach, clinical observations may also aid in the assessment of preschool anxiety. Previous work has demonstrated the clinical utility of standardized observational assessments for preschool disruptive behavior disorders (Wakschlag et al., 2008) and autism spectrum disorders (Lord et al., 2000). Recent work has extended observational assessments to preschool anxiety disorders with the Anxiety Dimensional Observation Scale (ANX-DOS); a standardized observational measurement of behaviors such as fear arousal, physical avoidance, and startle response (Mian et al., 2015). The preliminary data on the ANX-DOS demonstrated good inter-rater reliability and internal consistency, and modest, but significant, associations with parent-reported anxiety symptoms (Briggs-Gowan et al., 2015; Mian et al., 2015). It will be important for future work to determine whether observational assessments of preschool anxiety contribute unique information, over and above informant reports, that will increase diagnostic accuracy and benefit treatment planning. In addition, limited work has investigated the reliability and validity of preschoolers' self-reports of their anxiety given that young children's ability to verbalize their thoughts, feelings, and behaviors is nascent. However, preliminary findings offer promising results. For example, Luby and colleagues (2007) demonstrated that preschoolers' self-reported anxiety symptoms on the Berkeley Puppet Interview (Ablow & Measelle, 1993), a developmentally-appropriate clinical interview with preschool-age children, were associated with parent-reported internalizing symptoms. Further research into the reliability, validity, and clinical utility of observational measures and preschoolers' self-reports of anxiety is warranted.

In summary, the assessment of preschool anxiety disorders has grown significantly over the past several decades, and emerging empirical data supports the reliability and validity of these instruments. However, much of the data is limited to research by a few groups or focuses on only a few interviews (e.g., the PAPA, ADIS, and K-SADS). In addition, future research should continue to improve developmentally sensitive measures to obtain the most accurate assessment possible, including parent-report, teacher-report, preschooler self-report, and possibly behavioral observations. Next, we review the rates, comorbidity, and stability of preschool anxiety disorders in light of these limitations.

Rates of Preschool Anxiety Disorders

Multiple epidemiological studies have been conducted to estimate rates of anxiety disorders across this developmental period, although studies have varied in the number of anxiety disorders assessed and the time frame over which they were assessed (past three months versus lifetime prevalence). Prevalence rates for anxiety disorders in unselected community samples are reported in Table 1.1. Overall, rates of any anxiety disorder in preschool-age children range from 9.4% to 19.2% in community samples in the United States (Bufferd et al., 2011, 2012; Egger, Erkanli, et al., 2006; for a review see Dougherty et al., 2015) and from 1.5% to 6.6% in community samples outside the United States (Ezpeleta et al., 2014; Gudmundsson et al., 2013; Gleason et al., 2011; Wichstrøm et al., 2012); rates also fall within this range for samples selected based on elevated parental psychopathology or clinic-referrals, both within and outside of the United States (Birmaher et al., 2009, Coskun & Kaya, 2016). Specific phobia (0.3–9.1%), separation anxiety (0.3–5.4%), and social anxiety (0.3–4.4%) are the most common disorders in preschool-age children in community samples (Bufferd et al., 2011, 2012; Carter et al., 2010; Egger, Erkanli, et al., 2006; Ezpeleta et al., 2014; Gleason et al., 2011; Lavigne et al., 2009; Wichstrøm et al., 2012). Prevalence rates also generally fall within these ranges for selected community samples (Birmaher et al., 2009; Coskun & Kaya, 2016; Keenan, Shaw, Walsh, Delliquadri, & Giovannelli, 1997). Prevalence rates for

Table 1.1 Prevalence rates of preschool anxiety disorders in unselected community samples assessed using clinical interviews

	Bufferd et al., 2011	Bufferd et al., 2012	Carter et al., 2010	Egger, Erkanli, et al., 2006	Ezpeleta et al., 2013	Gleason et al., 2011	Gudmundsson et al., 2013	Lavigne et al., 2009	Wichstrom et al., 2012
Sample Demographics									
Sample size	541	462	442	314	622	350	131	796	995
Child age in years: mean age (SD) [range]	3.6 (.3) [-]	6.1 (.4) [-]	6.6 (.4) [-]	- (-) [2–5]	3.8 (.33) [-]	3.30 (.08) [-]	5.08 (.15) [4.83–6.17]	4.44 (-) [3.92–5.08]	4.42 (.18) [3.86–5.73]
Sex (% female)	45.7	45.9	5.04	46	50	47.1	47.6	50.9	50.9
Clinical interview used	PAPA	PAPA	DISC-IV	PAPA	DICA-PPC	PAPA	KSADS-PL	DISC-YC	PAPA
Time frame assessed	3 months	3 months	6 months	3 months	Lifetime	3 months	–	3 months	3 months
Informant (% mothers)	parent (98.0)	parent (97.6)	parent (-)	parent (92.7)	parent (-)	parent (100)	parent (-)	parent (-)	parent (84.8)
Anxiety Disorder Prevalence Rates									
Any anxiety disorder (%)	19.6	15.6	–	9.4	6.6	4.5	5.7	–	1.5
Separation anxiety (%)	5.4	4.8	2.2	2.4	2.2	1.3	–	–	0.3
Social phobia (%)	4.4	2.2	0.3	2.1	1.9	0.6	–	–	0.5
Specific phobia (%)	9.1	8.2	9.0	2.3	3.7	0.3	–	–	0.7

Table 1.1 (Cont.)

	Bufferd et al., 2011	Bufferd et al., 2012	Carter et al., 2010	Egger, Erkanli, et al., 2006	Ezpeleta et al., 2013	Gleason et al., 2011	Gudmundsson et al., 2013	Lavigne et al., 2009	Wichstrom et al., 2012
Selective mutism (%)	1.5	0.6	–	0.6	–	0.2	–	–	0.1
GAD (%)	3.9	1.5	0.2	3.8	0.1	2.5	–	0.6	0.0
Agoraphobia (%)	3.5	1.7	0.1	–	–	–	–	–	–
Panic (%)	0.2	0.0	–	–	–	–	–	–	–
OCD (%)	–	–	0.2	–	–	–	–	–	–
PTSD (%)	–	–	0.3	–	0.0	0.2	–	–	–

Note: PAPA = Preschool Age Psychiatric Assessment; DISC-IV = Diagnostic Interview Schedule for Children, Version IV; DICA-PPC = Diagnostic Interview of Children and Adolescents for Parents of Preschool Children; KSADS-PL = Schedule for affective disorders and schizophrenia for school aged children present and lifetime version; DISC-YC = Diagnostic Interview Schedule for Children – Young Child Version: GAD = Generalized Anxiety Disorder; OCD = Obsessive Compulsive Disorder; PTSD = Post-Traumatic Stress Disorder.

GAD (0.0–3.9%), agoraphobia (0.1–3.5%), selective mutism (0.1–1.5%), panic disorder (0.2%), OCD (0.2%), and PTSD (0.0–0.3%) are much lower in this age group (Bufferd et al., 2011, 2012; Carter et al., 2010; Egger, Erkanli, et al., 2006; Ezpeleta et al., 2014; Gleason et al., 2011; Lavigne et al., 2009; Wichstrøm et al., 2012), and rates are similar in selected community samples (Birmaher et al., 2009; Coskun & Kaya, 2016). Consistent with the normative decrease in fear across early childhood, younger preschoolers (ages 3 to 4) appear to demonstrate more anxious symptoms than older children (ages 5 to 6) during early childhood (Wang & Zhao, 2015).

Although higher rates of anxiety disorders are observed in females compared with males in later childhood (Costello, Egger, Copeland, Erkanli, & Angold, 2011), preschool anxiety disorders have largely demonstrated no sex differences across both selected and unselected community samples (Bufferd et al., 2011, 2012; Carter et al., 2010; Ezpeleta et al., 2014; Lavigne et al., 2009; Wichstrøm et al., 2012), with the exception of two studies. First, in a sample of 917 children ages two to five years from the United States, Franz and colleagues (2013) found that female preschoolers were more likely to meet criteria for separation anxiety disorder on the PAPA compared with male preschoolers, but did not find gender differences for social anxiety disorder or GAD. Second, in a German sample of 1,342 children ages four to seven years, Paulus and colleagues (2015) found that female preschoolers had higher rates of social and specific phobia on the DISYPS-II (a German questionnaire based on DSM-IV diagnoses) compared with male preschoolers, but males had higher rates of separation anxiety disorder compared with females. Given that these findings are inconsistent with one another, and given the lack of sex differences found in other studies, sex differences in preschool anxiety disorders require further investigation.

The various measures that are used to assess preschool psychopathology (e.g., structured and semi-structured interviews, questionnaires) may contribute to the differing prevalence rates reported in the literature. For example, higher rates of anxiety disorders have been reported when diagnostic interviews use longer time-frame references (Costello et al., 2011). Moreover, many diagnostic interviews assess the past three months (e.g., PAPA), which may be problematic and underrepresent disorders that require longer duration criteria (e.g., GAD, social anxiety, separation anxiety). Prevalence rates for preschool anxiety disorders also vary depending on the sample (clinical vs. unselected community sample), whether impairment is required for a diagnosis (Carter et al., 2010; Costello et al., 2011; Rijlaarsdam et al., 2015; Wichstrøm et al., 2012), and the number of anxiety disorders assessed in a given study (Dougherty et al., 2015). Finally, as few studies have assessed rates of preschool agoraphobia (Bufferd et al., 2011, 2012; Wichstrøm et al., 2012), panic disorder (Bufferd et al., 2011, 2012), and OCD (Gudmundsson et al., 2013), these estimates should be interpreted with caution.

Comorbidity

Preschool anxiety disorders demonstrate significant comorbidity with other anxiety, mood, and behavioral disorders. For example, in a community sample over-selected for children with anxiety, 23% met criteria for comorbidity between one anxiety disorder and another anxiety disorder (GAD, separation anxiety, or social anxiety), and 7% met criteria for all three disorders (Franz et al., 2013). Preschoolers with separation anxiety have higher rates of specific phobia (OR = 4.2–4.4), GAD (OR = 8.5), and social anxiety (OR = 11.2–14.4), while preschoolers with social anxiety have higher rates of agoraphobia (OR = 13.3) and specific phobia (OR = 8.4–10.4) (Bufferd et al., 2012; Ezpeleta et al., 2014). Among GAD, separation anxiety, and social anxiety, GAD demonstrated the greatest comorbidity with non-anxious disorders (i.e., depression, ADHD, and/or disruptive behavior disorders; 51%), followed by separation anxiety (41%) and social anxiety (32%) (Franz et al., 2013). Preschool anxiety is also associated with higher rates of depression (OR = 6.5–7.1; Bufferd et al., 2011; Dougherty et al., 2013; Wichstrøm et al., 2012), suggesting that the pattern of comorbidity between anxiety and depression observed in adults may be seen as early as the preschool years. Lastly, preschool anxiety demonstrates significant comorbidity with behavioral disorders, similar to the associations observed in older children (Costello et al., 2003). Any preschool anxiety disorder is associated with increased likelihood of comorbid ADHD (OR = 4.5; Wichstrøm et al., 2012), and these associations have also been documented specifically between separation anxiety and ADHD (OR = 2.7), and specific phobia and ADHD (OR = 4.4; Ezpeleta et al., 2014). Furthermore, anxiety disorders demonstrate significant comorbidity with oppositional defiant disorder (ODD) (OR = 2.0–5.6; Bufferd et al., 2011; Dougherty et al., 2013; Wichstrøm et al., 2012) and conduct disorder (OR = 5.8; Wichstrøm et al., 2012).

The high rates of comorbidity observed in preschool anxiety disorders warrant clinical attention, given that increased comorbidity is associated with greater psychosocial impairment during the preschool period (Egger, Erkanli et al., 2006; von Klitzing et al., 2014) and across childhood (Johnco, Salloum, Lewin, McBridge, & Storch, 2015; Farmer, Burns, Phillips, Angold, & Costello, 2003). Preschool comorbid psychiatric conditions may significantly impact later functioning. As the preschool period is characterized by the coordination of behavioral and emotional systems, impairment in one domain may generalize to other domains, thus contributing to comorbidity (Egger & Angold, 2006). Of the approximately 7–27% of preschoolers who meet criteria for any psychiatric disorder, 20.8–

33.8% of these children meet criteria for two or more disorders (Bufferd et al., 2011; Dougherty et al., 2013; Egger, Erkanli, et al., 2006; Wichstrøm et al., 2012). Several studies have found that anxiety disorders show the least amount of comorbidity compared to other psychiatric disorders during the preschool period (e.g., Egger & Angold, 2006; Gudmundsson et al., 2013; Wichstrom et al., 2012), although others have found that anxiety has comparable comorbidity to the other disorders (e.g., Bufferd et al., 2011; Ezpeleta et al., 2013). These inconsistencies may be related to difficulty distinguishing between normative and abnormal anxiety during this preschool period (discussed below). Furthermore, anxiety often precedes other disorders in older children (Bittner et al., 2007), and thus it is possible that anxiety disorders have not been present long enough for preschoolers to develop a second disorder (Egger & Angold, 2006; Wichstrøm et al., 2012).

Stability

Despite limited longitudinal research, the emerging data suggest that preschool anxiety symptoms and related temperamental traits (namely behavioral inhibition, which is characterized by shyness and decreased exploration in unfamiliar contexts and with unfamiliar people; Degnan, Almas, & Fox, 2010) demonstrate stability over time and predict later emotional problems. For example, preschool anxiety symptoms evidence moderate stability across one year (Edwards et al., 2010a), and across early childhood and adolescence from ages five to 17 (Bosquet & Egeland, 2006). In addition, behavioral inhibition at age two predicted social reticence at age four (Rubin, Burgess, & Hastings, 2002), behavioral inhibition at age four predicted behavioral inhibition and anxiety at age six (Hudson, Dodd, Lyneham, & Bovopoulous, 2011), and a high-increasing trajectory of separation anxiety symptoms from age 1.5 to age six predicted separation anxiety at age six (Battaglia et al., 2016). Evidence also supports moderate stability of internalizing symptoms from ages one to four (Briggs-Gowan, Carter, Bosson-Heenan, Guyer, & Horwitz, 2006), and anxious symptoms at ages 2–3 predicted greater internalizing problems at ages 10–11 (Mesman, Bongers, & Koot, 2001).

   Preschool anxiety disorders also demonstrate homotypic (i.e., one anxiety disorder predicts that same anxiety disorder over time) and heterotypic (i.e., one anxiety disorder predicts a different anxiety disorder or other disorder) continuity, similar to that observed in older children (Costello et al., 2003). With respect to homotypic continuity, the presence of any anxiety disorder at age three was associated with a greater likelihood of having an anxiety disorder at age six (OR = 4.01; Bufferd et al., 2012) and at age ten (OR = 1.91; Luby, Gaffrey, Tillman, April, & Belden, 2014). With respect to the specific anxiety disorders, research has documented significant homotypic continuity in specific phobia, separation anxiety, social anxiety, agoraphobia, and selective mutism from preschool- to early school-age (OR = 2.87–60.14; Bufferd et al., 2012). In longitudinal studies of child psychopathology from age three to six, researchers have also found evidence for heterotypic continuity among the various anxiety disorders. For example, social anxiety at age three predicted specific phobia at age six; separation anxiety at age three predicted agoraphobia at age six; agoraphobia at age three predicted specific phobia, social phobia, GAD, and selective mutism at age six; and selective mutism at age three predicted GAD at age six (ORs = 4.42–15.89; Bufferd et al., 2012). Heterotypic continuity was also observed between preschool anxiety and later mood and behavioral disorders. For example, the presence of any anxiety disorder at age three was associated with greater likelihood of depression at age six (Bufferd et al., 2012) and age twelve (Finsaas, Bufferd, Dougherty, Carlson, & Klein, in press).

It should be noted that the majority of studies on the homotypic and heterotypic continuity of preschool anxiety have largely been conducted by one research group, and have used the PAPA to assess preschool psychopathology. Further work is needed to replicate these patterns of continuity. Taken together, these findings highlight that preschool anxiety disorders predict persistent psychopathology across childhood, and underscore the need for early intervention to improve child functioning. Moreover, although anxious symptoms have been examined with the CBCL from preschool to adolescence (Bosquet & Egeland, 2006; Mesman, Bongers, & Koot, 2001), no study has examined the stability of preschool anxiety disorders into adolescence and adulthood, and thus longitudinal studies with longer follow-up periods are necessary to assess enduring patterns of preschool anxiety diagnoses and associated impairment.

Cultural Considerations

It is important to consider the role that culture may play in the manifestation, assessment, and diagnosis of preschool anxiety disorders. Overall, rates of preschool psychopathology are relatively consistent when assessed using a clinical interview in both the United States (Birmaher et al., 2009; Bufferd et al., 2011, 2012; Carter et al., 2010; Egger, Erkanli, et al., 2006; Keenan et al., 1997; Lavigne et al., 2009) and samples in other countries, including Turkey (Coskun & Kaya, 2016), Iceland (Gudmundsson et al., 2013), Romania (Gleason et al., 2011), and Spain (Wichstrøm et al., 2012). Preliminary work has identified differences between anxiety symptoms in Western and non-Western preschool children using parent-report questionnaire measures. For example, preschool children in China exhibited higher levels of anxiety symptoms compared to Western (Dutch, Australian, and American) peers on the Preschool Anxiety Scale (Broeren & Muris, 2008; Spence, Rapee, McDonald, &

Ingram, 2001; Wang & Zhao, 2015) and Child Behavior Checklist 1.5–5 (Liu, Cheng, & Leung, 2011). In addition, South African preschoolers displayed higher levels of anxiety symptoms on the Preschool Anxiety Scale and higher levels of anxiety-proneness on the Behavioral Inhibition Questionnaire compared to Western preschoolers (Dutch, Australian, and American). Cultural factors likely play a role in these differences; for example, Wang and Zhao (2015) posit that higher levels of controlling parents and strict teachers in Asian cultures may contribute to increased frequency of anxiety symptoms. This is consistent with a larger body of work in older youth suggesting that Chinese socialization practices place a greater emphasis on self-control, discipline, and obedience to authority, which may play a role in increased internalizing symptoms such as anxiety (Chen, Rubin, & Li, 1997; Wang & Zhao, 2015). Moreover, from a cultural perspective, anxious symptoms in some cultures may exemplify a natural response to environmental influences and be adaptive to an extent (Liu, Cheng, & Leung, 2011; Wang & Zhao, 2015). Similarly, research in older South African youth has suggested that factors such as living conditions, crime rates, and poor parenting practices may contribute to increased rates of anxiety disorders (Howard et al., 2017; Muris et al., 2006; Muris, Schmidt, Engelbrecht, & Perold, 2002). Further research is needed examining cultural influences on the etiology and nosology of preschool anxiety disorders, particularly with the use of clinical interviews.

Challenges in the Assessment of Preschool Anxiety

Several challenges in the assessment of preschool anxiety are important to highlight. First, distinguishing between "normative" and "pathological" anxiety during the preschool period can be difficult, given that certain fears are considered developmentally appropriate at a given age (Beesdo et al., 2009; Muris, Meesters, Merckelbach, Sermon, & Zwakhalen, 1998; Muris & Field, 2011). For example, it is normal for preschool-age children to experience shyness around strangers, particularly new adults, or to have fears of storms, water, darkness, costumed characters, or specific animals. In school-age youth, fears of death, specific objects, germs/sickness, performances, and peer rejection are also considered typical (Beesdo et al., 2009). However, fears may reflect clinical levels of anxiety when they persist beyond the expected developmental period and/or are associated with clinical impairment. For example, child distress upon separating from his or her caregiver is typical, but may become pathological when it is excessive and persistent across contexts (e.g., bedtime, school drop-off, with babysitters) and/or interferes with the family's ability to meet obligations (e.g., child and parent consistently late for school and work, parents' inability to leave the child with a babysitter). The child and family's functional impairment is crucial to consider when determining whether behaviors are normative or problematic, specifically the child's level of distress across multiple domains, including disruption in family routines and activities, difficulties with peer relationships, and problems at school/daycare.

In order to take a developmentally sensitive measurement approach, researchers and clinicians must examine behaviors along a full spectrum from normal to abnormal (Arend, Lavigne, Rosenbaum, Binns & Kaufer Christoffel, 1996; Carter et al., 2013; Cole, Luby, & Sullivan, 2008; Wakschlag, Briggs-Gowan, et al., 2014), instead of merely rating behaviors as "absent" or "present" (Bufferd, Dyson, et al., 2016). The differentiation between normative fear and pathological anxiety is dependent on the frequency, intensity, duration, pervasiveness, and impairment associated with fears (Muris & Field, 2011). However, differentiation is complicated by vague descriptors used in the *DSM* such as "sometimes," "often," "recurrent," "persistent," and "excessive," which are not operationally defined, particularly for preschoolers' internalizing psychopathology. Therefore, it can be difficult for parents and interviewers to distinguish between whether behaviors occur "sometimes" or "often," and these subjective conclusions could vary significantly based on clinician training or parental experience with other children, cultural background, or parental stress levels and psychopathology. Empirically based norms must be established to ensure that evaluators and parents can accurately assess whether a given behavior is occurring more frequently compared with other children (Bufferd, Dougherty, & Olino, 2017). Notably, no work to date has established these norms for preschool anxiety behaviors, although work has been initiated for preschool disruptive behavior disorders (Wakschlag, Tolan, & Leventhal, 2010; Wakschlag et al., 2012) and depression (Bufferd, Dougherty, & Olino, 2017). Specific, developmentally sensitive definitions will be necessary to provide clear guidelines for clinicians and early interventionists.

Second, it is challenging to differentiate child temperament from psychopathology (Frick, 2004; Lahey, 2004; Tackett, 2006), particularly during the preschool period when changes in language, cognition, emotion, and social behaviors are rapidly occurring (Dougherty et al., 2011). There is a degree of fundamental overlap between the two constructs: children with anxiety disorders typically have increased levels of behavioral inhibition, high negative emotionality, and low positive affect (Anderson & Hope, 2008; Dougherty et al., 2011). In addition, many studies examining temperament-psychopathology associations in early childhood have used parent-report measures that may inflate associations due to shared method variance and overlapping items on both measures (Lemery, Essex, & Smider, 2002; Lengua, West, & Sandler, 1998). Laboratory observations of child temperament can help decrease these methodological confounds, and diagnostic interviews can further minimize overlap by examining the frequency, intensity, duration, and impairment level of each symptom (Dougherty et al., 2011). For example, children with a behaviorally inhibited temperament style are more likely to play alone and have difficulty approaching new peers, but could still be within the "normative" range and never develop social anxiety disorder. These inhibited behaviors may reflect clinical levels of social anxiety when a child evidences persistent social reticence, extreme difficulty creating and maintaining friendships, or excessive focus on internal experience (Bufferd, Dyson, et al., 2016; Degnan et al., 2010; Lonigan, Phillips, Wilson & Allan, 2011).

A third challenge in measuring preschool anxiety is preschoolers' limited cognitive and verbal ability. Cognitive components of anxiety that are present in older children and adults, such as anticipatory apprehension about future events, are less frequent in very young children (Bufferd et al., 2016). Preschoolers are more likely to experience concrete fears (e. g., physical safety) and are less likely to identify and verbalize anxious thoughts or worries (Cartwright-Hatton, Reynolds, & Wilson, 2011; Vasey, Crnic, & Carter, 1994). Given this limited cognitive ability, observer reports (parent and teacher) provide the basis for diagnoses in preschool-age children. However, parents may mistakenly attribute causes of the child's fearful behavior or inaccurately assume the child's cognitions. Furthermore, parent reports can be biased based on the parent's own psychopathology, stress, and personality (e.g., Najman et al., 2000; De Los Reyes et al., 2009; Kassam-Adams et al., 2006). Thus, researchers and clinicians should be careful to base preschool anxiety diagnoses solely on observable behaviors (e.g., distress, avoidance) or explicit child verbalizations of worry and physiological symptoms.

Fourth, high rates of co-occurrence between the anxiety disorders pose another challenge in the assessment of preschool anxiety disorders. Approximately one-fourth of preschool children with anxiety meet criteria for two or more anxiety disorder diagnoses (Dougherty et al., 2013; Franz et al., 2013; Wichstrøm et al., 2012). Although these rates are relatively similar to those observed in adolescents and adults (Brown, Campbell, Lehman, Grisham, & Mancill, 2001; Essau, 2003; Kaufman & Charney, 2000), differentiating among the anxiety disorders during the preschool years may be particularly challenging. An examination of the overlap between social anxiety and selective mutism provides an illustration of this difficulty. Approximately 65% of children with selective mutism also meet criteria for social anxiety disorder, and some researchers have proposed that selective mutism is an extreme manifestation of social anxiety (Kristensen, 2000; Schneier, 2003; see Bögels et al., 2010; Viana et al., 2009 for reviews). Indeed, selective mutism could be viewed as a pattern of social avoidance within social anxiety disorder, similar to the pattern of school avoidance observed in some children with social anxiety (Bögels et al., 2010; Viana et al., 2009). Further complicating the clinical picture, some anxiety symptoms appear to be attributable to one disorder, but additional examination clarifies its classification. For example, excessive distress when leaving one's parent may appear to be separation anxiety, but, when probed, the distress may be limited to when the child enters social contexts, and thus this symptom is better classified as social anxiety. It is therefore important for the interviewer to determine the function of the child's distress or avoidance, if possible. Some findings suggest that there is clinical utility in differentiating between the disorders, given that separate diagnoses provide information about specific patterns of problematic behavior, thus informing a more targeted treatment plan (Bögels et al., 2010). Moreover, different patterns of association are observed between each of the anxiety disorders and a number of factors, including parental psychopathology, child affect, and life stressors (Dougherty, Tolep, et al., 2013). More research is needed to determine how to measure and diagnose anxiety disorders, particularly when we observe overlap between the various anxiety disorders and symptoms.

Finally, there is a paucity of work examining the validity of low frequency disorders in preschoolers, such as agoraphobia, OCD, GAD, and panic disorder. In epidemiological studies, these disorders have primarily been diagnosed with the PAPA (e.g., Bufferd et al., 2011; Wichstrøm et al., 2012). However, it is possible that the PAPA may misdiagnose or overdiagnose these disorders in preschoolers. Similarly, although studies have documented agoraphobia using the PAPA and the DISC (0.1%–3.5%) (Bufferd et al., 2011, 2012; Carter et al., 2010) and panic disorder (0%–0.2%) using the PAPA (Bufferd et al., 2011; 2012) in preschool-aged children, these estimates may be due to methodological shortcomings of the measure used, and these disorders may not be present in early childhood. Panic disorder and agoraphobia typically onset in later adolescence (Beesdo et al., 2009), suggesting that there may be subtle differences between the PAPA algorithm for these diagnoses and the *DSM* criteria. Importantly, behaviors such as avoidance can be attributed to multiple anxiety disorders (e.g., agoraphobia, social, or separation anxiety disorder), which makes it difficult to differentiate and achieve accurate diagnoses. Relatedly, as raised above, parents often state that a child has many worries based on their own interpretation of their child's behavior, rather than the child's actual verbalization of worries. Given that preschoolers cannot reliably self-report on cognitions and likely do not experience the complex cognitions seen in older youth and adults, it is possible that there are high levels of false positives of these disorders. Thus, additional work is needed to determine normative levels of these symptoms and the validity of each of these diagnoses in preschool-age children.

Compared to the low-base rate disorders mentioned above, it is important to highlight that PTSD in preschoolers has received more scientific inquiry. Emerging research on PTSD in preschoolers has supported age-related differences in symptomatology, and modified diagnostic criteria were adopted in *DSM-5* (see Haag, Celi, & Landolt, Chapter 8, this volume). This developmental subtype of PTSD in preschool-age children exemplifies a key step for DSM classification, as it is among the first of its kind (Scheeringa, 2016). The developmental modifications include the following: the requirement of children to show extreme distress at the time of the event has been removed; the threshold for intrusive symptoms has been slightly lowered; and the required number of avoidance behaviors and negative alterations in cognitions/mood has been reduced from three to one. The modified criteria have been examined empirically (Scheeringa, Myers, Putman & Zeanah, 2012; Scheeringa, Zeanah, Drell, & Larrieu, 1995; Scheeringa, Zeanah, Myers, & Putnam, 2003) and are supported by experts in the field (Task Force on Research and Diagnostic Criteria: Infancy and Preschool, 2003). When using the modified criteria, three to eight times more preschoolers received a PTSD diagnosis compared with the DSM-IV criteria (Scheeringa, Zeanah, & Cohen, 2011; Scheeringa et al., 2012). Initial examinations of the modified preschool PTSD criteria have demonstrated adequate criterion, convergent, discriminant, and predictive validity (Scheeringa et al., 2011). A similar developmentally sensitive approach could be applied to the other anxiety disorders to improve diagnosis and treatment in preschoolers.

Summary and Recommendations

In summary, preschool anxiety disorders are diagnosed at rates similar to older children, demonstrate significant comorbidity and stability over time, are associated with substantial impairment, and confer risk for later psychopathology and functional impairment. The current framework for assessing and diagnosing preschool anxiety disorders has improved over the last several decades, and emerging developmentally sensitive assessment tools (e.g., clinical interviews, questionnaires) demonstrate preliminary evidence of reliability and validity. However, the accurate assessment of preschool anxiety disorders is complicated by challenges of this early developmental period, including unclear boundaries differentiating normal from pathological fear, limited cognitive ability, and diagnostic overlap.

Future research should seek to establish developmentally-sensitive, empirically-based norms for preschool anxiety symptoms so that parents and interviewers can better distinguish between normative and pathological fears and behaviors. Further, additional studies should be conducted to identify base rates of anxiety disorders using assessments that are developmentally sensitive and specific to unique components of various anxiety disorders. Furthermore, studies should directly compare rates of anxiety disorders obtained from different clinical interviews within the same sample. This will help elucidate whether all interviews are capturing the same phenomenon, or whether certain interviews reveal broader or narrower phenotypes for anxiety. In addition, further work is needed to better integrate teacher and co-parent data. Preschool and daycare reporters provide unique insight, especially in the assessment of social and separation anxiety and selective mutism (e.g., duration and intensity of distress once child separates from parent, whether or not the child is engaging with peers at school, quality of peer interaction, participation in circle time, ability to ask teacher for assistance); thus, integrating this information into standardized assessments could enhance accurate diagnoses. Finally, additional research is needed to investigate the homotypic and heterotypic continuity of preschool anxiety disorders using multiple diagnostic instruments and over longer follow-up periods, which will better characterize the trajectory of preschool anxiety disorders across childhood, adolescence, and into adulthood.

References

Achenbach, T. M., & Rescorla, L. (2001). *Manual for the ASEBA Preschool Forms & Profiles. An Integrated System of Multi-informant Assessment* (pp. 74–100). Burlington, VT: University of Vermont, Research Center for Children, Youth and Families.

Ablow, J. C., & Measelle, J. R. (1993). The Berkeley puppet interview. University of California, Berkeley, Berkeley, CA.

American Psychiatric Association. (2013). *Diagnostic and statistical manual of mental disorders* (5th ed.). Washington, DC: American Psychiatric Publishing.

Anderson, E. R., & Hope, D. A. (2008). A review of the tripartite model for understanding the link between anxiety and depression in youth. *Clinical Psychology Review, 28*, 275–287. doi:10.1016/j.cpr.2007. 05. 00doi:4

Angold, A., & Egger, H. L. (2007). Preschool psychopathology: Lessons for the lifespan. *Journal of Child Psychology and Psychiatry, 48*, 961–966. doi:10.1111/j.1469-7610.2007.01832.x

Angold, A., & Egger, H. L. (2004). Psychiatric diagnosis in preschool children. In R. DelCarmen-Wiggins & A. Carter (Eds.), *Handbook of infant, toddler, and preschool mental health assessment* (pp. 123–139). New York, NY: Oxford University Press.

Arend, R., Lavigne, J. V., Rosenbaum, D., Binns, H. J., & Kaufer Christoffel, K. (1996). Relation between taxonomic and quantitative diagnostic systems in preschool children: Emphasis on disruptive disorders. *Journal of Clinical Child Psychology, 25*, 388–397. doi:10.1207/s15374424jccp2504_4

Barlow, D. H. (2002). *Anxiety and its disorders: The nature and treatment of anxiety and panic* (2nd ed.). New York: Guilford Press.

Barlow, D. H., Allen, L. B., & Choate, M. L. (2004). Towards a unified treatment for emotional disorders . *Behavior Therapy, 35*, 205–230. doi:10.1016/S0005-7894(04)80036-4

Barrett, P., Fisak, B., & Cooper, M. (2015). The treatment of anxiety in young children: Results of an open trial of the Fun FRIENDS program. *Behavior Change, 32*, 231–242. doi:10.1017/bec.2015.12

Battaglia, M., Touchette, É., Garon-Carrier, G., Dionne, G., Côté, S. M., Vitaro, F., … & Boivin, M. (2016). Distinct trajectories of separation anxiety in the preschool years: Persistence at school entry and early-life associated factors. *Journal of Child Psychology and Psychiatry, 57*, 39–46. doi:10.1111/jcpp.12424

Beesdo, K., Knappe, S., & Pine, D. S. (2009). Anxiety and anxiety disorders in children and adolescents: developmental issues and implications for DSM-V. *Psychiatric Clinics of North America, 32*, 483–524. doi:10.1016/j.psc.2009. 06. 00doi:2

Belsky, J., & de Haan, M. (2011). Annual research review: Parenting and children's brain development: The end of the beginning. *Journal of Child Psychology and Psychiatry, 52*, 409–428. doi:10.1111/j.1469-7610.2010.02281.x

Bender, P. K., Reinholdt-Dunne, M. L., Esbjørn, B. H., & Pons, F. (2012). Emotion dysregulation and anxiety in children and adolescents: Gender differences. *Personality and Individual Differences, 53*, 284–288. doi:10.1016/j.paid.2012. 03. 02doi:7

Benga, O., Ţincaş, I., & Visu-Petra, L. (2010). Investigating the structure of anxiety symptoms among Romanian preschoolers using the Spence Preschool Anxiety Scales. *Cognition, Brain, Behavior, 14*, 159–182.

Birmaher, B., Ehmann, M., Axelson, D. A., Goldstein, B. I., Monk, K., Kalas, C., ... & Guyer, A. (2009). Schedule for Affective Disorders and Schizophrenia for School-age Children (K-SADS-PL) for the assessment of preschool children–a preliminary psychometric study. *Journal of Psychiatric Research, 43*, 680–686. doi:10.1016/j.jpsychires.2008. 10. 00doi:3

Bittner, A., Egger, H. L., Erkanli, A., Costello, J. E., Foley, D. L., & Angold, A. (2007). What do childhood anxiety disorders predict? *Journal of Child Psychology and Psychiatry, 48*, 1174–1183. doi:10.1111/j.1469-7610.2007.01812.x

Bögels, S. M., Alden, L., Beidel, D. C., Clark, L. A., Pine, D. S., Stein, M. B., & Voncken, M. (2010). Social anxiety disorder: Questions and answers for the DSM-V. *Depression and Anxiety, 27*, 168–189. doi:10.1002/da.20670

Bosquet, M., & Egeland, B. (2006). The development and maintenance of anxiety symptoms from infancy through adolescence in a longitudinal sample. *Development and Psychopathology, 18*, 517–550. doi:10.1017/S0954579406060275

Briggs-Gowan, M. J., Carter, A. S., Bosson-Heenan, J., Guyer, A. E., & Horwitz, S. M. (2006). Are infant-toddler social-emotional and behavioral problems transient? *Journal of the American Academy of Child & Adolescent Psychiatry, 45*, 849–858. doi:10.1097/01.chi.0000220849.48650.59

Briggs-Gowan, M. J., Pollak, S. D., Grasso, D., Voss, J., Mian, N. D., Zobel, E., ... & Pine, D. S. (2015). Attention bias and anxiety in young children exposed to family violence. *Journal of Child Psychology and Psychiatry, 56*, 1194–1201. doi:10.1111/jcpp.12397

Broeren, S., & Muris, P. (2008). Psychometric evaluation of two new parent-rating scales for measuring anxiety symptoms in young Dutch children. *Journal of Anxiety Disorders, 22*(6), 949–958. doi:10.1016/j.janxdis.2007. 09. 00doi:8

Brown, T. A., Campbell, L. A., Lehman, C. L., Grisham, J. R., & Mancill, R. B. (2001). Current and lifetime comorbidity of the DSM-IV anxiety and mood disorders in a large clinical sample. *Journal of Abnormal Psychology, 110*, 585–599. doi:10.1037/0021-843X.110. 4. 58doi:5

Bufferd, S. J., Dougherty, L. R., Carlson, G. A., & Klein, D. N. (2011). Parent-reported mental health in preschoolers: Findings using a diagnostic interview. *Comprehensive Psychiatry, 52*, 359–369. doi:10.1016/j.comppsych.2010. 08. 00doi:6

Bufferd, S. J., Dougherty, L. R., Carlson, G. A., Rose, S., & Klein, D. N. (2012). Psychiatric disorders in preschoolers: Continuity from ages 3 to 6. *American Journal of Psychiatry, 169*, 1157–1164. doi:10.1176/appi.ajp.2012.12020268

Bufferd, S. J., Dougherty, L. R., & Olino, T. M. (2017). Mapping the frequency and severity of depressive behaviors in preschool-aged children. *Child Psychiatry & Human Development*, doi:10.1007/s10578-017-0715-2

Bufferd, S. J., Dougherty, L. R., Olino, T. M., Dyson, M. W., Carlson, G. A., & Klein, D. N. (2016). Temperament distinguishes persistent/recurrent from remitting anxiety disorders across early childhood. *Journal of Clinical Child & Adolescent Psychology*, doi:10.1080/15374416.2016.1212362.

Bufferd, S. J., Dyson, M. W., Hernandez, I. ., & Wakschlag, L. S. (2016). Explicating the 'Developmental' in preschool psychopathology. In D. Cicchetti (Eds.), *Developmental Psychopathology*, Third Edition (152–186). Hoboken, NJ: John Wiley & Sons, Inc.

Cai, X., Kaiser, A. P., & Hancock, T. B. (2004). Parent and teacher agreement on child behavior checklist items in a sample of preschoolers from low-income and predominantly African American families. *Journal of Clinical Child and Adolescent Psychology*, 33, 303–312. doi:10.1207/s15374424jccp3302_12

Campbell, S. B. (1995). Behavior problems in preschool children: A review of recent research. *Journal of Child Psychology and Psychiatry*, 36, 113–149. doi:10.1111/j.1469-7610.1995.tb01657.x

Carter, A. S., Gray, S. A., Baillargeon, R. H., & Wakschlag, L. S. (2013). A multidimensional approach to disruptive behaviors: Informing life span research from an early childhood perspective. In *Disruptive behavior disorders* (pp. 103–135). New York, NY: Springer.

Carter, A. S., Wagmiller, R. J., Gray, S. A., McCarthy, K. J., Horwitz, S. M., & Briggs-Gowan, M. J. (2010). Prevalence of DSM-IV disorder in a representative, healthy birth cohort at school entry: Sociodemographic risks and social adaptation. *Journal of the American Academy of Child & Adolescent Psychiatry*, 49, 686–698. doi:10.1037/a0022435

Cartwright-Hatton, S., Reynolds, S., & Wilson, C. (2011). Adult models of anxiety and their application to children and adolescents. In Silverman, W. K., & Field, A. P. (Eds.), *Anxiety disorders in children and adolescents, second edition* (pp. 129–158). New York, NY: Cambridge University Press.

Chen, X., Rubin, K. H., & Li, B. S. (1997). Maternal acceptance and social and school adjustment in Chinese children: A four-year longitudinal study. *Merrill-Palmer Quarterly* (1982-), 663–681.

Chronis-Tuscano, A., Rubin, K. H., O'Brien, K. A., Coplan, R. J., Thomas, S. R., Dougherty, L. R., … & Menzer, M. (2015). Preliminary evaluation of a multimodal early intervention program for behaviorally inhibited preschoolers. *Journal of Consulting and Clinical Psychology*, 83, 534–540. doi:10.1037/a0039043

Cole, P. M., Luby, J., & Sullivan, M. W. (2008). Emotions and the development of childhood depression: Bridging the gap. *Child Development Perspectives*, 2, 141–148. doi:10.1111/j.1750-8606.2008.00056.x

Copeland, W. E., Angold, A., Shanahan, L., & Costello, E. J. (2014). Longitudinal patterns of anxiety from childhood to adulthood: The Great Smoky Mountains study. *Journal of the American Academy of Child & Adolescent Psychiatry*, 53, 21–33. doi:10.1016/j.jaac.2013. 09. 01doi:7

Copeland, W. E., Shanahan, L., Costello, J., & Angold, A. (2009). Childhood and adolescent psychiatric disorders as predictors of young adult disorders. *Archives of General Psychiatry*, 66, 764–772. doi:10.1001/archgenpsychiatry.2009.85

Copeland, W. E., Wolke, D., Shanahan, L., & Costello, E. J. (2015). Adult functional outcomes of common childhood psychiatric problems: A prospective, longitudinal study. *JAMA Psychiatry*, 72, 892–899. doi:10.1001/jamapsychiatry.2015.0730

Coskun, M., & Kaya, I. (2016). Prevalence and patterns of psychiatric disorders in preschool children referred to an outpatient psychiatric clinic. *Anatolian Clinic Journal of Medical Sciences*, 21, 42–47. doi:10.21673/aktbd.76943

Costello, E. J., Egger, H. L., & Angold, A. (2005). The developmental epidemiology of anxiety disorders: Phenomenology, prevalence, and comorbidity. *Child and Adolescent Psychiatric Clinics of North America*, 14, 631–648. doi:10.1016/j.chc.2005. 06. 00doi:3

Costello, E. J., Egger, H. L., Copeland, W., Erkanli, A., & Angold, A. (2011). The developmental epidemiology of anxiety disorders: Phenomenology, prevalence, and comorbidity. In W. K. Silverman & E. P. Field (Eds.), *Anxiety disorders in children and adolescents: Research, assessment and intervention* (pp. 56–75). Cambridge, United Kingdom: Cambridge University Press.

Costello, E. J., Mustillo, S., Erkanli, A., Keeler, G., & Angold, A. (2003). Prevalence and development of psychiatric disorders in childhood and adolescence. *Archives of General Psychiatry*, 60, 837–844. doi:10.1001/archpsyc.60. 8. 83doi:7

De Los Reyes, A., Henry, D., Tolan, P., & Wakschlag, L. S. (2009). Linking informant discrepancies to observed variations in young children's disruptive behavior. *Journal of Abnormal Child Psychology*, 37, 637–652. doi:10.1007/s10802-009-9307-3

Degnan, K., Almas, A., & Fox, N. (2010). Temperament and the environment in the etiology of childhood anxiety. *Journal of Child Psychology and Psychiatry*, 51, 497–517. doi:10.1111/j.1469-7610.2010.02228.x

DelCarmen-Wiggins, R., & Carter, A. S. (2004). *Handbook of infant, toddler, and preschool mental health assessment.* New York, NY: Oxford University Press.

Dirks, M. A., De Los Reyes, A., Briggs-Gowan, M., Cella, D., & Wakschlag, L. S. (2012). Annual Research Review: Embracing not erasing contextual variability in children's behavior – theory and utility in the selection and use of methods and informants in developmental psychopathology. *Journal of Child Psychology and Psychiatry*, 53(5), 558–574. doi:10.1111/j.1469-7610.2012.02537.x

Donovan, C. L., & March, S. (2014). Online CBT for preschool anxiety disorders: A randomised control trial. *Behavior Research and Therapy*, 58, 24–35. doi:10.1016/j.brat.2014. 05. 00doi:1

Dougherty, L. R., Bufferd, S. J., Carlson, G. A., Dyson, M., Olino, T. M., Durbin, C. E., & Klein, D. N. (2011). Preschoolers' observed temperament and psychiatric disorders assessed with a parent diagnostic interview. *Journal of Clinical Child & Adolescent Psychology*, 40, 295–306. doi:10.1080/15374416.2011.546046

Dougherty, L. R., Leppert, K. A., Merwin, S. M., Smith, V. C., Bufferd, S. J., & Kushner, M. R. (2015). Advances and directions in preschool mental health research. *Child Development Perspectives*, 9, 14–19. doi:10.1111/cdep.12099

Dougherty, L. R., Tolep, M. R., Bufferd, S. J., Olino, T. M., Dyson, M., Traditi, J., ... & Klein, D. N. (2013). Preschool anxiety disorders: Comprehensive assessment of clinical, demographic, temperamental, familial, and life stress correlates. *Journal of Clinical Child & Adolescent Psychology*, 42, 577–589. doi:10.1080/15374416.2012.759225

Dyson, M. W., Klein, D. N., Olino, T. M., Dougherty, L. R., & Durbin, C. E. (2011). Social and non-social behavioral inhibition in preschool-age children: Differential associations with parent-reports of temperament and anxiety. *Child Psychiatry & Human Development, 42*(4), 390–405. doi:10.1007/s10578-011-0225-6

Edwards, S. L., Rapee, R. M., & Kennedy, S. (2010a). Prediction of anxiety symptoms in preschool-aged children: examination of maternal and paternal perspectives. *Journal of Child Psychology and Psychiatry, 51*, 313–321. doi:10.1111/j.1469-7610.2009.02160.x

Edwards, S. L., Rapee, R. M., Kennedy, S. J., & Spence, S. H. (2010b). The assessment of anxiety symptoms in preschool-aged children: The revised Preschool Anxiety Scale. *Journal of Clinical Child & Adolescent Psychology, 39*, 400–409. doi:10.1080/15374411003691701

Egger, H. L., & Angold, A. (2004). The Preschool Age Psychiatric Assessment (PAPA): A structured parent interview for diagnosing psychiatric disorders in preschool children. In R. DelCarmen-Wiggins & A. Carter (Eds.), *Handbook of infant, toddler, and preschool mental health assessment* (pp. 223–243). New York, NY: Oxford University Press.

Egger, H. L., & Angold, A. (2006). Common emotional and behavioral disorders in preschool children: Presentation, nosology, and epidemiology. *Journal of Child Psychology and Psychiatry, 47*, 313–337. doi:10.1111/j.1469-7610.2006.01618.x

Egger, H. L., Ascher, B. H., & Angold, A. (1999). *The preschool age psychiatric assessment: Version 1.1.* Durham, NC: Center for Developmental Epidemiology, Department of Psychiatry and Behavioral Sciences, Duke University Medical Center.

Egger, H. L., Erkanli, A., Keeler, G., Potts, E., Walter, B. K., & Angold, A. (2006). Test-retest reliability of the Preschool Age Psychiatric Assessment (PAPA). *Journal of the American Academy of Child & Adolescent Psychiatry, 45*, 538–549. doi:10.1097/01.chi.0000205705.71194.b8

Eley, T. C., Bolton, D., O'Connor, T. G., Perrin, S., Smith, P., & Plomin, R. (2003). A twin study of anxiety-related behaviors in pre-school children. *Journal of Child Psychology and Psychiatry, 44*, 945–960. doi:10.1111/1469-7610.00179

Essau, C. A. (2003). Comorbidity of anxiety disorders in adolescents. *Depression and Anxiety, 18*, 1–6. doi:10.1002/da.10107

Ezpeleta, L., de la Osa, N., & Doménech, J. M. (2014). Prevalence of DSM-IV disorders, comorbidity and impairment in 3-year-old Spanish preschoolers. *Social Psychiatry and Psychiatric Epidemiology, 49*, 145–155. doi:10.1007/s00127-013-0683-1

Ezpeleta, L., de la Osa, N., Granero, R., Domenech, J. M., & Reich, W. (2011). The diagnostic interview of children and adolescents for parents of preschool and young children: psychometric properties in the general population. *Psychiatry Research, 190*, 137–144. doi:10.1016/j.psychres.2011. 04. 03doi:4

Ezpeleta, L., de la Osa, N., Granero, R., Penelo, E., & Domenech, J. M. (2013). Inventory of callous-unemotional traits in a community sample of preschoolers. *Journal of Clinical Child and Adolescent Psychology, 42*, 91–105. doi:10.1080/15374416.2012.734221

Farmer, E. M., Burns, B. J., Phillips, S. D., Angold, A., & Costello, E. J. (2003). Pathways into and through mental health services for children and adolescents. *Psychiatric Services, 54*, 60–66. doi:10.1176/appi.ps.54. 1. 60

Finsaas, M. C., Bufferd, S. J., Dougherty, L. R., Carlson, G. A., & Klein, D. N. (2019). Preschool psychiatric disorders: Homotypic and heterotypic continuity through middle childhood and early adolescence. *Psychological Medicine*.

Fox, J. K., Warner, C. M., Lerner, A. B., Ludwig, K., Ryan, J. L., Colognori, D., ... & Brotman, L. M. (2012). Preventive intervention for anxious preschoolers and their parents: Strengthening early emotional development. *Child Psychiatry & Human Development*, 43, 544–559. doi:10.1007/s10578-012-0283-4.

Franz, L., Angold, A., Copeland, W., Costello, E. J., Towe-Goodman, N., & Egger, H. (2013). Preschool anxiety disorders in pediatric primary care: prevalence and comorbidity. *Journal of the American Academy of Child & Adolescent Psychiatry*, 52, 1294–1303. doi:10.1016/j.jaac.2013. 09. 00doi:8

Frick, P. J. (2004). Special Selection: Temperament and childhood psychopathology. Integrating research on temperament and childhood psychopathology: Its pitfalls and promise. *Journal of Clinical Child and Adolescent Psychology*, 33, 2–7. doi:10.1207/S15374424JCCP3301_1

Gleason, M. M., Zamfirescu, A., Egger, H. L., Nelson, C. A., Fox, N. A., & Zeanah, C. H. (2011). Epidemiology of psychiatric disorders in very young children in a Romanian pediatric setting. *European Child & Adolescent Psychiatry*, 20, 527–535. doi:10.1007/s00787-011-0214-0

Goodman, R. (1997). The Strengths and Difficulties Questionnaire: A research note. *Journal of Child Psychology and Psychiatry*, 38, 581–586. doi:10.1111/j.1469-7610.1997.tb01545.x

Gudmundsson, O. O., Magnusson, P., Saemundsen, E., Lauth, B., Baldursson, G., Skarphedinsson, G., & Fombonne, E. (2013). Psychiatric disorders in an urban sample of preschool children. *Child and Adolescent Mental Health*, 18, 210–217. doi:10.1111/j.1475-3588.2012.00675.x

Hirshfeld-Becker, D. R., Masek, B., Henin, A., Blakely, L. R., Pollock-Wurman, R. A., McQuade, J., ... & Biederman, J. (2010). Cognitive behavioral therapy for 4- to 7-year-old children with anxiety disorders: A randomized clinical trial. *Journal of Consulting and Clinical Psychology*, 78, 498–510. doi:10.1037/a0019055

Hirshfeld-Becker, D. R., Masek, B., Henin, A., Blakely, L. R., Rettew, D. C., Dufton, L., ... & Biederman, J. (2008). Cognitive-behavioral intervention with young anxious children. *Harvard Review of Psychiatry*, 16, 113–125. doi:10.1080/10673220802073956

Howard, M., Muris, P., Loxton, H., & Wege, A. (2017). Anxiety-proneness, anxiety symptoms, and the role of parental overprotection in young South African children. *Journal of Child and Family Studies*, 26(1), 262–270. doi:10.1007/s10826-016-0545-z

Hudson, J. L., Dodd, H. F., Lyneham, H. J., & Bovopoulous, N. (2011). Temperament and family environment in the development of anxiety disorder: Two-year follow-up. *Journal of the American Academy of Child & Adolescent Psychiatry*, 50, 1255–1264. doi:10.1016/j.jaac.2011. 09. 00doi:9

Insel, T. R., & Fenton, W. S. (2005). Psychiatric epidemiology: it's not just about counting anymore. *Archives of General Psychiatry*, 62, 590–592. doi:10.1001/archpsyc.62. 6. 59doi:0

Johnco, C. J., Salloum, A., Lewin, A. B., McBride, N. M., & Storch, E. A. (2015). The impact of comorbidity profiles on clinical and psychosocial functioning in childhood anxiety disorders. *Psychiatry Research*, 229, 237–244. doi:10.1016/j. psychres.2015. 07. 02doi:7

Kassam-Adams, N., Garcia-Espana, J. F., Miller, V. A., & Winston, F. (2006). Parent-child agreement regarding children's acute stress: The role of parent acute stress reactions. *Journal of the American Academy of Child & Adolescent Psychiatry, 45,* 1485–1493. doi:10.1097/01.chi.0000237703.97518.12

Kaufman, J., Birmaher, B., Brent, D., Rao, U. M. A., Flynn, C., Moreci, P., ... & Ryan, N. (1997). Schedule for Affective Disorders and Schizophrenia for School-age Children-Present and Lifetime Version (K-SADS-PL): Initial reliability and validity data. *Journal of the American Academy of Child & Adolescent Psychiatry, 36,* 980–988. doi:10.1097/00004583-199707000-00021

Kaufman, J., & Charney, D. (2000). Comorbidity of mood and anxiety disorders. *Depression and Anxiety, 12,* 69–76.

Keenan, K., Shaw, D. S., Walsh, B., Delliquadri, E., & Giovannelli, J. (1997). DSM-III-R disorders in preschool children from low-income families. *Journal of the American Academy of Child & Adolescent Psychiatry, 36,* 620–627. doi:10.1097/00004583-199705000-00012

Kennedy, S. J., Rapee, R. M., & Edwards, S. L. (2009). A selective intervention program for inhibited preschool-aged children of parents with an anxiety disorder: Effects on current anxiety disorders and temperament. *Journal of the American Academy of Child & Adolescent Psychiatry, 48,* 602–609. doi:10.1097/CHI.0b013e31819f6fa9

Kessler, R. C., Aguilar-Gaxiola, S., Alonso, J., Chatterji, S., Lee, S., Ormel, J., ... & Wang, P. S. (2009a). The global burden of mental disorders: an update from the WHO World Mental Health (WMH) surveys. *Epidemiologia e Psichiatria Sociale, 18,* 23–33. doi:10.1017/S1121189X00001421

Kessler, R. C., Ruscio, A. M., Shear, K., & Wittchen, H. U. (2009b). Epidemiology of anxiety disorders. In M.B. Stein & T. Steckler (Eds.), *Behavioral neurobiology of anxiety and its treatment* (pp. 21–35). Berlin Heidelberg: Springer.

Kristensen, H. (2000). Selective mutism and comorbidity with developmental disorder/delay, anxiety disorder, and elimination disorder. *Journal of the American Academy of Child & Adolescent Psychiatry, 39,* 249–256. doi:10.1097/00004583-200002000-00026

Lahey, B. B. (2004). Commentary: Role of temperament in developmental models of psychopathology. *Journal of Clinical Child and Adolescent Psychology, 33,* 88–93. doi:10.1207/S15374424JCCP3301_9

Lavigne, J. V., Arend, R., Rosenbaum, D., Binns, H. J., Christoffel, K. K., & Gibbons, R. D. (1998). Psychiatric disorders with onset in the preschool years: I. Stability of diagnoses. *Journal of the American Academy of Child & Adolescent Psychiatry, 37,* 1246–1254. doi:10.1097/00004583-199812000-00007

Lavigne, J. V., Cicchetti, C., Gibbons, R. D., Binns, H. J., Larsen, L., & DeVito, C. (2001). Oppositional defiant disorder with onset in preschool years: Longitudinal stability and pathways to other disorders. *Journal of the American Academy of Child & Adolescent Psychiatry, 40,* 1393–1400. doi:10.1097/00004583-200112000-00009

Lavigne, J. V., Lebailly, S. A., Hopkins, J., Gouze, K. R., & Binns, H. J. (2009). The prevalence of ADHD, ODD, depression, and anxiety in a community sample of 4-year-olds. *Journal of Clinical Child and Adolescent Psychology, 38,* 315–328. doi:10.1080/15374410902851382

Lemery, K. S., Essex, M. J., & Smider, N. A. (2002). Revealing the relation between temperament and behavior problem symptoms by eliminating measurement confounding: Expert ratings and factor analyses. *Child Development, 73,* 867–882. doi:10.1111/1467-8624.00444

Lengua, L. J., West, S. G., & Sandler, I. N. (1998). Temperament as a predictor of symptomatology in children: Addressing contamination of measures. *Child Development, 69*, 164–181. doi:10.2307/1132078

Lépine, J. (2002). The epidemiology of anxiety disorders: Prevalence and societal costs. *The Journal of Clinical Psychiatry, 63*(Suppl14), 4–8.

Liu, J., Cheng, H., & Leung, P. W. (2011). The application of the preschool Child Behavior Checklist and the Caregiver–Teacher Report Form to mainland Chinese children: Syndrome structure, gender differences, country effects, and inter-informant agreement. *Journal of Abnormal Child Psychology, 39*(2), 251–264. doi:10.1007/s10802-010-9452-8

Lonigan, C. J., Phillips, B. M., Wilson, S. B., & Allan, N. P. (2011). Temperament and anxiety in children and adolescents. In Silverman, W. K., & Field, A. P. (Eds.), *Anxiety disorders in children and adolescents, second edition* (pp. 198–226). New York, NY: Cambridge University Press.

Lord, C., Risi, S., Lambrecht, L., Cook, E. H., Leventhal, B. L., DiLavore, P. C., ... & Rutter, M. (2000). The Autism Diagnostic Observation Schedule— Generic: A standard measure of social and communication deficits associated with the spectrum of autism. *Journal of Autism and Developmental Disorders, 30*, 205–223. doi:10.1023/A:1005592401947

Luby, J. L., Belden, A., Sullivan, J., & Spitznagel, E. (2007). Preschoolers' contribution to their diagnosis of depression and anxiety: Uses and limitations of young child self-report of symptoms. *Child Psychiatry and Human Development, 38*, 321–338. doi:10.1007/s10578-007-0063-8

Luby, J. L., Gaffrey, M. S., Tillman, R., April, L. M., & Belden, A. C. (2014). Trajectories of preschool disorders to full DSM depression at school age and early adolescence: Continuity of preschool depression. *American Journal of Psychiatry, 171*, 768–776. doi:10.1176/appi.ajp.2014.13091198

Mesman, J., Bongers, I. L., & Koot, H. M. (2001). Preschool developmental pathways to preadolescent internalizing and externalizing problems. *Journal of Child Psychology and Psychiatry, 42*, 679–689. doi:10.1111/1469-7610.00763

Mian, N. D., Carter, A. S., Pine, D. S., Wakschlag, L. S., & Briggs-Gowan, M. J. (2015). Development of a novel observational measure for anxiety in young children: The Anxiety Dimensional Observation Scale. *Journal of Child Psychology and Psychiatry, 56*, 1017–1025. doi:10.1111/jcpp.12407

Mian, N. D., Godoy, L., Briggs-Gowan, M. J., & Carter, A. S. (2012). Patterns of anxiety symptoms in toddlers and preschool-age children: Evidence of early differentiation. *Journal of Anxiety Disorders, 26*, 102–110. doi:10.1016/j.janxdis.2011. 09. 00doi:6

Muris, P. & Field, A. P (2011). The normal development of fear. In Silverman, W. K., & Field, A. P. (Eds.), *Anxiety disorders in children and adolescents, second edition* (pp. 76–89). New York, NY: Cambridge University Press.

Muris, P., Loxton, H., Neumann, A., du Plessis, M., King, N., & Ollendick, T. (2006). DSM-defined anxiety disorders symptoms in South African youths: Their assessment and relationship with perceived parental rearing behaviors. *Behaviour Research and Therapy, 44*, 883–896. doi:10.1016/j.brat.2005. 06. 00doi:2

Muris, P., Meesters, C., Merckelbach, H., Sermon, A., & Zwakhalen, S. (1998). Worry in normal children. *Journal of the American Academy of Child & Adolescent Psychiatry, 37*, 703–710. doi:10.1097/00004583-199807000-00009

Muris, P., Schmidt, H., Engelbrecht, P., & Perold, M. (2002). DSM-IV-defined anxiety disorder symptoms in South African children. *Journal of the American Academy of Child & Adolescent Psychiatry, 41,* 1360–1368. doi:10.1590/2237-6089-2015-0027

Najman, J. M., Williams, G. M., Nikles, J., Spence, S. U. E., Bor, W., O'Callaghan, M., … & Andersen, M. J. (2000). Mothers' mental illness and child behavior problems: Cause-effect association or observation bias? *Journal of the American Academy of Child & Adolescent Psychiatry, 39,* 592–602. doi:10.1097/00004583-200005000-00013

Paulus, F. W., Backes, A., Sander, C. S., Weber, M., & von Gontard, A. (2015). Anxiety disorders and behavioral inhibition in preschool children: a population-based study. *Child Psychiatry & Human Development, 46,* 150–157. doi:10.1007/s10578-014-0460-8

Pincus, D. B., Santucci, L. C., Ehrenreich, J. T., & Eyberg, S. M. (2008). The implementation of modified parent-child interaction therapy for youth with separation anxiety disorder. *Cognitive and Behavioral Practice, 15,* 118–125. doi:10.1016/j.cbpra.2007. 08. 00doi:2

Rapee, R. M., Kennedy, S., Ingram, M., Edwards, S., & Sweeney, L. (2005). Prevention and early intervention of anxiety disorders in inhibited preschool children. *Journal of Consulting and Clinical Psychology, 73,* 488–497. doi:10.1037/0022-006X.73. 3. 48doi:8

Rijlaarsdam, J., Stevens, G. W., van der Ende, J., Hofman, A., Jaddoe, V. W., Verhulst, F. C., & Tiemeier, H. (2015). Prevalence of DSM-IV disorders in a population-based sample of 5- to 8-year-old children: The impact of impairment criteria. *European Child & Adolescent Psychiatry, 24,* 1339–1348. doi:10.1007/s00787-015-0684-6

Rubin, K. H., Burgess, K. B., & Hastings, P. D. (2002). Stability and social–behavioral consequences of toddlers' inhibited temperament and parenting behaviors. *Child Development, 73,* 483–495. doi:10.1111/1467-8624.00419

Scheeringa, M. S. (2016). *Treating PTSD in preschoolers: A clinical guide.* New York, NY: Guilford Press.

Scheeringa, M. S., & Haslett, N. (2010). The reliability and criterion validity of the Diagnostic Infant and Preschool Assessment: A new diagnostic instrument for young children. *Child Psychiatry and Human Development, 41,* 299–312. doi:10.1007/s10578-009-0169-2

Scheeringa, M. S., Myers, L., Putnam, F. W., & Zeanah, C. H. (2012). Diagnosing PTSD in early childhood: An empirical assessment of four approaches. *Journal of Traumatic Stress, 25,* 359–367. doi:10.1002/jts.21723

Scheeringa, M. S., Zeanah, C. H., & Cohen, J. A. (2011). PTSD in children and adolescents: toward an empirically based algorithm. *Depression and Anxiety, 28,* 770–782. doi:10.1002/da.20736

Scheeringa, M. S., Zeanah, C. H., Drell, M. J., & Larrieu, J. A. (1995). Two approaches to the diagnosis of posttraumatic stress disorder in infancy and early childhood. *Journal of the American Academy of Child and Adolescent Psychiatry, 34,* 191–200. doi:10.1097/00004583-199502000-00014

Scheeringa, M. S., Zeanah, C. H., Myers, L., & Putnam, F. W. (2003). New findings on alternative criteria for PTSD in preschool children. *Journal of the American Academy of Child and Adolescent Psychiatry, 42,* 561–570. doi:10.1097/01.CHI.0000046822.95464.14

Schneier, F. R. (2003). Social anxiety disorder: Is common, underdiagnosed, impairing, and treatable. *British Medical Journal, 327*, 515–517. doi:10.1136/bmj.327.7414.515

Silverman, W.K. & Ollendick, T.H. (2008). Child and adolescent anxiety disorders. In J. Hunsley & E.J. Mash (Eds.), *A guide to assessments that work* (pp. 181–206). New York: Oxford University Press.

Silverman, W. K., Saavedra, L. M., & Pina, A. A. (2001). Test-retest reliability of anxiety symptoms and diagnoses with the Anxiety Disorders Interview Schedule for DSM-IV: child and parent versions. *Journal of the American Academy of Child & Adolescent Psychiatry, 40*, 937–944. doi:10.1097/00004583-200108000-00016

Spence, S. H., Rapee, R., McDonald, C., & Ingram, M. (2001). The structure of anxiety symptoms among preschoolers. *Behaviour Research and Therapy, 39*(11), 1293–1316. doi:10.1016/S0005-7967(00)00098-X

Sprafkin, J., Volpe, R. J., Gadow, K. D., Nolan, E. E., & Kelly, K. (2002). A DSM-IV–referenced screening instrument for preschool children: The Early Childhood Inventory-4. *Journal of the American Academy of Child & Adolescent Psychiatry, 41*, 604–612. doi:10.1097/00004583-200205000-00018

Sterba, S., Egger, H. L., & Angold, A. (2007). Diagnostic specificity and non-specificity in the dimensions of preschool psychopathology. *Journal of Child Psychology and Psychiatry, 48*, 1005–1013. doi:10.1111/j.1469-7610.2007.01770.x

Tackett, J. L. (2006). Evaluating models of the personality–psychopathology relationship in children and adolescents. *Clinical Psychology Review, 26*, 584–599. doi:10.1016/j.cpr.2006. 04. 00doi:3

Task Force on Research Diagnostic Criteria: Infancy and Preschool. (2003). Research diagnostic criteria for infants and preschool children: The process and empirical support. *Journal of the American Academy of Child and Adolescent Psychiatry, 42*, 1504–1512. doi:10.1097/00004583-200312000-00018

van der Heiden, C., Melchior, K., Muris, P., Bouwmeester, S., Bos, A. E., & van der Molen, H. T. (2010). A hierarchical model for the relationships between general and specific vulnerability factors and symptom levels of generalized anxiety disorder. *Journal of Anxiety Disorders, 24*, 284–289. doi:10.1016/j.janxdis.2009. 12. 00doi:5

Vasey, M. W., Crnic, K. A., & Carter, W. G. (1994). Worry in childhood: A developmental perspective. *Cognitive Therapy and Research, 18*, 529–549. doi:10.1007/BF02355667

Viana, A. G., Beidel, D. C., & Rabian, B. (2009). Selective mutism: A review and integration of the last 15 years. *Clinical Psychology Review, 29*, 57–67. doi:10.1016/j.cpr.2008. 09. 00doi:9

Von Klitzing, K., White, L. O., Otto, Y., Fuchs, S., Egger, H. L., & Klein, A. M. (2014). Depressive comorbidity in preschool anxiety disorder. *Journal of Child Psychology and Psychiatry, 55*, 1107–1116. doi:10.1111/jcpp.12222

Wakschlag, L. S., Briggs-Gowan, M. J., Choi, S. W., Nichols, S. R., Kestler, J., Burns, J. L., ... Henry, D. (2014). Advancing a multidimensional, developmental spectrum approach to preschool disruptive behavior. *Journal of the American Academy of Child and Adolescent Psychiatry, 53*, 82–96. doi:10.1016/j.jaac.2013. 10. 011

Wakschlag, L. S., Choi, S. W., Carter, A. S., Hullsiek, H., Burns, J., McCarthy, K., ... & Briggs-Gowan, M. J. (2012). Defining the developmental parameters of temper loss in early childhood: implications for developmental psychopathology. *Journal of Child Psychology and Psychiatry, 53*, 1099–1108. doi:10.1111/j.1469-7610.2012.02595.x

Wakschlag, L. S., & Danis, B. (2009). Characterizing early childhood disruptive behavior: Enhancing developmental sensitivity. In C. Zeanah (Ed.), *Handbook of infant mental health* (3rd ed., pp. 392–408). New York, NY: Guilford Press.

Wakschlag, L. S., Hill, C., Carter, A. S., Danis, B., Egger, H. L., Keenan, K., ... Briggs-Gowan, M. J. (2008). Observational assessment of preschool disruptive behavior, part I: Reliability of the Disruptive Behavior Diagnostic Observation Schedule (DB-DOS). *Journal of the American Academy of Child & Adolescent Psychiatry, 47*, 622–631. doi:10.1097/CHI.0b013e31816c5bdb

Wakschlag, L. S., Tolan, P. H., & Leventhal, B. L. (2010). Research Review: 'Ain't misbehavin': Towards a developmentally-specified nosology for preschool disruptive behavior. *Journal of Child Psychology and Psychiatry, 51*, 3–22. doi:10.1111/j.1469-7610.2009.02184.x

Wang, M., & Zhao, J. (2015). Anxiety disorder symptoms in Chinese preschool children. *Child Psychiatry & Human Development, 46*, 158–166. doi:10.1007/s10578-014-0461

Watson, D. (1999). Dimensions underlying the anxiety disorders: A hierarchical perspective. *Current Opinion in Psychiatry, 12*, 181–186.

Watson, D. (2005). Rethinking the mood and anxiety disorders: A quantitative hierarchical model for DSM-V. *Journal of Abnormal Psychology, 114*, 522–536. doi:10.1037/0021-843X.114. 4. 52doi:2

Weems, C. F. (2008). Developmental trajectories of childhood anxiety: Identifying continuity and change in anxious emotion. *Developmental Review, 28*, 488–502. doi:10.1016/j.dr.2008. 01. 00doi:1

Weems, C. F., & Costa, N. M. (2005). Developmental differences in the expression of childhood anxiety symptoms and fears. *Journal of the American Academy of Child & Adolescent Psychiatry, 44*, 656–663. doi:10.1097/01.chi.0000162583.25829.4b

Wichstrøm, L., Berg-Nielsen, T. S., Angold, A., Egger, H. L., Solheim, E., & Sveen, T. H. (2012). Prevalence of psychiatric disorders in preschoolers. *Journal of Child Psychology and Psychiatry, 53*, 695–705. doi:10.1111/j.1469-7610.2011.02514.x

2 Preschool Anxiety
Risk and Protective Factors

Nicholas D. Mian and Sarah A.O. Gray

Anxiety disorders in young children have become well recognized as an important condition to understand, treat, and prevent. This rise in interest coincides with several empirical findings: (1) these disorders are equally, if not more, prevalent in preschool-age children compared to older peers (Egger & Angold, 2006a, 2006b; Franz et al., 2013), (2) anxiety disorders in preschool-age children have been shown to reflect changes at the neurobiological level, including reduced connectivity between brain structures integral to emotion regulation (Carpenter et al., 2015), and (3) young children who experience high levels of anxiety in early childhood are at higher risk for emotional and behavioral conditions (Bittner et al., 2007; Karevold, Roysamb, Ystrom, & Mathiesen, 2009; Mesman & Koot, 2001; Mian, Wainwright, Briggs-Gowan, & Carter, 2011). Consequently, effectively treating or preventing anxiety disorders in preschool-age children could have substantial, long-lasting public health benefits (Bayer et al., 2011; Farrell & Barrett, 2007; Hirshfeld-Becker & Biederman, 2002; Mian, 2013; Pahl & Barrett, 2010).

Anxiety disorders in preschool-aged children have been identified as prime candidates for selective prevention (Rapee, 2002), wherein children are identified as "at risk" according to specific risk factors, and then targeted for prevention trials. The efficacy of such prevention models depends on the accuracy with which we are able to identify children at high levels of risk. Most prospective research to date has investigated middle childhood or adolescence as the developmental period for the measured outcome. However, this chapter focuses on the recent research on risk and protective factors associated with anxiety disorders in *preschool*-age children. Hence, we focus on risk factors that can be identified in infants and toddlers younger than age four years. As a broad overview of risk and protective factors is beyond the scope of this chapter (for further reading, see Navsaria, Gilbert, Lenze, & Whalen, 2017), we focus on those factors that are specific to – or most relevant for – anxiety disorders, rather than general risk factors (e.g., poverty).

Defining Risk and Protective Factors

In the field of developmental psychopathology, risk and protective factors have been inconsistently defined. In the context of resilience research, which focuses on how one adapts to adversity (i.e., "risk"), the terms *vulnerability* and *protective factors* are used to refer to moderating indices that have either a negative effect (amplifying negative outcomes) or positive effect (reducing negative outcomes) on adaptation (Luthar & Cicchetti, 2000). In the context of studying resilience, it can be appropriate to refer to vulnerability and protective factors as two ends of the same spectrum (e.g., intelligence) when one end constitutes a positive consequence and the other constitutes a negative consequence in regard to adaptation (Luthar & Cicchetti, 2000).

In more general psychiatric contexts, the terms "risk factor" and "protective factor" simply refer to whether the index increases or decreases the likelihood of a negative outcome (e.g., developing a disorder). Generally, the two terms do *not* refer to the opposite end of the same spectrum, suggesting instead that protective factors should emphasize a *mechanism* that has a protective effect, rather than an attribute (Rutter, 1990). As this chapter is focused on risk and protective factors for preschool anxiety disorders in the general population, we define a *risk factor* as any index that increases the likelihood of a young child developing an anxiety disorder or increases symptom severity. Consistent with the resilience framework, we define a *protective factor* as a variable or index that buffers or mitigates the effect of risk, increasing the likelihood of a more favorable outcome (i.e., reducing the likelihood of developing an anxiety disorder or reducing symptom severity). As such, protective factors are of little importance in the absence of risk. Finally, we assert that a protective factor cannot be identified simply by the absence of a risk factor, or vice versa.

Both risk and protective factors can originate in the individual (e.g., personal attributes), the family context (e.g., parenting styles), or in the community (e.g., exposure to community violence) (Bronfenbrenner & Ceci, 1994; Luthar & Cicchetti, 2000; Navsaria et al., 2017). Further, risk and protective factors affect one another across these levels through transactional processes. As argued by Gregory and Eley (2007), understanding gene-by-environment interactions is key in understanding risk factors for anxiety disorders. For example, if behavioral inhibition represents a genetically-influenced temperamental trait, then other factors, including parenting and attention biases, could act as moderators, explaining why only a portion of inhibited children develop anxiety disorders (Fox, Hane, & Pine, 2007). Examining the dynamic interplay between risk factors, rather than studying them in isolation, will likely yield a more accurate depiction of the etiology of anxiety disorders.

Genetic Risk

It has long been apparent that children of anxious parents were more likely to be anxious themselves, but for decades, it was unclear if this observation was due to genetic factors, the childrearing of anxious parents, or some other factor. A robust body of literature has now confirmed that much (although not all) of this phenomenon can be attributed to genetic factors (Gregory & Eley, 2007).

Twin studies enable the estimation of genetic risk for specific characteristics based on the different degrees of genetic relatedness for monozygotic (100%) versus dizygotic (50% on average) twin pairs (for a review, see Gregory & Eley, 2007). Using an approach that differentiated anxiety symptoms in four-year-olds into several types, Eley and colleagues (2003) estimated heritability at 50% for general distress, 39% for separation anxiety, 52% for fear, 54% for obsessive-compulsive behaviors, and 64% for shyness. Heritability was comparable (ranging from 50–61% across similar constructs) for the same sample at age seven (Hallett, Ronald, Rijsdijk, & Eley, 2009). It is interesting that shyness had the highest heritability, as this trait (further defined below) has long been considered a temperamental variation present in toddlers that confers risk for anxiety disorders (Kagan, Reznick, & Snidman, 1988). While this research is very exciting, it is important to remember that estimates of heritability do vary from one study to the next, in part due to varying methods and approaches to assessment of the phenotype (focusing on anxiety symptoms versus diagnoses, parent versus child report, etc.), each with unique sources of error (Gregory & Eley, 2007).

Some molecular genetics studies have investigated certain genes that may be involved in the development of anxiety disorders. Once a candidate gene has been identified, different polymorphisms of that gene can be studied to elucidate potential risk or protective roles. One example is the corticotrophin releasing hormone (CRH) gene, which was specifically linked to behavioral inhibition in one study (Smoller et al., 2005). Most genetic studies using this technique have focused on genes linked to serotonin on the basis that medications that affect reuptake of serotonin appear to be effective for treating anxiety. Studies investigating polymorphisms of the serotonin transporter gene (5-HTT) have received much attention (e.g., Fox, Nichols, et al., 2005), but controversy remains over seemingly contradictory results upon replication (for a review, see Gregory & Eley, 2007).

Current thinking is that there is no single gene responsible for anxiety disorders, but rather a host of genes contributing small effects that interact with one another and with environmental factors. Based on a recent accumulation of research, it appears misguided to consider genetic influence to be a static risk factor unaffected by experience. The burgeoning field of epigenetics has demonstrated that there is a dynamic interplay between life experiences and gene expression (Kundakovic & Champagne, 2015). In short, epigenetics refers to how certain gene activity is altered over the life of an individual, often due to the influence of life experiences. Some research has demonstrated that early caregiving behaviors are associated with epigenetic effects, leading to differences in the genome that are not apparent at birth (Kundakovic & Champagne, 2015). This is an exciting, new area that may lead to an improved understanding of the role of genetic influence on the development of anxiety disorders.

Temperamental Risk: Behavioral Inhibition

Behavioral inhibition (BI) has been defined as a consistent tendency to display shyness or withdrawal in novel or unfamiliar situations (Kagan, 1984; Kagan, Reznik, & Snidman, 1999). Behavioral inhibition has been assessed through behavioral observation with tests that place children in unfamiliar situations (such as a room with many unfamiliar toys) or confront them with an unfamiliar stimulus (a strange adult). In such situations, assessment may be based on the number of toys a child plays with or the amount of behavioral resistance to the situation (Biederman et al., 2001).

BI is considered a temperamental construct, meaning it is present in infants with assumed genetic origin and can be reliably assessed in toddlers. Although temperament was initially conceptualized as a collection of varying dimensions (Thomas, Chess, Birch, Hertzig, & Korn, 1963), Kagan and colleagues (and others) have consistently adopted a typological or categorical approach, identifying children at the extreme end of the temperamental dimension of BI (Kagan, 1984; Kagan & Snidman, 1999). Although this technique is reliable and effective in identifying those who are most likely to display BI-related impairment, one could argue that this method misrepresents a dimensional construct. However, as Fox and colleagues point out, this categorical approach has led to a fruitful and productive collaboration between psychologists and neuroscientists (Fox, Henderson, Marshall, Nichols, & Ghera, 2005). Differences between inhibited and uninhibited toddlers have been traced back as young as four months; infants classified as "high reactive" at four months have been shown to be more likely to be behaviorally inhibited at two years old (Fox, Henderson, Rubin, Calkins, & Schmidt, 2001) and also at four years old (Kagan, Snidman, & Arcus, 1998).

Toddlers and young children with BI have been consistently shown to be more likely to develop an anxiety disorder later in childhood. In a large, longitudinal study of children at risk of developing anxiety by virtue of parental diagnosis, children who were identified in preschool as being inhibited were approximately twice as likely to develop social phobia (now social anxiety disorder) five years later (Hirshfeld-Becker et al., 2007). Results from one meta-analysis suggested that children with BI have a fourfold increase in risk of developing social anxiety disorder (Blackford & Clauss, 2013; Clauss & Blackford, 2012). Interestingly, BI was found to be inversely related to disruptive or externalizing disorders, suggesting the specificity of it as a risk factor for social anxiety (Biederman et al., 2001). Another longitudinal study demonstrated impressive developmental continuity and specificity; children who had been rated as behaviorally inhibited at two years old showed greater tendency of being diagnosed with social anxiety disorder 11 years later, at the age of 13 (Schwartz, Snidman, & Kagan, 1999).

It has been established that BI in toddlers is physiologically-based, as exhibited by increased secretion of salivary cortisol (a hormone secreted during sympathetic arousal), faster heart rate, quicker heart rate acceleration, and increased pupil dilation up to five years later (Kagan et al., 1988). These physiological characteristics appear to be reliable and stable over time (Kagan et al., 1988). Differences in behavior between inhibited and uninhibited children have been explained through the excitability of the amygdala and associated circuits. This has been supported by early research using animal models in which lesions to the amygdala, significantly decreased startle responses in rats, suggesting that the amygdala is specifically involved in the initial fear responses of unfamiliar situations and the "fight or flight" response of the sympathetic nervous system (Davis & Lee, 1998). More recent research supports the notion that differences in BI are associated with amygdala functioning; for example, one study using functional magnetic resonance imaging (fMRI) identified that adults with a history of BI in early childhood exhibited disruptions in amygdala circuitry, compared to those without a history of BI (Roy et al., 2014). Even in newborns, differences in amygdala connectivity (using resting state fMRI) have been shown to predict internalizing symptoms (including inhibition to novelty) in toddlerhood (Rogers et al., 2017).

Despite its value as a risk factor, the majority of children identified with BI still do not develop anxiety disorders, which begs the question of how to more precisely identify risk in this population. Buss (2011) identified subgroups of BI toddlers based on displays of inhibition to different levels of threat. High threat conditions included interaction with a remote-controlled spider or robot toy; low threat conditions included being invited to play by two friendly puppets or a female clown (without make-up). Those demonstrating inhibition in low-threat conditions were identified by exhibiting "dysregulated fear," which was in turn more strongly predictive of anxiety symptoms in kindergarten, even when controlling for anxiety symptoms and BI in toddlerhood. These findings suggest that it may not be the BI *per se* that puts certain toddlers at risk, but their inaccuracy in assessing risk in novel or ambiguous situations.

Anxiety Symptoms in Toddlers

Although BI is a temperamental risk factor, it is unclear if the behaviors traditionally associated with BI could be more accurately described as early manifestations of anxiety symptoms (Egger & Angold, 2006a). It is important to recall that foundational research on BI was done at a time when internalizing psychopathology was rarely considered in preschool-age children. More recent work with toddlers suggests that anxiety symptoms can be identified in children much younger than previously thought (Mian, Carter, Pine, Wakschlag, & Briggs-Gowan, 2015; Mian, Godoy, Briggs-Gowan, & Carter, 2012). It is quite challenging to differentiate between toddlers and preschool-aged children presenting with elevated symptoms and those with BI (Rapee & Coplan, 2010; Sylvester & Pine, 2017). As one of the core manifestations of anxiety is interpreting neutral situations as overly threatening, young children with anxiety disorders will often present as wary, shy and inhibited in a novel situation. Rapee and Coplan (2010) offer some hypotheses and guidance in differentiating these two constructs; for example, BI should be more heritable and stable over time, as well as less susceptible to external agents, compared to anxiety disorders. In clinical practice however, probably the most meaningful way to determine if an anxiety disorder is present is based on level of impairment, regardless of BI status.

Unsurprisingly, toddlers with elevated anxiety symptoms are also at increased risk for preschool anxiety disorders. Although anxiety symptoms were once considered "undifferentiated" in young children, current research supports the conceptualization of differentiated symptoms (generalized anxiety, separation anxiety, social anxiety, and OCD symptoms) even in toddlers (Mian et al., 2012). Longitudinal research has demonstrated that anxiety symptoms, when measured in infancy and toddlerhood, are relatively stable, increasing the risk of anxiety symptoms or disorders in the preschool years (Karevold et al., 2009; Mesman, Bongers, & Koot, 2001). However, there is significant heterogeneity regarding stability of anxiety symptoms during the preschool period. In one longitudinal study of children ages one to three years, separation distress and parent-reported inhibition to novelty both significantly declined, while general anxiety symptoms increased over this period (Carter, Godoy, et al., 2010). These results suggest that as toddlers mature, they become better at tolerating parental separation and novel situations; however, at the same time, they gain the capacity to worry about the future or develop fears related to safety. In a study on trajectories of internalizing symptoms from ages two to seven years, 13% of boys and 21% of girls fell into a trajectory class with elevated symptoms, which remained largely stable (Sterba, Prinstein, & Cox, 2007). In another study using anxiety symptom trajectories among boys from ages two to six years, 8% fell into an elevated, stable/increasing class, while 32.5% fell into a class that started elevated and then decreased

(Feng, Shaw, & Silk, 2008), suggesting a significant portion of toddlers with anxious symptoms will not maintain elevated symptoms throughout early childhood.

Given the significant overlap between anxiety symptoms and BI in toddlers, one approach is to combine these two in a single risk indicator, which can be done with factor analysis. In one longitudinal study, child factors in toddlers (including parent-reported BI and anxiety symptoms) were the most robust predictors of anxiety symptoms in both kindergarten and second grade (Mian et al., 2011). Other risk factors in the model included maternal factors (anxiety and depression symptoms) and community factors (cumulative sociodemographic risk and violence exposure). Whether considered symptoms or temperamental traits, such child-level factors are apparent in toddlers, and confer significant risk.

Information Processing in Young Children

Information processing is an important aspect of anxiety etiology, as theoretical models suggest that achieving a sense of control in the early environment is of utmost importance for early development (Barlow, Chorpita, & Turovsky, 1996; Chorpita, 2001; Chorpita & Barlow, 1998; Ollendick & Benoit, 2012). According to the models proposed by Barlow and Chorpita, young children need to be able to explore their early environments in such a way that they develop a belief that the world is safe and predictable, gaining a sense of control and mastery to act on it through early autonomous experiences. In addition, to presenting with a temperament that puts them at risk by virtue of a lower threshold for biological arousal, behaviorally inhibited toddlers also are at increased risk because behavioral avoidance limits these early mastery experiences, and therefore may contribute to information processing biases that interpret situations as unpredictable, threatening, or out of their control. Ollendick and Benoit (2012) suggest that changes in information processing may partially explain the link between parenting practices and child anxiety symptoms.

Of course, it is difficult to study information processing in toddlers due to developmental limitations in language and metacognition. One way to study how young children process novel stimuli is by measuring what they pay attention to in such situations. Although several theoretical models posit that attention is a key dimension on which information processing differs for anxious versus non-anxious individuals, some controversy remains as to the nature and direction of attentional processes (for a review, see Bar-Haim, Lamy, Pergamin, Bakermans-Kranenburg, & van Ijzendoorn, 2007). While some models had suggested that anxious individuals would be expected to show a bias *away* from threat, as anxiety disorders are associated with avoidance, studies have consistently found that anxious individuals show a bias *toward* threat, likely due to hypervigilance (Bar-Haim et al., 2007; Nozadi et al., 2016).

While several methods exist for measuring attention bias, we focus on the affective dot-probe technique, which relies on reaction time as related to threatening stimuli briefly appearing on a computer screen (Bar-Haim et al., 2007; Pérez-Edgar et al., 2010; Pine, 2007). In the dot-probe, participants look at a computer screen that shows two images (e.g., either threatening, like an angry face, or non-threatening, like a neutral face), which are followed by a visual probe that appears on one side of the screen. Participants respond as quickly as possible to the probe, indicating its location or orientation. If participants were attending to the threatening image, then they are expected to react more quickly to the presence of the probe when it appears in the location where the threatening image previously appeared, thus providing a way to reliably ascertain the degree to which a participant was attending to threat. Those who spend more time looking at the threatening stimuli are said to exhibit an (implicit) attention bias to threat. Several studies have found an association between attention bias to threat (angry faces) and anxiety symptoms in older children (Bar-Haim et al., 2007; Nozadi et al., 2016); one study demonstrated a relationship between attention bias toward threat and observed anxiety symptoms in preschool-aged children (Mian, Carter, et al., 2015).

Studying attention biases may be one way to understand the relationship between BI and anxiety disorders, and a growing body of research has focused on attention biases as a moderator of BI (Fox & Pine, 2012; Nozadi et al., 2016). One series of studies with six- to nine-year-old children demonstrated that BI moderated the relationship between (1) threat information and attentional bias and (2) threat information and behavioral avoidance (Field, 2006). In these two experiments, children were either told that novel animals were friendly (no threat condition) or nasty (threat condition). Children who scored higher on the measure of BI took longer to reach into a box to touch the animal – showing higher behavioral avoidance – in the threat condition (compared to the no-threat condition). The same moderating result was found for attention bias; as BI scores increased, so did children's attention bias toward threat (looking more at pictures of an animal described as threatening compared to one described in a positive way).

Consistent with the notion that attention bias may moderate other risk factors, adolescents with a history of BI as toddlers were more likely to demonstrate an attention bias to threat (angry faces) in adolescence, which was shown to moderate the relationship between BI and social withdrawal in adolescence (Pérez-Edgar et al., 2010). One recent longitudinal study provides perhaps the strongest evidence of attention bias as a moderator to date: the association between BI in toddlers and anxiety symptoms at age 10 was only apparent for children who exhibited attention bias to threat at five years old (Nozadi et al., 2016). Attention bias to threat has also been shown to moderate the relationship between exposure to violence and anxiety symptoms in preschool-age children, suggesting attention bias may be a particularly important moderator for community-level risk factors (Briggs-Gowan et al., 2015). Unfortunately, few studies have included preschool-age children due to developmental complications with participating in the task. While three-year-olds participated in the Briggs-Gowan et al. study above, they tended to have difficulty with the demands of the task, producing an insufficient number of accurate trials to calculate reliable estimates of attention bias. Ongoing challenges include the difficulty of assessing threat-related bias in young children, as well as the small number of prospective, longitudinal studies.

Parenting Behavior

As mentioned above, certain styles of parenting have been implicated as a risk factor for childhood anxiety disorders. It is generally thought that parental information processing (e.g., interpreting ambiguous situations as being potentially dangerous), is associated with "anxious parenting" behaviors, which sequentially influence the child's information processing and associated anxiety symptoms (Ollendick & Benoit, 2012). The type of parenting behavior that has received the most attention and empirical support in relation to child anxiety is over-control (sometimes referred to as over-protection or over-intrusiveness) (Möller, Nikolić, Majdandžić, & Bögels, 2016). Theoretical models suggest that such parenting limits children's opportunities to explore their environment, take risks, and develop a sense of mastery and the ability to accurately evaluate threat (Chorpita & Barlow, 1998; McLeod, Wood, & Weisz, 2007; Wood, McLeod, Sigman, Hwang, & Chu, 2003). Additionally, parenting that deprives children of experiencing challenging situations through parental intervention or accommodation may prevent opportunities to develop appropriate tolerance for both situational uncertainty and emotional distress (Fialko, Bolton, & Perrin, 2012).

Parental modelling of anxiety – displays of anxious responses to certain situations, including avoidant coping and catastrophizing, often a result of parents' own anxiety – is distinguished from the above parenting behaviors, as these behaviors are not directed at the child (Fisak & Grills-Taquechel, 2007; Wood et al., 2003). In one review, Fisak and Grills-Taquechel (2007) propose that anxiety may be transmitted from parent to child by way of social referencing; the process by which toddlers learn by referencing others' reactions to novel stimuli. This is also consistent with above referenced models of information processing in young children, as parental modeling could amplify perceptions of threat information. Parental modeling is associated with child anxiety in older children (Fliek, Dibbets, Roelofs, & Muris, 2016; Wood et al., 2003), but there is a lack of studies with preschool-age children; modeling was not included in a recent meta-analysis on parenting and anxiety in preschool-age children (Möller et al., 2016).

While correlational data certainly supports an association between parenting behaviors and preschool anxiety, the interplay between the two is complex (Ollendick & Benoit, 2012). A traditional assertion was that anxious parenting leads to anxious children (and correlational research supports this), but the strong evidence of genetic influence allows us to reject any claim that parenting behavior *alone* causes child anxiety (Eley, Napolitano, Lau, & Gregory, 2010). There are three remaining hypotheses: (1) a third variable, such as shared genetic risk for both variables, causes both child anxiety and parental control, (2) child anxiety elicits parental control, and (3) there are reciprocal effects: child anxiety elicits parental control, which maintains child anxiety symptoms (Eley et al., 2010). Most consistent with the third model, Fox and colleagues have argued that a transactional model is most appropriate to understand the relationship between environmental effects and abnormal brain development, which is especially important in the first two years of life due to enhanced neuroplasticity in this developmental stage (Fox, Calkins, & Bell, 1994). Similarly, a model for Social Anxiety Disorder put forth by Ollendick and Benoit (2012) suggests that parenting practices could have a moderating effect on BI. That is, toddlers with BI may be more likely to develop anxiety symptoms later in childhood if their parents exhibit intrusive or controlling behaviors.

Research does suggest that anxious children are more likely to elicit more controlling behaviors from parents. In one study, mothers were paired with eight-year-old children (either clinically anxious or non-anxious) who were not their own (Hudson, Doyle, & Gar, 2009). Mothers were observed to be more highly involved in children's play when they were interacting with clinically anxious children, compared to non-anxious. This is consistent with research on parental accommodations (efforts to help anxious children by avoiding or alleviating anxiety-related distress), which are thought to be performed in response to child anxiety. Such accommodations have been shown to mediate the relationship between parental and child anxiety symptoms (in school-age children) (Jones, Lebowitz, Marin, & Stark, 2015).

There is also research to support a relationship between insecure attachment (a lack of security in the parent-infant relationship) and child anxiety symptoms/disorders later in childhood (Brumariu & Kerns, 2010; Ollendick & Benoit, 2012; Warren, Huston, Egeland, & Sroufe, 1997). For the purposes of this chapter, we do not focus on attachment as a risk factor, as we agree with Ollendick and Benoit (2012) that other factors – namely parental anxiety and associated factors – are precursors to insecure attachment. As such, insecure attachment may be an important moderator of these more primary risk factors. Parenting stress has also been identified as a risk factor for anxiety symptoms in young children (Pahl, Barrett, & Gullo, 2012). This is not surprising as it is established that parent stress is associated with negative parenting behaviors that are more proximal risk factors (e.g., Puff & Renk, 2014). In addition, parent stress is considered a non-specific risk factor, likely increasing risk for a host of child problems.

Finally, it is important to note two limitations. First, meta-analysis suggests that effect sizes for parenting behaviors predicting child anxiety have generally been small-to-medium, with r ranging from .20 to .26 (one exception was $r = .42$ for autonomy granting), and accounting for only 4% of the variance in child anxiety symptoms (McLeod et al., 2007). This suggests parenting may play a less robust role in anxiety etiology than once assumed. Second, parenting effects may increase with age; as children grow older, there is more time for the parenting behaviors to have an effect. Indeed, effects for parenting behaviors on anxiety have been found to be especially small in the toddler and preschool years (r ranging from .06 to .14 for mothers) (Möller et al., 2016). In one study, parenting did show modest relationships to child anxiety in four-year-olds, but showed no relation in the same families' two-year-old children, for whom anxiety was instead explained largely by temperamental factors (Majdandžić, Möller, de Vente, Bögels, & van den Boom, 2014). Nevertheless, as parenting remains one of the most proximal and malleable risk factors, it is crucial to target in treatment and prevention programs (Hirshfeld-Becker et al., 2010; Puliafico, Comer, & Pincus, 2012; Rapee, Kennedy, Ingram, Edwards, & Sweeney, 2005). Treatment and prevention efforts are described in Chapters 6 and 10 in this book.

Exposure to Trauma

Exposure to early adversity has been identified as a broad risk factor for emergent psychopathology across the lifespan, including during the early childhood period (Copeland, Keeler, Angold, & Costello, 2007). Here, we will focus specifically on risk conferred for anxiety disorders, for which exposure to potentially traumatic events is an established risk factor. Among a sample of preschool-aged children who experienced Hurricane Katrina, for example, 17% of children demonstrated a non-PTSD anxiety disorder (Scheeringa & Zeanah, 2008), which is notably higher than rates of anxiety disorders identified in epidemiological work with young children (Carter, Wagmiller, et al., 2010). Clinically, it is critical to consider post-traumatic stress when evaluating anxiety presentation in the context of exposures to trauma, as the two are highly comorbid; in a sample of preschool-aged children with trauma exposure, for example, only 5% of children developed anxiety disorders in the absence of PTSD (Scheeringa, 2015). Among a sample of preschool-aged children diagnosed with PTSD, 63% met criteria for separation anxiety disorder – significantly higher than observed rates in a group of children with trauma exposure who did not meet clinical criteria for PTSD (Scheeringa, Zeanah, Myers, & Putnam, 2003). In longitudinal models, avoidance-related symptoms that emerge during the toddler period have been shown to be a pathway through which early violence exposures impact internalizing symptoms in kindergarten (Briggs-Gowan, Carter, & Ford, 2012). Trauma exposure has also been linked to attentional biases in young children (Briggs-Gowan et al., 2015).

Importantly, distinct types of exposures to potentially traumatic events have shown unique pathways to emergent anxiety disorders. For example, exposure to violence-related events, including family violence, during the toddler period has been associated with separation anxiety. In contrast, non-interpersonal exposures, such as car accidents and injuries, have been associated with specific phobias. These associations between exposure to trauma and risk for anxiety outcomes remain even when taking into consideration other known risks for anxiety, including socioeconomic status and parents' anxiety symptoms (Briggs-Gowan et al., 2010). Also of note, not surprisingly, experiences of stress and trauma appear to have a cumulative effect on children's risk for anxiety. For example, cumulative levels of trauma exposure – e.g., repeated exposures – are associated with higher levels of internalizing symptoms in young children (Hagan, Sulik, & Lieberman, 2016). Additionally, evidence suggests that experiences of early trauma may place children at risk for anxiety symptoms when exposed to non-traumatic life stressors (Grasso, Ford, & Briggs-Gowan, 2013).

As with other risk factors described above, exposure to trauma can be exacerbated by other factors. At the child level, for example, high negative emotionality has been shown to interact with exposure to family conflict to predict later anxiety symptoms (Shaw, Keenan, Vondra, Delliquadri, & Giovannelli, 1997). Additionally, among children with experiences of family violence, children's attention bias towards threat was associated with higher levels of anxiety symptoms in young children (Briggs-Gowan et al., 2015). At the family level, mothers' own psychopathologies have been shown to be a vulnerability factor, exacerbating the likelihood of the emergence of children's internalizing behavior in young children exposed to domestic violence (Ahlfs-Dunn & Huth-Bocks, 2014).

Protective Factors

More research has been focused on risk factors relative to protective factors for anxiety. As stated above, for an index to be defined as a protective factor, it must be studied in the context of risk. For example, this could be a factor that reduces the likelihood of developing an anxiety disorder in children designated as behaviorally inhibited.

Certain parenting behaviors have been proposed as protective factors for children who are at risk (i.e., by virtue of BI or family history). *Autonomy granting* – parenting that grants children age-appropriate independence and autonomy (Silk, Morris, Kanaya, & Steinberg, 2003) – has been found to have a larger effect on anxiety symptoms than other hypothesized parenting variables (McLeod et al., 2007). Moreover, it has been demonstrated to be distinct (i.e., *not* the opposite end of the same spectrum) from psychological control (Silk et al., 2003).

A more recent construct that has been proposed is *challenging parenting behavior* (Möller et al., 2016). This refers to parenting that may be considered the opposite of overprotection, and perhaps a more extreme version of autonomy granting – parenting that playfully encourages risk taking and challenges (Lazarus et al., 2016). Part of the support for this idea can be found in the research on cognitive-behavioral therapy for children – the leading evidence-based treatment for anxiety disorders – which places a significant emphasis on exposure to threatening situations (Kendall, 2006; Kendall et al., 2005; Kendall, Settipani, & Cummings, 2012). It is thought that such exposure (or "practice") reduces problematic cognitions by teaching (through experience) that the feared situation is not dangerous. Secondly, and perhaps more important for young children, such exposure builds tolerance for distress, teaching (to both children and parents) that anxiety is safe and the experience of anxiety does not mean the situation must be avoided. Consistent with this concept, there is a growing body of evidence for treatment programs for preschool-age children that focus on exposure principles (see Chapter 6 in this book), and encourage parents to engage children in approach versus avoidance of anxiety-provoking situations (Hirshfeld-Becker et al., 2010; Pincus, Santucci, Ehrenreich, & Eyberg, 2008; Puliafico et al., 2012).

If such exposure is therapeutic, it follows that regular "exposures" in daily life would buffer other sources of risk. Indeed, there is some evidence that challenging parenting behavior is negatively correlated with anxiety in preschool-age children (Lazarus et al., 2016). Furthermore, this relationship has been demonstrated longitudinally in fathers (but not mothers) in relation to social anxiety (Majdandžić et al., 2014). In this study, four-year-old children and their parents were observed for challenging and over-involved parenting behaviors, as well as child anxiety-related behaviors (approaching a stranger). Fathers' challenging behavior predicted lower anxiety six months later. Interestingly, challenging parenting behavior may serve a different role for fathers than mothers, as mothers' challenging behavior was associated with higher social anxiety in the child six months later (Majdandžić et al., 2014). As with other parenting variables, interpretation is complex. For example, it could be that observed challenging behavior in mothers is a function of mothers' interpretation of what their child needs. In this sense, providing challenging behavior to young children could be a response to BI or early emerging anxiety symptoms. Indeed, this response from parents would be precisely what most experts would prescribe.

From the perspective of resilience research in contexts of early trauma exposure, very little data is available with anxiety disorders as outcomes of interest. However, with regard to the broader dimension of early-emerging internalizing symptomatology in contexts of early trauma exposure, some protective factors have been identified. At the individual child level, strong emergent emotion regulation and prosocial skills have been identified as protective factors (Howell, Graham-Bermann, Czyz, & Lilly, 2010). At the family level, parent-child relationship processes can provide a buffering impact against symptom development in contexts of trauma exposure (Gray, Forbes, Briggs-Gowan, & Carter, 2015; Katz, Hessler, & Annest, 2007).

The recognition of protective factors is apparent in the development of the Fun FRIENDS program that, in addition to reducing symptoms in preschool-aged children, is also designed to promote resilience (Barrett, Fisak, & Cooper, 2015). This universal prevention program (see Chapter 10 in this book) is based on the notion that most (not only "high risk") children will encounter emotionally stressful situations, and that the ability to effectively cope with emotional challenges can help all partici-pants be more resilient in the face of future adversity (Pahl & Barrett, 2007). To this end, the program aims to enhance skills associated with, for example, being brave when feeling anxious, regulating emotions, and problem solving.

Conclusions

Many indices have been identified as conferring risk for anxiety disorders in young children. It is now clear that sources of risk can be found in genetic inheritance, parenting approaches, information processing style, life experiences (e.g., traumatic experiences), as well as early manifesta-tions of temperament and symptoms. Figure 2.1 illustrates one way to organize these risk factors according to child-level versus environmental-level factors, with risk factors closer to the bottom of the figure repre-senting constructs "downstream" in development. Risk factors that have been studied as targets for treatment are identified with an asterisk. Conceptually speaking, we view environmental risk factors as potential moderators of child-level factors. However, child-level factors could also moderate other child-level factors or environmental factors (e.g., atten-tional biases moderating the effect of trauma exposure). It is also impor-tant to note that risk factors tend to be highly correlated with one another in statistical models (Mian et al., 2011; Pahl et al., 2012), sug-gesting that the future of research in this area should avoid considering risk factors in isolation. Research on protective factors is less advanced, but suggests that certain parenting practices or programs that enhance approach-oriented coping responses in children, problem solving, emo-tion regulation, and increased distress tolerance in anxiety provoking

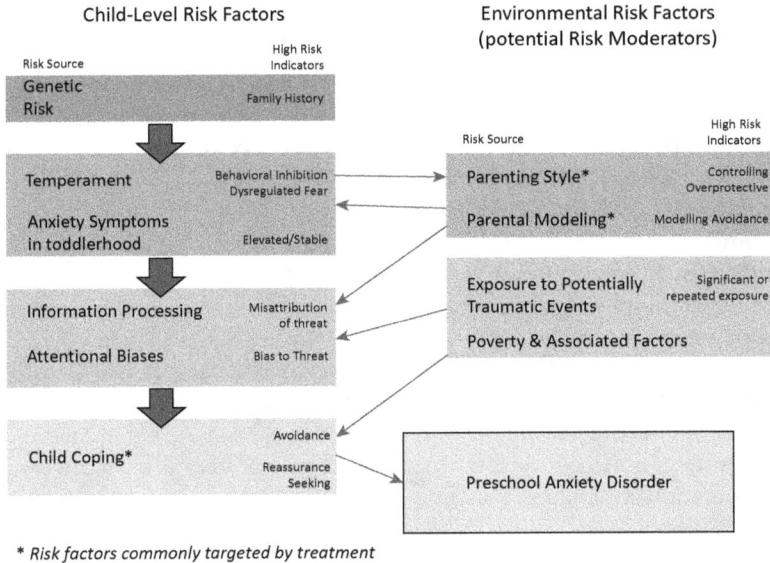

Figure 2.1 Risk factors for anxiety disorders in young children

situations could buffer risk (Pahl & Barrett, 2007). As such, these are often the goals of anxiety-focused early intervention and prevention programs (Elkins, Mian, Comer, & Pincus, 2016; Fisak, 2014; Kendall et al., 2005; Pahl & Barrett, 2010).

Being true to the theoretical proposition that risk factors are reciprocal in nature, we assert that children are an active part of this transactional process. Hence, the manner in which they cope likely plays a significant role in their confidence in such situations and the development of disorders (Kendall et al., 2005). Cognitive-behavioral models suggest that children who engage in coping that fundamentally allows them to avoid the arousal associated with anxiety-inducing situations, are more likely to experience ongoing symptoms. This includes children who engage in avoidant responses, as well as children who engage in excessive reassurance seeking (a safety behavior, which leads to avoidance of anxious arousal). With the paucity of research in this area, coping behavior in young children is proposed as a "downstream" risk factor that warrants further attention. The limited research that does exist suggests, as would be expected, that anxiety is associated with "negative" coping styles akin to withdrawal and giving up in preschool-age children (Yeo, Frydenberg, Northam, & Deans, 2014).

For the purposes of identifying children who are at risk for selective prevention, early manifestations of anxiety/shyness, as measured by laboratory assessments, have been used successfully (Rapee, 2013; Rapee et al., 2005). However, this has clear drawbacks for screening purposes as lab-based assessments are time consuming and present a barrier for many families (Mian, 2013). Fortunately, all risk indices reported on in this chapter (with the exception of attentional biases) can be measured by parent-report, and several research groups have taken this approach (Anticich, Barrett, Silverman, Lacherez, & Gillies, 2013; LaFreniere & Capuano, 1997; Mian, Eisenhower, & Carter, 2015).

In summary, the relationship between various risk factors and anxiety disorders in young children is complex, and likely includes many reciprocal and transactional processes. Even those risk factors once treated as static, such as genetic inheritance, are now considered malleable. It is also clear from the literature that the effects of risk factors can already be seen in young children, increasing the likelihood of developing an anxiety disorder by the preschool years. These findings make clear that the case for early intervention – and even targeted prevention – is stronger than ever, and should be a top priority.

References

Ahlfs-Dunn, S. M., & Huth-Bocks, A. C. (2014). Intimate partner violence and infant socioemotional development: The moderating effects of maternal trauma symptoms. *Infant Mental Health Journal*, 35(4), 322–335. doi:10.1002/imhj.21453

Anticich, S. A. J., Barrett, P. M., Silverman, W., Lacherez, P., & Gillies, R. (2013). The prevention of childhood anxiety and promotion of resilience among pre-school-aged children: A universal school based trial. *Advances in School Mental Health Promotion*, 6(2), 93–121. doi:10.1080/1754730X.2013.784616

Bar-Haim, Y., Lamy, D., Pergamin, L., Bakermans-Kranenburg, M. J., & van Ijzendoorn, M. H. (2007). Threat-related attentional bias in anxious and non-anxious individuals: A meta-analytic study. *Psychological Bulletin*, 133(1), 1–24. doi:10.1037/0033-2909.133.1.1

Barlow, D. H., Chorpita, B. F., & Turovsky, J. (1996). Fear, panic, anxiety, and disorders of emotion. In D. A. Hope (Ed.), *Nebraska Symposium on Motivation, 1995: Perspectives on anxiety, panic, and fear* (pp. 251–328). Lincoln, NE: University of Nebraska Press.

Barrett, P., Fisak, B., & Cooper, M. (2015). The treatment of anxiety in young children: Results of an open trial of the Fun FRIENDS program. *Behavior Change*, 32(4), 231–242. doi:10.1017/bec.2015.12

Bayer, J. K., Rapee, R. M., Hiscock, H., Ukoumunne, O. C., Mihalopoulos, C., & Wake, M. (2011). Translational research to prevent internalizing problems early in childhood. *Depression and Anxiety*, 28(1), 50–57. doi:10.1002/da.20743

Biederman, J., Hirshfeld-Becker, D. R., Rosenbaum, J. F., Hérot, C., Friedman, D., Snidman, N., … Faraone, S. V. (2001). Further evidence of association between behavioral inhibition and social anxiety in children. *American Journal of Psychiatry*, 158(10), 1673–1679.

Bittner, A., Egger, H. L., Erkanli, A., Costello, E. J., Foley, D. L., & Angold, A. (2007). What do childhood anxiety disorders predict? *Journal of Child Psychology and Psychiatry*, 48(12), 1174–1183.

Blackford, J. U., & Clauss, J. A. (2013). 'Risks interpreting odds': Dr. Blackford and Ms. Clauss reply. *Journal of the American Academy of Child & Adolescent Psychiatry*, 52(3), 319–320. doi:10.1016/j.jaac.2012. 12. 00doi:9

Briggs-Gowan, M. J., Carter, A. S., Clark, R., Augustyn, M., McCarthy, K. J., & Ford, J. D. (2010). Exposure to potentially traumatic events in early childhood: differential links to emergent psychopathology. *Journal of Child Psychology & Psychiatry*, 51(10), 1132–1140. doi:10.1111/j.1469-7610.2010.02256.x

Briggs-Gowan, M. J., Carter, A. S., & Ford, J. D. (2012). Parsing the effects violence exposure in early childhood: Modeling developmental pathways. *Journal of Pediatric Psychology*, 37(1), 11–22. doi:10.1093/jpepsy/jsr063

Briggs-Gowan, M. J., Pollak, S. D., Grasso, D., Voss, J., Mian, N. D., Zobel, E., … Pine, D. S. (2015). Attention bias and anxiety in young children exposed to family violence. *Journal of Child Psychology and Psychiatry*, 56(11), 1194–1201. doi:10.1111/jcpp.12397

Bronfenbrenner, U., & Ceci, S. J. (1994). Nature-nurture reconceptualized in developmental perspective: A bioecological model. *Psychological Review*, 101(4), 568–586.

Brumariu, L. E., & Kerns, K. A. (2010). Parent-child attachment and internalizing symptoms in childhood and adolescence: A review of empirical findings and future directions. *Development and Psychopathology*, 22(1), 177–203.

Buss, K. A. (2011). Which fearful toddlers should we worry about? Context, fear regulation, and anxiety risk. *Developmental Psychology*, 47(3), 804–819. doi:10.1037/a0023227

Carpenter, K. L. H., Angold, A., Chen, N., Copeland, W., Gaur, P., Pelphrey, K., … Egger, H. (2015). Preschool anxiety disorders predict different patterns of amygdala-prefrontal connectivity at school-age. *PLoS ONE*, 10(1), e0116854. doi:10.1371/journal.pone.0116854

Carter, A. S., Godoy, L., Wagmiller, R. L., Veliz, P., Marakovitz, S., & Briggs-Gowan, M. J. (2010). Internalizing trajectories in young boys and girls: The whole is not a simple sum of its parts. *Journal of Abnormal Child Psychology*, 38(1), 19–31. doi:10.1007/s10802-009-9342-0

Carter, A. S., Wagmiller, R. J., Gray, S. A. O., McCarthy, K. J., Horwitz, S. M., & Briggs-Gowan, M. J. (2010). Prevalence of DSM-IV disorder in a representative, healthy birth cohort at school entry: Sociodemographic risks and social adaptation. *Journal of the American Academy of Child & Adolescent Psychiatry*, 49(7), 686–698.

Chorpita, B. F. (2001). Control and the development of negative emotion. In M. W. Vasey & M. R. Dadds (Eds.), *The developmental psychopathology of anxiety* (pp. 112–142). New York, NY: Oxford University Press.

Chorpita, B. F., & Barlow, D. H. (1998). The development of anxiety: The role of control in the early environment. *Psychological Bulletin*, 124(1), 3–21.

Clauss, J. A., & Blackford, J. U. (2012). Behavioral inhibition and risk for developing social anxiety disorder: A meta-analytic study. *Journal of the American Academy of Child & Adolescent Psychiatry*, 51(10), 1066–1075. doi:10.1016/j. jaac.2012. 08. 00doi:2

Copeland, W. E., Keeler, G., Angold, A., & Costello, E. J. (2007). Traumatic events and posttraumatic stress in childhood. *Archives of General Psychiatry*, 64(5), 577–584. doi:10.1001/archpsyc.64. 5. 57doi:7

Davis, M., & Lee, Y. (1998). Fear and anxiety: Possible roles of the amygdala and bed nucleus of the stria terminalis. *Cognition & Emotion*, 12(3), 277–305.

Egger, H. L., & Angold, A. (2006a). Anxiety disorders. In J. L. Luby (Ed.), *Handbook of preschool mental health: Development, disorders, and treatment* (pp. 137–164). New York, NY: Guilford Press.

Egger, H. L., & Angold, A. (2006b). Common emotional and behavioral disorders in preschool children: Presentation, nosology, and epidemiology. *Journal of Child Psychology and Psychiatry*, 47(3), 313–337.

Eley, T. C., Bolton, D., O'Connor, T. G., Perrin, S., Smith, P., & Plomin, R. (2003). A twin study of anxiety-related behaviors in pre-school children. *Journal of Child Psychology and Psychiatry*, 44(7), 945–960.

Eley, T. C., Napolitano, M., Lau, J. Y. F., & Gregory, A. M. (2010). Does childhood anxiety evoke maternal control? A genetically informed study. *Journal of Child Psychology and Psychiatry*, 51(7), 772–779.

Elkins, R. M., Mian, N. D., Comer, J. S., & Pincus, D. B. (2016). Parent-Child Interaction Therapy (PCIT) and its adaptations. In J. L. Luby (Ed.), *Handbook of preschool mental health: Development, disorders, and treatment* (2nd ed.). New York, NY: Guilford Press.

Farrell, L. J., & Barrett, P. M. (2007). Prevention of childhood emotional disorders: Reducing the burden of suffering associated with anxiety and depression. *Child and Adolescent Mental Health*, 12(2), 58–65. doi:10.1111/j.1475-3588.2006.00430.x

Feng, X., Shaw, D. S., & Silk, J. S. (2008). Developmental trajectories of anxiety symptoms among boys across early and middle childhood. *Journal of Abnormal Psychology*, 117(1), 32–47.

Fialko, L., Bolton, D., & Perrin, S. (2012). Applicability of a cognitive model of worry to children and adolescents. *Behavior Research and Therapy*, 50(5), 341–349. doi:10.1016/j.brat.2012. 02. 00doi:3

Field, A. P. (2006). The behavioral inhibition system and the verbal information pathway to children's fears. *Journal of Abnormal Psychology*, 115(4), 742–752.

Fisak, B. (2014). The prevention of anxiety in preschool-aged children: Development of a new program and preliminary findings. *Mental Health and Prevention*, 2(1–2), 18–25. doi:10.1016/j.mhp.2014. 07. 00doi:1

Fisak, B., & Grills-Taquechel, A. E. (2007). Parental modeling, reinforcement, and information transfer: Risk factors in the development of child anxiety? *Clinical Child and Family Psychology Review*, 10(3), 213–231. doi:10.1007/s10567-007-0020-x

Fliek, L., Dibbets, P., Roelofs, J., & Muris, P. (2016). Cognitive bias as a mediator in the relation between fear-enhancing parental behaviors and anxiety symptoms in children: A cross-sectional study. *Child Psychiatry and Human Development*. doi:10.1007/s10578-016-0655-2

Fox, N. A., Calkins, S. D., & Bell, M. A. (1994). Neural plasticity and development in the first two years of life: Evidence from cognitive and socioemotional domains of research. *Development and Psychopathology*, 6(4), 677–696.

Fox, N. A., Hane, A. A., & Pine, D. S. (2007). Plasticity for affective neurocircuitry: How the environment affects gene expr. *Current Directions in Psychological Science*, 16(1), 1–5. doi:10.1111/j.1467-8721.2007.00464.x

Fox, N. A., Henderson, H. A., Marshall, P. J., Nichols, K. E., & Ghera, M. M. (2005). Behavioral inhibition: Linking biology and behavior within a developmental framework. *Annual Review of Psychology*, 56, 235–262.

Fox, N. A., Henderson, H. A., Rubin, K. H., Calkins, S. D., & Schmidt, L. A. (2001). Continuity and discontinuity of behavioral inhibition and exuberance:

Psychophysiological and behavioral influences across the first four years of life. *Child Development*, 72(1), 1–21.

Fox, N. A., Nichols, K. E., Henderson, H. A., Rubin, K., Schmidt, L., Hamer, D., … Pine, D. S. (2005). Evidence for a gene-environment interaction in predicting behavioral inhibition in middle childhood. *Psychological Science*, 16(12), 921–926.

Fox, N. A., & Pine, D. S. (2012). Temperament and the emergence of anxiety disorders. *Journal of the American Academy of Child & Adolescent Psychiatry*, 51 (2), 125–128. doi:10.1016/j.jaac.2011. 10. 00doi:6

Franz, L., Angold, A., Copeland, W., Costello, E. J., Towe-Goodman, N., & Egger, H. (2013). Preschool anxiety disorders in pediatric primary care: Prevalence and comorbidity. *Journal of the American Academy of Child & Adolescent Psychiatry*, 52(12), 1294–1303.

Grasso, D. J., Ford, J. D., & Briggs-Gowan, M. J. (2013). Early life trauma exposure and stress sensitivity in young children. *Journal of Pediatric Psychology*, 38(1), 94–103.

Gray, S. A. O., Forbes, D., Briggs-Gowan, M. J., & Carter, A. S. (2015). Caregiver insightfulness and young children's violence exposure: Testing a relational model of risk and resilience. *Attachment & Human Development*, 17(6), 615–634.

Gregory, A. M., & Eley, T. C. (2007). Genetic influences on anxiety in children: What we've learned and where we're heading. *Clinical Child and Family Psychology Review*, 10(3), 199–212. doi:10.1007/s10567-007-0022-8

Hagan, M. J., Sulik, M. J., & Lieberman, A. F. (2016). Traumatic life events and psychopathology in a high risk, ethnically diverse sample of young children: A person-centered approach. *Journal of Abnormal Child Psychology*, 44(5), 833–844. doi:10.1007/s10802-015-0078-8

Hallett, V., Ronald, A., Rijsdijk, F., & Eley, T. C. (2009). Phenotypic and genetic differentiation of anxiety-related behaviors in middle childhood. *Depression and Anxiety*, 26(4), 316–324.

Hirshfeld-Becker, D. R., & Biederman, J. (2002). Rationale and principles for early intervention with young children at risk for anxiety disorders. *Clinical Child and Family Psychology Review*, 5(3), 161–172.

Hirshfeld-Becker, D. R., Biederman, J., Henin, A., Faraone, S. V., Davis, S., Harrington, K., & Rosenbaum, J. F. (2007). Behavioral inhibition in preschool children at risk is a specific predictor of middle childhood social anxiety: A five-year follow-up. *Journal of Developmental & Behavioral Pediatrics*, 28(3), 225–233.

Hirshfeld-Becker, D. R., Masek, B., Henin, A., Blakely, L. R., Pollock-Wurman, R. A., McQuade, J., … Biederman, J. (2010). Cognitive behavioral therapy for 4- to 7-year-old children with anxiety disorders: A randomized clinical trial. *Journal of Consulting and Clinical Psychology*, 78(4), 498–510.

Howell, K. H., Graham-Bermann, S. A., Czyz, E., & Lilly, M. (2010). Assessing resilience in preschool children exposed to intimate partner violence. *Violence and Victims*, 25(2), 150–164. doi:10.1891/0886-6708.25.2doi:150

Hudson, J. L., Doyle, A. M., & Gar, N. (2009). Child and maternal influence on parenting behavior in clinically anxious children. *Journal of Clinical Child and Adolescent Psychology*, 38(2), 256–262. doi:10.1080/15374410802698438

Jones, J. D., Lebowitz, E. R., Marin, C. E., & Stark, K. D. (2015). Family accommodation mediates the association between anxiety symptoms in mothers and children. *Journal of Child and Adolescent Mental Health*, 27(1), 41–51. doi:10.2989/17280583.2015.1007866

Kagan, J. (1984). Behavioral inhibition to the unfamiliar. *Child Development*, 55(6), 2212–2225.

Kagan, J., Reznick, J. S., & Snidman, N. (1988). Biological bases of childhood shyness. *Science*, 240(4849), 167–171.

Kagan, J., Reznik, J. S., & Snidman, N. (1999). Biological basis of childhood shyness. In A. Slater & D. Muir (Eds.), *The Blackwell reader in development psychology* (pp. 65–78). Malden, MA: Blackwell Publishing.

Kagan, J., & Snidman, N. (1999). Early childhood predictors of adult anxiety disorders. *Biological Psychiatry*, 46(11), 1536–1541.

Kagan, J., Snidman, N., & Arcus, D. (1998). Childhood derivatives of high and low reactivity in infancy. *Child Development*, 69(6), 1483–1493.

Karevold, E., Roysamb, E., Ystrom, E., & Mathiesen, K. S. (2009). Predictors and pathways from infancy to symptoms of anxiety and depression in early adolescence. *Developmental Psychology*, 45(4), 1051–1060.

Katz, L. F., Hessler, D. M., & Annest, A. (2007). Domestic violence, emotional competence, and child adjustment. *Social Development*, 16(3), 513–538. doi:10.1111/j.1467-9507.2007.00401.x

Kendall, P. C. (2006). *Child and adolescent therapy: Cognitive-behavioral procedures* (3rd ed.). New York, NY: Guilford Press.

Kendall, P. C., Robin, J. A., Hedtke, K. A., Suveg, C., Flannery-Schroeder, E., & Gosch, E. (2005). Considering CBT with anxious youth? Think exposures. *Cognitive and Behavioral Practice*, 12(1), 136–150. doi:10.1016/S1077-7229(05)80048-3

Kendall, P. C., Settipani, C. A., & Cummings, C. M. (2012). No need to worry: The promising future of child anxiety research. *Journal of Clinical Child and Adolescent Psychology*, 41(1), 103–115. doi:10.1080/15374416.2012.632352

Kundakovic, M., & Champagne, F. A. (2015). Early-life experience, epigenetics, and the developing brain. *Neuropsychopharmacology*, 40(1), 141–153. doi:10.1038/npp.2014.140

LaFreniere, P. J., & Capuano, F. (1997). Preventive intervention as means of clarifying direction of effects in socialization: Anxious-withdrawn preschoolers case. *Development and Psychopathology*, 9(3), 551–564.

Lazarus, R. S., Dodd, H. F., Majdandžić, M., de Vente, W., Morris, T., Byrow, Y., … Hudson, J. L. (2016). The relationship between challenging parenting behavior and childhood anxiety disorders. *Journal of Affective Disorders*, 190, 784–791. doi:10.1016/j.jad.2015. 11. 03doi:2

Luthar, S. S., & Cicchetti, D. (2000). The construct of resilience: Implications for interventions and social policies. *Development and Psychopathology*, 12(4), 857–885. doi:10.1017/S0954579400004156

Majdandžić, M., Möller, E. L., de Vente, W., Bögels, S. M., & van den Boom, D. C. (2014). Fathers' challenging parenting behavior prevents social anxiety development in their 4-year-old children: A longitudinal observational study. *Journal of Abnormal Child Psychology*, 42(2), 301–310. doi:10.1007/s10802-013-9774-4

McLeod, B. D., Wood, J. J., & Weisz, J. R. (2007). Examining the association between parenting and childhood anxiety: A meta-analysis. *Clinical Psychology Review*, 27(2), 155–172. doi:10.1016/j.cpr.2006. 09. 00doi:2

Mesman, J., Bongers, I. L., & Koot, H. M. (2001). Preschool developmental pathways to preadolescent internalizing and externalizing problems. *Journal of Child Psychology and Psychiatry*, 42(5), 679–689.

Mesman, J., & Koot, H. M. (2001). Early preschool predictors of preadolescent internalizing and externalizing DSM-IV diagnoses. *Journal of the American Academy of Child & Adolescent Psychiatry*, 40(9), 1029–1036.

Mian, N. D. (2013). Little children with big worries: Addressing the needs of young, anxious children and the problem of parent engagement. *Clinical Child and Family Psychology Review*. doi:10.1007/s10567-013-0152-0

Mian, N. D., Carter, A. S., Pine, D. S., Wakschlag, L. S., & Briggs-Gowan, M. J. (2015). Development of a novel observational measure for anxiety in young children: The anxiety dimensional observation scale. *Journal of Child Psychology and Psychiatry*, 56(9), 1017–1025. doi:10.1111/jcpp.12407

Mian, N. D., Eisenhower, A. S., & Carter, A. S. (2015). Targeted prevention of childhood anxiety: Engaging parents in an underserved community. *American Journal of Community Psychology*, 55(1–2), 58–69. doi:10.1007/s10464-014-9696-5

Mian, N. D., Godoy, L., Briggs-Gowan, M. J., & Carter, A. S. (2012). Patterns of anxiety symptoms in toddlers and preschool-age children: Evidence of early differentiation. *Journal of Anxiety Disorders*, 26(1), 102–110. doi:10.1016/j.janxdis.2011. 09. 00doi:6

Mian, N. D., Wainwright, L., Briggs-Gowan, M. J., & Carter, A. S. (2011). An ecological risk model for early childhood anxiety: The importance of early child symptoms and temperament. *Journal of Abnormal Child Psychology*, 39(4), 501–512. doi:10.1007/s10802-010-9476-0

Möller, E. L., Nikolić, M., Majdandžić, M., & Bögels, S. M. (2016). Associations between maternal and paternal parenting behaviors, anxiety and its precursors in early childhood: A meta-analysis. *Clinical Psychology Review*, 45, 17–33. doi:10.1016/j.cpr.2016. 03. 00doi:2

Navsaria, N., Gilbert, K., Lenze, S. N., & Whalen, D. J. (2017). Effects of early environment and caregiving: Risk and protective factors in developmental psychopathology. In J. Luby (Ed.), *Handbook of preschool mental health: Development, disorders, and treatment* (2nd ed.). New York, NY: Guilford Press.

Nozadi, S. S., Troller-Renfree, S., White, L. K., Frenkel, T., Degnan, K. A., Bar-Haim, Y., ... Fox, N. A. (2016). The moderating role of attention biases in understanding the link between behavioral inhibition and anxiety. *Journal of Experimental Psychopathology*, 7(3), 451–465.

Ollendick, T. H., & Benoit, K. E. (2012). A parent–child interactional model of social anxiety disorder in youth. *Clinical Child and Family Psychology Review*, 15 (1), 81–91. doi:10.1007/s10567-011-0108-1

Pahl, K. M., & Barrett, P. M. (2007). The development of social-emotional competence in preschool-aged children: An introduction to the Fun FRIENDS Program. *Australian Journal of Guidance and Counselling*, 17(1), 81–90. doi:10.1375/ajgc.17. 1. 81

Pahl, K. M., & Barrett, P. M. (2010). Preventing anxiety and promoting social and emotional strength in preschool children: A universal evaluation of the Fun FRIENDS program. *Advances in School Mental Health Promotion*, 3(3), 14–25. doi:10.1080/1754730x.2010.9715683

Pahl, K. M., Barrett, P. M., & Gullo, M. J. (2012). Examining potential risk factors for anxiety in early childhood. *Journal of Anxiety Disorders*, 26(2), 311–320. doi:10.1016/j.janxdis.2011. 12. 01doi:3

Pérez-Edgar, K., Bar-Haim, Y., McDermott, J. M., Chronis-Tuscano, A., Pine, D. S., & Fox, N. A. (2010). Attention biases to threat and behavioral inhibition in early childhood shape adolescent social withdrawal. *Emotion*, 10(3), 349–357.

Pincus, D. B., Santucci, L. C., Ehrenreich, J. T., & Eyberg, S. M. (2008). The implementation of modified parent-child interaction therapy for youth with Separation Anxiety Disorder. *Cognitive and Behavioral Practice*, 15(2), 118–125.

Pine, D. S. (2007). Research review: A neuroscience framework for pediatric anxiety disorders. *Journal of Child Psychology and Psychiatry*, 48(7), 631–648.

Puff, J., & Renk, K. (2014). Relationships among parents' economic stress, parenting, and young children's behavior problems. *Child Psychiatry and Human Development*, 45(6), 712–727. doi:10.1007/s10578-014-0440-z

Puliafico, A. C., Comer, J. S., & Pincus, D. B. (2012). Adapting parent-child interaction therapy to treat anxiety disorders in young children. *Child and Adolescent Psychiatric Clinics of North America*, 21(3), 607–619. doi:10.1016/j.chc.2012. 05. 00doi:5

Rapee, R. M. (2002). The development and modification of temperamental risk for anxiety disorders: Prevention of a lifetime of anxiety? *Biological Psychiatry*, 52(10), 947–957.

Rapee, R. M. (2013). The preventative effects of a brief, early intervention for preschool-aged children at risk for internalising: follow-up into middle adolescence. *Journal of Child Psychology and Psychiatry*, 54(7), 780–788. doi:10.1111/jcpp.12048

Rapee, R. M., & Coplan, R. J. (2010). Conceptual relation between anxiety disorder and fearful temperament. In H. Gazelle & K. Rubin (Eds.), *Social anxiety in childhood: Bridging developmental and clinical perspectives. New directions for child and adolescent development*. San Francisco: Jossey-Bass.

Rapee, R. M., Kennedy, S., Ingram, M., Edwards, S., & Sweeney, L. (2005). Prevention and early intervention of anxiety disorders in inhibited preschool children. *Journal of Consulting and Clinical Psychology*, 73(3), 488–497.

Rogers, C. E., Sylvester, C. M., Mintz, C., Kenley, J. K., Shimony, J. S., Barch, D. M., & Smyser, C. D. (2017). Neonatal amygdala functional connectivity at rest in healthy and preterm infants and early internalizing symptoms. *Journal of the American Academy of Child & Adolescent Psychiatry*, 56(2), 157–166. doi:10.1016/j.jaac.2016. 11. 00doi:5

Roy, A. K., Benson, B. E., Degnan, K. A., Perez-Edgar, K., Pine, D. S., Fox, N. A., & Ernst, M. (2014). Alterations in amygdala functional connectivity reflect early temperament. *Biological Psychology*, 103, 248–254. doi:10.1016/j.biopsycho.2014. 09. 00doi:7

Rutter, M. (1990). Psychosocial resilience and protective mechanisms. In J. E. Rolf, A. S. Masten, D. Cicchetti, K. H. Nuechterlein, S. Weintraub, J. E. Rolf, A. S. Masten, D. Cicchetti, K. H. Nuechterlein, & S. Weintraub (Eds.), *Risk and protective factors in the development of psychopathology* (pp. 181–214). New York, NY: Cambridge University Press.

Scheeringa, M. S. (2015). Untangling psychiatric comorbidity in young children who experienced single, repeated, or Hurricane Katrina traumatic events. *Child & Youth Care Forum*, 44(4), 475–492. doi:10.1007/s10566-014-9293-7

Scheeringa, M. S., & Zeanah, C. H. (2008). Reconsideration of harm's way: Onsets and comorbidity patterns of disorders in preschool children and their caregivers following Hurricane Katrina. *Journal of Clinical Child and Adolescent Psychology*, 37(3), 508–518. doi:10.1080/15374410802148178

Scheeringa, M. S., Zeanah, C. H., Myers, L., & Putnam, F. W. (2003). New findings on alternative criteria for PTSD in preschool children. *Journal of the American Academy of Child & Adolescent Psychiatry, 42*(5), 561–570.

Schwartz, C. E., Snidman, N., & Kagan, J. (1999). Adolescent social anxiety as an outcome of inhibited temperament in childhood. *Journal of the American Academy of Child & Adolescent Psychiatry, 38*(8), 1008–1015.

Shaw, D. S., Keenan, K., Vondra, J. I., Delliquadri, E., & Giovannelli, J. (1997). Antecedents of preschool children's internalizing problems: A longitudinal study of low-income families. *Journal of the American Academy of Child & Adolescent Psychiatry, 36*(12), 1760–1767.

Silk, J. S., Morris, A. S., Kanaya, T., & Steinberg, L. (2003). Psychological control and autonomy granting: Opposite ends of a continuum or distinct constructs? *Journal of Research on Adolescence, 13*(1), 113–128. doi:10.1111/1532-7795.1301004

Smoller, J. W., Yamaki, L. H., Fagerness, J. A., Biederman, J., Racette, S., Laird, N. M., ... Sklar, P. B. (2005). The corticotropin-releasing hormone gene and behavioral inhibition in children at risk for panic disorder. *Biological Psychiatry, 57*(12), 1485–1492.

Sterba, S. K., Prinstein, M. J., & Cox, M. J. (2007). Trajectories of internalizing problems across childhood: Heterogeneity, external validity, and gender differences. *Development and Psychopathology, 19*(2), 345–366.

Sylvester, C., & Pine, D. S. (2017). Anxiety disorders. In J. Luby (Ed.), *Handbook of preschool mental health: Development, disorders, and treatment* (2nd ed.). New York, NY: The Guilford Press.

Thomas, A., Chess, S., Birch, H. G., Hertzig, M. E., & Korn, S. (1963). *Behavioral individuality in early childhood.* Oxford, England: New York University Press.

Warren, S. L., Huston, L., Egeland, B., & Sroufe, L. A. (1997). Child and adolescent anxiety disorders and early attachment. *Journal of the American Academy of Child & Adolescent Psychiatry, 36*(5), 637–644. doi:10.1097/00004583-199705000-00014

Wood, J. J., McLeod, B. D., Sigman, M., Hwang, W.-C., & Chu, B. C. (2003). Parenting and childhood anxiety: Theory, empirical findings, and future directions. *Journal of Child Psychology and Psychiatry, 44*(1), 134–151.

Yeo, K., Frydenberg, E., Northam, E., & Deans, J. (2014). Coping with stress among preschool children and associations with anxiety level and controllability of situations. *Australian Journal of Psychology, 66*(2), 93–101. doi:10.1111/ajpy.12047

3 Normative Fears in Preschool-Aged Children

Lauren Phillips, Natalie Games, Jennifer Scheurich, Paula Barrett, and Brian Fisak

Fear can be considered normative, developmentally appropriate, and often adaptive in young children. For example, Muris, Merckelbach, Gadet, and Moulaert (2000) found that 71% of preschool-aged children were able to identify at least one specific fear. As with other developmental norms, it is important for professionals working with young children and caregivers to have a basic understanding of normative fears, as this understanding can assist in the identification of atypical or excessive fears (Muris, 2006, 2007). Conversely, a basic knowledge of norms can help professionals and caregivers set realistic expectations and prevent the over-pathologizing of typical behaviors, which, in turn, may prevent unnecessary referrals to mental health professionals.

Normative Fears: Developmental Trends and Considerations

From the available data, it is apparent that normative fears differ based on developmental level in terms of content and frequency, which may be related to age and level of cognitive development. In preschool years, children are typically in the preoperational stage of cognitive development, where reasoning is less abstract (Muris et al., 2000). Consequently, fears tend to be consistent with more concrete thinking, such as fears of the dark, strangers, being alone, separating from caregivers, sleeping away from parents, monsters, water, storms, new foods, and physical harm including medical procedures and falling (Biederman et al., 2001; Field, 2006; Kagan, 2000).

As children grow older, fears that require more abstract reasoning become more common, including performance-related and social fears (Gullone, 1999; Gullone & King, 1993; Ferrari, 1986; King, Gullone & Tonge, 1991). Examples of these fears include trying new tasks, delivering presentations, and being accepted in friendship groups. Further, an age-related reduction in fears associated with animals, the dark, and supernatural phenomena is often observed (e.g., Draper & James, 1985; Gullone & King, 1992, 1993). Although normative fears change across developmental stages, some fears seem to be experienced consistently across age groups, including fears of certain animals, natural disasters, and death.

Assessment of Normative Fears

Numerous research strategies have been used to assess normative fears in children, including child interviews, self-report measures, parent-reports, and observational data (Gullone, 1999). Although the concept of normative fears in children has been extensively researched, most studies have focused on school-aged children. One reason for this, from a developmental perspective, is that preschool-aged children may not possess the cognitive ability to accurately complete certain assessment measures. For example, the second edition of the Fear Survey Schedule for Children (FSSC-II) is typically administered to children between the ages of seven and sixteen years (Gullone & King, 1992). Preschool-aged children have occasionally completed the FSSC-II; however, limited information is available regarding specific norms for this age group, and the reliability of preschool children's self-reports of fears is also questionable (Edelbrock, Costello, Dulcan, Kalas & Conover, 1985). Bouldin and Pratt (1998) modified the FSSC-II to be used as a parent measure designed to evaluate fears of preschool-aged children as well as school-aged children. The modified instrument is the Fear Survey Schedule for Children-II Parent version (FSSC-IIP). In contrast to previous studies, the authors found an increase in reported fears over time rather than a decrease. This difference may reflect the fact that the FSSC-IIP is based on parent perceptions rather than child self-report.

It is noteworthy that a number of other assessment measures have been designed specifically to assess anxiety and fear in preschool-aged children. These measures can be used as resources to differentiate normative fears from atypical fears, as these measures often include data from normative, nonclinical samples in addition to data from clinical samples. One example is the Spence Preschool Anxiety Scale (Spence, Rapee, McDonald & Ingram, 2001), which is normed for preschool-aged children. This parent-report measure consists of 34 items and is appropriate for children aged 2.5 to 6.5 years. Another example is the Children's Moods, Fears and Worries Questionnaire (Bayer, Sanson, & Hemphill, 2006). More information on the assessment of preschool anxiety can be found in Chapters 4 and 5 of this book.

Specific Fears

Stranger Fear

At around six months of age, children begin to identify the presence of strangers and may begin to react to strangers with fear (Field, 2006). The typical development of this fear increases throughout the first year of life, and typically stabilizes by the second year (Brooker et al., 2012; Sroufe, 1977). Furthermore, mild stranger fear is believed to be an adaptive quality for the development of a secure attachment system (Ainsworth,

1973). However, studies have linked extreme and persistent stranger fear to the development of social anxiety (e.g., de Rosnay, Cooper, Tsigaras, & Murray, 2006; Kagan, 2000). As with other fears, normative stranger fear can be differentiated from more problematic fears based on duration and intensity.

Behavioral inhibition may be related to elevated stranger fears and related social fears (Brooker et al., 2012; Hirshfeld et al., 1992). Further, an association has been found between high maternal stress reactivity and infants with high levels of stranger fear (Biederman et al., 2001). This pattern has two possible explanations; one explanation is that maternal negative affect (such as anxiety, stress or depression) may predict anxiety risk in children (Biederman et al., 2001; Brooker et al., 2012). An alternative explanation is that fearfulness in infants may evoke symptoms in parents, and the heightened maternal negative affect is a direct result of the pattern of fearfulness of their infant (Brooker et al., 2012; Hirshfeld et al., 1992).

Separation Fears

Attachment experiences are foundational to multiple areas of a child's development including self-reliance, emotional regulation, and interpersonal competence (Sroufe, 2005). Children often look to their attachment figures for a sense of familiarity and comfort. Most children form an attachment to a caregiver by the age of one, and assuming secure attachment, fear of separation from primary caregivers typically emerges at this time (Gullone, 2000; Gullone & King, 1993; Schaffer & Emerson, 1964). Separation distress may manifest when the child anticipates separation, or while the child is actually separated from their attachment figures. The child may worry about losing them, harm befalling them, and being away from them. It is noteworthy that these fears are normative and DSM-5 criteria for separation anxiety disorder are only met if the fear is "developmentally inappropriate and excessive" (APA, 2013).

The literature suggests that separation concerns are prevalent amongst preschool-aged children, and typically reduce in intensity over time. In one study (Muris et al., 2000), four- to twelve-year-old children were surveyed about their fears and worries. Among specific fears reported by children, separation fear ranked rather low, with only 0.5% of the sample identifying separation from parents as being one of their specific fears. However, when broken down by age, approximately half of the four- to six-year-old children identified separation from parents as being their most intense worry, whilst separation worries did not even rank in the top three among older children. In summary, separation fears are present in a small subset of school-aged children, whereas worries about separation are rather common among preschool children who experience worry.

When separation fear, anxiety, or avoidance last in excess of four weeks, and cause significant distress or impairment in academic or social domains, or daily activities, then a diagnosis of separation anxiety disorder may be warranted (APA, 2013). This is the most commonly diagnosed childhood anxiety disorder (Cartwright-Hatton, McNicol, & Doubleday, 2006). A child suffering from separation anxiety will frequently tantrum, express somatic complaints, experience nightmares or sleep problems, and/or refuse to separate from their attachment figures (Schniering, Hudson, & Rapee, 2000). For young children, distress may only occur during the actual separation phase (APA, 2013). As the cognitive capacity to worry develops, children may begin to worry about dangerous situations in which they would not be reunited with their attachment figures (e.g., kidnapping, accidents, death) (APA, 2013; Muris et al., 2000).

Certain genetic, temperamental and biological risk factors have been found to contribute to clinically significant levels of separation fear and anxiety, and there is also substantial evidence for the involvement of environmental factors (Ehrenreich, Santucci & Weiner, 2008). Specifically, family and parenting variables have been implicated in the development of anxiety in children, including over-control, overprotection, rejection/criticism, and modeling or reinforcement of anxious/avoidant behaviors (Ginsburg, Siqueland, Masia-Warner & Hedtke, 2004). Accordingly, mechanisms of effective intervention may include increasing the child's autonomy, reinforcing brave behaviors, and improving parent-child attachment (Choate, Pincus, Eyberg, & Barlow, 2005).

Regarding the trajectory of separation fear, Battaglia and colleagues (2017) investigated the long-term outcomes of separation anxiety among preschool-aged children. The subset of young children with high levels of separation anxiety that increased over time had higher levels of internalizing behavior, poorer academic achievement, and worse physical health (i.e., headaches and asthma) in mid-childhood and preadolescence. Thus, intervention is recommended when separation distress persists outside of the typical developmental period and has a negative impact on the child's daily functioning, such as school, friendships, and daily routines.

Nighttime Fears

Bedtime difficulties are one of the most common presenting problems in young children. A significant number of infants and young children have difficulties with falling asleep, staying asleep, or rising early. Many children experience sleep-related difficulties associated with worries about noises, shadows, monsters, intruders, burglars, kidnappers, and being left alone at night (Gordon, King, Gullone, Muris, & Ollendick, 2007; King, Ollendick, & Tonge, 1997). The ongoing development of imagination in preschool-aged children may result in fears of monsters or creatures in the dark, which may then lead to nighttime fears (Meltzer & McLauglin Crabtree, 2015).

Other sleep-related difficulties associated with nighttime fears include nightmares and sleep terrors. Nightmares are common for children aged three to six years, of both sexes (Adair & Bauchner, 1993). Occasional nightmares are typical, but recurrent nightmares, or those with disturbing content, may indicate underlying stress during the day. Intervention is recommended to eliminate or reduce the child's exposure to the feared stimuli.

Sleep-terrors occur in 1% to 6% of children aged 18 months, and these normally disappear by six years of age (Anders & Eiben, 1997). It is recommended that children suffering from sleep-terrors are redirected back to bed, as children are extremely difficult to arouse and may not remember the incident when woken. When children refuse to go to bed for fear of being alone, or due to nightmares about being separated for an extended period of time, and this affects their ability to engage in normal activities, then the behavior has become atypical and intervention is recommended.

Monsters and Fantasy

When children feel fearful, the source can originate from a real situation (e.g., there is a spider in their room) or from their imagination (e.g., they say they saw a monster under their bed). Research has found that a child's ability to distinguish reality from fantasy occurs at around three years of age (Bourchier & Davis, 2002). Sayfan and Lagattuta (2009) reported that the majority of children aged three to five years understand that ghosts, witches, dragons and monsters are not real. A more sophisticated knowledge of people's fear reactions develops at around seven years of age, where the distinction between real- and imaginary-threat situations is demonstrated (Bourchier & Davis, 2002).

Normative Worry and Rituals

Worry

Fear is the unpleasant feeling experienced by an individual who is faced with danger or threat to survival (Gullone, King, & Ollendick, 2000; Marks, 1987). Worry, on the other hand, refers to the thought process around the possible occurrence of negative events in the future (Borkevec, Robinson, Pruzinsky, & DePree, 1983). Whilst fear is primarily based in the here and now, worry involves concerns about the future. As with fear, worry can be adaptive, as anticipation of problems and consideration of alternative solutions are helpful for planning. For example, worry may be related to problem-solving and may prepare individuals for negative outcomes (Silverman, La Greca, & Wasserstein, 1995). Further, older children have reported on the potential positive features of worrying, including more effective coping (Muris, Meesters, Merckelbach, Sermon & Zwakhalen, 1998).

The frequency and content of worry may be influenced by cognitive development, as children become more capable of worry as their cognitive abilities and structures develop (Vasey, 1993). Specifically, skills such as abstract reasoning are necessary for the elaboration and representation of concepts required for worrying. For example, between the ages of three and five years, Lagattuta (2007) found a significant improvement in the ability to consider possibilities of future negative events based on past negative events – a skill that may be necessary for worry about abstract concepts. Other researchers have focused on worry elaboration, defined as the ability to generate potential negative outcomes, which may be a fundamental ability required for engagement in worry (Muris, Merckelbach, Meesters, & van den Brand, 2002). Muris et al. (2002) found that, among three- to seven-year-old children, cognitive development has been found to mediate the relationship between age and worry elaboration. In a similar study, Grist & Field (2012) found that specific cognitive abilities mediated the relationship between age and worry elaboration, including the acknowledgement of multiple possibilities, the development of concrete operational skills, and the development of theory of mind.

The frequency of worry and changes in worry-related content seem to follow a predictive developmental pattern. Specifically, the aforementioned study by Muris et al. (2002) found that the percentage of children who reported worry increased by age group (3- to 6-year-olds: 48.2%, 7- to 9-year-olds: 56.8%, and 10- to 14-year-olds: 74.7%). Similarly, researchers found from another study that approximately half of four- to six-year-old children report specific worries, and this number essentially doubles among seven- to nine-year-old children (Muris et al., 2000). Further, Vasey, Crnic, & Carter (1994) found that the worrying of children aged eight years and older was not only more common than the worrying of younger children, but it was also more varied and elaborative. Additional support has been found for shifts in worry content over time. In particular, the content of worries has been found to shift from concerns about physical wellbeing to psychological wellbeing, behavioral competence, and social evaluation between the ages of five and twelve years (Vasey, Crnic, & Carter, 1994). For example, worries among four- to six-year-old children include separation from parents and dying or death of others, while the top worries among seven- to nine-year-old children include personal harm or harm to others, dying or death of others, and test performance (Muris et al., 2000). Despite the rapid changes in the content and nature of worry that occurs in early childhood, there is some evidence to suggest that worry is relatively stable in school-aged children. For example, Silverman, La Greca, and Wasserstein (1995) found that, between the ages of seven and twelve years, various parameters of worry (e.g., number, content, intensity, perception of frequency) appear to be relatively stable. Further, there is some research to suggest that the intensity and susceptibility to intrusive, uncontrollable thoughts may even reduce around this time (Laing, Fernyhough, Turner, & Freeston, 2009).

Rituals

Some level of ritualistic behavior is common in young, typically developing children between the ages of two and five years (Gesell, Ilg, & Ames, 1974; Zohar & Dahan, 2016). Consequently, it can be difficult to distinguish obsessive-compulsive behaviors more indicative of psychopathology from normative, ritualistic behaviors in young children. For example, magical thinking and rigidity tend to be interconnected with pretend play, and these behaviors are considered normative in preschoolers (King, Muris, & Ollendick, 2005). It is noteworthy that ritualistic behaviors typically subside after the age of five due to general maturation and frontal lobe development (Boyer & Liénard, 2006; Zohar & Dahan, 2016).

A number of considerations can aid in the distinction between normative rituals and obsessive compulsive disorder (OCD). Specifically, disruptions to normative ritualistic behaviors may cause some distress to most children, but the inability of a child suffering from OCD to engage in their ritual will likely cause high level distress and anxiety. Another consideration relates to the function of the ritual. With OCD, compulsions or repetitive behaviors such as checking or washing are performed to reduce anxiety and to neutralize maladaptive thoughts that are perceived as being uncontrollable (APA, 2013; Evans et al., 1997). Furthermore, compulsions or repetitive behaviors may be attempts made by children with OCD, to control their environments, or to ward off harm to self or others (King & Noshpitz, 1991).

Overall, if the ritualistic behaviors persist, lead to substantial distress, and/or are excessive (e.g., more than one hour per day), then clinical intervention may be necessary. Please refer to Chapter 7 for further information regarding the assessment and treatment of OCD in preschool children. Finally, it is worth pointing out that other medically related problems can be associated with problematic ritualistic behaviors, including autism spectrum disorder and Pediatric Autoimmune Neuropsychiatric Disorders Associated with Streptococcal Infections (PANDAS), and thus, specialist intervention and diagnosis may be necessary.

Factors that Influence the Development of Problematic Fear

Early childhood anxiety (four- to six-year-old children) continues to be an understudied area. Given the long life-course of anxiety and depression, it is important to understand potential risk factors for early childhood anxiety. An overview is provided in this section. See Chapter 2 of this book for a more detailed review of risk and protective factors related to the development and maintenance of anxiety in young children.

Temperament

Behavioral inhibition, or inhibited temperament, is described as marked behavioral restrain or fearfulness with unfamiliar people and situations (Kagan, Reznick, & Snidman, 1988), and a large body of research provides support for a robust association between behavioral inhibition and child anxiety. For example, in a meta-analytic review, children with behavioral inhibition were seven times more likely to develop social anxiety over time than children without behavioral inhibition (Clauss & Blackford, 2012). Whilst 15% of children with typical development display behavioral inhibition, not all children with behavioral inhibition will develop a disorder (Fox, Hendersen, Marshall, Nichols & Ghera, 2005). Consequently, environmental factors also appear to be relevant to the development of excessive fears and anxiety (Pahl, Barrett, & Gullo, 2012).

Role of Parents

Further to behavioral inhibition, numerous studies have found support for the role of parenting behaviors and parent-child interactions in the development and maintenance of child anxiety (Pahl, Barrett, & Gullo, 2012). In particular, many studies have consistently found parental overcontrol and overprotection to be associated with child anxiety (Möller, Nikolić, Majdandžić, & Bögels, 2016; Murray, Creswell, & Cooper, 2009; Yap, Pilkington, Ryan, & Jorm, 2014). For example, in a meta-analytic review by Möller et al. (2016), a small but significant effect was found for the relationship between parenting behavior and anxiety in young children. In addition to overcontrol and overprotection, specific learning pathways may account for the transmission of anxiety from parent to child, including reinforcement, modeling/vicarious learning, and information transfer (Fisak & Grills-Taquechel, 2007; Rachman, 1989). Parents may inadvertently reinforce their child's anxiety; rather than encouraging an anxious child to face his or her fears, the parent may enable avoidance by allowing the child to avoid feared situations, or the parent may quickly remove the child from an anxiety-inducing situation. Children may also learn anxiety through parental modeling of anxious behavior and avoidance of certain situations that may produce anxiety. Further, negative information transfer occurs when parents verbally communicate a sense of danger to their children. Overall, various transactional learning pathways may be involved in the development and maintenance of excessive fear.

Other Risk Factors

Other possible pathways for the development of excessive fear and anxiety are noteworthy. For example, several studies have linked child internalizing difficulties to traumatic events, conflict between parents, low social support, daily hassles with parenting, and low socioeconomic status (Ashford, Smit, van Lier, Cuijpers, & Koot, 2008; Cicchetti & Toth, 1998).

Demographic Variations

Cultural Variations in Children's Fears

A number of studies have examined children from different cultures from two perspectives. The first is the comparison of children from various ethnic backgrounds within one country, and the second is the comparison of children from various countries and nationalities. Interestingly, most investigations examining cross-cultural comparisons between children's fears found more similarities than differences (Burnham & Gullone, 1997). However, some specific cross-cultural differences have been observed (Burnham & Gullone, 1997; Burnham, Hooper, & Ogorchock, 2011). For example, Burnham and colleagues (2011) found that both Israeli Bedouin and Israeli Jewish youths were fearful of snakes, which may have been explained by their close proximity to deserts where snakes live. Another example includes the observation that Australian children reported a fear of sharks as being amongst their top ten fears, whereas this has not been reported as a common fear in children from other countries (Ollendick, Yang, King, Dong, & Akande, 1996). Given that most populated areas of Australia are coastal, where sharks may pose a real threat, then this likely explains why sharks are among Australian children's top ten fears compared with children from other countries. Kayyal and Widen (2015) compared the fears of children between the ages of three and seven years from Palestine and America. The authors found that, in both groups, imaginary creatures were cited as the most common cause of fear, suggesting a similarity in fears. However, differences between the samples were also observed. When the children were asked to generate possible causes of fear for a male or female hero in a story, imaginary causes were primarily identified as being fearful by the American children, whereas the Palestinian sample generated more realistic causes (Kayyal & Widen, 2015).

Gender Variations in Children's Fears

Overall, girls consistently report a higher intensity and greater number of self-reported fears than boys (Mellon, Koliadis, & Paraskevopoulos, 2004; Muris, 2007; Muris, Merckelbach, & Collaris, 1997). Boys and girls across cultures report fears of different objects and situations relative to members of the opposite sex. However, when the differences were examined, gender-influenced fears were not strong in young children (Spence et al., 2001).

Treatment and Early Intervention – Information for Parents, Educators, and Practitioners

If a child is experiencing fears, regardless of whether the fears are normative or excessive, it is important to encourage feelings of confidence and control, as children learn to handle fears better when they are given support to be autonomous and independent (Matthews, 2010). Related to this point, it is imperative that parents and educators listen to, and show empathy and support for the child, while exploring different strategies to overcome his or her fears. It is equally important that children are encouraged to, and allowed to talk about their fears and feelings, and build relationships of trust and support. Furthermore, it is vital that parents and educators do not make fun of a child's fears, nor discipline behaviors relating to those fears. Providing a secure, nurturing relationship from which the child can explore and develop confidence to try new coping strategies will enhance the effectiveness of a child's ability to deal with his or her fears. In relation to this point, early intervention provides increased opportunities for learning, and there is less chance that avoidance can develop. For more information about early intervention, please see Chapter 10 of this book, which is focused on the prevention of anxiety.

When children's fears are excessive, then clinical diagnoses follow observations and/or parent and teacher reports of fears across settings, questionnaires completed by parents and teachers, and comparative analyses of symptoms with DSM-5 criteria. In these cases, the early involvement of professionals can be implemented to help children cope with excessive fears, and treatment may include graduated exposure to feared objects and situations, as well as participation and reinforcement from parents (King, Muris, & Ollendick, 2005). Evidence-based treatment programs for preschool-aged children include parent-only programs (such as the *Timid to Tiger* program, developed by Cartwright-Hatton, Laskey, Rust, & McNally, 2010), and combined parent and child treatments (such as the *Fun FRIENDS* program, developed by Barrett, 2007). Please refer to Chapter 6 of this book for further information.

Summary

The early identification of an atypical trajectory in a young child's mental health status can have a long-term impact on well-being into adolescence and adulthood. Consequently, it is important to understand age- and stage-appropriate fears if we are to identify and successfully assist children in dealing with excessive fears (Matthews, 2010).

Whilst fears do vary in frequency, intensity and duration, they are typically mild, age-specific, and transitory (Ollendick, King, & Muris, 2002). However, markers suggesting that intervention may be necessary include fear that is excessive (relative to same-aged children), persistent (especially outside of the typical developmental window), and cause significant distress

Table 3.1 A summary of children's fears by age

Age	Fear
0–6 months	Loss of support, loud noises, sudden movement
7–12 months	Strangers, sudden appearance of large objects, loud noises
1 year	Separation from parent, strangers, injury, toilet
2 years	Large animals, dark rooms, large objects and machines, loud noises, sudden changes in routine
3–4 years	Dark rooms, masks, large animals, snakes, separation from parent, noises at night
5 years	Wild animals, bodily injury (e.g., medical procedures), dark, bad people, separation from parent
6–7 years	Ghosts, monsters, witches, dark, being alone, thunder and lightning, storms, being lost, kidnapping

Adapted from Robinson, Rotter, Fey, & Robinson, 1991. Permission granted by the American School Counselor Association.

or disruption in functioning (and this can include family functioning). Under these circumstances, it is important that caregivers promptly acknowledge the difficulties and seek professional assistance for an assessment, so that early invention can inform a suitable treatment plan. A summary of typical fears by developmental stage is provided in Table 3.1.

References

Adair, R. H., & Bauchner, H. (1993). Sleep problems in childhood. *Current Problems in Pediatrics*, 23, 147–170. doi:10.1016/0045–9380(93)90011-Z

Ainsworth, M. (1973). The development of infant-mother attachment. In B. Caldwell & H. Ricciuti (Eds.), *Review of child development research* (Vol. 3, pp. 1–94). Chicago: University of Chicago Press.

American Psychiatric Association (APA). (2013). *Diagnostic and statistical manual of mental disorders* (5th ed.). Washington, DC: APA.

Anders, T. F., & Eiben, L. A. (1997). Pediatric sleep disorders: A review of the past 10 years. *Journal of the American Academy of Child and Adolescent Psychiatry*, 36, 9–20. doi:10.1097/00004583–199701000–00012

Ashford, J., Smit, F., van Lier, P. A., Cuijpers, P., & Koot, H. M. (2008). Early risk indicators of internalizing problems in late childhood: A 9-year longitudinal study. *Journal of Child Psychology and Psychiatry*, 49, 774–780. doi:10.1111/j.1469–7610.2008.01889.x

Barrett, P.M. (2007). *Fun Friends. The teaching and training manual for group leaders*. Brisbane, Australia: Fun Friends Publishing.

Battaglia, M., Garon-Carrier, G., Côté, S. M., Dionne, G., Touchette, E., Vitaro, F., & ... Boivin, M. (2017). Early childhood trajectories of separation anxiety: Bearing on mental health, academic achievement, and physical health from mid-childhood to preadolescence. *Depression and Anxiety*, 34, 918–927. doi:10.1002/da.22674

Bayer, J. K., Sanson, A. V., & Hemphill, S. A. (2006). Children's moods, fears, and worries: Development of an early childhood parent questionnaire. *Journal of Emotional and Behavioral Disorders*, 14(1), 41–49. doi:10.1177/10634266060140010401

Biederman, J., Hirshfeld-Becker, D. R., Rosenbaum, J. F., Herot, C., Friedman, D., Snidman, N., Kgan, J., & Faraone, S.V. (2001). Further evidence of association between behavioral inhibition and social anxiety in children. *American Journal of Psychiatry*, 158, 1673–1679. doi:10.1176/appi.ajp.158.10.1673

Borkovec, T. D., Robinson, E., Pruzinsky, T., & DePree, J. A. (1983). Preliminary exploration of worry: Some characteristics and processes. *Behaviour Research and Therapy*, 21, 9–16. doi:10.1016/0005-7967(83)90121-90123

Bouldin, P., & Pratt, C. (1998). Utilizing parent report to investigate young children's fears: a modification of the Fear Survey Schedule for Children–II: A research note. *Journal of Child Psychology and Psychiatry*, 39, 271–277. doi:10.1017/S0021963097001881

Bourchier, A., & Davis, A. (2002). Children's understanding of the pretence-reality distinction: A review of current theory and evidence. *Developmental Science*, 5, 397–413. doi:10.1111/1467-7687.00236_1

Boyer, P., & Liénard, P. (2006). Why ritualized behavior? Precaution systems and action parsing in developmental, pathological and cultural rituals. *Behavioral & Brain Sciences*, 29, 595–613. doi:10.1017/S0140525X06009332

BrookerR. J., Neiderhiser, J. M., Ganiban, J. M., Leve, L. D., Shaw, D. S., & Reiss, D. (2012). Difficult temperament in infancy evokes changes in parent anxiety symptoms over time. Paper presented at the biennial meeting of the International Society on Infant Studies. Minneapolis, MN.

Burnham, J. J. & Gullone, E. (1997). The fear survey schedule for children-II: A psychometric investigation with American data. *Behaviour Research & Therapy*, 35, 165–173. doi:10.1016/S0005-7967(96)00089-7

Burnham, J.J., Hooper, L.M. & Ogorchock, H.N. (2011). Differences in the fears of elementary school children in North and South America: A cross-cultural comparison. *International Journal of Advanced Counseling*, 33, 235–251. doi:10.1007/s10447–10011–9131–9137

Cartwright-Hatton, S., Laskey, B., Rust, S., & McNally, D. (2010). *From timid to tiger: A treatment manual for parenting the anxious child*. Chichester: Wiley-Blackwell. doi:10.1002/9780470970331

Cartwright-Hatton, S., McNicol, K., & Doubleday, E. (2006). Anxiety in a neglected population: prevalence of anxiety disorders in preadolescent children. *Clinical Psychology Review*, 26(7), 817–833. doi:10.1016/j.cpr.2005. 12. 00doi:2

Choate, M. L., Pincus, D. B., Eyberg, S. M., & Barlow, D. H. (2005). Parent-child interaction therapy for treatment of separation anxiety disorder in young children: A pilot study. *Cognitive and Behavioral Practice*, 12(1), 126–135. doi:10.1016/S1077-7229(05)80047-80041

Cicchetti, D., & Toth, S. L. (1998). The development of depression in children and adolescents. *American Psychologist*, 53(2), 221–241. doi:10.1037/0003-0066X.53.2.221

Clauss, J. A., & Blackford, J. U. (2012). Behavioral inhibition and risk for developing social anxiety disorder: A meta-analytic study. *Journal of the American Academy of Child & Adolescent Psychiatry*, 51, 1066–1075. doi:10.1016/j.jaac.2012. 08. 00doi:2

de Rosnay, M., Cooper, P. J., Tsigaras, N., & Murray, L. (2006). Transmission of social anxiety from mother to infant: An experimental study using a social referencing paradigm. *Behaviour Research and Therapy*, 44, 1165–1175. doi:10.1016/j.brat.2005. 09. 00doi:3

Draper, T. W., & James, R. S. (1985). Preschool fears: Longitudinal sequence and cohort changes. *Child Study Journal*, 15(2), 147–156.

Edelbrock, C., Costello, A. J., Dulcan, M. K., Kalas, R., & Conover, N. C. (1985). Age differences in the reliability of the psychiatric interview of the child. *Child Development*, 56, 265–275. doi:10.2307/1130193

Ehrenreich, J. T., Santucci, L. C., & Weiner, C. L. (2008). Separation anxiety disorder in youth: Phenomenology, assessment, and treatment. *Behavioral Psychology*, 16, 389–412.

Evans, D. W., Leckman, J. F., Carter, A., Reznick, J. S., Henshaw, D., King, R. A., & Pauls, D. (1997). Ritual, habit and perfectionism: The prevalence and development of compulsive-like behaviour in normal young children. *Child Development*, 68, 58–68. doi:10.2307/1131925

Ferrari, M. (1986). Fears and phobias in childhood: Some clinical and developmental considerations. *Child Psychiatry and Human Development*, 17, 75–87. doi:10.1007/BF00706646

Field, A. P. (2006). Watch out for the beast: Fear information and attentional bias in children. *Journal of Clinical Child and Adolescent Psychology*, 35, 431–439. doi:10.1207/s15374424jccp3503_8

Fisak, B., & Grills-Taquechel, A. E. (2007). Parental modeling, reinforcement, and information transfer: Risk factors in the development of child anxiety? *Clinical Child and Family Psychology Review*, 10, 213–231. doi:10.1007/s10567-007-0020-x

Fox, N. A., Henderson, H. A., Marshall, P. J., Nichols, K. E., & Ghera, M. M. (2005). Behavioral inhibition: Linking biology and behaviour within a developmental framework. *Annual Review of Psychology*, 56, 235–262. doi:10.1146/annurev.psych.55.090902.141532

Gesell, A., Ilg, F. L., & Ames, L. B. (1974). *Infant and child in the culture of today*. London: Harper & Row.

Ginsburg, G. S., Siqueland, L., Masia-Warner, C., & Hedtke, K. A. (2004). Anxiety disorders in children: Family matters. *Cognitive and Behavioral Practice*, 11(1), 28–43. doi:10.1016/S1077-7229(04)80005-1

Gordon, J., King, N., Gullone, E., Muris, P., & Ollendick, T. H. (2007). Nighttime fears of children and adolescents: Frequency, content, severity, harm expectations, disclosure, and coping behaviours. *Behaviour Research and Therapy*, 45(10), 2464–2472. doi:10.1016/j.brat.2007. 03. 01doi:3

Grist, R. M., & Field, A. P. (2012). The mediating effect of cognitive development on children's worry elaboration. *Journal of Behavior Therapy and Experimental Psychiatry*, 43(2), 801–807. doi:10.1016/j.jbtep.2011.11.002

Gullone, E. (2000). The development of normal fear: A century of research. *ClinicalPsychology Review*, 20(4), 429–451. doi: 10.1016/S0272–7358(99)33–34

Gullone, E. (1999). The assessment of normal fear in children and adolescents. *Clinical Child and Family Psychology Review*, 2, 91–106. doi:10.1023/A:1021895630678

Gullone, E., & King, N. J. (1992). Psychometric evaluation of a revised fear survey schedule for children and adolescents. *Journal of Child Psychology and Psychiatry*, 33, 987–999. doi:10.1111/j.1469-7610.1992.tb00920.x

Gullone, E., & King, N. J. (1993). The fears of youth in the 1990s: Contemporary normative data. *The Journal of Genetic Psychology*, 154(2), 137–153. doi:10.1080/00221325.1993.9914728

Gullone, E., King, N. J., & Ollendick, T. H. (2000). The development and psy-chometric evaluation of the Fear Experiences Questionnaire: An attempt to disentangle the fear and anxiety constructs. *Clinical Psychology & Psychotherapy*, 7, 61–75. doi:10.1002/(SICI)1099–0879(200002)7:1<61:AID-CPP227>3.0.CO;2-P

Hirshfeld, D. R., Rosenbaum, J. F., Biederman, J., Bolduc, E. A., Faraone, S.V., Snidman, N., Reznick, J.S., & Kagan, J. (1992). Stable behavioral inhibition and its association with anxiety disorder. *Journal of the American Academy of Child and Adolescent Psychiatry*, 31, 103–111. doi:10.1097/00004583-199201000-00016

Kagan, J. (2000). Inhibited and uninhibited temperaments: Recent developments. In W. R. Crozier (Ed.), *Shyness: Development, consolidation and change* (pp. 22–29). London: Routledge.

Kagan, J., Reznick, J. S., & Snidman, N. (1988). Biological bases of childhood shyness. *Science*, 240, 167–171. doi:10.1126/science.3353713

Kayyal, M., & Widen, S. (2015). What made Sahar scared? Imaginary and realis-tic causes in Palestinian and American children's concept for fear. *Journal of Cognition and Culture*, 15, 32–44. doi:10.1163/15685373–12342139

King, N. J., Gullone, E., & Tonge, R. J. (1991). Childhood fears and anxiety dis-orders. *Behaviour Change*, 8, 124–135.

King, N. J., Muris, P., & Ollendick, T. H. (2005). Childhood fears and phobias: Assessment and treatment. *Child and Adolescent Mental Health*, 10(2), 50–56. doi:10.1111/j.14753588.2005.00118.x

King, R. A., & Noshpitz, J. D. (1991). *Pathways of growth. Essentials of child psy-chiatry: Vol. 2. Psychopathology*. New York: Wiley.

King, N., Ollendick, T. H., & Tonge, B. J. (1997). Children's nighttime fears. *Clinical Psychology Review*, 17(4), 431–443. doi:10.1016/S0272-7358(97)00014-7

Lagattuta, K. H. (2007). Thinking about the future because of the past: Young children's knowledge about the causes of worry and preventative decisions. *Child Development*, 78, 1492–1509. doi:10.1111/j.1467-8624.2007.01079.x

Laing, S. V., Fernyhough, C., Turner, M., & Freeston, M. H. (2009). Fear, worry, and ritualistic behavior in childhood: Developmental trends and interrelations. *Infant and Child Development*, 18(4), 351–366. doi:10.1002/icd.627

Marks, I. M. (1987). *Fears, phobias, and rituals: Panic, anxiety, and their disorders*. Oxford: Oxford University Press.

Matthews, S. N. (2010). *Children's fears: Developmental or disorder?*Pittsburgh: Uni-versity of Pittsburgh School of Education.

Mellon, R., Koliadis, E., & Paraskevopoulos, T. (2004). Normative development of fears in Greece: Self-reports on the Hellenic Fear Survey Schedule for Children. *Journal of Anxiety Disorders*, 18, 233–254. doi:10.1016/S0887-6185(03)00011-2

Meltzer, L. J., & McLaughlin Crabtree, V. (2015). Nighttime fears, anxiety, and recurrent nightmares. In *Pediatric, sleep problems: A clinician's guide to behavioral interventions* (pp. 119–141). Washington, DC: American Psychological Associa-tion. doi:10.1037/14645–14009

Möller, E. L., Nikolić, M., Majdandžić, M., & Bögels, S. M. (2016). Associations between maternal and paternal parenting behaviors, anxiety and its precursors in early childhood: A meta-analysis. *Clinical Psychology Review*, 45, 17–33. doi:10.1016/j.cpr.2016.03.002

Muris, P. (2006). The pathogenesis of childhood anxiety disorders: considerations from a developmental psychopathology perspective. *International Journal of Behavioral Development*, 31, 4–10. doi:10.1177/0165025406059967

Muris, P. (2007). *Normal and abnormal fear and anxiety in children and adolescents.* Oxford: Elsevier.

Muris, P., Meesters, C., Merckelbach, H., Sermon, A., & Zwakhalen, S. (1998). Worry in normal children. *Journal of the American Academy of Child & Adolescent Psychiatry*, 37, 703–710. doi:10.1097/00004583–199807000–00009

Muris, P., Merckelbach, H., & Collaris, R. (1997). Common childhood fears and their origins. *Behaviour Research and Therapy*, 35, 929–937. doi:10.1016/S0005–7967(97)00050–00058

Muris, P., Merckelbach, H., Gadet, B., & Moulaert, V. (2000). Fears, worries, and scary dreams in 4- to 12-year-old children: Their content, developmental pattern, and origins. *Journal of Clinical Child Psychology*, 29(1), 43–52. doi:10.1207/S15374424jccp2901_5

Muris, P., Merckelbach, H., Meesters, C., & van den Brand, K. (2002). Cognitive development and worry in normal children. *Cognitive Therapy and Research*, 26(6), 775–787. doi:10.1023/A:1021241517274

Murray, L., Creswell, C., & Cooper, P. J. (2009). The development of anxiety disorders in childhood: An integrative review. *Psychological Medicine*, 39, 1413–1423. doi:10.1017/S0033291709005157

Ollendick, T., King, N., & Muris, P. (2002). Fears and phobias in children: Phenomenology, epidemiology, and aetiology. *Child and Adolescent Mental Health*, 7, 98–106.

Ollendick, T. H., Yang, B., King, N. J., Dong, Q., & Akande, A. (1996). Fears in American, Australia, Chinese, and Nigerian children and adolescents: A cross-cultural study. *Journal of Child Psychology and Psychiatry*, 37, 213–220. doi:10.1111/1475–3588.00019

Pahl, K. M., Barrett, P. M., & Gullo, M. J. (2012). Examining potential risk factors for anxiety in early childhood. *Journal of Anxiety Disorders*, 26, 311–320. doi:10.1016/janxdis.2011.12.013

Rachman, S. J., (1989). The return of fear: Review and prospect. *Clinical Psychology Review*, 9, 147–168. doi:10.1016/0272-7358(89)90025-1

Robinson, E. H., Rotter, J. C., Fey, M. A., & Robinson, S. L. (1991). Children's fears: Toward a preventive model. *School Counselor*, 38(3), 187–202.

Sayfan, L., & Lagattuta, K. H. (2009). Scaring the monster away: What children know about managing fears of real and imaginary creatures. *Child Development*, 80(6), 1756–1774. doi:10.1111/j.1467-8624.2009.01366.x

Schaffer, H. R., & Emerson, P. E. (1964). The development of social attachments in infancy. *Monographs of the Society for Research in Child Development*, 29(3), 1–77. doi:10.2307/1165727

Schniering, C. A., Hudson, J. L., & Rapee, R. M. (2000). Issues in the diagnosis and assessment of anxiety disorders in children and adolescents. *Clinical Psychology Review*, 20(4), 453–478. doi:10.1016/S0272–7358(99)00037–00039

Silverman, W. K., La Greca, A. M., & Wasserstein, S. (1995). What do children worry about? Worries and their relation to anxiety. *Child Development*, 66, 671–686. doi:10.2307/1131942

Spence, S. H., Rapee, R., McDonald, C., & Ingram, M. (2001). The structure of anxiety symptoms among preschoolers. *Behaviour Research and Therapy*, 39, 1293–1316. doi:10.1016/S0005–7967(00)00098-X

Sroufe, L. A. (1977). Wariness of strangers and the study of infant development. *Child Development*, 48, 731–746. doi:10.2307/1128323

Sroufe, L. A. (2005). Attachment and development: A prospective, longitudinal study from birth to adulthood. *Attachment & Human Development*, 7, 349–367. doi:10.1080/14616730500365928

Vasey, M. W. (1993). Development and cognition in childhood anxiety: The example of worry. *Advances in Clinical Child Psychology*, 15, 1–39.

Vasey, M. W., Crnic, K. A., & Carter, W. G. (1994). Worry in childhood: A developmental perspective. *Cognitive Therapy and Research*, 18(6), 529–549. doi:10.1007/BF02355667

Yap, M. H., Pilkington, P. D., Ryan, S. M., & Jorm, A. F. (2014). Parental factors associated with depression and anxiety in young people: A systematic review and meta-analysis. *Journal of Affective Disorders*, 156, 8–23. doi:10.1016/j.jad.2013. 11. 00doi:7

Zohar, A. H., & Dahan, D. (2016). Young children's ritual compulsive-like behavior and executive function: A cross section study. *Child Psychiatry and Human Development*, 47, 13–22. doi:10.1007/s10578-015-0539-x

4 Assessment of Fear and Anxiety in Preschool Children
Parent and Teacher Report

Susan H. Spence

Introduction

This chapter provides a pragmatic overview of the empirical literature regarding parent and teacher report methods for the assessment of anxiety in preschool children. As noted in previous chapters, the relatively high prevalence of anxiety problems among preschoolers and the potential adverse consequences if left untreated mean that it is imperative that we can identify anxious children as early in life as possible, to ensure that they receive interventions designed to treat current or prevent future anxiety disorders.

The Purpose of the Assessment and Practical Considerations

Various types of assessment methods can be used to obtain information about anxiety, including questionnaires/surveys/rating scales, clinical interviews, direct behavioral observation (in naturalistic settings or the lab/clinic), and physiological recordings. However, the present chapter is limited to questionnaires/surveys/rating scales and clinical interviews in which parents, caregivers or teachers are the informants. The methods used vary according to the purpose and context. There are many situations in which anxious young children may come to the attention of professionals, such as day care/preschool, foster care and child custody situations, and contact with pediatricians, general practitioners, family services, and community nurses, to mention just a few. Depending on the context, the assessment may be designed to:

i   screen young children in community settings (e.g., preschools) to identify those with elevated but subclinical levels of anxiety who may benefit from early intervention or targeted prevention, and for whom a more in-depth assessment is justified;

ii assess young children who are at increased risk of developing anxiety problems (e.g., having experienced trauma, abuse, neglect, parental loss, parental mental illness, or an early temperament of behavioral inhibition) to identify those who may benefit from a targeted prevention program;

iii determine whether a child is experiencing anxiety symptoms that are of sufficient severity, frequency, and duration, and associated with sufficient impairment to functioning that the problem cannot be regarded as a normal part of the child's development, and thus, justifies clinical treatment;

iv conduct a more in-depth assessment to clarify the nature of the presenting problem and other comorbid disorders, to inform the case formulation, the decision to treat, and the form of treatment;

v establish a baseline from which to (a) monitor anxiety symptoms during therapy to inform whether changes in treatment are required, and (b) compare the post-treatment and follow-up results to determine the effectiveness of the intervention; and

vi assess the nature and severity of anxiety symptoms as a component of research studies that examine the developmental psychopathology of anxiety, such as epidemiology, trajectories, risk and protective factors, causes, consequences and comorbidity.

Measures vary in terms of the purpose for which they were designed, the length, the focus (broad range versus specific mental health problems), and the informant (children, parents, teachers, carers, or clinicians). In some instances, measures that were designed for intensive research studies are less practical for school or clinical contexts, where less time is available for their completion, and where it is not feasible to use long, comprehensive assessment batteries with multiple informants. The selection of measures may also be influenced by the requirements for training of staff in the use of the measure. For example, administration of the Schedule for Affective Disorders and Schizophrenia for School-Age Children (KSADS: Kaufman et al., 1997) is restricted to mental health clinicians who have completed appropriate training, in order to enhance the reliability of the measure.

Collecting Information for the Case Formulation

In addition to information about frequency, duration, and severity of anxiety symptoms and their impact upon the child's functioning, the assessment process generally obtains data about the emotional/affective, cognitive, behavioral and physiological components of anxiety. Information is collected about how the child feels, what they think/worry about, what they do, and how their body reacts in situations that provoke anxiety. In clinical contexts, the information typically derives from the diagnostic interview, questionnaire data, background information and other assessment data. These data are then integrated to produce a case formulation that determines whether a problem exists of sufficient severity, duration, frequency and impairment to warrant intervention. It clarifies the specific cognitive, behavioral, affective and physiological symptoms, the situations in which they occur, the likely causal and maintaining factors, and whether these are potentially modifiable (McLeod, Weisz, & Wood, 2007). The collated assessment information then enables the clinician to design a treatment plan that addresses the presenting problem. A good understanding of the developmental psychopathology, and risk and protective factors associated with early childhood anxiety is required in order to identify potential causal and maintaining factors that could be addressed during treatment, or which may have an influence on the treatment process (Dougherty et al., 2013; Garro, 2016; Muris, 2007; see also Chapter 2). Spence (2017) outlined some key factors that should be examined during the assessment process, including:

i   Parental mental health problems suggesting potential genetic and biological factors and/or a challenging family environment
ii Early childhood temperament, including behavioral inhibition or neuroticism
iii Parenting behavior (e.g., modelling of anxiety, threat communication, rewarding of avoidance, excessive criticism, harsh discipline, and/or overcontrol/intrusiveness)
iv The child's experience of life or family stressors (e.g., parental absence, serious illness of the child or family member, death, family violence, parent conflict, parent separation/divorce, high levels of parent stress)
v   The child's experience of trauma, abuse, neglect, or fear conditioning events
vi Peer or sibling victimization or isolation
vii The child's developmental and behavioral skills deficits or impairments (e.g., social skills, externalizing problems, attention deficits, developmental delays, physical, sensory or motor skills impairments)
viii Strengths or protective factors within the child, family, and environment that can be drawn on during the treatment process, such as parental warmth, positive and supportive relationships with parents, family, significant others, peers, siblings or teachers, and the child's coping strategies and emotional regulation skills.

The treatment plan should then be informed by knowledge of evidence-based treatment approaches to ensure that they have demonstrable effectiveness in the treatment of the specific type(s) of anxiety relevant to the preschool population.

Data from Different Informants

Parents, caregivers, and teachers tend to be the most frequently used informants in the assessment of anxiety in preschool children, but the young child him/herself can also contribute to the assessment process as outlined by Muris in Chapter 5. The use of different informants has implications for the data obtained. Children vary in the locations in which they experience anxiety, such as home versus preschool, and thus, mothers, fathers and teachers will have different perspectives and awareness of the child's anxiety. Parents may be unaware of their child's anxious presentation at school, and similarly, teachers generally have limited knowledge of a child's anxiety outside of the school setting (Headley & Campbell, 2011). Mothers and fathers may differ in their perceptions of their child's behavior depending on their level of contact with the child (Moreno et al., 2008). Parents' own mental health problems may also influence their reporting, with negative affectivity being associated with an over-estimation of the child's anxiety symptoms (Fjermestad et al., 2017). Social stereotyping is another factor that may impact on parents' and teachers' judgements about whether or not anxiety is regarded as being a problem for a particular child, with anxiety symptoms being more likely to be seen as problematic when they occur in boys, rather than girls, for whom anxiety may be regarded as a more "normal" occurrence (Headley & Campbell, 2011). Not surprisingly, the level of agreement between different informants regarding the presence and severity of anxiety problems tends to be relatively modest (Rescorla et al., 2014). Clinicians, therefore, need to use their clinical judgement to integrate information from different informants. Smith (2007) suggests that, where discrepancies occur between informants in the assessment of younger children, priority should be given to data from those who spend most time with the child in the setting concerned.

Evidence-based Measures/Psychometric Criteria – What Do We Look for?

Wherever possible, evidence-based assessment measures should be used with careful attention paid to their psychometric properties (Hunsley & Mash, 2008). In terms of validity, there should be evidence that the measure assesses the construct that it purports to measure, and not other constructs. This includes convergent validity (the results of the measure correlate highly with those from other measures of the same construct) and divergent validity (the results do not correlate so strongly with measures of other constructs). There should also be evidence of good construct validity as reflected by factor analytic data, indicating that the items within the scale (or subscales) cluster together in the manner predicted by the theoretical underpinnings of the scale(s). Strong internal consistency of the measure is also important, showing that items within the scale are measuring the same construct. Measures need good test-retest reliability over time, and yet, they should be sufficiently sensitive to changes in anxiety symptoms to provide a valid measure of treatment effects. If instruments are to be used to make decisions about clinical diagnoses, then one would expect them to show high levels of sensitivity and specificity. That is, the scale should have a high level of accuracy in correctly identifying those who do have the disorder of concern (sensitivity) and yet should also be accurate in not identifying those who do not have the disorder (specificity) with a low false alarm rate.

Finally, given the rapid and variable rate of development of children's language, motor, emotional and interpersonal skills during early childhood, it is important that measures have well-established norms by gender and age, suitable for the preschool population. Measures also need to assess the child's behavior across different contexts, given the variability in children's behavior in different locations (e.g., home, preschool, visiting other families, shopping, playgrounds, etc.) and with different individuals (e.g., family members, teachers, peers, familiar adults, strangers, etc.). The cultural background of the family and language spoken at home also need to be taken into account to ensure that the norms are appropriate for the child concerned.

Diagnostic Interviews

There is significant debate in the literature regarding the validity and ethics of diagnosing anxiety disorders among children below the age of five years, given rapid changes in the development of emotions that normally occur during early childhood (Gardner & Shaw, 2009). The main criticisms generally reflected views that preschoolers do not show clusters of symptoms in line with diagnostic categories in the same way that older children do, that their presenting problems tend to be transient, that diagnostic systems do not sufficiently consider what is normal child behavior at different stages of development, and that early labelling of children with psychiatric diagnoses may produce long-term, adverse, and stigmatizing consequences. Egger and Angold (2006) pointed out, however, that there is a lack of evidence to confirm these viewpoints, and the evidence suggests that mental health symptoms in preschool children do indeed cluster in a manner consistent with current diagnostic classification systems (Eley et al., 2003; Gadow, Sprafkin, & Nolan, 2001; Spence et al., 2001). Concern about the appropriateness of systems such as DSM or ICD led to the development of Zero to Three, an alternative diagnostic classification system for infants (DC-0-3), developed by an expert working group of psychiatrists and psychologists (Zero to Three, 1994). The system is currently being adapted for Zero to Five, and it is unclear whether this will include recommendations about the diagnostic classification of anxiety disorders in preschool children.

Whilst accepting that we need to avoid any adverse consequences that could arise from early labelling of a child as having a particular disorder, and recognizing the importance of taking developmental considerations into account, there are benefits to be gained from formulating clinical diagnoses with young children. For example, a clinical diagnosis may be of value in communicating information to other professionals about the pattern of anxiety symptoms, and in informing the selection of treatment based on empirical evidence regarding effective interventions for the disorder(s) concerned.

Where possible, the process of diagnosis should be informed by an evidence-based structured or semi-structured clinical interview. Given the high level of comorbidity between anxiety disorders and other mental health conditions, it is important that the interview also assesses the presence of other disorders (including conduct disorders, OCD, and depression), plus developmental disorders, physical disabilities, and medical conditions, all of which will need to be addressed or considered in the treatment plan. A variety of such interviews have been used in the assessment of anxiety in preschoolers. In some instances, researchers or clinicians have assessed preschoolers using an interview schedule that is normally used with older children, such as the Anxiety Disorders Interview Schedule for Children/Parents (ADIS-C/P, Silverman & Albano, 1996a), or the Schedule for Affective Disorders and Schizophrenia for School-Age Children (K-SADS, Kaufman, Birmaher, Axelson, et al., 2016; Kaufman et al., 1997). In other instances, the interview content has been adapted for use with preschoolers from an existing interview schedule for older children, such as the Diagnostic Interview Schedule for Children – Young Child Edition (DISC–YC, Lucas, Fisher, & Luby, 2008), the Diagnostic Interview for Children and Adolescents for Parents of Preschool and Young Children (DICA-PPYC, Ezpeleta et al., 2011) or the Preschool Psychiatric Assessment (PAPA, Egger & Angold, 2004). There are also examples in which the interview content has been designed for preschool assessment but based on DSM criteria, such as the Diagnostic Infant and Preschool Assessment (DIPA, Scheeringa & Haslett, 2010).

The change from DSM-IV to DSM-5 has meant that some changes are required to these measures to bring them into line with the most recent version of this diagnostic classification system. The K-SADS and DIPA have been adapted for DSM-5, and work will undoubtedly be in progress for other interviews. A non-exhaustive list of diagnostic interviews that have been used to assess anxiety in preschoolers is provided in Table 4.1. There has been substantially less research into the reliability and validity of diagnostic interview schedules for preschoolers, when compared to the evidence-base with older children, making it difficult to compare instruments. Table 4.1 provides a pragmatic overview of the psychometric properties of the various instruments, and the findings illustrate the strong need for ongoing research.

Based on the limited evidence to date, some tentative comments can be made about the relative strengths and weaknesses of these interviews for assessing anxiety in preschoolers. For example, the ADIS-C/P has tended to be used in research studies and treatment trials that relate specifically to anxiety disorders in young children. It has been less commonly used in community-based epidemiological studies or in clinic-based studies where the clinic population covers the full spectrum of emotional and

Table 4.1 Examples of diagnostic interviews used in the assessment of anxiety in preschoolers

Title and Key Reference	Brief Description	Evidence-base
Anxiety Disorders Interview Schedule for Children/Parents (Silverman & Albano, 1996b)	• Semi-structured interview, Current version based on DSM-IV-TR (American Psychiatric Association, 1994). Assesses anxiety, mood and externalizing disorders, with particularly strong assessment of anxiety disorders. • Includes screening questions and skip options that enable shorter administration time (around 60–90 mins per informant). • Includes clinician severity ratings for degree of impairment and interference in functioning, plus ratings of youth's fear and avoidance of situations relating to anxiety disorders. • Intended for use by mental health clinicians. It was originally designed for youth, aged 6–7 years	*Inter-Assessor Agreement* (from taped interviews): Kappas: SEP = .84, SOC = .86, SpecPh = .83, GA= .77 (Rapee et al., 2005). Kappas: .56 and greater (Kennedy et al., 2009) Large UK twin study 6 year olds – Kappas = SAD .91, social phobia .96, specific phobia .82, GAD .85 (Bolton et al., 2006). *Convergent and divergent validity:* Significant difference between diagnosed anxious pre-schoolers and non-anxious on threat-related attentional bias tasks (Dodd et al., 2015), insecure attachment and behavioral inhibition (Shamir-Essakow, Ungerer, & Rapee, 2005). *Treatment sensitivity* Evidence of sensitivity to intervention effects in treatment and prevention trials (Donovan & March, 2014; Rapee et al., 2010). *Availability:* https://global.oup.com

The Schedule for Affective Disorders and Schizophrenia for School-Age Children – Present and Lifetime Version (K-SADS-PL) (Kaufman et al., 1997)

- Semi-structured interview.
- Originally developed for youth aged 6–8 years
- Recently been adapted in line with DSM-5 (Kaufman, Birmaher, Axelson, et al., 2016).
- Uses a modular approach, with screening questions and skip options that enable shorter administration time.
- Around 60–90 mins per informant.
- Interviewers are expected to be clinicians who have completed KSADS training. Anxiety diagnoses cover Panic, Agoraphobia, SEP, SOC, GAD, SpPh, Selective Mutism and Generalized Anxiety Disorder.

Inter-Assessor Agreement:
> .80 in 204, 1.5- to 5-year-olds, offspring of parents with bipolar disorder of which 32 received an anxiety disorder diagnosis (Birmaher et al., 2009).

Convergent and divergent validity:
Correlation between anxiety disorder diagnosis and the anxious/depressed and internalizing CBCL subscales, rho = .31 and .24 respectively (Birmaher et al., 2009). Correlation between any anxiety disorder and attention and aggressive subscales were significantly lower (rho = .06, and rho = .16, Z = 2.46, respectively) (Birmaher et al., 2009).

Discriminant validity:
Children with a K-SADS-PL anxiety disorder diagnosis received significantly lower ECI4 scores than those without a disorder (p = .001) (Birmaher et al., 2009).

Table 4.1 (Cont.)

Title and Key Reference	Brief Description	Evidence-base
Diagnostic interview schedule for children–parent scale–young child version (DISC–YC) (Lucas et al., 2008)	<ul><li>Developmentally appropriate adaptation of the DISC-IV parent report version (Shaffer et al., 2000).</li><li>Aligned with DSM-IV and ICD-10.</li><li>Aged 3–6 years.</li><li>Fully structured, respondent-based, interview with Yes/No responses.</li><li>Can be conducted by trained interviewers without extensive clinical experience.</li><li>If threshold is met for a diagnosis, questions about onset, impairment and treatment are included.</li><li>Computer derived diagnoses using algorithms.</li><li>Separate modules may be administered for SOC, GAD, SEP, SpPh.</li></ul>	*Convergent validity:* Agreement with Child Symptom Checklist on presence of GAD polychoric correlation = .65 with small number of cases (Lavigne et al., 2009). *Use in Research Studies:* Used in several research studies as indicator of anxiety, examining causal factors, trajectories, epidemiology etc. e.g. (Hopkins et al., 2013; Lavigne et al., 2015; Ringoot et al., 2017; Silberg et al., 2015). *Availability:* contact original developers.
Diagnostic Interview for Children and Adolescents for Parents of Preschool and Young Children (DICA-PPYC) (Ezpeleta et al., 2011)	<ul><li>Semi-structured interview for parents.</li><li>Assesses common mental health disorders of children 3–7 years including SEP, SOC, GAD and SpPh.</li><li>Adapted from Diagnostic Interview for Children and Adolescents-IV (DICA-IV) (Reich, Leacock, & Shanfeld, 1997).</li><li>A computerized instrument, with algorithms to determine diagnoses. Aligned to DSM-IV as relevant to preschoolers, informed by Research Diagnostic Criteria – Preschool Age (RDC-PA, Task Force on Research Diagnostic Criteria: Infancy and Preschool, 2003).</li><li>Administration time around 45 mins.</li><li>Spanish validation.</li></ul>	*Test-retest reliability:* Mean 8.8 days: any anxiety diagnosis kappa = .76, sub-types of anxiety kappas .50–.76. (Ezpeleta et al., 2011). *Convergent and divergent validity:* Weak agreement between specific DICA-PPYC DSM-IV anxiety disorder diagnoses and CBCL-Anx-Dep subscale (correlations .02–.28) (Ezpeleta et al., 2011) in a community sample. *Availability:* Contact Dr Ezpeleta (first author).

Preschool Psychiatric
Assessment
(PAPA)
(Egger & Angold, 2004)

- Semi-structured interview for parents of children 2 to 5 years. Paper and electronic versions Adapted from the Child and Adolescent Psychiatric Assessment (CAPA) (Angold & Costello, 2000).
- Aligned with DSM-IV criteria and DC:0–3.
- Includes diagnoses for SAD, GAD, SOC, and SpPh, selective mutism, agoraphobia and panic disorder.
- Administration qualifications: Trained lay interviewers (bachelor's degree or above) or mental health professionals. Paper and electronic versions.
- Assesses presence of symptoms, date of onset, duration, frequency over previous 3 months.
- Includes impairment ratings across 30 areas of functioning, at home, school/daycare and out of home.
- DSM-IV diagnoses derived using developmentally appropriate algorithms. Provides diagnoses and dimensional scores.
- Interview does not include self-contained modules and questions for some disorders are interspersed.
- Administration time ~ 110 minutes.

Re-test agreement/Inter-assessor:
Mean of 11 day interval, primary care clinics, kappas for any anxiety disorder = .49, SAD = .60; GAD = .30, SpPh = .36, SOC = .54, Sel Mutism = .53. Scale test-retest reliabilities ICCs – SAD = .63; GAD = .61, SpPh = .57, SOC = .73 (Egger et al., 2006).
Inter-assessor agreement:
Independent rating of 12 interviews from videotapes, anxiety symptom score ICC = 1.0, and anxiety diagnosis kappa = 1.0 (Bufferd et al., 2011).
Internal consistency:
For anxiety dimension score, alpha = .83 (Bufferd et al., 2011).

Construct validity:
Confirmatory factor analysis of symptom scores supported 3 inter-correlated factors for emotional symptoms consistent with SOC, SEP, and GAD/Depression (Sterba, Egger, & Angold, 2007).
Availability: http://devepi.duhs.duke.edu/papa.html

Table 4.1 (Cont.)

Title and Key Reference	Brief Description	Evidence-base
The Diagnostic Infant and Preschool Assessment (DIPA) (Scheeringa & Haslett, 2010)	• Parent structured interview. • 1–6 year olds. • Recently revised to align with DSM-5. • New version assesses 16 disorders, including: Self-contained modules for SEP, SOC, GAD and SpecPh • Stem questions, then follow-up questions regarding onset, frequency, and duration of symptoms, and functional impairment. • Assesses child behavior over past 4 weeks relative to other children his/her own age.	Limited published psychometric research *Inter-Assessor Agreement:* Small clinical sample, with few anxiety disorder diagnoses: reported weak 1–3 week test-retest reliability for SEP (.37–.50). *Convergent and divergent validity:* Fair to good agreement between SEP diagnosis (with and without impairment criteria) and CBCL-AD criterion, kappa = .45/.53 respectively. Insufficient numbers of other anxiety diagnoses for valid interpretation (Scheeringa & Haslett, 2010). *Availability:* https://www2.tulane.edu/som/departments/psychiatry/ScheeringaLab/dipa.cfm

Notes: SAD = separation anxiety disorder, SOC = social anxiety disorder, GAD = generalized anxiety disorder, SpPh = specific phobia behavioral disorders, even though it includes modules for assessing other disorders. There is good evidence of its sensitivity to detect anxiety treatment effects in studies involving preschoolers, but limited evidence regarding inter-rater agreement and its reliability and validity with this younger age group.

In contrast, the K-SADS has more evidence regarding its psychometric properties with preschoolers, but this is much less than that for older children. It also requires detailed training of interviewers who should have clinical qualifications. The DISC-YC has the advantage of its computer scoring and strict algorithms, and it can be administered by non-clinicians. These factors facilitate its use in community-based epidemiological research into early childhood mental health issues. However, its very tight structure can also be a disadvantage in clinical contexts where clinical judgement might indicate a deviation from the strictly controlled questioning. The PAPA has probably the strongest evidence-base regarding its psychometric properties with preschool populations, but it tends to have a longer administration time than some of the other interviews, and it is not modularized into stand-alone diagnoses. Rather, all questions from the interview must be asked and DSM-IV diagnoses are then derived from algorithms created by the PAPA developers (PAPA, Egger & Angold, 2004).

Questionnaires and Rating Scales

There are numerous rating scales to assess anxiety in young people that can be completed by parents and/or teachers. These vary in terms of the degree of specificity, assessing (i) the construct of anxiety more broadly, or as a brief subscale within a comprehensive assessment of emotional and behavioral problems, (ii) the multi-dimensional constructs of anxiety, covering symptoms across a range of disorders, with a total score plus subscale scores associated with specific anxiety disorders, or (iii) a specific type of anxiety problem, such as social anxiety, separation anxiety, generalized anxiety or specific phobias. As such, the different types of scale play different roles in the assessment process. They differ in terms of the depth and breadth of anxiety symptoms assessed, and in the type of information provided about severity and frequency of symptoms. However, they do not provide sufficient information about severity, frequency and duration of symptoms, the range of symptoms, and the degree of associated impairment to enable a reliable clinical diagnosis to be made. They are of value in identifying young children who show elevated symptoms of anxiety and for whom early intervention may be warranted, or who may benefit from a more in-depth assessment in order to determine whether clinical intervention is justified. They enable the clinician to form hypotheses about presenting clinical problems, which then should be supported by clinical interview and more in-depth assessment of specific areas (Grills-Taquechel, Ollendick, & Fisak, 2008). They may also be of value in measuring change in anxiety over time, for research or treatment evaluation purposes.

A Multi-dimensional Approach to Assessing Anxiety

The Preschool Anxiety Scale (Spence et al., 2001) is a widely used clinical measure that focuses specifically on anxiety symptoms in the 3–6 year age group. It is a parent report, multi-dimensional scale, with 28 items that provide 5 subscales aligned with DSM-IV anxiety diagnoses, namely separation anxiety, social anxiety, generalized anxiety, physical injury fears, and obsessive-compulsive disorder. Parents rate how true each statement is for their child (5-point scale). Table 4.2 outlines the psychometric research relating to the PAS. The originally proposed 5-factor structure has been supported in multiple factor analytic studies, including justification for the higher order anxiety factor assessed by the total anxiety scale that recognizes the high level of comorbidity between the subtypes of anxiety. Internal consistency is high for the total score, and adequate for the subscale scores. As the scale was originally aligned with DSM-IV, research is now underway to adapt the PAS in line with DSM-5 key diagnostic categories. The scale, normative data, scoring information and translations into multiple languages may be downloaded from the website: www.scaswebsite.com. There is a teacher version of the PAS, although published norms are not yet available, and research is needed to evaluate its psychometric properties.

The Children's Moods, Fears and Worries Questionnaire (CMFWQ, Bayer, Sanson, & Hemphill, 2006) is a parent report instrument that focuses on young children's anxiety, worries, and symptoms of depressed mood. Although it does not align with specific anxiety diagnoses, it offers promise as an instrument that assesses the broader construct of anxiety and internalizing problems, with strong psychometric properties (see Table 4.2).

Preschool adaptations of the Fear Survey Schedule for Children – Revised (FSSC-R, Ollendick, 1983) also warrant acknowledgement, as this provides a general indication of fearfulness across a broad range of situations (fear of failure and criticism, the unknown, minor injury and small animals, danger and death, and medical procedures). The preschool versions of the FSSC-R have not been included in Table 4.2, as there is not yet sufficient research to draw firm conclusions regarding their psychometric properties. There are at least two versions; for example, Warren, Ollendick, and Simmens (2008) adapted the 80-item FSSC-R for completion by parents of children aged 18 months to five years. They removed 17 items and added in 29 new items to produce a 92-item scale relevant to preschoolers' fears. The internal consistency of the fear score was high, alpha = .94, with 6-month test-retest reliability, r = .67. The fear score correlated with parent report on the CBCL 1/12–5 Anxiety Problems subscale, r = .46, and with the Infant Toddler Social and

Table 4.2 Parent/teacher questionnaires and rating scales

Title and Key Reference	Brief Description	Evidence-base
Preschool Anxiety Scale (PAS) (Spence et al., 2001)	• Parent report • 3–6 yr olds • 28 items • Assess symptoms aligned with DSM-IV disorders • SEP, GAD, SOC, Physical Injury Fears and OCD • Produces a total score and subscale scores • Revision included minor modifications resulting in marginal improvement to psychometric properties (Edwards et al., 2010). Most clinicians and researchers continue to use the original PAS.	*Internal consistency:* Total score alpha = .86, subscale alphas = .59–.81 (Broeren & Muris, 2008). Total score alpha = .87, subscale alphas = .60–.77 (Benga, Tincas, & Visu-Petra, 2010). Total score alpha = .87, subscale alphas = .55–.75 (Wang & Zhao, 2015). *Test-Retest:* 6-month Total score r = .59, subscale rs = .37–.59 (Benga et al., 2010). 1 month Total score r = .73, subscale rs = .58–.71 (Wang & Zhao, 2015). *Convergent and divergent validity:* Correlation between mother total PAS score and CBCL Internalizing = .68 (subscales .42–.60). Lower correlations with CBCL Externalizing score, r = .21, (subscales − .08–.20) (Spence et al., 2001). Significant correlations between PAS and CBCL-INT, all rs > .42 and lower correlations with CBCL externalizing scale (Balaj et al., 2011). Significant correlations between PAS and ECI4, SEP r = .71; GAD r = .58 (Balaj et al., 2011). Significant correlation Total PAS and CMFWQ fear and anxiety factor, r = .75 (Broeren & Muris, 2008). Correlations with CBCL-Int significantly greater than those with CBCL-Ext for all scales of the PAS (Wang & Zhao, 2015). *Discriminant validity:* Significantly higher PAS total scores comparing children with normal vs clinical range on CBCL-Anx/Dep (Broeren & Muris, 2008). *Construct validity:* Confirmatory factor analyses support the proposed 5, correlated factor model (Benga et al., 2010; Edwards et al., 2010; Spence et al., 2001; Wang & Zhao, 2015). *Treatment sensitivity:* Evidence of sensitivity to intervention effects in treatment and prevention trials (Barrett, Fisak, & Cooper, 2015; Donovan & March, 2014; Fox et al., 2012; Morgan et al., 2017). *Availability:* www.scaswebsite.com

Table 4.2 (Cont.)

Title and Key Reference	Brief Description	Evidence-base
Children's Moods, Fears and Worries Questionnaire (CMFWQ) (Bayer et al., 2006)	• Parent-report rating scale assessing broad range of internalizing symptoms, relating to anxiety, worry and depressive mood. 1.5–7 yr olds. • The item content has changed over time. Current versions typically limited to the internalizing subscale. • 35 items at 1.5–2 years; 38 items at 3–5 years; 34 items at 6–7 years. • Assesses frequency with which symptoms occur on a 5-point scale.	*Internal consistency:* Total internalizing scale, alpha = .92 (Bayer et al., 2006), alpha = .95 (Antonucci & Bayer, 2017). *Convergent and divergent validity:* Significant correlation with inhibition subscale of Short Temperament Scale for Children (at age 4), r = .50 (Bayer et al., 2006). In inhibited 5 year olds: significant correlation with SDQ emotional symptoms r = .71, and .49 with conduct problems (Antonucci & Bayer, 2017). In 1.5–7 year olds (small clinical sample) significant correlation with CBCL internalizing, r = .61 and BASC-2 internalizing, r = .65 (Andrijic, Bayer, & Bretherton, 2013). Significant correlation between CMFWQ fear and anxiety score and total PAS score, r = .75 (Broeren & Muris, 2008). *Discriminant validity:* Children with anxiety disorder diagnoses had significantly higher CMFWQ scores than those without (Antonucci & Bayer, 2017). Good sensitivity but poor specificity for agreement between clinical cut on CMFWQ and ADIS-C anxiety disorders (Antonucci & Bayer, 2017). Note: Broeren and Muris (2008) reported good psychometric properties for the CMFWQ but they used a version with more items and comparability with the current version is unclear. *Availability:* Contract original developer.

| Child Behavior Checklist 1½ to 5 years (CBCL/1½ – 5) (Achenbach & Rescorla, 2000) | • 99 item parent completed rating scale covering broad range of child behavior problems.
• Teacher/Caregiver version.
• 1.5–5 year olds.
• 3 response options (0, not true; 1, somewhat or sometimes true; 2, very true or often true), plus one open-ended item for adding problems that are not listed.
• Of relevance to anxiety assessment are the 36 item internalizing scale (CBCL-INT), the anxious-depressed (CBCL-AD) and the DSM aligned 10-item anxiety problems subscale (CBCL-AP) which have recently been adapted for DSM-5 (Achenbach & Rescorla, 2001). | *Internal consistency:*
Alphas for parent report AD score = ~.71, AP score = ~.65, (de la Osa et al., 2016); alpha (parent) internalizing score = .87, teacher = .88 (Kristensen, Henriksen, & Bilenberg, 2010).
Convergent and divergent validity:
Significant correlation with the total score on FSSC-R preschool adaptation, r = 44 (Kushnir et al., 2015).
Discriminant validity:
Sensitivity and specificity for detection of diagnosed anxiety disorders: moderate to good diagnostic accuracy (with DICA-PPYC) in identifying anxiety disorders in preschoolers with screened behavior problems: AUC for CBCL-AP (with any anxiety disorder) = .75 (age 3yrs), .71 (age 4yrs), 80 (age 5yrs), slightly lower AUC for CBCL-AD scores (de la Osa et al., 2016).
*Availability:*http://www.aseba.org/ |

Table 4.2 (Cont.)

Title and Key Reference	Brief Description	Evidence-base
Early Childhood Inventory-5 (ECI-5) (de la Osa et al., 2016)	• Recent DSM-5 compatible adaptation of the ECI-4 (Sprafkin & Gadow, 2017). • Includes minor changes and no new norms. • Parent rating scale – 108 items. • Teacher version – 94 items screening for 13 emotional and behavioral disorders (doesn't include SEP). • 3–5 year olds. • Covers 15 emotional and behavioral disorders. • Includes GAD, SOC, SEP, SpecPh, Selective Mutism. • Can be scored to derive Symptom count scores (diagnostic model) or Symptom severity scores (normative data model). • Includes impairment question for each DSM disorder. • Research to date is limited to ECI4 (noting that the changes to ECI-5 are few). • The norm sample for the Parent Checklist (N = 531) and the Teacher Checklist (N = 398) included 3- and 5-years-olds who attended day care, preschool, and Head Start programs.	*Internal consistency:* ECI-4 symptom score for anxiety problems (parent) alphas – GAD = .63, SAD = .81; (teacher) GAD = .74 (Gadow & Sprafkin, 1997); SAD = .83 (Gadow et al., 2001). *Test-Retest:* 3 month correlations of symptom severity score (parent), r = GAD [.77], SAD [.65] (Sprafkin et al., 2002). 8 month (teacher) test-retest correlation of symptom severity scores for SOC r = .59, GAD r = .22. (Gadow et al., 2001). 4 month (40 clinical cases) for GAD (parent) r = .92, (teacher) r = .92; SEP (parent) r = .97, SOC (parent) r = .73, (teacher) r = .73 (Gadow et al., 2001). *Convergent and divergent validity:* Significant correlation between SEP subscale and CBCL-AnxDep r = .44 (Balaj et al., 2011); SEP (parent) subscale correlated .44 with CBCL Anx-Dep; Lower for unrelated CBCL subscales (Sprafkin et al., 2002). Significant correlations between ECI-4 symptom scale and Preschool Anxiety Scale (PAS), SEP r = .71; GAD r = .58. (Balaj et al., 2011). *Discriminant validity:* Significantly higher identified cases with GAD and SEP in clinical sample vs community (Balaj et al., 2011). *Availability:*http://www.checkmateplus.com/product/eci-4.htm

| Behavior Assessment System for Children – Third Edition (BASC-3) (Gadow et al., 2001) | • Assesses broad range of child emotional and behavioral problems.
• Parent and teacher reports.
• Includes a 2–5 years version with specific norms for this age group.
• T-scores are provided for eight clinical scales including anxiety and four adaptive scales (Activities of Daily Living, Adaptability, Functional Communication, Social Skills), as well as four composite scales: Externalizing problems, Internalizing problems, Behavioral Symptoms Index, and Adaptive skills.
• Also includes an F index, which is a validity scale designed to detect excessively negative responses made by a parent. | *Internal consistency:*
13 items BASC-2 anxiety subscale, alpha = .71 (Huang et al., 2012).
Convergent and divergent validity:
13 items BASC-2 anxiety subscale correlated with PAS subscales GAD r = .46, SOC, r = .31 (Huang et al., 2012).
*Availability:*http://www.pearsonclinical.com |

Notes: SAD = separation anxiety disorder, SOC = social anxiety disorder, GAD = generalized anxiety disorder, SpPh = specific phobia

Emotional Assessment (Carter & Briggs-Gowan, 2000), r = .57, supporting convergent validity. The psychometric properties were slightly stronger if a high fear scoring system was used that summed items rated as "a lot" of fear. Kushnir, Gothelf, and Sadeh (2015) developed a 52-item version of the FSSC-R for parents of preschoolers. The total score correlated, r = .44, with the CBCL 1/12–5 Anxious-Depressed subscale, with internal consistency Cronbach's alpha = .79. Measures such as the FSSC-R are valuable where the aim is to evaluate a child's overall level of fearfulness, but they provide less information about specific types of anxiety.

Measures of Emotional and Behavioral Problems in which Anxiety is a Dimension

There are various parent and teacher measures of emotional and behavioral problems among preschoolers that include an internalizing dimension and some items relating specifically to anxiety. They differ in terms of the number of anxiety-related items and the depth and breadth of anxiety assessment, and whether an anxiety subscale is extracted in addition to the broader internalizing dimension. Generally, the information produced provides only a rough screen to suggest the presence of anxiety problems that would warrant further investigation using a more extensive anxiety measure or a structured interview, depending on the purpose of the assessment.

For example, the Child Behavior Checklist $1^1/_2$ to five years (CBCL/ 1.5–5, Achenbach & Rescorla, 2000), provides three scores that are of relevance to the assessment of anxiety, namely, the internalizing composite (CBCL-Int), the empirically derived anxiety-depression score (CBCL-AD), and the DSM-aligned, 6-item anxiety problems subscale (CBCL-AP) (Achenbach, Dumenci, & Rescorla, 2003). A summary of key points relating to its psychometric properties is provided in Table 4.2. The Early Childhood Inventory-5 (ECI-5, de la Osa et al., 2016) and the Behaviour Assessment System for Children (BASC, Gadow et al., 2001) also provide an anxiety symptom severity score. All three of the above measures have parent and teacher versions for the preschool population. To date, research into their psychometric properties lags behind that available for similar measures for older children. A further measure to mention is the Infant Toddler Social and Emotional Assessment (ITSEA, Carter & Briggs-Gowan, 2000) developed to assess socio-emotional dysfunction in infants aged one to three years. This measure has not been included in Table 4.2, as it focuses on infants aged three years and below, but it includes an internalizing dimension that may be of value in the assessment of three-year-olds.

Assessing Specific Types of Anxiety

Scales that assess specific types of anxiety are of value in research studies that focus on a particular anxiety disorder, or for providing a more detailed assessment to clarify the nature of a child's presenting problem in a clinical context. Although instruments such as the PAS provide an indication of subtypes of anxiety, a more detailed assessment of particular areas may be required. There are still relatively few measures of specific types of anxiety in preschoolers that have established psychometric properties and demonstrated validity with this younger age group. The majority are measures that were developed for older children and have been applied to preschoolers. For example, parent report measures such as the Children's Separation Anxiety Scale (Méndez et al., 2014), the Separation Anxiety Assessment Scale (Eisen & Schaefer, 2005), the Social Phobia and Anxiety Inventory for Children (Beidel, Turner, & Morris, 1995), and the Social Anxiety Scale for Children (La Greca et al., 1988) can be used to assess specific aspects of anxiety in preschoolers, but research is needed into the psychometric properties, and to ensure that the content is developmentally appropriate. There are few measures that have been adapted specifically for preschoolers and for which psychometric data are available. One example is the Social Worries Anxiety Index for Young Children (Stuijfzand & Dodd, 2017), a parent-report measure developed for four- to eight-year-olds. It showed strong internal consistency, alpha = 0.92, and good test-retest reliability (average of 13 day interval), r = 0.87.

Selective mutism is a problem not covered sufficiently in most broadband emotional and behavioral questionnaires for preschoolers. Although assessment of this disorder is generally included in structured diagnostic interviews, specific parent-report measures, such as the Selective Mutism Questionnaire (Bergman et al., 2008), have also been developed to provide more detailed information for the assessment process. This scale has been used in several studies that included preschoolers (e.g. Muris, Heniks, & Bot, 2016). More detailed assessment may also be warranted regarding specific phobias, but again, the research into such assessment measures has generally focused on older children. Some examples include the assessment of fears relating to spiders (Kindt, Brosschot, & Muris, 1996), the dark (Cornwall, Spence, & Schotte, 1996), dental procedures (Buchanan, 2005) and painful medical procedures (McMurtry et al., 2011). Their psychometric properties with preschoolers need to be investigated, and they should be used with caution until sufficient data are available.

Assessing Anxiety in Sub-populations

It is important that anxiety measures are appropriate to the needs of particular groups of young children in terms of gender, culture, language, learning difficulties, other comorbid mental health conditions, and physical impairments. There is minimal research into the generalizability of pre-school anxiety assessment methods to different populations. For example, whereas research has been conducted supporting the psychometric proper-ties of the parent version of the Spence Children's Anxiety Scale for older children with autism spectrum disorders (Jitlina et al., 2017; Russell & Sofronoff, 2005; Wigham & McConachie, 2014; Zainal et al., 2014), this type of research is yet to be conducted for the PAS with younger children with ASD. The psychometric properties and generalizability of the PAS and other measures of anxiety need to be examined with other subgroups of preschoolers, such as those with hearing and vision impairments, learning difficulties, and those who have experienced trauma or abuse. There are also potential differences in the presentation of anxiety that need to be taken into account when assessing children from different cultural backgrounds. Most of the research to date regarding the assessment of preschool anxiety has involved children from Western cultures, including those from Spanish speaking countries. The generalizability of measures to other cultures needs to be determined, given evidence of cultural differences in the presentation of anxiety problems in older children (Essau, Ishikawa, & Sasagawa, 2011; Essau, Sasagawa, et al., 2011).

Assessment of Impairment

The decision about whether intervention is warranted for an anxious child is partly determined by the degree to which the anxiety problem results in impairment to the child's functioning. Most clinical diagnostic interviews require that an impairment criterion is met before a diagnosis of a clinical disorder can be given. Anxiety may impair functioning across various areas of a child's life, such as in the home, at preschool/daycare, and in forming relationships with peers. It may also lead to considerable disruption to family functioning and the lives of parents. The assessment of the child's functioning is built into most clinical interviews (e.g., PAPA and DISC) and included in some child behavior questionnaires, such as the CBCL. There are also stand-alone measures that assess children's adaptive functioning across a range of domains, but these are typically developed for older chil-dren. One exception is the Preschool and Early Childhood Functional Assessment Scale (PECFAS) Interview (Hodges, 1994; Murphy et al., 1999) that provides a detailed assessment of functioning across seven domains. However, it is lengthy and requires interviewer training. There is a need for a brief, reliable and valid, parent report measure of adaptive functioning for preschoolers that covers the key domains of functioning, and that has well-established norms for this age group.

Some scales focus more specifically on the impact of the child's anxiety problems upon child functioning and parents' lives. This can be of value both in informing treatment decisions and in contributing to the evalua-tion of treatment outcome. For example, Lyneham et al. (2013) developed parent and child versions of the Child Anxiety Life Interference Scale (CALIS). The parent version has been modified for preschooler populations (Kennedy, Rapee, & Edwards, 2009), with good internal consistency for both mother and father reports (Gilbertson et al., 2017).

Assessment of Behavioral Inhibition

Behavioral inhibition (BI) represents a tendency to respond with heightened sensitivity to novel auditory and visual stimuli, and to avoid unfamiliar situations and people (Kagan et al., 1984). A critical component of BI is behavioral withdrawal and avoidance, and a characteristic pattern of behavior during social interactions includes poor eye contact, maintained proximity to attachment (safety) figures, lack of verbal utterances, and avoidance of threat stimuli (Kagan et al., 1984; Rapee, 2002). An early childhood temperament of BI has been identified in multiple studies as a risk factor for the development of anxiety later in childhood and adolescence (Broeren et al., 2013; Clauss & Blackford, 2012; Rapee, 2014). Indeed, the significant overlap in presentation of behavioral inhibition and childhood anxiety (and social anxiety disorder in particular) led Rapee and Spence (2004) to question whether BI can be distinguished from anxiety, or whether it is simply an early manifestation of anxiety that, when present at a more severe level and associated with impairment or disruption to daily living, is labeled a disorder. However, Rapee and Coplan (2010), in a detailed review of the literature, concluded that there was sufficient evidence to suggest that BI can be conceptually distinguished from clinical syndromes of anxiety, such as SAD, although they noted the strong overlap and lack of clear evidence.

The strong association between BI and anxiety in young children, and the role of BI as a risk factor for the later development of anxiety, means that it is important to have well-designed and psychometrically sound measures of BI in young children. This enables the identification of children with high BI, who may benefit from targeted prevention approaches designed to break the trajectory from BI to anxiety problems. Ideally, the assessment of BI should include data from direct observation in laboratory, clinic, home or preschool settings, and measurements of psychophysiological indicators that are characteristic of BI. Observational assessment is discussed in more detail in Chapter 5. In most routine clinical contexts or population-based screening programs, observational methods and psychophysiological measurements are not feasible, and the assessment must rely on questionnaire data from parents and teachers.

Several such measures have been developed. In some instances, the construct of BI is assessed as one component of a multi-dimensional measure of temperament, and the relevant subscale can be used independently to assess BI or closely associated constructs. For example, the shyness and fear dimensions of the Child Behavior Questionnaire (Rothbart et al., 2001) tap into the social and physical dimensions of BI (Dyson et al., 2011). Other measures include the shyness subscale of the Emotionality Activity Sociability Temperament Survey (Buss & Plomin, 1984), the approach/withdrawal scale of the Temperament Assessment Battery for Children (Martin, 1994) and the inhibition scale of the TABC-R, to mention just a few.

Some measures have focused more specifically on the assessment of BI. For example, Bishop, Spence, and McDonald (2003) developed a 30-item parent- and 28-item teacher-report measure of BI. Subscales assess children's BI across six different contexts reflecting three domains: response to novelty (unfamiliar adults, peer situations, performing in front of others), situational novelty (separation/preschool, unfamiliar situations), and novel physical activities with minor risk (physical challenges). Confirmatory factor analysis supported six distinct, but correlated factors, with a higher order factor model providing a good fit, justifying the use of the total BI score in addition to the subscale scores. Internal consistency of the total score and subscales was high (exceeding .80 for all mother, father and teacher report, with the exception of physical challenges for father report). Test-retest reliability for the total score over 12 months was good (r = .78, .74, .58 for mother, father and teacher report respectively). Convergent validity with the TABC-R inhibition subscale and the BIQ total score was high, r = .87, .86, and .85 for mother, father and teacher report respectively, and the BIQ correlated significantly with independent observations of BI in a naturalist preschool context. Findings regarding the strong psychometric properties of the BIQ have been replicated by Kim et al. (2011) and Broeren and Muris (2010). The instrument may be downloaded from http://www.scaswebsite.com/index.php?p=1_56. The Behavioral Inhibition Scale for children aged three to six years (Ballespí, Jané, & Riba, 2012) is another stand-alone instrument for assessment of BI in preschool children.

Discussion

This chapter has illustrated the advances that have been made in the assessment of anxiety among preschoolers, although the research still lags a long way behind that conducted with older children. Nevertheless, although there is a need for continued research, there is now evidence to guide us in the selection of clinical diagnostic interviews, and parent and teacher questionnaire measures in younger children. Measures vary in the degree to which they are suited to particular contexts, depending upon whether the aim is one of initial screening, more in-depth assessment of a specific disorder, clinical diagnosis, or treatment evaluation. In selecting measures, clinicians also need to consider their psychometric properties and the degree to which the results generated can be generalized to the population of interest. Where possible, it is advantageous to obtain data from multiple informants, and a task of the clinician is to use their skills, knowledge and experience to integrate the information to create the case formulation and intervention plan. Data from questionnaire measures provide valuable information to identify young people with a "probable" anxiety problem, and for whom a more in-depth assessment, using clinical interview or further questionnaire measures, may be warranted. However, they are not intended for, nor capable of, generating a highly reliable clinical diagnosis. There has also been good progress in the development of measures for the assessment of impairment associated with anxiety in preschoolers, and associated constructs such as behavioral inhibition. There is still a particular need for the development and evaluation of instruments for assessing specific forms of anxiety in younger children. Meanwhile, we should be cautious about using measures that were originally designed for older children, in the absence of psychometric evidence with preschool children.

References

Achenbach, T. M., Dumenci, L., & Rescorla, L. A. (2003). DSM-oriented and empirically based approaches to constructing scales from the same item pools. *Journal of Clinical Child and Adolescent Psychology, 32*(3), 328–340.

Achenbach, T. M., & Rescorla, L. A. (2000). *Manual for the ASEBA preschool forms & profiles*. Burlington, VT: University of Vermont, Research Centre for Children, Youth, & Families.

Achenbach, T. M., & Rescorla, L. A. (2001). *Manual for the ASEBA school-age forms and profiles*. Burlington, VT: University of Vermont, Research Centre for Children, Youth and Families.

American Psychiatric Association. (1994). *Diagnostic and statistical manual of mental disorders*, 4th Edition (DSM-IV). Washington, DC: American Psychiatric Association.

Andrijic, V., Bayer, J., & Bretherton, L. (2013). Validity of the Children's Moods, Fears and Worries Questionnaire in a clinical setting. *Child and Adolescent Mental Health, 18*(1), 11–17.

Angold, A., & Costello, E. J. (2000). The Child and Adolescent Psychiatric Assessment (CAPA). *Journal of the American Academy of Child and Adolescent Psychiatry, 39*(1), 39–48.

Antonucci, M., & Bayer, J. K. (2017). Children's Moods, Fears and Worries Questionnaire: Validity with young children at risk for internalizing problems. *Infant and Child Development, 26*(2), 1–15. https://doi-org.ezproxy.net.ucf.edu/10.1002/icd.1966.

Balaj, A., Albu, M., Porumb, M., & Miclea, M. (2011). The standardization of Early Childhood Inventory-4 on Romanian Population – A preliminary report. *Cognitie, Creier, Comportament/Cognition, Brain, Behavior, 15*(1), 95.

Ballespí, S., Jané, M. C., & Riba, M. D. (2012). The Behavioural Inhibition Scale for Children Aged 3 to 6 (BIS 3–6): Validity based on its relation with observational measures. *Journal of Psychopathology and Behavioral Assessment, 34*(4), 487–496.

Barrett, P., Fisak, B., & Cooper, M. (2015). The treatment of anxiety in young children: Results of an open trial of the Fun FRIENDS Program. *Behaviour Change, 32*(4), 231–242.

Bayer, J. K., Sanson, A. V., & Hemphill, S. A. (2006). Children's moods, fears, and worries: Development of an early childhood parent questionnaire. *Journal of Emotional and Behavioral Disorders*, 14(1), 41–49.

Beidel, D. C., Turner, S. M., & Morris, T. L. (1995). A new inventory to assess childhood social anxiety and phobia: The Social Phobia and Anxiety Inventory for Children. *Psychological Assessment*, 7(1), 73–79.

Benga, O., Tincas, I., & Visu-Petra, L. (2010). Investigating the structure of anxiety symptoms among Romanian preschoolers using the Spence Preschool Anxiety Scales. *Cognition, Brain, Behavior: An Interdisciplinary Journal*, 14(2), 159–182.

Bergman, R. L., Keller, M. L., Piacentini, J., & Bergman, A. J. (2008). The development and psychometric properties of the Selective Mutism Questionnaire. *Journal of Clinical Child and Adolescent Psychology*, 37(2), 456–464.

Birmaher, B., Ehmann, M., Axelson, D. A., Goldstein, B. I., Monk, K., Kalas, C., ... Brent, D. A. (2009). Schedule for affective disorders and schizophrenia for school-age children (K-SADS-PL) for the assessment of preschool children – A preliminary psychometric study. *Journal of Psychiatric Research*, 43(7), 680–686.

Bishop, G., Spence, S. H., & McDonald, C. (2003). Can parents and teachers provide a reliable and valid report of behavioral inhibition? *Child Development*, 74(6), 1899–1917.

Bolton, D., Eley, T. C., O'Connor, T. G., Perrin, S., Rabe-Hesketh, S., Rijsdijk, F., & Smith, P. (2006). Prevalence and genetic and environmental influences on anxiety disorders in 6-year-old twins. *Psychological Medicine*, 36(3), 335–344.

Broeren, S., & Muris, P. (2008). Psychometric evaluation of two new parent-rating scales for measuring anxiety symptoms in young Dutch children. *Journal of Anxiety Disorders*, 22(6), 949–958.

Broeren, S., & Muris, P. (2010). A psychometric evaluation of the behavioral inhibition questionnaire in a non-clinical sample of Dutch children and adolescents. *Child Psychiatry and Human Development*, 41(2), 214–229.

Broeren, S., Muris, P. E. H. M., Diamantopoulou, S., & Baker, J. (2013). The course of childhood anxiety symptoms: Developmental trajectories and child-related factors in normal children. *Journal of Abnormal Child Psychology*, 41(1), 81–95.

Buchanan, H. (2005). Development of a computerised dental anxiety scale for children: validation and reliability. *British Dental Journal*, 199(6), 359–362.

Bufferd, S. J., Dougherty, L. R., Carlson, G. A., & Klein, D. N. (2011). Parent-reported mental health in preschoolers: Findings using a diagnostic interview. *Comprehensive Psychiatry*, 52(4), 359–369.

Buss, A., & Plomin, R. (1984). *Temperament: Early developing personality traits*. Hillsdale, NJ: Lawrence Erlbaum.

Carter, A. S., & Briggs-Gowan, M. (2000). The Infant–Toddler Social and Emotional Assessment (ITSEA). New Haven, CT: Unpublished Manual. University of Massachusetts Boston Department of Psychology, Boston, MA. Yale University.

Clauss, J. A., & Blackford, J. U. (2012). Behavioral inhibition and risk for developing social anxiety disorder: a meta-analytic study. *Journal of the American Academy of Child and Adolescent Psychiatry*, 51(10), 1066–1075.

Cornwall, E., Spence, S. H., & Schotte, D. (1996). The effectiveness of emotive imagery in the treatment of darkness phobia in children. *Behaviour Change*, 13(4), 223–229.

de la Osa, N., Granero, R., Trepat, E., Domenech, J. M., & Ezpeleta, L. (2016). The discriminative capacity of CBCL/1/2;-5-DSM5 scales to identify disruptive and internalizing disorders in preschool children. *European Child and Adolescent Psychiatry*, 25(1), 17–23.

Dodd, H. F., Hudson, J. L., Williams, T., Morris, T., Lazarus, R. S., & Byrow, Y. (2015). Anxiety and attentional bias in preschool-aged children: An eyetracking study. *Journal of Abnormal Child Psychology*, 43(6), 1055–1065.

Donovan, C. L., & March, S. (2014). Online CBT for preschool anxiety disorders: A randomised control trial. *Behaviour Research and Therapy*, 58(1), 24–35.

Dougherty, L. R., Tolep, M. R., Bufferd, S. J., Olino, T. M., Dyson, M., Traditi, J., ... Klein, D. N. (2013). Preschool anxiety disorders: comprehensive assessment of clinical, demographic, temperamental, familial, and life stress correlates. *Journal of Clinical Child and Adolescent Psychology: The Official Journal for the Society of Clinical Child and Adolescent Psychology, American Psychological Association, Division 53*, 42(5), 577–589.

Dyson, M. W., Klein, D. N., Olino, T. M., Dougherty, L. R., & Durbin, C. E. (2011). Social and non-social behavioral inhibition in preschool-age children: Differential associations with parent-reports of temperament and anxiety. *Child Psychiatry and Human Development*, 42(4), 390–405.

Edwards, S. L., Rapee, R. M., Kennedy, S. J., & Spence, S. H. (2010). The assessment of anxiety symptoms in preschool-aged children: The Revised Preschool Anxiety Scale. *Journal of Clinical Child and Adolescent Psychology*, 39(3), 400–409.

Egger, H. L., & Angold, A. (2004). The Preschool Age Psychiatric Assessment (PAPA): A structured parent interview for diagnosing psychiatric disorders in preschool children. In R. DelCarmen-Wiggins & A. Carter (Eds.), *Handbook of infant, toddler, and preschool mental assessment* (pp. 223–243). New York: Oxford University Press.

Egger, H. L., & Angold, A. (2006). Common emotional and behavioral disorders in preschool children: Presentation, nosology, and epidemiology. *Journal of Child Psychology and Psychiatry*, 47(3–4), 313–337.

Egger, H. L., Erkanli, A., Keeler, G., Potts, E., Walter, B. K., & Angold, A. (2006). Test-retest reliability of the Preschool Age Psychiatric Assessment (PAPA). *Journal of the American Academy of Child and Adolescent Psychiatry*, 45(5), 538–549.

Eisen, A. R., & Schaefer, C. E. (2005). *Separation anxiety in children and adolescents: an individualized approach to assessment and treatment*. New York: Guilford Press.

Eley, T. C., Bolton, D., O'Connor, T. G., Perrin, S., Smith, P., & Plomin, R. (2003). A twin study of anxiety-related behaviours in pre-school children. *Journal of Child Psychology and Psychiatry*, 44(7), 945–960.

Essau, C. A., Ishikawa, S. I., & Sasagawa, S. (2011). S10–02 - Early learning experience and adolescent anxiety: A cross-cultural comparison between Japan and England. *European Psychiatry*, 26, 2046–2046.

Essau, C. A., Sasagawa, S., Anastassiou-Hadjicharalambous, X., Guzman, B. O., & Ollendick, T. H. (2011). Psychometric properties of the Spence Child Anxiety Scale with adolescents from five European countries. *Journal of Anxiety Disorders*, 25(1), 19–27.

Ezpeleta, L., de la Osa, N., Granero, R., Domènech, J. M., & Reich, W. (2011). The Diagnostic Interview of Children and Adolescents for Parents of Preschool and Young Children: Psychometric properties in the general population. *Psychiatry Research*, 190(1), 137–144.

Fjermestad, K. W., Nilsen, W., Johannessen, T. D., & Karevold, E. B. (2017). Mothers' and fathers' internalizing symptoms influence parental ratings of adolescent anxiety symptoms. *Journal of Family Psychology*, 31(7), 939–944. http s://doi-org.ezproxy.net.ucf.edu/10.1037/fam0000322.

Fox, J. K., Warner, C. M., Lerner, A. B., Ludwig, K., Ryan, J. L., Colognori, D., ... Brotman, L. M. (2012). Preventive intervention for anxious preschoolers and their parents: Strengthening early emotional development. *Child Psychiatry and Human Development*, 43(4), 544–559.

Gadow, K. D., & Sprafkin, J. (1997). *Early Childhood Inventory-4 Norms Manual*. Stony Brook, NY: Checkmate Plus.

Gadow, K. D., Sprafkin, J., & Nolan, E. E. (2001). DSM-IV symptoms in community and clinic preschool children. *Journal of the American Academy of Child and Adolescent Psychiatry*, 40(12), 1383–1392.

Gardner, F., & Shaw, D. S. (2009). Behavioral problems of infancy and preschool children (0–5). In *Rutter's Child and adolescent psychiatry* (pp. 882–893). Oxford: Blackwell Publishing Ltd.

Garro, A. (2016). Assessment of anxiety disorders, PTSD, OCD, and depression in young children. In Garro, A. (Ed.)*Early childhood assessment in school and clinical child psychology* (pp. 233–260). New York, NY: Springer Science + Business Media.

Gilbertson, T. J., Morgan, A. J., Rapee, R. M., Lyneham, H. J., & Bayer, J. K. (2017). Psychometric properties of the Child Anxiety Life Interference Scale Preschool Version. *Journal of Anxiety Disorders*, 52, 62–71.

Grills-Taquechel, A. E., Ollendick, T. H., & Fisak, B. (2008). Reexamination of the MASC factor structure and discriminant ability in a mixed clinical outpatient sample. *Depression and Anxiety*, 25(11), 942–950.

Headley, C., & Campbell, M. A. (2011). Teachers' recognition and referral of anxiety disorders in primary school children. *Australian Journal of Educational & Developmental Psychology*, 11, 78–90.

Hodges, K. (1994). *The Preschool and Early Childhood Functional Assessment Scale (PECFAS) Interview*. Ypsilanti, MI: Eastern Michigan University, Department of Psychology.

Hopkins, J., Lavigne, J. V., Gouze, K. R., LeBailly, S. A., & Bryant, F. B. (2013). Multi-domain models of risk factors for depression and anxiety symptoms in preschoolers: Evidence for common and specific factors. *Journal of Abnormal Child Psychology*, 41(5), 705–722.

Huang, K.-Y., Cheng, S., Calzada, E., & Brotman, L. M. (2012). Symptoms of anxiety and associated risk and protective factors in young Asian American children. *Child Psychiatry and Human Development*, 43(5), 761–774.

Hunsley, J., & Mash, E. J. (2008). *A guide to assessments that work*. New York: Oxford University Press.

Jitlina, K., Zumbo, B., Mirenda, P., Ford, L., Bennett, T., Georgiades, S., ... Elsabbagh, M. (2017). Psychometric properties of the Spence Children's Anxiety Scale: Parent report in children with Autism Spectrum Disorder. *Journal of Autism and Developmental Disorders*, 1–10.

Kagan, J., Reznick, J. S., Clarke, C., Snidman, N., & Garcia-Coll, C. (1984). Behavioral inhibition to the unfamiliar. *Child Development*, 55(6), 2212–2225.

Kaufman, J., Birmaher, B., Axelson, D., Perepletchikova, F., Brent, D., & Ryan, N. (2016). *The Schedule for Affective Disorders and Schizophrenia for School-Age Children – Present and Lifetime Version for DSM5 (K-SADS-PL-DSM5)*. Pittsburgh: Western Psychiatric Institute and Clinic.

Kaufman, J., Birmaher, B., Brent, D., Rao, U. M. A., Flynn, C., Moreci, P., ... Ryan, N. (1997). Schedule for Affective Disorders and Schizophrenia for School-Age Children-Present and Lifetime Version (K-SADS-PL): Initial reliability and validity data. *Journal of the American Academy of Child and Adolescent Psychiatry*, 36(7), 980–988.

Kennedy, S. J., Rapee, R. M., & Edwards, S. L. (2009). A selective intervention program for inhibited preschool-aged children of parents with an anxiety disorder: effects on current anxiety disorders and temperament. *Journal of the American Academy of Child and Adolescent Psychiatry*, 48(6), 602–609.

Kim, J., Klein, D. N., Olino, T. M., Dyson, M. W., Dougherty, L. R., & Durbin, C. E. (2011). Psychometric properties of the Behavioral Inhibition Questionnaire in preschool children. *Journal of Personality Assessment*, 93(6), 545–555.

Kindt, M., Brosschot, J. F., & Muris, P. (1996). Spider Phobia Questionnaire for children (SPQ-C): A psychometric study and normative data. *Behaviour Research and Therapy*, 34(3), 277–282.

Kristensen, S., Henriksen, T. B., & Bilenberg, N. (2010). The Child Behavior Checklist for Ages 1.5–5 (CBCL/1/12-5): Assessment and analysis of parent- and caregiver-reported problems in a population-based sample of Danish preschool children. *Nordic Journal of Psychiatry*, 64(3), 203–209.

Kushnir, J., Gothelf, D., & Sadeh, A. (2015). Assessing fears of preschool children with nighttime fears by a parent version of the fear survey schedule for preschool children. *The Israel Journal of Psychiatry and Related Sciences*, 52(1), 61.

La Greca, A. M., Dandes, S. K., Wick, P., Shaw, K., & Stone, W. L. (1988). Development of the Social Anxiety Scale for Children: Reliability and concurrent validity. *Journal of Clinical Child Psychology*, 17(1), 84–91.

Lavigne, J. V., Hopkins, J., Gouze, K. R., & Bryant, F. B. (2015). Bidirectional influences of anxiety and depression in young children. *Journal of Abnormal Child Psychology*, 43(1), 163–176.

Lavigne, J. V., LeBailly, S. A., Hopkins, J., Gouze, K. R., & Binns, H. J. (2009). The prevalence of ADHD, ODD, depression, and anxiety in a community sample of 4-year-olds. *Journal of Clinical Child and Adolescent Psychology*, 38(3), 315–328.

Lucas, C. P., Fisher, P., & Luby, J. L. (2008). *Young child DISC-IV: Diagnostic interview schedule for children.* New York, NY: Columbia University, Division of Children Psychiatry, Joy and William Ruane Center to Identify and Treat Mood Disorders.

Lyneham, H. J., Sburlati, E. S., Abbott, M. J., Rapee, R. M., Hudson, J. L., Tolin, D. F., & Carlson, S. E. (2013). Psychometric properties of the Child Anxiety Life Interference Scale (CALIS). *Journal of Anxiety Disorders*, 27(7), 711–719.

Martin, R. P. (1994). Temperament assessment battery for children (TABC). *Infant Mental Health Journal*, 15(2), 238–238.

McLeod, B. D., Weisz, J. R., & Wood, J. J. (2007). Examining the association between parenting and childhood depression: A meta-analysis. *Clinical Psychology Review*, 27(8), 986–1003.

McMurtry, C. M., Noel, M., Chambers, C. T., & McGrath, P. J. (2011). Children's fear during procedural pain: preliminary investigation of the Children's Fear Scale. *Health Psychology: Official Journal of the Division of Health Psychology, American Psychological Association*, 30(6), 780–788.

Méndez, X., Espada, J. P., Orgilés, M., Llavona, L. M., & García-Fernández, J. M. (2014). Children's Separation Anxiety Scale (CSAS): Psychometric properties. *PloS One*, 9(7), e103212.

Moreno, J., Silverman, W. K., Saavedra, L. M., & Phares, V. (2008). Fathers' ratings in the assessment of their child's anxiety symptoms: A comparison to mothers' ratings and their associations with paternal symptomatology. *Journal of Family Psychology*, 22(6), 915–919.

Morgan, A. J., Rapee, R. M., Salim, A., Goharpey, N., Tamir, E., McLellan, L. F., & Bayer, J. K. (2017). Internet-delivered parenting program for prevention and early intervention of anxiety problems in young children: Randomized controlled trial. *Journal of the American Academy of Child and Adolescent Psychiatry*, 56(5), 417–425.

Muris, P. (2007). *Normal and abnormal fear and anxiety in children and adolescents*. Amsterdam; Boston: Elsevier.

Muris, P., Heniks, E., & Bot, S. (2016). Children of few words: relations among selective mutism, behavioral inhibition, and (social) anxiety symptoms in 3-to 6-year-olds. *Child Psychiatry and Human Development*, 47(1), 94–101.

Murphy, J. M., Pagano, M. E., Ramirez, A., Anaya, Y., Nowlin, C., & Jellinek, M. S. (1999). Validation of the Preschool and Early Childhood Functional Assessment Scale (PECFAS). *Journal of Child and Family Studies*, 8(3), 343–356.

Ollendick, T. H. (1983). Reliability and validity of the Revised Fear Survey Schedule for Children (FSSC-R). *Behaviour Research and Therapy*, 21(6), 685–692.

Rapee, R. M. (2002). The development and modification of temperamental risk for anxiety disorders: prevention of a lifetime of anxiety? *Biological Psychiatry*, 52(10), 947–957.

Rapee, R. M. (2014). Preschool environment and temperament as predictors of social and nonsocial anxiety disorders in middle adolescence. *Journal of the American Academy of Child and Adolescent Psychiatry*, 53(3), 320.

Rapee, R. M., & Coplan, R. J. (2010). Conceptual relations between anxiety disorder and fearful temperament. *New Directions for Child and Adolescent Development*, 2010(127), 17–31.

Rapee, R. M., Kennedy, S., Ingram, M., Edwards, S., & Sweeney, L. (2005). Prevention and early intervention of anxiety disorders in inhibited preschool children. *Journal of Consulting and Clinical Psychology*, 73(3), 488–497.

Rapee, R. M., Kennedy, S. J., Ingram, M., Edwards, S. L., & Sweeney, L. (2010). Altering the trajectory of anxiety in at-risk young children. *American Journal of Psychiatry*, 167(12), 1518–1525.

Rapee, R. M., & Spence, S. H. (2004). The etiology of social phobia: Empirical evidence and an initial model. *Clinical Psychology Review*, 24(7), 737–767.

Reich, W., Leacock, N., & Shanfeld, K. (1997). DICA-IV Diagnostic Interview for Children and Adolescents-IV [Computer software]. Toronto, Ontario: Multi-Health Systems, Inc.

Rescorla, L. A., Bochicchio, L., Achenbach, T. M., Ivanova, M. Y., Almqvist, F., Begovac, I., … Verhulst, F. C. (2014). Parent–teacher agreement on children's problems in 21 societies. *Journal of Clinical Child and Adolescent Psychology*, 43(4), 627–642.

Ringoot, A. P., Jansen, P. W., Rijlaarsdam, J., So, P., Jaddoe, V. W. V., Verhulst, F. C., & Tiemeier, H. (2017). Self-reported problem behavior in young children with and without a DSM-disorder in the general population. *European Psychiatry*, 40, 110–115.

Rothbart, M. K., Ahadi, S. A., Hershey, K. L., & Fisher, P. (2001). Investigations of temperament at three to seven years: The Children's Behavior Questionnaire. *Child Development*, 72(5), 1394–1408.

Russell, E., & Sofronoff, K. (2005). Anxiety and social worries in children with Asperger syndrome. *Australian and New Zealand Journal of Psychiatry*, 39(7), 633–638.

Scheeringa, M. S., & Haslett, N. (2010). The reliability and criterion validity of the Diagnostic Infant and Preschool Assessment: A new diagnostic instrument for young children. *Child Psychiatry and Human Development*, 41(3), 299–312.

Shaffer, D., Fisher, P., Lucas, C. P., Dulcan, M. K., & Schwab-Stone, M. E. (2000). NIMH Diagnostic Interview Schedule for Children Version IV (NIMH DISC-IV): Description, differences from previous versions, and reliability of some common diagnoses. *Journal of the American Academy of Child and Adolescent Psychiatry*, 39(1), 28–38.

Shamir-Essakow, G., Ungerer, J. A., & Rapee, R. M. (2005). Attachment, behavioral inhibition, and anxiety in preschool children. *Journal of Abnormal Child Psychology*, 33(2), 131–143.

Silberg, J. L., Gillespie, N., Moore, A. A., Eaves, L. J., Bates, J., Aggen, S., ... Canino, G. (2015). Shared genetic and environmental influences on early temperament and preschool psychiatric disorders in Hispanic twins. *Twin Research and Human Genetics: The Official Journal of the International Society for Twin Studies*, 18(2), 171–178.

Silverman, W. K., & Albano, A. M. (1996a). *Anxiety Disorders Interview schedule for children for DSM-IV: Child and parent versions*. San Antonio, TX: The Psychological Corporation, Harcourt, Brace & Company.

Silverman, W. K., & Albano, A. M. (1996b). *Anxiety Disorders Interview schedule for DSM-IV – Child Version: Parent Interview Schedule*. San Antonio: The Psychological Corporation, Harcourt, Brace & Company.

Smith, S. R. (2007). Making sense of multiple informants in child and adolescent psychopathology: A guide for clinicians. *Journal of Psychoeducational Assessment*, 25(2), 139–149.

Spence, S. H. (2017). Review-measurement issues: Assessing anxiety disorders in children and adolescents. *Child and Adolescent Mental Health*, doi:10.1111/camh.12251

Spence, S. H., Rapee, R., McDonald, C., & Ingram, M. (2001). The structure of anxiety symptoms among preschoolers. *Behaviour Research and Therapy*, 39(11), 1293–1316.

Sprafkin, J., & Gadow, K. D. (2017). *Early Childhood Inventory-5 Norms Manual*. Stony Brook, NY: Checkmate Plus.

Sprafkin, J., Volpe, R. J., Gadow, K. D., Nolan, E. E., & Kelly, K. (2002). A DSM-IV–referenced screening instrument for preschool children: The Early Childhood Inventory-4. *Journal of the American Academy of Child and Adolescent Psychiatry*, 41(5), 604–612.

Sterba, S., Egger, H. L., & Angold, A. (2007). Diagnostic specificity and nonspecificity in the dimensions of preschool psychopathology. *Journal of Child Psychology and Psychiatry, and Allied Disciplines*, 48(10), 1005–1013.

Stuijfzand, S., & Dodd, H. F. (2017). Young children have social worries too: Validation of a brief parent report measure of social worries in children aged 4–8 years. *Journal of Anxiety Disorders*, 50, 87–93.

Task Force on Research Diagnostic Criteria: Infancy and Preschool. (2003). Research diagnostic criteria for infants and preschool children: The process and empirical support. *Journal of the American Academy of Child and Adolescent Psychiatry*, 42(12), 1504–1512.

Wang, M., & Zhao, J. (2015). Anxiety disorder symptoms in Chinese preschool children. *Child Psychiatry and Human Development*, 46(1), 158–166.

Warren, S. L., Ollendick, T. H., & Simmens, S. J. (2008). Reliability and validity of the fear survey schedule for infants—preschoolers. *Depression and Anxiety*, 25(12), E205–E207.

Wigham, S., & McConachie, H. (2014). Systematic review of the properties of tools used to measure outcomes in anxiety intervention studies for children with autism spectrum disorders. *PloS One*, 9(1), e85268.

Zainal, H., Magiati, I., Tan, J. W.-L., Sung, M., Fung, D. S., & Howlin, P. (2014). A preliminary investigation of the Spence Children's Anxiety Parent Scale as a screening tool for anxiety in young people with autism spectrum disorders. *Journal of Autism and Developmental Disorders*, 44(8), 1982–1994.

Zero to Three. (1994). *Diagnostic classification: 0–3: Diagnostic classification of mental health and developmental disorders of infancy and early childhood*. Arlington, VA: National Center for Clinical Infant Programs.

5 Assessment of Fear and Anxiety in Preschool Children
Self-report and Observational Measures

Peter Muris

Introduction

Fear and anxiety are common phenomena during the childhood years. This has been primarily documented in samples of non-referred school-aged children and adolescents, where up to 95% report signs of a fear, worry, or scary dream (Muris, Merckelbach, Gadet, & Moulaert, 2000), and about 1 in 10 youngsters have been found to fulfill the diagnostic criteria of an anxiety disorder (Costello, Mustillo, Erkanli, Keeler, & Angold, 2003). Prevalence studies in preschool children are more sparse, but the available epidemiological evidence is showing that a similar percentage of anxiety disorders can be found at an early age. For example, the investigation of Egger et al. (2006) in which the parents of 1073 preschoolers aged 2 to 5 years were subjected to a two-step screening procedure consisting of the Child Behavior Checklist 1/12-5 (Achenbach & Rescorla, 2000), a parent-rated screening questionnaire for psychopathological symptoms, and the Preschool Age Psychiatric Assessment (Egger & Angold, 1999), a structured clinical interview for assessing psychiatric diagnoses, indicated that 9.4% of the children consistently met the criteria of any anxiety disorder. Generalized anxiety disorder was the most common (3.8%), followed by separation anxiety disorder (2.4%), specific phobia (2.3%), social anxiety disorder (2.1%), and selective mutism (0.6%), this clearly being the least frequently occurring anxiety problem.

Given the limited cognitive capacities of preschool children, it seems logical that previous investigations have mainly relied on parent-administered questionnaires and interviews to assess fear, anxiety, and their disorders in this age group. This does not necessarily imply that other types of assessment cannot be employed in this population. For example, observational measures can be useful as there are some fear and anxiety symptoms (e.g., shyness, avoidance behavior) that are so readily observable. In addition, self-report instruments can also be applied and may yield information about the child's internal or "hidden" fear- and anxiety-related experiences. In this chapter, an overview of these two types of assessment methods in preschool children as well as a discussion of their psychometric properties will be provided.

Observational Measures

A number of observational measures can be used to assess fear, anxiety, or related phenomena in preschool children (Table 5.1). One instrument is the *Strange Situation procedure* as developed by Ainsworth, Blehar, Waters, and Wall (1978) to assess the quality of the attachment relationship between parent and child. During a 20-minutes play session, caregivers and strangers enter and leave the room, thereby simulating the presence of familiar and unfamiliar persons in children's daily lives. Based on systematic observations of children's (a) explorative behavior displayed in the playroom, (b) reactions to the departure of the parent, (c) amount of anxiety in response to the stranger, and (d) reunion behavior with the caregiver, they can be categorized into three attachment groups: (1) a secure attachment group that consists of children who use the caregiver as a secure base to regulate anxiety and distress, (2) an avoidant attachment group that is composed of children who do not use the caregiver as a source of comfort to regulate their negative affect, and (3) an ambivalent attachment group that contains children who display signs of distress and anxiety in response to the new situation even before the separation from the parent, and then are difficult to comfort on the caregiver's return. There is evidence for the test-retest reliability of the attachment classifications as obtained by means of the Strange Situation procedure (Main & Cassidy, 1988). Research also supports its validity (e.g., Richters, Waters, & Vaughn, 1988), but it is good to keep in mind that this assessment method does not represent a pure anxiety measure. Nevertheless, it is clear that the insecure attachment patterns observed in preschoolers are intimately linked with separation anxiety (Dallaire & Weinraub, 2005; Shouldice & Stevenson-Hinde, 1992), and there is also evidence showing that such early attachment problems are predictive of a broad range of anxiety disorders in later childhood. For example, Warren, Huston, Egeland, and Sroufe (1997) followed a group of infants who at the age of 12-months, were subjected to the Strange Situation procedure and had been classified as either securely, avoidantly, or ambivalently attached. When children reached the age of 17 years, current and past anxiety disorders were assessed by means of a structured diagnostic interview. Results indicated that 15% of the youths had developed one past or present anxiety disorder, including social phobia, separation anxiety disorder, generalized anxiety disorder, and panic disorder. Most importantly, insecurely attached children, and in particular the ambivalently attached, were twice as much at risk of suffering from an anxiety disorder than children who were securely attached.

Table 5.1 Items included in the Preschool Observation Scale of Anxiety (POSA)

1	*Physical complaint:* Child says he or she has a headache, stomach ache, or has to go to the bathroom
2	Desire to leave: Child says he or she wants to leave the testing room or makes excuses about why he or she must leave; desire or "need" to leave must be explicit
3	Expression of fear or worry: Child complains about being afraid of or worried about something; must use the word "afraid", "scared", "worried", or a synonym
4	Cry: Tears should be visible
5	Scream
6	Whine or whimper
7	Trembling voice
8	Stutter
9	Whisper: Child speaks softly, without vocal cords, should not be a playful whisper
10	Silence to one question in the interval
11	Silence to more than one question during the interval
12	Nail-biting: Child actually bites his or her nails in the testing room
13	Lip-licking: Tongue should be visible
14	Fingers touching mouth area: Not counted if bites nails why touching mouth
15	Sucking or chewing object: Not fingernails
16	Lip contortions
17	Trembling lip
18	Gratuitous hand movement at ear area
19	Gratuitous hand movement on top of head
20	Gratuitous hand movement at an object separate from body or at a part of clothing separate from body
21	Gratuitous hand movement at some part of body (not ear, hair, mouth, or genitals)
22	Gratuitous hand movement
23	Gratuitous leg movement
24	Gratuitous foot movement: Below ankles, distinguish from foot merely moving along with leg
25	Trunk contortions
26	Rigid posture: Part of body is held unusually stiff or motionless for the entire 30-sec interval
27	Masturbation: Touches genital area
28	Fearful facial expression
29	Distraction: Must be indicated by a verbal reminder by the examiner to the child to pay attention
30	Avoidance of eye contact: Examiner should be having clear trouble making eye contact with child

Note: Items taken from Table 1 in Glennon and Weisz (1978).

Kagan's (1994) temperamental concept of *Behavioral Inhibition to the Unfamiliar* (BIU) is another operationalization of children's anxiety proneness. It pertains to a subgroup of children who show a consistent tendency to interrupt ongoing behavior and to react with vocal restraint and withdrawal when confronted with unknown people or novel settings. Although BIU can be efficiently assessed by means of parent- and teacher-report questionnaires (e.g., Vreeke et al., 2012), this temperamental characteristic has been typically measured by observing children's responses in a laboratory setting where they are exposed to unfamiliar objects (e.g., a robot animal) and persons (e.g., meeting a new or a dressed-up person; Kagan, Reznick, & Snidman, 1988). Latency to approach, spontaneous talk, frequency of smiling, and encouragements by the experimenter are examples of variables that are assessed via observation, ultimately defining a child's level of BIU. The inter-rater reliability of observational BIU variables is generally good (Van Brakel, Muris, & Bögels, 2004), but the method is time-consuming especially because one needs to observe the child in multiple contexts to obtain a valid impression of the trait (Majdandzic & Van den Boom, 2007). Nevertheless, there is convincing evidence for a link between BIU and anxiety problems in children (see for a review: Fox, Henderson, Marshall, Nichols, & Ghera, 2005). One of the first investigations showing this explicitly was conducted by Biederman et al. (1990) who compared the presence of anxiety disorders in preschool children who had been classified as either inhibited or uninhibited by means of a laboratory assessment. It was found that the inhibited children clearly exhibited higher levels of anxiety disorders relative to the uninhibited children. Even more interestingly, at a follow-up assessment three year later (Biederman et al., 1993), it was noted that the inhibited children displayed a significant increase in anxiety problems from baseline to follow-up, whereas such a marked increase was not observed for the uninhibited group. More than 25 years later, it has become clear that BIU has a special relationship with social anxiety disorder (Clauss & Blackford, 2012) and selective mutism (Muris & Ollendick, 2015), which suggests that this temperamental trait becomes particularly apparent in response to social cues.

Other observational instruments have borrowed elements from the procedures used to assess attachment insecurity and behavioral inhibition. One example is the recently developed *Anxiety Dimensional Observation Scale* (Anx-DOS; Mian, Carter, Pine, Wakschlag, & Briggs-Gowan, 2015), which employs four tasks to be conducted by the child in the presence of the parent: (1) mystery jar: the child is asked to explore the content of an opaque pot, (2) spider: the child is asked to play with a remote controlled tarantula robot toy, (3) bell: the child is exposed to the suddenly occurring sound of an electronic bell signaling the transition to the next task, and (4) separation: the parent leaves the room and the child is left behind with an unknown person. Observers have to code the child's behavior during each of the four tasks on dimensions of anxiety such as fear arousal, physical avoidance, and exaggerated startle, using a clinical continuum with 0 = no evidence, 1 = mild, 2 = of concern, and 3 = atypical. The inter-rater reliability and internal consistency of the Anx-DOS proved to be good in a sample of 403 preschool children, and there was also evidence for its convergent validity as shown by the expected positive correlations with parent-reported anxiety symptoms, observed BIU, and attention bias to threat (Mian et al., 2015). Another illustration concerns the *Laboratory Temperament Assessment Battery* (Lab-TAB; Gagne, Van Hulle, Aksan, Essex, & Goldsmith, 2011; http://www.uta.edu/fa culty/jgagne/labtab/labtab_page.htm), which essentially intends to measure a broad range of temperament features of which fear and (lack of) sociability are particularly relevant within the context of childhood anxiety. The Lab-TAB consists of a series of tasks of which some are pre-eminently suitable for studying fear reactions and social wariness, such as the risk room – where the child is left alone with a set of novel and ambiguous stimuli (e.g., scary mask, large black box with eyes and teeth), the stranger approach – during which an unknown person enters the room and speaks to the child while slowly walking closer, and scary animals – which requires the child to explore pretend mice in a cage and a mechanical spider and bird. The child's behavior during such tasks is coded into reliable temperament scores, of which parents have reported that they are highly typical representations of behavior outside of the laboratory, thereby supporting the ecological validity of this observational assessment (e.g., Lo, Vroman, & Durbin, 2015). Work by Dougherty and colleagues (2011, 2013) has indeed confirmed that the Lab-TAB produces a prototypical temperament profile for preschool children with anxiety disorders, which confirms that this instrument yields valuable information on this type of psychopathology.

The most direct way to assess fear and anxiety is to observe these behaviors in the situations in which they occur. Specific behaviors reflective of a fear or anxiety problem are operationally defined and then recorded (King, Ollendick, & Murphy, 1997). For example, one can reliably assess the amount of speech produced in the classroom at school by a child with selective mutism (e.g., Conn & Coyne, 2014) or establish the number of minutes required to go to bed after being asked in a child with separation anxiety and/or nighttime fears (Graziano & Mooney, 1980). Otherwise, *behavioral approach tests* can be employed during which the child is asked to move towards the feared object in a standardized, stepwise manner. The fear and anxiety level of a child can be inferred from the steps taken during the test: the lower the number of steps, the more avoidant and thus fearful the child is. Hamilton and King (1991) applied such an assessment in 14 dog phobic children, of whom the youngest was two years of age, and noted that the test-retest reliability (over the period of one week) of this type of test appears to be good. Finally, one can also try to quantify behavioral indicators of fear and anxiety of children when they are exposed to a stressful situation. Noteworthy in this regard is the *Preschool Observation Scale of Anxiety* (POSA; Glennon & Weisz, 1978), which can be used to assess the frequency of behaviors such as nail biting, crying, trembling, and fearful facial expression (for a full list of the POSA items, see Table 5.2) in two- to four-year-old children using a time-sampling observation procedure. The psychometric evaluation showed that the POSA has satisfactory interrater reliability and good validity as established via positive correlations with parent- and teacher-ratings of anxiety.

In spite of the fact that behavioral observational measures yield reliable information about fear and anxiety in preschool children, this assessment method is not very popular because it is often considered to be too time-consuming and costly. However, it should be stressed that these observations provide unique information on childhood fear and anxiety. Too often researchers and clinicians only rely on ratings of parents and teachers to evaluate these internalizing symptoms on the basis of which they draw conclusions about their intensity, severity, and need for treatment. The addition of an observational assessment can be extremely valuable as one can establish how the young child is actually handling fear-and anxiety-provoking stimuli and situations.

Self-report Instruments

As noted in the previous section, some fear and anxiety symptoms are readily observable, but it should be kept in mind that most of these internalizing experiences remain hidden for the environment and are only open to child introspection. This is why, at least in older children, self-report instruments are considered to be an important element in the assessment of anxiety problems (Stallings & March, 1995). In preschoolers, however, self-report measures have not enjoyed great popularity, likely because they are considered to be less suitable given that the cognitive capacities of young children are still limited. In other words, the disadvantage of this method is that – at this age – questions are often too difficult and that the response format is not properly understood, which poses serious problems in relation to validity (Warren & Dadson, 2001).

Despite these concerns, some researchers have used self-report questionnaires originally developed for older children to assess anxiety in youngsters at a preschool age (Table 5.3). For example, Ialongo, Edelsohn, Werthamer-Larsson, Crockett, and Kellam (1995) examined anxiety symptoms in five- and six-year-olds by means of an interview version of the *Revised Children's Manifest Anxiety Scale* (RCMAS; Reynolds & Richmond, 1978) using symbols (i.e., pictures of shapes and objects) to help children find the correct spot on the answer sheet. The results of the study were quite encouraging as data indicated that the RCMAS measurement was reliable in terms of internal consistency as well as valid, because preschoolers' anxiety scores were predictive of anxiety

Table 5.2 Overview of the *observational measures* (including parent-rating scales) that can be used to assess fear, anxiety, and related constructs in preschool children

Measure	Procedure	Type of fear/anxiety measured
Strange situation test (Ainsworth et al., 1978)[1]	Systematic observation of the behavior and emotional reactions of one-year-old children who undergo a structured procedure involving separation and reunion from the mother and interaction with a stranger	Attachment types: secure, avoidant, and ambivalent, of which the latter two are associated with (separation) anxiety symptoms
Behavioral Inhibition to the Unfamiliar (Kagan, 1994)[2]	Relevant behaviors (such as latency to approach, spontaneous speech, frequency of smiling) are observed in children exposed to novel objects and unknown persons	Anxiety-prone temperament
Anxiety Dimensional Observation Scale (Mian et al., 2015)	Children's anxiety-related reactions during four challenging experimental tasks are directly scored	Fear arousal, physical avoidance, and exaggerated startle
Laboratory Temperament Assessment Battery (Gagne et al., 2011)[3]	Children's fear reactions and social behavior are coded during a series of ambiguous or mildly threatening experimental tasks	The temperament features of fear and social wariness
Behavioral approach tests	Quantifying avoidance by asking the child to approach the feared stimulus or situation in a standardized, stepwise manner	Fear- or phobia-related avoidance behavior
Preschool Observation Scale of Anxiety (Glennon & Weisz, 1978)	Quantifying behavioral indicators of fear and anxiety (nail biting, crying, trembling, and fearful facial expression) in children who are exposed to a stressful situation	Situation-related (state) fear and anxiety

Notes: [1] See https://www.bing.com/videos/search?q=strange+situation+test&&view=detail&mid=E13B86AB51F8E1CC9128E13B86AB51F8E1CC9128&&FORM=VDRVRV; [2] https://www.bing.com/videos/search?q=behavioral+inhibition+to+the+unfamiliar&&view=detail&mid=199A440DE0E80EDDD195199A440DE0E80EDDD195&&FORM=VDRVRV; [3] http://www.uta.edu/faculty/jgagne/labtab/labtab_page.htm; https://www.bing.com/videos/search?q=lab-tab&&view=detail&mid=5FF3598364CFADC258DA5FF3598364CFADC258DA&&FORM=VDRVRV.

Table 5.3 Overview of the *self-report scales* that can be employed to measure fear and anxiety in preschool children

Measure	Description	Type of fear/anxiety measured
Revised Children's Manifest Anxiety Scale (Reynolds & Richmond, 1978; age-adjusted interview version by Ialongo et al., 1995)[1]	37 items are read aloud by the interviewer while children indicate yes-no responses on answer sheet; pictures of common shapes (circle and square) and objects (ball, apple, etc.) help children to indicate answer choices and to show the right place of items on the answer sheet	Physiological anxiety, worry and oversensitivity, problems with fear and concentration
Anxiety Interview (Muris et al., 2000)	The child is interviewed about his/her experience with various anxiety phenomena; a brief description is read and a picture of each phenomenon is shown to the child	Fear/anxiety, worry, scary dreams
Koala Fear Questionnaire (Muris et al., 2003)	31 items of fear-provoking stimuli or situations that are illustrated with pictures, for which the child indicates his/her fear level using a visual scale depicting Koala bears expressing various degrees of fear (none, some, a lot)	Fears and fearfulness
Picture Anxiety Test (Dubi & Schneider, 2009)	21 items each consisting of two pictures of a similar situation (one threatening, one neutral); the child has to select the picture most applicable to him/her and then indicates levels of anxiety/avoidance in the selected situation	Symptoms of specific phobias, social phobia, generalized anxiety disorder, and separation anxiety disorder
Dominic (Valla, Bergeron, & Smolla, 2000)[2]	Computerized test showing 91 cartoon pictures of a gender- and ethnic-neutral character who experiences a broad range of behavioral and emotional (including anxiety) symptoms; the child indicates whether he/she has similar symptoms	Symptoms of specific phobias, generalized anxiety disorder, and separation anxiety disorder
Berkeley Puppet Interview (Ablow et al., 2003)	Semi-structured interview during which two identical dog hand puppets are used who make opposing statements regarding psychopathology (including anxiety symptoms); the child indicates which puppet most resembles him/her and is then questioned to establish the intensity of symptomatology	Symptoms of generalized anxiety disorder and separation anxiety disorder

[1] https://www.wpspublish.com/store/p/2934/rcmas-2-revised-children-s-manifest-anxiety-scale-second-edition; [2] http://www.dominic-interactive.com/index_fr.jsp; [3] http://pages.uoregon.edu/dslab/BPI.html; https://www.bing.com/videos/search?q=berkeley+puppet&view=detail&mid=7E04EF4F84C4A87DEA8F7E04EF4F84C4A87DEA8F&FORM=VIRE.

symptoms and adaptive functioning at a follow-up assessment when children had reached the age of 10. However, there is likely doubt as to
whether such young children fully understand the content of items such
as "I feel nervous when things don't go the right way," "Often I have
trouble getting my breath," and "I worry a lot of the time."

Fortunately, a number of alternative instruments are available that have
been especially construed for assessing fear and anxiety in preschool
children, and thus, make use of more developmentally acceptable mate-
rials. A straightforward method is the *Anxiety Interview* (Muris, Merckelbach, Gadet, & Moulaert, 2000) which simply asks children to report
the stimuli and situations that they fear or worry about. To prompt the
child a brief description and a picture are used to make the anxiety phenomena (i.e., fear, worry, and scary dreams) more comprehensible.
Although this method has yielded interesting information regarding the
content of young children's fear and anxiety (e.g., Stevenson-Hinde &
Shouldice, 1995), this approach is less suitable for evaluating the frequency, severity, and intensity of symptoms.

Scales that are more appropriate in this regard are the *Koala Fear
Questionnaire* (KFQ; Muris et al., 2003) and the *Picture Anxiety Test* (PAT;
Dubi & Schneider, 2009). The KFQ consists of 31 potentially fear-pro-
voking stimuli and situations that are all illustrated with pictures. Children rate their intensity of fear to each of these stimuli and situations by
using a visual scale depicting koala bears expressing various levels of fear
(no fear, some fear, a lot of fear). In a first psychometric evaluation,
Muris and colleagues (2003) found that the KFQ is a reliable measure in
terms of internal consistency and test-retest stability, which also displays
reasonable validity as established by a positive correlation with an alternative anxiety assessment (the Anxiety Interview). A second investigation,
carried out on a small island in the Caribbean (Saint Martin, Netherlands
Antilles; Muris, 2002), demonstrated that KFQ scores of four- to six-year-
old children were significantly correlated with a highly relevant fear in
this part of the world, namely fear of storms and hurricanes. Finally,
Kushnir, Gothelf, and Sadeh (2014) administered the KFQ in four- to six-
year-olds with and without severe nighttime fears. It was found that the
young children with severe nighttime fears displayed significantly higher
fear levels than their counterparts without such problems, which supports the discriminant validity of the scale.

Just like the KFQ, the PAT consists of pictures to make the fear and
anxiety items more comprehensible for the children. However, a difference is that the PAT employs two pictures for each item, which are presented simultaneously to the child: one picture depicts the critical
symptom (e.g., a fearful child running away from a dog), whereas in the
other picture the symptom is not shown (i.e., a calm child seeking contact with a dog). The child first selects the picture that is most applicable
to him or her and then indicates the level of anxiety and the level of

avoidance for that stimulus or situation, which results in four-point ratings ranging from 0 = "no anxiety/avoidance at all" to 3 = "a lot of anxiety/avoidance." The PAT contains 21 items that primarily assess symptoms of specific phobias (e.g., blood, spiders, heights), social phobia (e.g., talk/play with unfamiliar children), generalized anxiety disorder (e.g., worry), and separation anxiety disorder (e.g., going to school). The PAT displays good internal consistency, test-retest stability, convergent validity (as indicated by positive correlations with other self- and parent-rated anxiety scales), and discriminant validity (as shown by differences in scores between anxiety disorder and control children; Dubi, Lavallee, & Schneider, 2012; Dubi & Schneider, 2009). Meanwhile, there is little evidence for the added value of the distinction between anxiety and avoidance scores, which only seems to complicate the administration of this scale in the youngest children.

A number of other instruments that can be used to study anxiety symptoms from the child's perspective should be mentioned here. The *Dominic* (Valla, Bergeron, & Smolla, 2000) is a computerized self-report questionnaire containing 91 questions assessing symptoms of DSM-defined mental health problems in children. The test shows cartoon pictures of a character named Dominic (whose appearance can be adjusted to the gender and ethnicity of the child) who faces various situations that reflect a number of behavioral and emotional problems. The child is asked whether he/she encounters similar problems in his/her own life ("Do thunderstorms make you feel scared, like Dominic?"). Responses are scored as 0 ("No") or 1 ("Yes") and summed to a total score that can be interpreted as "No problem," "There may be a problem," or "There is a problem," using empirically derived cut-off points. Besides depression and disruptive behavior disorders, this questionnaire can be used to assess three categories of anxiety disorders (i.e., specific phobias, generalized anxiety disorder, and separation anxiety disorder). The psychometric properties are satisfactory in samples including children as young as six years of age (Valla et al., 2000; Kuijpers, Otten, Vermulst, & Engels, 2014), but given its content the Dominic might also be applicable to younger children.

The *Berkeley Puppet Interview* (BPI; Ablow et al., 2003; Measelle, Ablow, Cowan, & Cowan, 1998) is a semi-structured interview technique to obtain self-reports of emotional-behavioral, social, and academic functioning from young children. The BPI originally consists of 17 scales of which the so-called symptomatology scales are most relevant here, as two of them directly assess anxiety symptoms (i.e., separation anxiety, overanxiousness). During the interview – which is videotaped for scoring purposes, the child is invited to engage in a conversation/interaction with two identical dog hand puppets, Iggy and Ziggy. The puppets always make opposing statements about themselves; for example, when Iggy says "I worry about mom or dad when I am at school," Ziggy puts forward "I do not worry about mom or dad when I am at school." Subsequently, the puppets ask the child to indicate which statement applies most to him/her ("How about you?"). The natural dialogue that follows is coded by independent raters using a 7-point scale, with 1 indicating that the symptom is totally absent, and 7 indicating that the symptom is strongly present. By combining the ratings of relevant items, BPI scale scores are obtained. So far, a handful of studies have been conducted to investigate the reliability and validity of the BPI; they have demonstrated that the symptomatology scales of this instrument can be reliably coded, and have sufficient test-retest stability as well as reasonable validity (Luby, Belden, Sullivan, & Spitznagel, 2007; Ringoot et al., 2013; Stone et al., 2014). The BPI is a promising measure that could easily be extended to assess symptoms of anxiety disorders that are presently not covered by this instrument (e.g., specific phobias, social anxiety disorder).

Taken together, a number of developmentally appropriate measures are available for assessing fear and anxiety symptomatology from the preschool child's perspective. Research suggests that these instruments are reliable and valid, but more studies are needed to examine the relations among these measures and to establish their incremental validity beyond other types of assessment.

Conclusion

With the growing consensus that dysregulated fear and anxiety during early childhood reflect relevant clinical phenomena that are predictive for later internalizing problems (e.g., Bosquet & Egeland, 2006), there is increasing interest in standardized assessment instruments of these phenomena at a preschool age. So far, parent-report scales are by far most popular, but the sole reliance on such measures may be problematic in the assessment of fear and anxiety problems because caregivers may be less aware of these internalizing symptoms. This chapter addressed two types of assessment for gaining a more valid impression of fear and anxiety in preschool children, which can be added to the psychological assessment of fear and anxiety. Observational measurement is particularly important, as we know from the literature that subjective reporting of fear and anxiety and the behavioral assessment of these phenomena are often discordant (Ollendick, Allen, Benoit, & Cowart, 2011). Observations can be particularly valuable because they give a valid impression of children's actual avoidance and escape behaviors, which according to behaviorally oriented therapists and scholars are considered as the key mechanism in the maintenance of phobias and anxiety disorders (Ollendick & Muris, 2015).

So far, few studies have explored the additional value of self-reports in the assessment of fear and anxiety in preschool children. One exception is a study by Luby et al. (2007) who showed that young children, aged three to five years can accurately report anxiety phenomena such as being shy with peers, having bad dreams, and missing parents while being at school, and that these self-reports (obtained with the BPI) were more predictive of diagnostic status than a comparable parent-report of the same symptoms. Meanwhile, these researchers also noted that when symptoms were more complex and abstract, the predictive value of self-reports clearly attenuated, suggesting that the value of this method in young children is limited to the core and basic fear and anxiety symptoms.

Finally, it is good clinical and research practice to include multiple informants in the assessment of childhood psychopathology – and anxiety disorders are no exception to this rule (Silverman & Ollendick, 2005). The idea is to obtain as much information as possible on the child's symptomatology and functioning across different contexts, thereby producing a complete picture of its problems. Interestingly, not only converging information is important, but even informant discrepancies may yield relevant knowledge on the problems and difficulties of the child (De Los Reyes & Kazdin, 2005). More research embracing the multi-informant assessment methodology would be particularly welcome, to further advance our knowledge on the value of observational and self-report instruments for assessing fear and anxiety in young children.

References

Ablow, J.C., Measelle, J.R., and the MacArthur Working Group on Outcome Assessment (2003). *Manual for the Berkeley Puppet Interview: Symptomatology, social, and academic modules (BPI 1.0)*. Pittsburgh, PA: University of Pittsburgh.

Achenbach, T.M., & Rescorla, L.A. (2000). *Manual for the ASEBA preschool forms and profiles: An integrated system of multi-informant assessment*. Burlington, VT: University of Vermont, Department of Psychiatry.

Ainsworth, M.D.S., Blehar, M.C., Waters, E., & Wall, S. (1978). *Patterns of attachment: A psychological study of the strange situation*. Hillsdale, NJ: Erlbaum.

Biederman, J., Rosenbaum, J.F., Bolduc-Murphy, E.A., Faraone, S.V., Chaloff, J., Hirshfeld, D.R., & Kagan, J. (1993). A 3-year follow-up of children with and without behavioral inhibition. *Journal of the American Academy of Child and Adolescent Psychiatry, 32*, 814–821.

Biederman, J., Rosenbaum, J.F., Hirshfeld, D.R., Faraone, S.V., Bolduc, E.A., Gersten, M., Meminger, S.R., Kagan, J., Snidman, N., & Reznick, J.S. (1990). Psychiatric correlates of behavioral inhibition in young children of parents with and without psychiatric disorders. *Archives of General Psychiatry, 47*, 21–26.

Bosquet, M., & Egeland, B. (2006). The development and maintenance of anxiety symptoms from infancy through adolescence in a longitudinal sample. *Development and Psychopathology, 18*, 517–550.

Clauss, J.A., & Blackford, J.U. (2012). Behavioral inhibition and risk for developing social anxiety disorder: A meta-analytic study. *Journal of the American Academy of Child and Adolescent Psychiatry, 51*, 1066–1075.

Conn, B.M., & Coyne, L.W. (2014). Selective mutism in early childhood: Assessment and treatment of an African American preschool boy. *Clinical Case Studies, 13*, 487–500.

Costello, E.J., Mustillo, S., Erkanli, A., Keeler, G., & Angold, A. (2003). Prevalence and development of psychiatric disorders in childhood and adolescence. *Archives of General Psychiatry*, 60, 837–844.

Dallaire, D.H., & Weinraub, M. (2005). Predicting children's separation anxiety at age 6: The contributions of infant-mother attachment security, maternal sensitivity, and maternal separation anxiety. *Attachment and Human Development*, 7, 393–408.

De Los Reyes, A., & Kazdin, A.E. (2005). Informant discrepancies in the assessment of childhood psychopathology: A critical review, theoretical framework, and recommendations for further study. *Psychological Bulletin*, 131, 483–509.

Dougherty, L.R., Bufferd, S.J., Carlson, G.A., Dyson, M., Olino, T.M., Durbin, C.E., & Klein, D.N. (2011). Preschoolers' observed temperament and psychiatric disorders assessed with a parent diagnostic interview. *Journal of Clinical Child and Adolescent Psychiatry*, 40, 295–306.

Dougherty, L.R., Tolep, M.R., Bufferd, S.J., Olino, T.M., Dyson, M., Traditi, J., Rose, S., Carlson, G.A., & Klein, D.N. (2013). Preschool anxiety disorders: Comprehensive assessment of clinical, demographic, temperamental, familial, and life stress correlates. *Journal of Clinical Child and Adolescent Psychiatry*, 42, 577–589.

Dubi, K., Lavallee, K.L., & Schneider, S. (2012). The Picture Anxiety Test (PAT): Psychometric properties in a community sample of young children. *Swiss Journal of Psychology*, 71, 73–81.

Dubi, K., & Schneider, S. (2009). The Picture Anxiety Test (PAT): A new pictorial assessment of anxiety symptoms in young children. *Journal of Anxiety Disorders*, 23, 1148–1157.

Egger, H.L., & Angold, A. (1999). The Preschool Age Psychiatric Assessment (PAPA): A structured parent interview for diagnosing psychiatric disorders in preschool children. In R. DelCarmen-Wiggins, & A. Carter (Eds.), *Handbook of infant, toddler, and preschool mental assessment* (pp. 223–243). New York: Oxford University Press.

Egger, H.L., Erkanli, A., Keeler, G., Potts, E., Walter, B.K., & Angold, A. (2006). Test-retest reliability of the Preschool Age Psychiatric Assessment (PAPA). *Journal of the American Academy of Child and Adolescent Psychiatry*, 45, 538–549.

Fox, N.A., Henderson, H.A., Marshall, P.J., Nichols, K.E., & Ghera, M.M. (2005). Behavioral inhibition: Linking biology and behavior within a developmental framework. *Annual Review of Psychology*, 56, 235–262.

Gagne, J.R., Van Hulle, C.A., Aksan, N., Essex, M.J., & Goldsmith, H.H. (2011). Deriving childhood temperament measures from emotion-eliciting behavioral episodes: Scale construction and initial validation. *Psychological Assessment*, 23, 337–353.

Glennon, B., & Weisz, J.R. (1978). An observational approach to the assessment of anxiety in young children. *Journal of Consulting and Clinical Psychology*, 46, 1246–1257.

Graziano, A.M., & Mooney, K.C. (1980). Family self-control instruction for children's nighttime fear reduction. *Journal of Consulting and Clinical Psychology*, 48, 206–213.

Hamilton, D.I., & King, N.J. (1991). Reliability of a behavioral avoidance test for the assessment of dog phobic children. *Psychological Reports*, 69, 18.

Ialongo, N., Edelsohn, G., Werthamer-Larsson, L., Crockett, L., & Kellam, S. (1995). The significance of self-reported anxious symptoms in first grade children: Prediction to anxious symptoms and adaptive functioning in fifth grade.

Journal of Child Psychology and Psychiatry, 36(3), 427–437, https://doi-org.ezp roxy.net.ucf.edu/10.1111/j.1469-7610.1995.tb01300.x.

Kagan, J. (1994). *Galen's prophecy. Temperament in human nature.* New York: Basic Books.

Kagan, J., Reznick, J.S., & Snidman, N. (1988). Biological basis of childhood shyness. *Science*, 240, 167–171.

King, N.J., Ollendick, T.H., & Murphy, G.C. (1997). Assessment of childhood phobias. *Clinical Psychology Review*, 17, 667–687.

Kuijpers, R., Otten, R., Vermulst, A.A., & Engels, R. (2014). Reliability and construct validity of a child self-report instrument. *European Journal of Psychological Assessment*, 30, 40–47.

Kushnir, J., Gothelf, D., & Sadeh, A. (2014). Nighttime fears of preschool children: A potential disposition marker for anxiety? *Comprehensive Psychiatry*, 55, 336–341.

Lo, S.L., Vroman, L.N., & Durbin, C.E. (2015). Ecological validity of laboratory assessments of child temperament: Evidence from parent perspectives. *Psychological Assessment*, 27, 280–290.

Luby, J.L., Belden, A., Sullivan, J., & Spitznagel, E. (2007). Preschoolers' contribution to their diagnosis of depression and anxiety: Uses and limitations of young child self-report of symptoms. *Child Psychiatry and Human Development*, 38, 321–338.

Main, M., & Cassidy, J. (1988). Categories of response to reunion with the parent at age 6: Predictable from infant attachment classifications and stable over a 1-month period. *Developmental Psychology*, 24, 415–426.

Majdandzic, M., & Van den Boom, D. (2007). Multimethod longitudinal assessment of temperament in early childhood. *Journal of Personality*, 75, 121–167.

Measelle, J.R., Ablow, J.C., Cowan, P.A., & Cowan, C.P. (1998). Assessing young children's views of their academic, social, and emotional lives: An evaluation of the self-perception scales of the Berkeley Puppet Interview. *Child Development*, 69, 1556–1576.

Mian, N.D., Carter, A.S., Pine, D.S., Wakschlag, L.S., & Briggs-Gowan, M.J. (2015). Development of a novel observational measure for anxiety in young children: The Anxiety Dimensional Observation Scale. *Journal of Child Psychology and Psychiatry*, 56, 1017–1025.

Muris, P. (2002). The Koala Fear Questionnaire: Its relationship with fear of storms and hurricanes in 4- to 14-year-old Antillean children. *Journal of Psychopathology and Behavioral Assessment*, 24, 145–150.

Muris, P., Meesters, C., Mayer, B., Bogie, N., Luijten, M., Geebelen, E., Bessems, J., & Smit, C. (2003). The Koala Fear Questionnaire: A standardized self-report scale for assessing fears and fearfulness in preschool and primary school children. *Behaviour Research and Therapy*, 41, 597–617.

Muris, P., Merckelbach, H., Gadet, B., & Moulaert, V. (2000). Fears, worries, and scary dreams in 4- to 12-year-old children: Their content, developmental pattern, and origins. *Journal of Clinical Child Psychology*, 29, 43–52.

Muris, P., & Ollendick, T.H. (2015). Children who are anxious in silence: A review on selective mutism, the new anxiety disorder in DSM-5. *Clinical Child and Family Psychology Review*, 18, 151–169.

Ollendick, T.H., Allen, B., Benoit, K., & Cowart, M. (2011). The tripartite model of fear in children with specific phobias: Assessing concordance and discordance using the behavioral approach test. *Behavior Research and Therapy*, 49, 459–465.

Ollendick, T.H., & Muris, P. (2015). The scientific legacy of Little Hans and Little Albert: Future directions for research on specific phobias in youth. *Journal of Clinical Child and Adolescent Psychology*, 44, 689–706.

Reynolds, C. R., & Richmond, B. O. (1978). What I think and feel: A revised measure of children's manifest anxiety. *Journal of Abnormal Child Psychology*, 6(2), 271–280. https://doi-org.ezproxy.net.ucf.edu/10.1007/BF00919131.

Richters, J.E., Waters, E., & Vaughn, B.E. (1988). Empirical classification of infant-mother relationships from interactive behavior and crying during reunion. *Child Development*, 59, 512–522.

Ringoot, A.P., Jansen, P.J., Steenweg-de Graaff, J., Measelle, J.R., Van der Ende, J., Raat, H., Jaddoe, V.W.V., Hofman, A., Verhulst, F.C., & Tiemeier, H. (2013). Young children's self-reported emotional, behavioral, and peer problems: The Berkeley Puppet Interview. *Psychological Assessment*, 25, 1273–1285.

Shouldice, A., & Stevenson-Hinde, J. (1992). Coping with security distress. The separation anxiety test and attachment classification at 4.5 years. *Journal of Child Psychology and Psychiatry*, 33, 331–348.

Silverman, W.K., & Ollendick, T.H. (2005). Evidence-based assessment of anxiety and its disorders in children and adolescents. *Journal of Clinical Child and Adolescent Psychology*, 34, 380–411.

Stallings, P., & March, J.S. (1995). Assessment. In J.S. March (Ed.), *Anxiety disorders in children and adolescents* (pp. 125–147). New York: Guilford Press.

Stevenson-Hinde, J., & Shouldice, A. (1995). 4.5 to 7 years: Fearful behavior, fears, and worries. *Journal of Child Psychology and Psychiatry*, 36, 1027–1038.

Stone, L.L., Van Daal, C., Van der Maten, M., Engels, R., Janssens, J., & Otten, R. (2014). The Berkeley Puppet Interview: A screening instrument for measuring psychopathology in young children. *Child Youth Care Forum*, 43, 211–225.

Valla, J.P., Bergeron, L., & Smolla, N. (2000). The Dominic-R: A pictorial interview for 6- to 11-year-old children. *Journal of the American Academy of Child and Adolescent Psychiatry*, 39, 85–93.

Van Brakel, A.M., Muris, P., & Bögels, S.M. (2004). Relations between parent- and teacher-reported behavioral inhibition and behavioral observations of this temperamental trait. *Journal of Clinical Child and Adolescent Psychology*, 33, 579–589.

Vreeke, L.J., Muris, P., Mayer, B., Huijding, J., Bos, A.E.R., Van der Veen, M., Raat, H., & Verheij, F. (2012). The assessment of an inhibited, anxiety-prone temperament in a Dutch multi-ethnic population of preschool children. *European Child and Adolescent Psychiatry*, 21, 623–633.

Warren, S.L., & Dadson, N. (2001). Assessment of anxiety in young children. *Current Opinion in Pediatrics*, 13, 580–585.

Warren, S.L., Huston, L., Egeland, B., & Sroufe, L.A. (1997). Child and adolescent anxiety disorders and early attachment. *Journal of the American Academy of Child and Adolescent Psychiatry*, 36, 637–641.

6 The Treatment of Anxiety Disorders in Preschool-Aged Children

Paula Barrett, Natalie Games, Brian Fisak, Paul Stallard, and Lauren Phillips

Although rates of anxiety disorders found in epidemiological studies have varied and may reflect differences in methodology, up to 19% of preschool-aged children may meet criteria for an anxiety disorder (Bufferd, Dougherty, Carlson, & Klein, 2011). In addition to a high prevalence rate, untreated anxiety disorders can potentially disrupt a child's normal developmental trajectory leading to negative outcomes (Merikangas et al., 2010; Langley, Bergman, McCracken, & Piacentini, 2004). Serious, untreated anxiety often persist or worsen over time. Often this is because children learn avoidance tactics and families reinforce this avoidance to prevent triggering the anxiety.

Normative childhood fears are distinguished from anxiety disorders by their transient nature which diminishes over time. In contrast, for a diagnosis of an anxiety disorder: (a) the duration of the fear must be beyond the appropriate developmental stage for a particular fear, (b) the anxiety must interfere with functioning, and (c) the symptoms are often pervasive across settings (APA, 2013). The most common anxiety disorders in children are separation anxiety disorder, specific phobias, generalized anxiety disorder, and social phobia (Bufferd et al., 2011; Egger & Angold, 2006; Wichstrøm et al., 2012). A brief description of these disorders is provided below.

Separation Anxiety Disorder

According to the DSM-5 (APA, 2013), the essential feature of separation anxiety disorder (SAD) is excessive fear or anxiety concerning separation from home or from main attachment figures. Children with SAD may experience emotional distress in the form of crying, withdrawal, the refusal to eat or engage, the inability to self-soothe, problems with sleep, and psychosomatic symptoms (e.g., headaches, stomach aches, and related somatic symptoms) when separation from an attachment figure occurs or is anticipated. Other symptoms may include extreme homesickness, school refusal, excessive anxiety about sleepovers, or requests for company at bedtime. It is noteworthy that anxiety exceeds what is expected at the child's developmental level.

Children with SAD typically become very distressed when faced with actual or anticipated separation from their main attachment figure. Going to school, daycare, or being left with a babysitter or relative are common situations that can trigger the child's anxiety. Young children often exhibit worry that their main attachment figure will not return, that the main attachment figure may be harmed, and/or that they will not be able to cope without their parent. When faced with possible separation, the child's concerns can result in behaviors such as excessive clinginess, crying, complaining of feeling unwell, refusing to join in with play or activities, and tantrums.

Specific Phobia

The DSM-5 defines specific phobia as a marked fear or anxiety about a specific object or situation (APA, 2013). For example, the fear may be in response to a situation such as flying, an object such as a public toilet, or a living creature, such as a dog. This fear will prevent the child from engaging in and enjoying normal life experiences (APA, 2013). Children with a specific phobia often cry, cling, avoid, or complain of headaches and/or stomach aches to avoid the situation or thing they fear. Unlike adults, children do not usually recognize that their fear is irrational. Additionally, the fear or anxiety is out of proportion to the actual danger posed by the specific object or situation, and to the sociocultural context.

The most common types of phobia are related to animals (e.g., dogs, spiders, snakes), natural events (e.g., thunder, the dark, heights), injury or medical tests (e.g., blood, vomiting, injections), specific situations (e.g., elevators, trains, planes) and other things (e.g., buttons, clowns). The child's response is typically extreme and may involve uncontrollable crying, screaming, shaking, panic or running away in terror.

Generalized Anxiety Disorder (GAD)

According to the DSM-5 criteria for generalized anxiety disorder (GAD), an essential feature is a marked, or intense, fear or anxiety about a number of events or activities (APA, 2013). The content of the worry includes a range of areas such as family, relationships, natural disasters, health, grades, performance and punctuality, which meet the criteria for GAD. Children with GAD worry about what has happened, what will happen, how things will go wrong and whether they will be able to cope. The specific focus of their worries will regularly change. In children, the worry or anxiety must include one of the following symptoms which have been present for more days than not within a 6-month period: restlessness or feeling on edge, fatigue, lack of concentration, irritability, tension and/or sleep disturbance (APA, 2013). Children with GAD regularly voice their worries, and seek excessive reassurance and approval from others. They also tend to strive for perfection, and are often self-critical. They frequently appear unhappy and in a constant state of anxiety, which can interfere with their ability to concentrate and engage in activities.

Social Phobia

Social anxiety disorder, or social phobia, is characterized by a marked or intense fear or worry about social situations that significantly disrupt a child's school performance, attendance and ability to develop and maintain relationships with peers (APA, 2013). According to the DSM-5, an essential feature of social anxiety disorder is that the experience of anxiety of social situations leads an individual to believe that they may be scrutinized by others. Furthermore, this scrutiny is perceived as negative, and potentially humiliating or embarrassing (APA, 2013). Criterion A in the DSM-5 stipulates that in children with social phobia, the fear or anxiety must occur in peer settings and not just during interactions with adults. Children may have difficulties with public speaking, reading aloud or being called on in class. Pre-school children with social phobia tend to avoid playing with other children. They may play on their own or spend time playing with, or being in close proximity to adults, rather than interacting with their peers. In social situations, they may withdraw when others arrive, appear quiet, and/or not talk or respond to questions from other children.

Treatment

Risk and Protective Factors

There is no one cause in the development of an anxiety disorder in children. In fact, etiological models emphasize a more complex interaction between two types of risk factors. Firstly, there are risk factors which are internal to the individual child, including temperament and negative affectivity. The second type of risk factors are those which are within the individual's environment including poverty, trauma or school stress. When considering the etiology of anxiety disorders in children, an individual's protective factors can mediate the interaction between the two types of risk factors. Protective factors can be seen to buffer the individual against onset, or reduce the likelihood that an anxiety disorder will develop when exposed to the risk (Rutter, 1985). Like risk factors, protective factors are internal or external to the individual. Therefore, the major consideration for many treatment programs is to identify and target malleable risk and protective factors to enhance the number of protective factors which in turn exert a stronger influence and decrease or eliminate risk factors (Rutter, 1985). To review all the risk and protective factors of relevance is beyond the scope of this chapter. See Figure 6.1 for a depiction of a theoretical model of risk and protective factors.

Background: Treatment Protocols for School-Aged Children

The evidence-based treatment of anxiety disorders in school-aged children typically involves mixed or trans-diagnostic protocols, which can be adapted to treat most anxiety disorders. These interventions are typically cognitive-behavioral, as they focus on the interaction between an individual's dysfunctional cognitions presumed to affect emotions and behavioral responses. Further, two basic approaches have been developed. The first is Individual Cognitive Behavioral Therapy (ICBT), in which intervention is generally child-based with limited parent involvement, and Family-based Cognitive Behavioral Therapy (FCBT), which involves both parents and children (Creswell & Cartwright-Hatton, 2007).

In one of the first randomized clinical trials (RCTs) for anxiety in school-aged children, Kendall (1994) developed an ICPT trans-diagnostic protocol. Based on the results of two RCTs, treating anxious children between nine and 13 years of age, the Coping Cat was found to be effective. In the first RCT, Kendall (1994) tested the 16-session manual-based CBT protocol (*The Coping Cat Workbook*) with 47 children with anxiety disorders, who were randomly assigned to either the CBT or wait-list control condition. The results revealed that 64% of the participants in the CBT condition no longer met their principal diagnosis following intervention.

In a follow-up study, Kendall & Southam-Gerow (1996) conducted a randomized clinical trial with 94 children (aged nine to 13 years) with an anxiety disorder diagnosis pre-treatment. Significant gains were reported

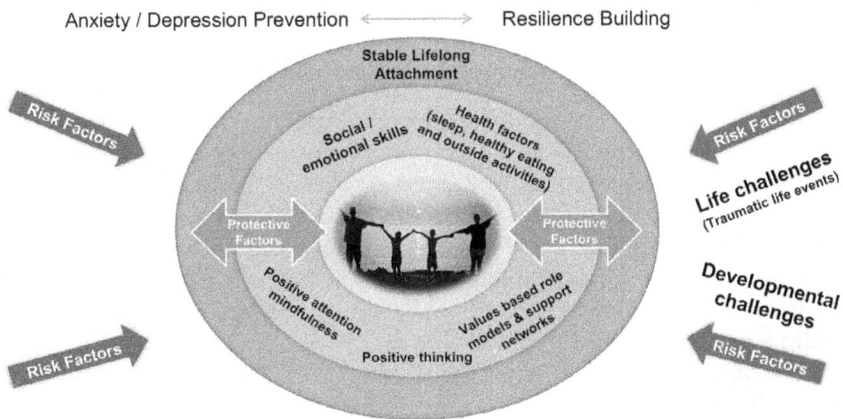

Figure 6.1 Theoretical model for anxiety/depression prevention
Based on: Barrett (2018). Friends Resilience Programs

at post-intervention, which were maintained at one-year follow-up. Kendall's (1994) initial focus was on working individually with children, as it was thought that children could not engage in groups. One criticism of this program came from whether young children were cognitively able to engage in the activities and whether they have the emotional capacity to self-regulate (Rueda, Posner, & Rothbart, 2005).

In contrast to IBCT, the FCBT approach operates under the premise that parents are in a pivotal position to assist children with new experiences to process day-to-day events from different perspectives (Wood, Piacentini, Southam-Gerow, Chu, & Sigman, 2006). In 1996, Barrett and colleagues adapted and extended Kendall's work to design the *Coping Koala* program, which treated children for anxiety in a group format with family involvement. In this adaptation of the *Coping Cat* program, the study included a family intervention (FAM). In conjunction with a variation of the CBT *Coping Cat* program being implemented with the children, the parents were trained in contingency management strategies, communication, and problem-solving skills, as well as being taught to recognize and address their own emotions and anxious responses to stimuli. Results revealed that 60% of the children in both treatment conditions, CBT or combined CBT and FAM, no longer met their principal diagnosis at post-treatment assessment, compared with less than 30% of the wait-list children. Furthermore, results suggested that this effect was best for younger children (Barrett et al., 1996). In conjunction with a team of researchers, the *Coping Koala* program was revised and expanded as an early intervention and prevention strategy (Barrett et al., 1996). Following the initial studies in the 1990s, over 50 randomized clinical trials have been conducted that examine the effectiveness of treatment for anxiety, and overall, it appears that these programs are effective (Warwick et al., 2017).

Treatment Programs for Preschool-Aged Children

A growing body of research has focused on the efficacy of treatment programs designed to address anxiety in preschool-aged children. A majority of studies have utilized trans-diagnostic treatment programs or mixed protocol treatments, which are focused on treating a range of anxiety disorders, and initial results suggest positive outcomes of CBT and other forms of psychological intervention for this age group. A summary of treatment programs and features are provided below, and additional detail is provided in Table 6.1.

Parent-Only Programs. Cartwright-Hatton et al. (2005; 2011) developed a parent-based program to treat younger anxious children, called the *Timid to Tiger* program. Following promising results from a pilot study (Cartwright-Hatton et al., 2005), Cartwright-Hatton et al. (2011) conducted a RCT with the parents of anxious children in the age range of two to nine years. Results showed that 57% of children whose parents were in the

Table 6.1 Summary of treatment programs

Study	Treatment approach (program name)	Participants	Disorder Treated	Format (group vs. individual)	Sample Size (intervention group)	Design	Results	Cohen'd Effect Size (between-groups)*
Cartwright-Hatton et al. (2011)	CBT (Timid to Tiger)	Parents only	Anxiety Disorders (transdiagnostic sample)	Group	37	RTC	Reduction of diagnosed anxiety disorders	-.39
Donovan & March (2014)	CBT	Parents only	Anxiety Disorders (transdiagnostic sample)	Internet-based	23	RTC	Reduction in clinical severity, anxiety symptoms and internalizing problems	-.44
Hirshfeld-Becker et al., 2010	CBT (Being Brave)	Parents & children	Anxiety Disorders (transdiagnostic sample)	Individual	34	RTC	Reduction of anxiety diagnosis compared to control group. Maintained at 12-month follow up	-.58

Table 6.1 (Cont.)

Study	Treatment approach (program name)	Participants	Disorder Treated	Format (group vs. individual)	Sample Size (intervention group)	Design	Results	Cohen'd Effect Size (between-groups)*
Santacruz et al. (2006) (play therapy & exposure)	Book and games play therapy& exposure therapy	Parents**	Darkness Phobia	Individual	27	RTC & treatment comparison	Reduction of children's darkness phobia both post-treat-ment and at 12-month follow up	-1.53
Santacruz et al. (2006) (play therapy & exposure)	Emotive per-formance play therapy & exposure therapy	Parents**	Darkness Phobia	Individual	28	RTC & treatment comparison	Reduction of children's darkness phobia both post-treat-ment and at 12-month follow up	-2.59

Study	Intervention	Participants	Disorder	Format	N	Design	Outcome	Effect size
Schneider et al. (2011)	Separation anxiety family therapy	Parents & children	Separation Anxiety	Individual	15	RTC	Significant improvement in the intervention group, with 76.19% no longer meeting diagnostic criteria for separation anxiety disorder	-1.08
Waters et al. (2009) (Parent Only Condition)	CBT (take ACTION program)	Parents only	Anxiety Disorders (transdiagnostic sample)	Group	25	RTC & treatment comparison	Reduction in anxiety symptoms from pre to post-intervention. Similar outcomes for both treatments	-.79

Table 6.1 (Cont.)

Study	Treatment approach (program name)	Participants	Disorder Treated	Format (group vs. individual)	Sample Size (intervention group)	Design	Results	Cohen'd Effect Size (between-groups)*
Waters et al. (2009) (Parent + Child Condition)	CBT (take ACTION program)	Parents & children	Anxiety Disorders (transdiagnostic sample)	Group	24	RTC & treatment comparison	Reduction in anxiety symptoms from pre to post-intervention. Similar outcomes for both treatments	-.96
Monga et al. (2015) (Parent + Child)	CBT (Taming Sneaky Fears)	Parents & children	Anxiety Disorders (transdiagnostic sample)	Group	45	Randomized treatment comparison	Improvement from pre to post-intervention. Greater recovery rate relative to parent only intervention	—

Study	Intervention	Participants	Population	Format	N	Design	Outcomes	
Monga et al. (2015) (Parent Only)	CBT (Taming Sneaky Fears)	Parents only	Anxiety Disorders (transdiagnostic sample)	Group	32	Randomized treatment comparison	Improvement from pre to post-intervention. Lower recovery rate relative to parent-child intervention	—
Barrett et al. (2015)	CBT (Fun FRIENDS)	Parents & children	Anxiety Disorders (transdiagnostic sample)	Group	31	Pretest-posttest	Decreased anxiety and behavioral inhibition. Improved resilience	—
Cartwright-Hatton et al. (2005)	CBT (Timid to Tiger)	Parents only	Anxiety Disorders (transdiagnostic sample) Group	Group	43	Pretest-posttest	Reduction in internalizing symptoms from pre- to post-intervention.	—

Table 6.1 (Cont.)

Study	Treatment approach (program name)	Participants	Disorder Treated	Format (group vs. individual)	Sample Size (intervention group)	Design	Results	Cohen'd Effect Size (between-groups)*
Carlyle (2014)	CBT (Fun FRIENDS)	Parents & children	Anxiety Disorders (transdiagnostic sample)	Group	6	Pretest-posttest	Greater emotional and social skills development. Improved anxiety scores post intervention	–
Choate et al. (2005)	Parent Child Interaction Therapy (PCIT)	Parents & children	Separation Anxiety Disorder	Individual	3	Multiple-baseline	Decrease in SAD symptoms. All children in treatment group did not meet SAD diagnosis post-treatment	–

Study	Intervention	Participants	Disorder	Format	N	Design	Results	
Fisak et al. (2018)	CBT (Fun FRIENDS)	Parents & children	Anxiety Disorders (transdiagnostic sample)	Group	111	Pretest-posttest	Fun FRIENDS delivered in conjunction with the Adult Resilience program to parents resulted in reductions in internalizing symptoms and increases in resilience for children and parents	—
Hirshfeld-Becker et al. (2008)	CBT	Parents & children	Anxiety Disorders (transdiagnostic sample)	Individual	9	Pretest-posttest	A majority of children rated as clinically improved at post-intervention	—

Table 6.1 (Cont.)

Study	Treatment approach (program name)	Participants	Disorder Treated	Format (group vs. individual)	Sample Size (intervention group)	Design	Results	Cohen'd Effect Size (between-groups)*
Monga et al. (2009)	CBT (Taming Sneaky Fears)	Parents & children	Anxiety Disorders (transdiagnostic sample)	Group	32	Pretest-posttest	Significant reduction in anxiety symptoms from pre- to post-intervention	–
Pincus et al. (2008)	Parent Child Interaction Therapy (PCIT)	Parents & children	Separation Anxiety Disorder	Individual	10	Pretest-posttest	Decrease in SAD symptoms, and improved parenting skills. However, SAD was not reduced to nonclinical levels at post-intervention	–

van der Sluis et al. (2012)	CBT (Confident Kids Program)	Parents only	Anxiety Disorders (transdiagnostic sample)	Group	26	Pretest-posttest	Effective in reducing child anxiety and behavioral inhibition. Reduction in clinical severity, anxiety symptoms and internalizing problems	–

Note: *Effect sizes for studies including a comparison group. **In Santacruz et al. parents were provided with instructions to engage in play therapy and subsequently carried out intervention with children in the home.

intervention group, no longer met the diagnostic criteria for their primary anxiety diagnosis, and 32% of children were free from any anxiety diagnosis. It was found that 15% and 6% of children in the waitlist control group no longer met the diagnostic criteria for their primary diagnosis and any anxiety diagnosis, respectively. Although this program is not specific to preschool-aged children, the findings indicate that this program can be effectively implemented with the parents of preschool-aged children. The *Timid to Tiger* treatment manual is available for purchase (see: Cartwright-Hatton, Laskey, Rust, & McNally, 2010).

Another study of anxiety in young children conducted by van der Sluis and colleagues (2012) found that the *Confident Kids* program was effective in reducing child anxiety and behavioral inhibition. The study investigated the efficacy of an eight-week CBT program which was presented to parents, and facilitated by clinical psychologists. The first four two-hour sessions were presented in a group format and focused on teaching parents about childhood anxiety and the concept of inadvertent reinforcement through use of avoidant- and/or over-controlling parenting strategies. The program also taught parents how to be aware of and manage their own anxiety. The next four sessions were via weekly telephone consultations, aimed at providing individual attention and support. Whilst the results of this brief parent-directed CBT intervention showed reduction in behavioral inhibition, fear and anxiety symptoms in children between four and seven years of age, there is a need to replicate this study to increase the sample size and include a control group.

Online treatment programs for adults, adolescents, and older children (seven- to 13-year-olds) are being developed as a means of overcoming financial and social barriers, as well as increasing treatment accessibility. To date, it appears that only one computer-based study has focused on the treatment of anxiety in preschool-aged children. In particular, Donovan and March (2014) reported significant reduction in clinical severity, anxiety symptoms, and internalizing problems of the children whose parents completed the online *Brave* CBT program. However, the study was not able to demonstrate a reduction in the number of clinical anxiety diagnoses.

Combined Parent and Child Treatments. Studies investigating both specific and various anxiety disorders in young children have also focused on the efficacy of combined parent and child involvement. Pincus, Santucci, Ehrenreich, and Eyberg (2008) and Choate, Pincus, Eyberg, and Barlow (2005) examined the effectiveness of parent-child interaction therapy (PCIT) modified to treat SAD. Although Pincus et al. (2008) found a decrease in symptoms, the severity of symptoms did not decrease to nonclinical levels. However, in an expanded follow-up study, Choate et al. (2005) found a clinically significant decrease in SAD symptoms, and all children in the treatment group did not meet criteria for SAD following treatment. Schneider and colleagues (2011) found similar results with their study of children aged five to seven years. After a 16-session individual-format CBT program that included parent, child, and family sessions, the children from the family session group had significantly reduced symptoms of SAD.

Hirshfeld-Becker and colleagues (2010) investigated the efficacy of a CBT program designed with sessions for both parents and young children, aged from four to seven years, through a pilot study and a RCT. The results of the RCT showed 59% of the children in the CBT parent-child group had a significant reduction in anxiety diagnoses compared with 18% of children in the control group. Results at one-year follow-up revealed that the improvement was maintained, with 83% of children being rated as "much" or "very much improved" and 59% of children no longer meeting diagnostic criteria for any anxiety diagnosis.

The *Fun FRIENDS* program (Barrett, 2007) was developed for pre-school-aged children to target the common symptoms of anxiety experienced by young children, and to provide them with a base of coping skills that would help prevent more serious anxiety symptoms as they grow older. Since its development in 2007, several studies have been conducted to investigate the efficacy of the *Fun FRIENDS* program. Studies have found that the program has been efficacious in decreasing anxiety and behavioral inhibition, and increasing the emotional and behavior strengths of preschool-aged children (Barrett, Fisak, & Cooper, 2015; Carlyle 2014; Pahl & Barrett, 2010). Additionally, the *Fun FRIENDS* program has been shown to decrease parenting distress and improve parent-child interactions, with improvements maintained at 12-month follow up (Anticich, Barrett, Silverman, Lacherez, & Gillies, 2013). More recent research has shown that the effectiveness of the program may be enhanced when parents participate in a concurrent adult resilience program (Fisak, Gallegos, Verreynne, & Barrett, 2018).

Two studies compared the effectiveness of parent-only intervention relative to intervention with both parent and child participation. In the first study, Waters and colleagues (2009) allocated 60 children to one of three conditions: waitlist, parent only, or parent/child group. Under the latter conditions, intervention appeared to be effective, and similar recovery rates were observed in both groups. Following a successful pilot study of a program called *Taming Sneaky Fears* (Monga, Young, & Owens, 2009), Monga, Rosenbloom, Tanha, Owens, & Young (2015) conducted a RCT comparing the effectiveness of parent-child CBT to parent-only CBT. Although both groups demonstrated significant improvement, greater improvements were found in the parent-child condition relative to the parent-only condition.

In addition to the above-mentioned trans-diagnostic studies, Santacruz et al. (2006) conducted a trial focused on treating children with a darkness phobia. In particular, the authors utilized play therapy combined with exposure therapy with 78 children, aged four to eight years of age

(Santacruz, Méndez, and Sánchez-Meca, 2006). The parents of the children were trained over five sessions, delivered over a period of one month. One group received instruction on exposure therapy with play, emphasizing emotive performance, and the second group received instruction on exposure therapy with play, emphasizing books and games. For both groups, the authors found positive results immediately following treatment, and at 12-month follow up, with decreased darkness phobia in both groups when compared with a control group.

The Effectiveness of Anxiety Treatment Programs

As a general measure of effectiveness of preschool anxiety treatment programs, between-group effect sizes were calculated for studies with comparison groups, and measures of anxiety and shyness were used as the primary outcome variables. Five trans-diagnostic studies compared intervention to a non-active comparison group. The mean weighted effect size for these studies at post-intervention was significant (Cohen's $d =$ -.58, $Z =$ -.42, $p < .001$). More specifically, across all studies, intervention groups scored an average of .58 standard deviation units lower on measures of anxiety and shyness symptoms at post-intervention relative to non-intervention comparison groups.

In addition to the above-mentioned trans-diagnostic studies, between-group effect size data was available for two studies that focused on the examination of specific anxiety-related problems. In particular, Schneider et al. (2011) conducted a RCT in which a CBT intervention for SAD was compared to a non-active comparison group. At post-intervention, the intervention group exhibited lower scores on a measure of SAD symptoms relative to the comparison group (Cohen's $d =$ -.93, $Z =$ -2.79, $p < .001$).

Santacruz et al. (2006) compared two similar treatments for darkness fears using a combination of play therapy and exposure. Effect sizes for measures of darkness fear and avoidance were statistically significant in both the bibliotherapy, games, plus exposure group (Cohen's $d =$ -1.59, Z = -4.69, $p < .001$), and the emotive performance plus exposure group (Cohen's $d =$ -2.59, $Z =$ -6.80, $p < .001$), indicating that both forms of play therapy plus exposure were effective.

Finally, two studies provided direct comparisons between parent-only intervention and combined parent and child intervention (Monga et al., 2015; Waters et al., 2009). Interestingly, a summary of the recovery rates in these studies highlight disparate findings. In particular, Waters et al. (2009) found similar recovery rates for the parent only group (55.3%), and the parent-child group (54.8%). In contrast, Monga et al. (2015) found a much higher recovery rate for the parent-child group (48.9%), relative to the parent-only group (12.5%). Overall, based on the current evidence, it appears that preschool-based interventions, most of which are CBT-based, lead to a reduction in shyness and anxiety symptoms at post-intervention. However, it is noteworthy that relatively few studies include a comparison group. The only two studies focused on the effectiveness of parent-only treatment relative to parent-child treatment have yielded mixed results.

Modifications and Challenges in Working with Preschoolers

There are many factors that need to be considered when working with preschool age children. Generally, adjustments need to be made based on the level of cognitive development of this age group. Related to this point, preschool age children are not able to read fluently, and consequently, they cannot engage in reading and writing activities. At the same time, the attention span of these children can also be short. For this reason, it is important to emphasize the play-based aspects of interventions. This will help to increase child engagement and allow them to learn complicated skills in simple ways that they can understand and relate to (reference). Play-based techniques can include games, dress-ups, role playing, drawing, story-telling, video clips, puppets, bubbles, etc. Interventions can also be rotated between teaching, activities, games, stories, and video clips to ensure that the children are never forced to focus their attention on one task for too long. Another consideration has to do with parent involvement in preschool intervention. With school-aged children, the added benefit of parent involvement is unclear. For example, in a meta-analysis, Thulin, Svirsky, Serlachius, Andersson, and Öst (2014) found that parent involvement yielded no added benefit. However, due to developmental considerations, parent involvement appears to be an essential component of the treatment of anxiety in preschool-aged children. All studies discussed above include some level of parent involvement, and for a number of studies, intervention is parent-only. Another consideration when working with young children with anxiety is the mode of delivery. Although this issue has not been systematically studied in anxious preschool-aged children, group-based intervention may have some specific advantages over individual intervention (see Table 6.2).

Specific Intervention Strategies: *Fun FRIENDS* as an Example

The *Fun FRIENDS* program is utilized to illustrate interventions that can be used to address anxiety-related difficulties in young children for a number of reasons. Firstly, it is noteworthy that there is a general paucity of early intervention studies focused on both anxiety prevention and resilience building. In this area, *Fun FRIENDS* appears to be among the most extensively studied program, with at least three trials providing support for the effectiveness of *Fun FRIENDS* (Anticich, Barrett, Silverman, Lacherez, & Gillies, 2013; Barrett, Fisak, & Cooper, 2015; Pahl & Barrett, 2010). Secondly, this program is easily disseminated, as it

Table 6.2 Advantages of groups-based vs. individual intervention

Group interventions	Individual treatment
- Normalizes experience of anxiety - Can learn from the experiences of others in the group - Able to practice skills with other group members - Exposure to social setting	- Able to focus on issues relevant to particular child - Able to discuss issues that may not be appropriate for a group setting - Treatment can be more in depth - Minimizes distractions from behavior management and disruptions that can occur within group settings

includes online training, interactive workbooks for children and parents, and manuals for facilitators. These features likely maximize the sustainability of the *Fun FRIENDS* programs in the community, which is an important factor in early intervention research (Cooper, Bumbarger, & Moore, 2015). Finally, the comprehensiveness is noteworthy, as this program provides an extensive array of evidence-based cognitive-behavioral and resilience-building coping skills. Both children and parents receive these skills-based interventions. The rationale behind this idea is that children are taught skills to help them manage their responses to anxiety and related negative emotions, but parents' responses to their children had a large impact on their anxiety, and thus also need to be addressed. Further, parents are able to facilitate the child's use of coping skills in the home setting.

Regarding direct intervention with children, the skills are presented to children in a developmentally appropriate manner, through play and interactive games rather than just through the use of pencil-and-paper worksheets (see Table 6.3). The program focuses on anxiety specific skills, along with more general resilience building and cognitive-behavioral coping skills. *FRIENDS* is an acronym used to emphasize the basic steps of the program (see Table 6.4). Further, it is notable that the program targets the five key areas of social and emotional competence: (1) Self-Awareness, (2) Self-Management, (3) Social Awareness, (4) Relationship Skills, and (5) Responsible Decision-Making (Collaborative for Academic, Social, and Emotional Learning, 2003).

As mentioned above, the parents also receive comprehensive, concurrent intervention. This consists of two parenting sessions and three Adult Resilience sessions covering specific concepts and skills. During the two parenting sessions, the program content is explained in detail, and behavior management strategies are discussed (e.g., planned ignoring, quiet time, time out). There are many benefits to providing parents with concurrent intervention. In particular, concurrent intervention helps parents facilitate the use of the coping skills with their children, and there is the added benefit of helping caregivers to manage their own stress. More specifically, the skills that are taught in the *FRIENDS* programs can

Table 6.3 Content and process factors in Fun FRIENDS

Content component	Process issues
- Simplifying complicated content - Play based teaching methods - Story telling and video clips - Take emphasis away from reading and writing so kids are not focusing on literacy issues but on practicing skills - Skills are practiced through a variety of activities - Shorter time spent focusing on one activity – rotating faster between different activities	- Behavior management - Difficulty separating from parents - Takes time for children to feel comfortable in the environment - Short attention span - Need higher ratio of adult to children (1:5) - More regular breaks to use bathroom and drink water - Fine motor co-ordination impacting on speed of activities that require coloring or writing etc. - Minimal reading or writing – reduce anxiety related to academic tasks

Table 6.4 Fun FRIENDS steps to treatment

Feelings	• *Understanding our feelings (e.g. identifying the four basic feelings (sad, happy, worried, angry), everyone takes turns making different facial expressions and guessing which feeling it is, giving examples of events and children have to show the facial expression of how they would feel in that situation)* • *All feelings are okay* • *We have choices about what we do with our feelings* • *Thumbs up vs. thumbs down choices*
Relaxation	• Identifying our body clues • Self-soothing skills, e.g. bubble breathing • Attention training skills, e.g. paying attention with the five senses
I can do it	• Understanding red and green thoughts • Learning how to change red thoughts to green thoughts • Understanding how our thoughts, feeling and actions are related • Values based role models • Values based support teams
Exploring solutions	• Setting goals • Coping step plans • Five ideas for solutions
Now reward yourself	• Rewarding ourselves • Rewarding other people
Do it every day	• How to keep using the FRIENDS skills for everyday situations

be compared to learning a new language, the language of resilience. If everyone in the family learns the same language and can practice it together, then the learning is efficient and consolidated. The intervention also teaches parents to understand their child's experience and to gain insight into how they contribute to their child's anxiety. The program does this

by building parent self-awareness and awareness of the power of modeling and their responses to their child (see Table 6.5). By understanding
the anxiety cycle and the value of reinforcing approach behaviors and
minimizing avoidance behaviors, catastrophizing, and negative thinking,
parents are able to adjust their responses to the child to empower them
in their journey to overcome their anxiety (Barrett, Lock & Farrell,
2005). Finally, parents benefit from the opportunity to engage with other
parents experiencing similar difficulties. This helps to normalize their
experience and provides them with the opportunity to learn from each
other's experiences. A description of the *Fun FRIENDS* group process
issues is provided in Appendix A.

Summary and Future Directions

Overall, a number of studies have focused on the treatment of anxiety in
preschool-aged children, and the findings of these studies suggest that
effective intervention programs have been developed for this age group.
A number of features of these studies are worthy of discussion. In particular, most programs are cognitive-behavioral and/or include some form
of exposure therapy. This observation highlights the importance of
including exposure therapy, which is also a key feature of treatment
programs for older children. Another important feature is that direct
interventions with this age group need to be designed to be developmentally appropriate, and as a result, are typically play-based. Finally,
based on the available literature, interventions appear to be either parent-
only, or to include both parents and children, as, considering the child's

Table 6.5 Adult Resilience Program overview: LIFE

Learn to be mindful	• *To identify feelings and develop empathy* • *How to control and regulate intense emotions* • *Relaxation techniques – like those used by athletes* • *Mindfulness skills and exercises to stay in the moment, focus and relax*
Inner helpful thoughts	• Understanding helpful and unhelpful thinking patterns
Feeling like a resilient person	• Prevent bullying for both victims and bullies • Resist peer pressure and develop positive relationships • To compromise in tricky situations and avoid conflict
Enjoying a healthy lifestyle	• To choose appropriate role models • Setting realistic and achievable life or study goals • Organisation and focus skills • Develop non-internet-based friendships and relationships

level of development, child-only intervention is not likely feasible in this age-group. A summary of resources is provided in Appendix B.

Despite the promising findings, a number of limitations to the current research literature and directions for future research should be highlighted. Although interventions for preschool-aged children have been found to be effective, more randomized clinical trials are needed, as mentioned above. Related to this point, additional research is needed to examine potential moderators of treatment effectiveness in order to determine the circumstances under which treatment is most effective. For example, more research is needed to compare the effectiveness of parent-only intervention and interventions including both parents and children, and to compare the effectiveness of individual intervention to group-based intervention. Additionally, issues for future research in child anxiety include systematic evaluation of the role of family members in maintaining and improving outcomes. For example, the potentially important role that fathers can play in the treatment of child anxiety has received limited attention in the research literature (Bögels & Phares, 2008). Continued research and the development of efficacious interventions are important for successful treatment of preschool-aged children's anxiety.

Appendix A *Fun FRIENDS* Group Process Issues

Fun Friends *Themes and Format*

The Fun FRIENDS program is tailored for children aged 4–7 years old. The Fun FRIENDS program is a developmentally sensitive cognitive-behavioral therapy (CBT) program to be used in small (i.e., target) or larger groups (i.e., classrooms). It aims to increase the resilience and emotional well-being of children. The Fun FRIENDS program teaches children and families cognitive, emotional, and behavioral skills for managing feelings and coping with life challenges with a positive and resilient attitude. The program also aims to promote important personal development concepts such as identify, self-esteem, problem solving, self-expression and guiding positive relationships (Barrett, 2007a).

The Fun FRIENDS program involves ten weeks of 1 to 1.5 hour sessions which have corresponding homework tasks for each session so the skills can be practiced at home within the family (Barrett, 2007a). Parents have an opportunity to support their children and learn more about *FRIENDS* themselves by attending two parent sessions. Each facilitator must first receive training prior to running the program.

Based on CBT principles the Fun FRIENDS program has three main components: (1) learning/behaviour, (2) cognitive and (3) physiological (Barrett, 2007a). All of the components are addressed using play-based activities. In addition, the child-centred Fun FRIENDS program maintains a focus on developing a child's individual strengths whilst also promoting family and community well-being (Barrett, 2007a, 2007b). The smaller group format enables the facilitator to vary the content of each session to meet the needs and preferences of the children. For example, if the group is made up of predominantly active children, then activities are tailored to be brief in length and incorporate movement, role play, stories, and music. However, if the children are more verbal, utilizing puppets, stories, games, and art activities may enhance learning the skills and concepts.

Fun FRIENDS program process

It is fundamentally important to consider process issues for the success of the Fun FRIENDS program delivery. There are three main process areas which are applicable to all settings.

Family and Community

Firstly, inclusion of parents, siblings and extended family where possible enhances the learning and application of skills and strategies in the home. Adult family members are invited to co-facilitate sessions as role models or mentors. It is helpful for those parents to work with other children and not their own during activities. If the program is being run in a school setting, positive mentors and role models from higher grades can be recruited. All teaching and other staff within the school setting are encouraged to participate in the training so a common language is shared. Parents are also encouraged to join the training.

Activities

Once the session aim has been introduced to the larger group, children can divide into smaller groups or pairs so activities can optimize learning opportunities. This allows children to discuss their ideas and increase their ability to participate. All children in the group are expected to listen encouragingly to each other. After a child has shared their idea the group and facilitator can give positive feedback such as "Thank you for sharing your idea using your brave voice" or "Super idea" or clapping. Be strategic in where you place children in your group to promote positive behaviors. Co-facilitators can be seated beside children who may be disruptive in the group. It is also recommended that siblings are not sitting together to foster independence. Facilitators and co-facilitators provide encouragement and support for those children who are shy or introverted for their effort or best estimate for participation in activities. They also need to ensure that all children are given an opportunity to talk and have their turn.

Behavior

As each group dynamic will be different, it is important that the facilitator and co-facilitators have clear and consistent behavior management strategies which have been agreed upon prior to commencement of the program. They need to know who is responsible for implementing the strategies if the disruptive behavior occurs and continues. Examples of strategies may start with planned ignoring for identified behaviors (i.e., moving around on the carpet, fidgeting etc.) and time-out for aggressive, physical behaviors (i.e., hitting, shouting, touching others etc.). Within the Fun FRIENDS groups positive behaviors can reinforced using reward charts.

List

Barrett, P. M. (2007a). Fun Friends. The teaching and training manual for group leaders. Brisbane, Australia: Fun Friends Publishing.

Barrett, P. M. (2007b). Fun Friends. Family learning adventure: Resilience building activities for 4-, 5- and 6-year-old children. Brisbane, Australia: Fun Friends Publishing.

Appendix B Resource List

Useful Websites

Anxiety BC
www.anxietybc.com
Anxiety BC is a website full of resources to help people learn and practice effective strategies to manage anxiety on their own, at their own pace. All content is grounded in scientific research and developed by professionals who specialize in helping people with anxiety. They have sections for children and parents. And the content includes information, videos, worksheets, and very clear, actionable skills to teach your children.
Coping Cat
www.copingcatparents.com/
Coping Cat Parents is a website which has evidence-based information and recommendations, symptom checker, and tools from experts in anxiety. Also, you can sign up for "Child Anxiety Tales." This is an online program for parents who would like to learn how to help their child better manage stress and anxiety.
FRIENDS Programs
www.friendsresilience.org
The FRIENDS programs are grounded in evidence-based research, and are kept up-to-date with current psychology expertise. The FRIENDS

Foundation is endorsed by the World Health Organisation as a leader in child psychology. Resources available for purchase online include the purchase of Workbooks, Manuals, Teacher Resource CD and posters.

From Timid to Tiger

This book is a manual for mental health professionals who work with young anxious children and their parents. Organized into a 10-session parenting-based course, the book provides parents with simple cognitive behavioral techniques for helping their children to manage their worries and fears.

The Brave Program

www.brave-online.com

The Brave Program is an online Cognitive Behavior Therapy (CBT) program for children or teens with anxiety and their parents. Any child who worries about things will find the program useful. The program also has a largely preventative and early intervention focus. It teaches children and parents about unhelpful thinking styles, body sensations of anxiety, and tools to cope more effectively and boost self-esteem.

Worry Wise Kids

www.worrywisekids.org/

Worry Wise Kids provides parents, educators, and mental health professionals with information on the full range of anxiety disorders. It includes how to identify symptoms, find effective treatments, and prevent anxiety from taking hold in a child's life.

Child Anxiety Apps

Smiling Mind

itunes.apple.com/au/app/smiling-mind/id560442518?mt=8&ign-mpt=uo%3D4

Smiling Mind is a meditation app. A simple tool that helps put a smile on your mind anytime and anywhere, teaching the important skill of mindfulness to ages 7+. You can track your progress, measure mood and tension levels, and have fun learning to be mindful.

Breathe, Think, Do with Sesame

itunes.apple.com/au/app/breathe-think-do-with-sesame/id721853597?mt=8

For use with young children (under 5), this simple app teaches kids the skills of problem solving, self-control, planning, and task persistence. The easy to remember slogan of Breathe, Think, Do, can be implemented in your daily life to encourage better emotion regulation and thinking clearly.

Books for Parents and Teachers

- *Helping Your Anxious Child: A Step-by-Step Guide for Parents* by Rapee, Wignall, Spence, Lyneham and Cobham (2008)

- *What to Do When You Worry Too Much: A Kid's Guide to Overcoming Anxiety* by Huebner and Matthews (2005)
- *Handbook of Resilience in Children* by Goldstein and Brooks (2006)
- *Little Mouse's Big Book of Fears* by Gravett (2008)
- *Parenting from the Inside Out* by Siegel & Hartzell (2004)
- *Raising an Emotionally Intelligent Child* by John Gottman (1997)
- *Toxic Childhood* by Sue Palmer (2006)
- *He'll Be Ok: Growing Gorgeous Boys into Good Men* by Celia Lashlie (2006)
- *Real Wired Child: What Parents Need to Know About Kids Online* by Michael Carr-Gregg.

References

American Psychiatric Association (APA) (2013). *Diagnostic and Statistical Manual of Mental Disorders* (5th ed.). Washington, DC: APA.

Anticich, S. A. J., Barrett, P. M., Silverman, W., Lacherez, P., Gillies, R. (2013). The prevention of childhood anxiety and promotion of resilience in preschool aged population: A universal school based trial. *Advances in School Mental Health*, 6, 93–121.

Barrett, P. M. (2007). *Fun Friends. The teaching and training manual for group leaders*. Brisbane, Australia: Fun Friends Publishing.

Barrett, P. M. (2018). *Fun FRIENDS: Online eBook- A facilitator's guide* (4th ed.). Brisbane, Australia: FRIENDS Resilience.

Barrett, P. M., Dadds, M. R., & Rapee, R. M. (1996). Family treatment of childhood anxiety: A controlled trial. *Journal of Consulting and Clinical Psychology*, 64, 333–342.

Barrett, P. M., Fisak, B., & Cooper, M. (2015). The treatment of anxiety in young children: Results of an open trial of the Fun FRIENDS program. *Behaviour Change*, 32(4), 231–242.

Barrett, P. M., Lock, S., & Farrell, L. J. (2005). Developmental differences in universal preventive intervention for child anxiety. *Clinical Child Psychology & Psychiatry*, 10, 539–555.

Bögels, S., & Phares, V. (2008). Fathers' role in the etiology, prevention and treatment of child anxiety: A review and new model. *Clinical Psychology Review*, 28, 539–558.

Bufferd, S. J., Dougherty, L. R., Carlson, G. A., & Klein, D. N. (2011). Parent-reported mental health in preschoolers: Findings using a diagnostic interview. *Comprehensive Psychiatry*, 52(4), 359–369. https://doi-org.ezproxy.net.ucf.edu/10.1016/j.comppsych.2010.08.006.

Carlyle, D. A. (2014). With a little help from FUN FRIENDS young children can overcome anxiety. *Community Practitioner: The Journal of the Community Practitioners & Health Visitors Association*, 87(8), 26–29.

Cartwright-Hatton, S., Laskey, B., Rust, S., & McNally, D. (2010). *From timid to tiger: A treatment manual for parenting the anxious child*. Chichester: Wiley-Blackwell

Cartwright-Hatton, S., McNally, D.Field, A. P., Rust, S., Laskey, B., Dixon, C., et al. (2011). A new parenting-based group intervention for young anxious children: results of a randomised controlled trial. *Journal of the American Academy of Child and Adolescent Psychiatry*, 50(3), 242–251.

Cartwright-Hatton, S., McNally, D., White, C., & Verduyn, C. (2005). Parenting skills training: an effective intervention for internalising symptoms in younger children? *Journal of Child and Adolescent Psychiatric Nursing*, 18(2), 45–52.

Choate, M. L., Pincus, D. B., Eyberg, S. M., & Barlow, D. H. (2005). Parent-child interaction therapy for treatment of separation anxiety disorder in young children: A pilot study. *Cognitive and Behavioural Practice*, 12(1), 126–135.

Collaborative for Academic, Social, and Emotional Learning. (2003). *Safe and sound: An educational leader's guide to evidence-based social and emotional learning programs*. Retrieved June 29, 2017 from http://casel.org/wp-content/uploads/1A_Safe_Sound-rev-2.pdf

Cooper, B. R., Bumbarger, B. K., & Moore, J. E. (2015). Sustaining evidence-based prevention programs: Correlates in a large-scale dissemination initiative. *Prevention Science*, 16(1), 145–157. doi:10.1007/s11121-013-0427-1

Creswell, C., & Cartwright-Hatton, S. (2007). Family treatment of child anxiety: Outcomes, limitations and future directions. *Clinical Child and Family Psychology Review*, 10, 235–252.

Donovan, C. L., & March, S. (2014). Online CBT for preschool anxiety disorders: A randomised control trial. *Behaviour Research and Therapy*, 58, 24–35.

Egger, H. L., & Angold, A. (2006). Common emotional and behavioral disorders in preschool children: Presentation, nosology, and epidemiology. *Journal of Child Psychology and Psychiatry*, 47(3–4), 313–337. Fisak, B., Gallegos, J., Verreynne, M., & Barrett, P. (2018). The results of a targeted open trial of the Fun FRIENDS combined with a concurrent parent-based intervention. *Mental Health and Prevention*, 10, 35–41.

Hirshfeld-Becker, D. R., & Masek, B., Henin, A., Blakely, I. R., Pollock-Wurman, R. A., McQuade, J., et al. (2010). Cognitive behavioural therapy for 4-to 7-year old children with anxiety disorders: A randomised clinical trial. *Journal of Consulting and Clinical Psychology*, 78(4), 498.

Hirshfeld-Becker, D. R., Malek, B., Henin, A., Blakely, L. R., Rettew, D. C., Dufton, L. et al. (2008). Cognitive-behavioural intervention with young anxious children. *Harvard Review of Psychiatry*, 16(2), 113–125.

Kendall, P. C. (1994). Treating anxiety disorders in children: Results of a randomized clinical trial. *Journal of Consulting and Clinical Psychology*, 62(1), 100–110.

Kendall, P. C., & Southam-Gerow, M. A. (1996). Long-term follow-up of a cognitive- behavioural therapy for anxiety-disordered youth. *Journal of Consulting and Clinical Psychology*, 64(4), 724–730.

Langley, A. K., Bergman, R. L., McCracken, J., & Piacentini, J. C. (2004). Impairment in childhood anxiety disorders: Preliminary examination of the child anxiety impact scale-parent version. *Journal of Child & Adolescent Psychopharmacology*, 14, 105–114. doi:10.1089/104454604773840544

Monga, S., Young, A., & Owens, M. (2009). Evaluating a cognitive behavioural therapy group program for anxious five to seven year old children: Evidence of early differentiation. *Journal of Anxiety Disorders*, 26(1), 102–110.

Monga, S., Rosenbloom, B. N., Tanha, A., Owens, M., & Young, A. (2015). Comparison of child–parent and parent-only cognitive-behavioral therapy programs for anxious children aged 5 to 7 years: Short- and long-term outcomes. *Journal of the American Academy of Child & Adolescent Psychiatry*, 54(2), 138–146. doi:10.1016/j.jaac.2014. 10. 00doi:8

Pahl, K. M., & Barrett, P. M. (2010). Preventing anxiety and promoting social and emotional strength in preschool children: A universal evaluation of the Fun FRIENDS Program. *Advances in School Mental Health Promotion*, 3(3), 14–25.

Pincus, D. B., Santucci, L. C., Ehrenreich, J. T., & Eyberg, S. M. (2008). The implementation of modified parent-child interaction therapy for youth with separation anxiety disorder. *Cognitive and Behavioural Practice*, 15(2), 118–125.

Rueda, M. R., Posner, M. I., & Rothbart, M. K. (2005). The development of executive attention: Contributions to the emergence of self-regulation. *Developmental Neuropsychology*, 28(2), 573–594.

Rutter, M. (1985). Resilience in the face of adversity: Protective factors and resistance to psychiatric disorder. *British Journal of Psychiatry*, 147, 598–611.

Santacruz, I., Méndez, F. J., & Sánchez-Meca, J. (2006). Play therapy applied by parents for children with darkness phobia: Comparison of two programmes. *Child and Family Behaviour Therapy*, 28(1), 19–35.

Schneider, S., Blatter-Meunier, J., Herren, C., Adornetto, C., In-Albon, T., & Lavallee, K. (2011). Disorder-specific cognitive-behavioral therapy for separation anxiety disorder in young children: A randomized waiting-list-controlled trial. *Psychotherapy and Psychosomatics*, 80(4), 206–215.

Thulin, U., Svirsky, L., Serlachius, E., Andersson, G., & Öst, L. (2014). The effect of parent involvement in the treatment of anxiety disorders in children: A meta-analysis. *Cognitive Behaviour Therapy*, 43(3), 185–200. doi:10.1080/16506073.2014.923928

van der Sluis, C. M., van der Bruggen, C. O., Brechman-Toussaint, M. L., Thissen, M. A. P., & Bögels, S. M. (2012). Parent-directed cognitive behavioural therapy for young anxious children: A pilot study. *Behaviour Therapy*, 43(3), 583–592.

Warwick, H., Reardon, T., Cooper, P., Murayama, K., Reynolds, S., Wilson, C., & Creswell, C. (2017). Complete recovery from anxiety disorders following Cognitive Behav Ther in children and adolescents: A meta-analysis. *Clinical Psychology Review*, 52, 77–91. doi:10.1016/j.cpr.2016. 12. 00doi:2

Waters, A. M., Ford, L. A., Wharton, T. A., & Cobham, V. E. (2009). Cognitive behavioural therapy for young children with anxiety disorders: Comparison of a child + parent condition versus a parent only condition. *Behaviour Research and Therapy*, 47(8), 654–662.

Wichstrøm, L., Berg, N. T. S., Angold, A., Egger, H. L., Solheim, E., & Sveen, T. H. (2012). Prevalence of psychiatric disorders in preschoolers. *Journal of Child Psychology and Psychiatry*, 53(6), 695–705. https://doi-org.ezproxy.net.ucf.edu/10.1111/j.1469-7610.2011.02514.x

Wood, J. J., Piacentini, J. C., Southam-Gerow, M., Chu, B. & Sigman, M. (2006). Family cognitive behavioral therapy for child anxiety disorders. *Journal of the American Academy of Child and Adolescent Psychiatry*, 45, 314–321.

7 Obsessive-Compulsive Disorder in Preschool-Aged Children[1]

Marina Iniesta-Sepúlveda and Eric A. Storch

Obsessive-compulsive disorder (OCD) is characterized by intrusive, unwanted and distress-provoking thoughts (obsessions) and/or repetitive or ritualistic behaviors (compulsions) aimed to neutralize distress; collectively such symptoms contribute to impaired functioning (American Psychiatric Association, 2013). Epidemiological studies have reported a lifetime prevalence of OCD of 1–2% in children and adolescents (Rapoport et al., 2000; Zohar, 1999). The prevalence of OCD in young children (under eight years) is unclear but may be underestimated due to the difficulties this age group has in accurately reporting their distress and symptoms (Freeman et al., 2012). However, there is increasing evidence that supports the appearance of OCD presentation in young children, as early as two or three years of age (Coskun & Zoroglu, 2009; Coskun, Zoroglu, & Ozturk, 2012). These results are concerning because although the phenomenological features of OCD are similar across the lifespan, cases with early childhood onset may present unique characteristics that have important clinical implications. Yet, this age group has been underrepresented across phenomenological, assessment, and treatment studies. With this in mind, the goal of the present chapter is to describe what is known related to OCD among young children.

Phenomenology

Core OCD features are shared among children, adolescents and adults although content of symptoms and presentation differs as a function of age (Geller et al., 2001; Selles, Storch, & Lewin, 2014). Some studies have suggested the existence of an early-onset OCD phenotype in which young patients present a clinical presentation different from those that experience first OCD manifestations in late adolescence or adulthood. This early-subtype would be characterized by male preponderance (Farrell, Barrett, & Piacentini, 2006; Geller et al., 2001), greater symptom severity (Lomax, Oldfield, & Salkovskis, 2009; Rosario-Campos et al., 2001), and higher comorbidity with tic disorders (Farrell et al., 2006; Geller et al., 2001; Rosario-Campos et al., 2001). However, these results have not always been confirmed (Kenyon & Eaton, 2015) and the question about the existence of an OCD subtype with early onset remains unclear.

Less is known regarding specific OCD features in preschool aged children and its differences with older children. Consideration of "young children" as participants presents variability across phenomenological studies, establishing age cut-off points at six (Coskun et al., 2012), eight (Garcia et al., 2009; Skriner et al., 2016) or nine years (Selles et al., 2014). In light of these different age cutoffs, we will distinguish studies as a function of age where appropriate. Among preschoolers, OCD gender distribution does not reflect the male preponderance observed in previous studies when comparing children with adolescents or adults (Farrell et al., 2006; Geller et al., 2001). Instead, OCD gender distribution shows similar percentages of males and females (e.g. Skriner et al., 2016; Selles et al., 2014), or even predominantly female samples (Garcia et al., 2009), although this may reflect differences in treatment presentation and/or diagnostic overshadowing (i.e., another diagnosis presents as more impairing/severe than OCD). Heritability rates are considerably elevated in children under six years of age with 68% of parents presenting a current or lifetime history of OCD (Coskun et al., 2012). In samples with children eight years and under, percentages of OCD family history in first-degree relatives decreased to 16–20% (Garcia et al., 2009; Skriner et al., 2016).

Within phenotypic differences, OCD symptom profiles in young children are characterized by a predominance of compulsions, especially before six years of age (Coskun et al., 2012) although the ratio of children reporting obsessions versus compulsions is greater in studies with children until eight years (Garcia et al., 2009). This may reflect that cognitive and verbal skills in children under six years of age are not developed sufficiently for them to recognize, comprehend, or verbalize obsessive thoughts. Likewise, obsessional content is linked to developmentally-related interests and activities. Contamination and aggressive/catastrophic thoughts were observed as the more frequent obsessive symptoms endorsed by young children, whereas sexual, superstitious or religious themes were less common (Garcia et al., 2009; Selles et al., 2014). Regarding compulsions, washing/cleaning, ordering, repeating, and rituals involving others (e.g., asking for reassurance) are common in preschool-aged children (Garcia et al., 2009; Coskun et al., 2012; Selles et al., 2014), and the majority of children report multiple compulsions (Skriner et al., 2016). Although there are no differences in symptom severity between younger and older children, younger children did exhibit lower intensity of symptoms, but also lower capability to resist and control their compulsions (Selles et al., 2014). In this sense, in comparison to adults, children appear to use less thought control strategies (Farrell & Barrett, 2006).

Cognitive biases and processes related to OCD have been studied in pediatric samples (Barrett & Farrell, 2003a; 2003b; Farrell & Barrett, 2006). Farrell and Barrett (2006) analyzed developmental differences in cognitive processes across children, adolescents, and adults with OCD. The group of children (from 6 to 13 years) exhibited anxious and depressive intrusive thoughts with less frequency and intensity than adolescents and adults. Also, children report less responsibility and perceived probability of harm than adults. Therefore, it appears that cognitive maturation is positively related to the development of OCD-specific biased appraisals, and hence to the increase of symptom severity.

Comorbidity patterns observed in young children reflect developmental trends. For example, Coskun et al. (2012) reported that attention deficit hyperactivity disorder (60%), separation anxiety disorder (52%), and oppositional defiant disorder (48%) were the most common comorbid conditions observed in children with OCD under the age of six. These disorders typically exhibit an early childhood onset. When studies included children under the age of eight to nine years, other anxiety disorders also emerged as frequent comorbidities (Garcia et al., 2009; Skriner et al., 2016; Selles et al., 2014). Comorbid tic disorder rates (22–27%) are similar across studies (Coskun et al., 2012; Garcia et al., 2009; Skriner et al., 2016) and common among young children with OCD. Finally, depressive symptoms presented lower prevalence (<10%) in young children with OCD (Coskun et al., 2012; Garcia et al., 2009; Skriner et al., 2016; Selles et al., 2014) and were significantly less common than in older youth (Selles et al., 2014).

Overall, clinical presentation of OCD presents some distinctive characteristics between younger and older children. OCD presentation in young children is particularly characterized with high heritability rates, less obsessive symptoms (likely due to lesser capability to articulate them), developmental-related obsessional content, poor capability of symptom resistance and control, and high comorbidity with attention deficit hyperactivity disorder, oppositional defiant disorder, tic disorders, and separation anxiety disorder. Although some differences are better explained by the natural course of development rather than by differences in the nature of OCD between age groups (Selles et al., 2014), these differences constitute important considerations for assessment and treatment of OCD in preschool populations.

Assessment

Evidence-based assessment of OCD in young children requires special attention to developmental and family factors across key assessment areas (i.e., diagnostic establishment, differential diagnosis, rating of symptom severity and evaluation of impairment and family functioning) to allow an effective case conceptualization (Lewin & Piacentini, 2010).

Diagnosis Establishment

Identifying OCD symptoms and conceptualizing those according to diagnostic criteria can be difficult due to the limited capability of young children to report obsessive symptoms and their underlying relationships with compulsions, rituals or avoidance responses. The *Anxiety Disorders Interview Schedule—Parent/Child* versions (ADIS-C/P; Silverman & Albano, 1996) is a widely used clinician-administered interview for diagnosing anxiety and related disorders in children and adolescents. The ADIS-C/P has demonstrated validity and inter-rater reliability in young children (Rapee, Kennedy, Ingram, Edwards & Sweeney, 2005). A widely used semi-structured interview for preschooler ages is the *Affective Disorders and Schizophrenia for School-Age Children-Present and Lifetime Version* (KSADS-PL, Kaufman et al., 1997). It is usually administered jointly to the child and parents, and assesses the presence of several common childhood disorders. Although parents are the main information source when assessing young children, the non-observable nature of obsessions may challenge parental reports of their child's obsessional thoughts. Thus, many times obsessive symptoms may be inferred by child behavior (APA, 2013). For example, children could verbalize obsessions during exposure exercises or obsessions could be inferred by observing specific situations that are avoided by children (Freeman et al., 2012).

Differential Diagnosis

Several issues gain special relevance when making OCD differential diagnosis in young children. In daily life, preschoolers are involved in several normative ritualized behaviors related to self-care, meal- and bed-time routines, arranging personal possessions, etc. (Evans, Milanak, Medeiros, & Ross, 2002). Therefore, it may be difficult to differentiate this normal behavior from pathological rituals present in OCD. Time spent, ritual function, interference with other activities, and distress – which are often provoked by ritual interruption – are important to consider when determining the adaptive or pathological nature of these behaviors (Choate-Summers et al., 2008). Also, due to young children's difficulties in describing the functional role of their compulsions, these may be perceived as very similar to other repetitive behaviors such as those presented in autism spectrum or tic disorders. For instance, to differentiate from autism spectrum disorder, such behaviors are gauged as being ego-dystonic and distressing for children with OCD (Neil & Sturmey, 2014). In addition, testing the presence of language delays and examining the difficulties these behaviors may cause in social relationships and restricted interests are recommended (Lewin & Piacentini, 2010). Also, a small percentage of youth have onset of obsessive-compulsive symptoms secondary to streptococcus, termed PANDAS (pediatric autoimmune neuropsychiatric disorders associated with streptococcus). PANDAS is characterized by a history of streptococcal infection, early abrupt onset, and an episodic course of symptoms (Murphy, Gerardi, & Leckman, 2014; Swedo, Leonard, & Rapoport, 2004). Specialized medical exploration, identifying drastic changes in symptom severity, and assessing characteristics of the symptoms, should guide clinicians to consider a PANDAS diagnosis (Murphy, et al., 2014).

Assessing Severity, Impairment, and Family Functioning

Due to the constraints of administering standardized measures to young children (i.e., poor insight, cognitive and literacy skills, etc.), the use of semi-structured clinical interviews, clinician-rated measures, and parent reports would be recommended for best practice (Johnco & Lewin, 2016). In addition, although there is a wide variety of research-based tools to assess different dimensions of OCD – including symptoms and severity, functional impairment, and family behavior (Iniesta-Sepúlveda et al., 2014) – there is a lack of research assessing psychometric properties of specific OCD measures in children under seven years. To assess severity, Children's Yale-Brown Obsessive Compulsive Scale (CY-BOCS; Scahill et al., 1997) is a well-established measure for OCD in youth (Storch et al., 2004; 2005). It is a clinician-administered semi-structured interview that includes a Symptom Checklist and a 10-item Severity Scale. Due to several barriers for its use in young children (understanding obsessions and compulsion definitions, use of anchors to rate time, distress, control, etc.), administration of the CY-BOCS relies primarily on parent report. Freeman et al. (2012) reported some developmentally sensitive modifications for the CY-BOCS in order to facilitate its application in children from five to eight years. They administered the Compulsions checklist prior to the Obsessions checklist, making it easy to identify potential obsessions. Specific obsession and compulsion descriptions were tailored using child-friendly expressions (e.g., *don't like touching sticky things* instead of *bothered by sticky substances or residues*). With these modifications, Freeman, Flessner, and Garcia (2011) observed that the complete scale and the Compulsion scale were valid and reliable for clinical and research purposes; however, the Obsession subscale should be administered with caution in this age group.

Other relevant areas to assess include functional impairment and family functioning. Level of impairment is crucial to determine the pathological nature of the child's behavior, and also constitutes a critical measure to gauge real change after treatment. The *Child Obsessive Compulsive Impact Scale-Revised* (COIS-R; Piacentini et al., 2007) assesses functional impairment related to OCD in children and adolescents across four domains: School Activities, Social Activities, Daily Living Skills, and Family Activities. Although a parallel version is available for parents and children, the parent version is preferred in working with young children (e.g., Freeman et al., 2014). Assessing the beliefs, behaviors, and attitudes of the family related to OCD is of particular importance in cases of young children. The presence of OCD in children affects family functioning and leads parents to develop high levels of distress and conflict, as well as blame, which can influence treatment response to CBT (Peris & Piacentini, 2013). Moreover, most families exhibit accommodation behaviors to OCD symptoms. Family accommodation includes a broad range of actions, in which family members facilitate the child's avoidance or compulsion performance. Through family accommodation, parents may help children complete rituals, modify family routines and activities, or provide reassurance and objects needed for compulsions (Caporino et al., 2012; Storch et al., 2007a). Accommodation should be assessed and considered an intervention target, since it contributes to the perpetuation of anxiety and symptoms via negative reinforcement (Rudy, Storch, & Lewin, 2015). The *Family Accommodation Scale for Obsessive–Compulsive Disorder* (FAS, Calvocoressi et al., 1995, 1999) is a clinician-administered scale that assesses the level of accommodation to OCD symptoms exhibited by relatives of family members, and distress generated by accommodation. The FAS has been widely used in OCD treatment studies with preschool-aged children (Freeman et al., 2014; Lewin et al., 2014a; Rosa-Alcázar et al., 2017). Also, the *Parental Attitudes and Beliefs Scale* (PABS; Peris et al., 2008) is a parent-report that can be used to assess accommodation, as well as other attitudes or emotional reactions to one's child's OCD symptoms, although psychometric properties of this measure has only been evaluated in one study.

Treatment

Cognitive-Behavioral Therapy (CBT), including exposure response prevention (ERP), is a well-established treatment approach for OCD in children and adolescents (Geller, March & AACAP, 2012). In recent meta-analytic studies regarding the treatment effectiveness for pediatric OCD, CBT exhibited large treatment effects, which was superior to pharmacological monotherapy (McGuire et al., 2015; Sánchez-Meca, Rosa-Alcázar, Iniesta-Sepúlveda, & Rosa-Alcázar, 2014). CBT is not only recommended as the first line of treatment in pediatric OCD (Geller et al., 2012), but also generally well accepted by parents, and preferred over medication (Lewin et al., 2014b).

Based on clinical lore and research findings about the influence of family behaviors and attitudes on the emergence and development of OCD in childhood – and the critical consequences it has on family relationships and interactions – standard CBT interventions have been modified to include structured parental involvement (Farrell & Barrett, 2007; Waters, Barrett, & March, 2001). Cognitive-Behavioral Family-Based

Treatments (CBFT) have demonstrated efficacy in RCTs (e.g., Barrett, Farrell, & March, 2004; Storch et al., 2007b) and superiority to interventions with limited parental involvement (Rosa-Alcàzar et al., 2015). For very young children with OCD, this approach is considered to be the standard of care, and includes developmental sensitive adaptations to address the unique requirements of the preschooler populations (Freeman & Garcia, 2009; Freeman et al., 2014; Lewin et al., 2014a). The core elements in CBFT programs for OCD include exposure with response prevention, which is usually accompanied by psychoeducation, parent training, and child tools meant to facilitate ERP and treatment adherence.

Intervention Components

Psychoeducation

Psychoeducation for parents usually involves explaining the OCD neurobiological model, correcting misattributions related to the disorder, and introducing the treatment rationale (Choate-Summers et al., 2008). The anxiety cycle is explained to parents so they understand that – although compulsions relieve distress caused by obsessions in the short term – obsessive thoughts always reappear, forcing the child to engage in compulsions even more frequently. The parent's understanding of the treatment rationale is crucial since they will be active providers of core CBT components. Depending on the child's developmental stage, a simplified psychoeducation could be provided to them. The concept of "being the boss" of OCD is usually introduced (Choate-Summers et al., 2008). Clear examples, visual elements, and metaphors are employed to facilitate understanding. With children from three to five years old, psychoeducation may not provide additional benefits, but instead it could be useful to use this time to increase ERP practice time (Lewin et al., 2014a).

Parent involvement

Given the anxiety-provoking nature of exposure treatment and developmentally-related difficulties of young children, the family is required to guide the child, promote their child's engagement across the intervention process, and practice treatment components. Therefore, parents are included in a structured way as active agents in treatment sessions and provided a set of strategies to help them comprehend, manage, and improve their child's obsessive compulsive symptoms (Choate-Summers et al., 2008; Freeman & Garcia, 2009). The purpose of this is so parents gradually become the child's primary "coaches" in treatment by administering treatment practices during and between sessions. The success of parent inclusion in enhancing the efficacy of CBT depends mostly on the extent to which exposure practice is facilitated (Taboas, McKay,

Whiteside, & Storch, 2015). In this sense, parents should be trained with three primary goals: (1) to guide homework ERP exercises, (2) to reduce family accommodation, and (3) to facilitate the engagement in ERP using behavior management techniques. Other family focused techniques to reduce parental anxiety, hostility, and criticism, and to improve problem solving skills, are commonly included in family-based protocols (Barmish & Kendall, 2005). However, adding non-exposure-focused parent components (e.g., emotional management techniques) may reduce the exposure dose in-session and provide less effective alternatives to manage anxiety and distress (Taboas et al., 2015).

In order to assist their child in the completion of exposures and facilitate between-session practice, parents are trained by the clinician to be the child's "coach." During in-session exposures, parents learn how to implement ERP, monitor anxiety, support their child and tolerate their own distress (Anderson, Freeman, Franklin, & Sapyta, 2015). At the beginning, the therapist leads the exposures, while parents observe. By learning how the clinician handles OCD symptoms in the context of ERP tasks and how they encourage the child, parents become gradually more confident to conduct exposures independently.

Family accommodation should be directly targeted in the early stages of treatment and thereafter, preferably as the first form of exposure (Lewin et al., 2014a). With accommodation, parents prevent the child from experiencing distress provoked by feared stimuli (e.g., open doors to avoid the child touching "contaminated" objects), impeding both the habituation process in daily-life situations and learning that feared outcomes do not occur. Studies have observed that family accommodation predicts worse symptom severity and treatment response (Rudy, Lewin, Geffken, Murphy, & Storch, 2014; Wu et al., 2016). During treatment, parents are encouraged to systematically abstain from participating in compulsions and facilitating avoidance of anxiety-provoking situations. They are instructed to use more adaptive responses instead of accommodation.

Given this, parents need to be trained in behavioral management techniques – such as differential attention, time out, and extinction – to cope with the child's oppositional behavior and tantrums, and to improve child engagement in treatment exercises. It is important that parents learn how to use these strategies. For example, time out should be applied to cope with disruptive behavior, but not as a punishment for engaging in compulsive behavior (Labouliere et al., 2014). Also, parents are trained to model adequate coping strategies to the child in the presence of fear stimuli instead of compulsions or avoidance (Freeman & Garcia, 2009). Finally, child participation and completion of exposures is usually rewarded through a token economy program and social reinforcement.

ERP and Complementary Child Tools

ERP is the primary active ingredient of the intervention for young children (as well as older children and adolescents) with OCD (Conelea & Freeman, 2015). During ERP trials, feared situations are gradually and systematically confronted and escape responses (compulsions and avoidance) are impeded. Allowing adequate time for exposures, the habituation process is activated and the child learns that feared outcomes do not occur.

Within intervention models for five- to eight-year-old children, cognitive techniques are developmentally tailored and focus is placed on ERP exercises. The goal of cognitive training is essentially the OCD externalization (Choate-Summers et al., 2008); the idea is that the child perceives OCD as something separate and independent from himself. In other words, the disorder is presented as a "mean" character that tries to make the child do things that he does not want to do. A common resource used to facilitate externalization is to allow the child to choose a funny or scary name for OCD and to then draw their OCD monster (Freeman & Garcia, 2009). ERP is introduced as a way to "fight back" against the OCD, using child-friendly explanations such as "don't listen to the lies of OCD," "do the opposite of what OCD says," or simply "say no! to OCD." Metaphors and clear examples are usually used to illustrate the habituation process, to explain that although fighting against OCD is hard at first, with practice it will be easier soon (e.g., like when you are learning to ride a bike). Also, the idea that the clinician and parents are on the child's team, and that they will be supported during the entire process in sessions and at home is emphasized. Regarding approaches for children under five years of age, cognitive techniques are almost eliminated; however, some simple self-instructions (e.g., don't listen to OCD) or positive self-talk (Lewin et al., 2014a) are maintained. In addition, exposures are implemented within a developmentally appropriate play context – using games, cartoon characters, toys, "fun" exposure tasks, etc. New applications also include computer games to enhance the child's treatment understanding and engagement (Comer et al., 2014).

A fear thermometer is the most common tool employed to monitor anxiety while developing a hierarchy and doing ERP tasks. In the case of young children, its use may be too complicated. Some children are not able to use rating scales, whereas others may have a dichotomous perception of anxiety occurrence (present vs. absent). Adaptations usually include the use of short rating scales (no more than three points), images (faces expressing different levels of distress), or manipulatives (items with different sizes representing high, low or no anxiety) (Choate-Summers et al., 2008).

Finalizing and Relapse Prevention

The last sessions of treatment are usually employed to work on a relapse prevention plan. Parents and children are instructed on how to proceed in cases where symptoms reappear or new symptoms emerge. They are encouraged to use all the strategies that they learned (recognizing OCD, keeping doing exposures, not engaging in accommodation, etc.) and come back for booster sessions, if necessary. This approach is not unique to young children with the exception perhaps of enhanced focus on parents.

Empirical Support for CBFT in very young children

In recent years, evidence on the effectiveness of CBFT in children from three to eight years old has grown (see Table 7.1). Overall, treatment protocols converge – including psychoeducation, ERP, and parent involvement – varying in the emphasis placed on cognitive elements (Freeman & Garcia, 2009; Ginsburg, Burstein, Becker, & Drake, 2011; Lewin et al., 2014a; Rosa-Alcázar et al., 2017). CBFT has demonstrated superiority to relaxation training in a RCT (Freeman et al., 2008) and in a multicenter RCT in children from five to eight years (Freeman et al., 2014). In younger children (3–5 years), Lewin et al. (2014a) reported significantly greater effectiveness for twice-weekly family-based ERP relative to a treatment as usual (TAU) condition. In Lewin et al. (2014a), cognitive strategies were minimized, placing emphasis in augmenting ERP practice and reducing family accommodation, given the cognitive limitations of very young children. More recently, a preliminary evaluation suggested the feasibility and preliminary efficacy of a parent-only intervention; no significant differences were observed between a CBFT – including children in sessions – and a parent-only training condition (Rosa-Alcázar et al., 2017). Also, an internet-based approach has yielded promising results (Comer et al, 2014; 2016), and no significant differences were observed in the efficacy, treatment engagement, and satisfaction between clinic- and internet-based conditions (Comer et al., 2016). In video teleconferencing sessions and interactive online activities, non-face-to-face interventions may contribute in addressing access barriers to trained mental health providers for this population. In addition to their effectiveness, family approaches for OCD in young children were well-accepted and parents showed a desire to participate actively in the treatment of their child's intervention (Lewin et al., 2014b; Rosa-Alcázar et al., 2017).

Challenges Unique to this Population

Developmental factors and the important role of family in the course, assessment, and treatment of OCD for preschooler ages makes it necessary to consider the challenges that are unique to this population across the therapeutic process.

Limited abstraction and meta-cognitive capabilities not only impede preschoolers' ability to express, identify, and differentiate obsessive thoughts, but also hinder their awareness towards the functional relationship between

Table 7.1 Empirical studies evaluating CBFT for OCD in young children

Study	N	Mean Age (yrs)	Design	Treatment Implementation	Child focused lements	Parent focused elements	Findings
Freeman et al. (2008)	16	7.11	RCT CBFT vs. RT	Clinic-based	Psychoeducation, Externalizing OCD, and ERP	Psychoeducation, behavior management training, parental ERP coaching, reducing accommodation, hostility and criticism, and problem solving	50% remitters[a] in CBFT vs. 20% remitters in RT
Ginsburg et al. (2011)	7	6.00	Case series	Clinic-based	Psychoeducation ERP	Psychoeducation, behavior management training, parental ERP coaching, reducing accommodation, and anxiety-enhancing behaviors, and problem solving	14.3% remitters[a] 85.71% responders[b]
Freeman et al. (2014)	59	7.40	Multicenter RCT CBFT vs. RT	Clinic-based	Psychoeducation, Externalizing OCD, and ERP	Psychoeducation, behavior management training, parental ERP coaching, reducing accommodation, hostility and criticism, and problem solving	72% responders[b] in CBFT vs. 41% responders in RT

	N		Design				Outcomes
(2014a)			vs. RT	talk		behavior management training, parental ERP coaching, and reducing accommodation	ters[a] in FB-ERP vs. 0% remitters in TAU
Comer et al. (2014)	5	6.50	Case series	VTC-delivered	Psychoeducation, Externalizing OCD, and ERP	Psychoeducation, behavior management training, parental ERP coaching, reducing accommodation, hostility and criticism, and problem solving	20% remitters[a] 60% responders[b]
Comer et al. (2016)	22	6.65	RCT VTC-CBFT vs. Clinic-based CBFT	VTC-delivered Clinic-based	Psychoeducation, Externalizing OCD, and ERP	Psychoeducation, behavior management training, parental ERP coaching, reducing accommodation, hostility and criticism, and problem solving	63.3% remitters[c] VTC-CBFT vs. 60% remitters in Clinic-based CBFT
Rosa-Alcázar et al. (2017)	20	6.62	Non-randomized comparison CBFT vs. PT	Clinic-based Parent-only	Psychoeducation, Externalizing OCD, and ERP	Psychoeducation, behavior management training, parental ERP coaching, and reducing accommodation	70% remitters[a] in CBFT vs. 60% in PT

N: sample size in the posttest for each group, RCT: randomized controlled trial, CBFT: cognitive-behavioral family-based treatment, ERP: exposure with response prevention, VTC: video teleconferencing, PT: parent training.
[a]Post-treatment CY-BOCS score ≤ 12 [b]*Much or very much improved* on CGI [c] No OCD diagnosis

obsessions and compulsions. Therefore, the understanding of the disorder and treatment rationale is very poor or non-existent in young children. A lack of insight (Lewin et al., 2010), and low capability to control and resist their compulsions (Selles et al., 2014) usually translate to limited motivation and treatment engagement. It is common for preschoolers to cry, have tantrums or outbursts when compulsions or avoidances are impeded. Likewise, oppositional disorder and ADHD (Coskun et al., 2012) are the most common comorbid conditions in young children with OCD. Disruptive behaviors derived from these conditions also contribute to complicated treatment implementation and compliance. When children are forced to do exposures or are punished for not participating in them, it is likely that they do not want to continue with the treatment and their oppositional behavior gets worse (Choate-Summers et al., 2008). In this sense, parent-training allows parents to learn how to engage with their child effectively during treatment, by using rewards and being supportive in exposure tasks.

As parents play a key role in the intervention process, their attitudes about the disorder and treatment may affect treatment success. First, high rates of heritability (Coskun et al., 2012) are indicative of a high probability for very young children with OCD to live within an environment where OCD behaviors may be supported (Choate-Summers et al., 2008). Parents' beliefs and attitudes toward OCD and psychotherapy may determine how their child responds to OCD symptoms. For example, parents can mistakenly believe that their child's behavior is part of either the normative developmental process, related to oppositional behavior, or that the child is "sick." Thus, parents could fail to seek appropriate treatment, or implement punitive or permissive parenting practices that may negatively affect the course of the disorder (Johnco & Lewin, 2016). Likewise, parents of young children may experience high levels of anxiety and/or distress due to the child's suffering; thus, it is common for parents to engage in accommodation behaviors (Freeman et al., 2003). When reducing accommodation, it is common that parents experience guilt feelings for allowing their child to suffer and cry, rather than take actions to reduce their distress. Many parents want to prevent their children from provoked suffering by exposures (and to reduce their own distress) and allow for some treatment inconsistencies – such as giving their child breaks from exposures at home, or finalizing ERP trials before the habituation occurs. To reduce potential inconsistencies in treatment, parents also receive an "exposure" during ERP trials, in which they learn to cope with their own anxieties (Freeman & Garcia, 2009). In order to avoid OCD symptom exacerbation, treatment should help parents in tolerating their own distress and teach them to be more confident when exposing their children to feared situations (Choate-Summers et al., 2008).

Summary of Recommendations and Resource List

The fully developed presentation of OCD can be observed in preschool-aged children, causing high levels of impairment and potential for a chronic course, if untreated. Early detection and treatment are warranted to limit the impact of the disorder in future academic, social and family life.

Table 7.2 presents recommendations and resources for assessment and treatment of OCD in young children. Obsessions and compulsions are usually difficult to identify as such in young children. Compulsions should be differentiated from normal ritualized or rigid behavior common to this age. Also, given the repetitive and rigid nature of OCD rituals – and the difficulty to determine if they are triggered by intrusive thoughts – differential diagnosis from ASD and tics disorders deserves special attention. In addition, the low capability of young children to report symptoms and distress

Table 7.2 Recommendations and resources for assessment and treatment of OCD in young children

---

Recommendations and resources for assessment

- Differentiate pathological rituals from normative ritualized behavior, attending time, interference, and distress.
- Make differential diagnosis from repetitive behaviors presented in ASD and tics disorders.
- Assess compulsions first, by using concrete examples and direct questioning.
- When children do not clearly articulate obsessions, these may be inferred by observing avoidance behavior and the child's reactions in ERP task.
- Consider behavioral observations and parent reports as the main resource of information.
- Some OCD-specific evidence-based measures to assess OCD and related responses in young children are:
  - For symptoms and severity, *Children's Yale Brown Obsessive Compulsive Scale* (CY-BOCS; Scahill et al., 1997).
  - For family accommodation, *Family Accommodation Scale* (FAS; Calvocoressi et al., 1999)
  - For functional impairment, *Child Obsessive Compulsive Impact Scale-Child and Parent Versions* (COIS-C/P; Piacentini & Jaffer, 1999).

Recommendations and resources for treatment

- Use CBT that focuses on ERP and reducing family accommodation.
- Include parent-training to guide and assist children in exposures, to reduce family accommodation and to learn behavior management strategies.
- Minimize focus on cognitive components of the intervention, especially in children under five years.
- Make child tools developmentally sensitive to young children (e.g., externalize drawing an OCD monster, fear thermometer with images or manipulatives, etc.).
- Apply treatment strategies within an appropriate play context (fun exposures, using toys, video games, etc.).

---

makes it necessary for behavioral observation and parent reports to become main pillars of the assessment. Obsessions should be inferred frequently while observing the child's specific fears and avoidance behavior. Although scarce, evidence-based assessment measures for OCD have been adapted and validated for the preschooler clinical population and are essential to achieve accurate and objective case conceptualization, as well as for monitoring treatment change.

Research on the effectiveness of CBFT for OCD in young children is a growing field and has demonstrated that family interventions including ERP are superior to active psychological control conditions. Parent involvement is the critical adaptation, in relation to standard CBT (which we believe should also include substantial family involvement), and should focus on parents' role of becoming "ERP coaches" and reducing family accommodation. Parallel behavioral interventions, targeting disruptive behavior, are also necessary to allow the application of specific OCD treatment techniques. Treatment should be implemented with a child-friendly approach, by using metaphors, clear examples, by playing, and allowing children to better understand why the intervention is needed – as well as their role throughout treatment. In addition, cognitive elements should be minimized for younger children, and focus should be placed in behavioral change mechanisms.

Note

1   Author Note: We acknowledge the contributions of Sandra Cepeda.

References

American Psychiatric Association (2013). *Diagnostic and statistical manual of mental disorders* (5th ed.). Washington, DC: American Psychiatric Publishing.

Anderson, L. M., Freeman, J. B., Franklin, M. E., & Sapyta, J. J. (2015). Family-based treatment of pediatric obsessive-compulsive disorder: Clinical considerations and application. *Child and Adolescent Psychiatric Clinics of North America*, 24(3), 535–555.

Barmish, A. J., & Kendall, P. C. (2005). Should parents be co-clients in cognitive-behavioral therapy for anxious youth? *Journal of Clinical Child and Adolescent Psychology*, 34(3), 569–581.

Barrett, P., Farrell, L., & March, J. S. (2004). Cognitive-behavioral family treatment of childhood obsessive-compulsive disorder: a controlled trial. *Journal of the American Academy of Child & Adolescent Psychiatry*, 43(1), 46–62.

Barrett, P. M., & Farrell, L. J. (2003a). An examination of the cognitive processes involved in childhood obsessive-compulsive disorder. *Behaviour, Research and Therapy*, 41, 285–299.

Barrett, P. M., & Farrell, L. J. (2003b). Perceived responsibility in childhood obsessive-compulsive disorder: An experimental manipulation. *Journal of Clinical Child and Adolescent Psychiatry*, 32, 430–441.

Calvocoressi, L., Lewis, B., Harris, M., Trufan, S., McDougle, C., & Price, L. (1995). Family accommodation in obsessive–compulsive disorder. *American Journal of Psychiatry*, 152, 441–443.

Calvocoressi, L., Mazure, C. M., Kasl, S. V., Skolnick, J., Fisk, D., Vegso, S. J., et al. (1999). Family accommodation of obsessive–compulsive symptoms: Instrument development and assessment of family behavior. *The Journal of Nervous and Mental Disease*, 187, 636–642.

Caporino, N. E., Morgan, J., Beckstead, J., Phares, V., Murphy, T. K., & Storch, E. A. (2012). A structural equation analysis of family accommodation in pediatric obsessive-compulsive disorder. *Journal of Abnormal Child Psychology*, 40(1), 133–143.

Choate-Summers, M. L., Freeman, J. B., Garcia, A. M., Coyne, L., Przeworski, A., & Leonard, H. L. (2008). Clinical considerations when tailoring cognitive behavioral treatment for young children with obsessive compulsive disorder. *Education and Treatment of Children*, 31(3), 395–416.

Comer, J. S., Furr, J. M., Cooper-Vince, C. E., Kerns, C. E., Chan, P. T., Edson, A. L., ... & Freeman, J. B. (2014). Internet-delivered, family-based treatment for early-onset OCD: a preliminary case series. *Journal of Clinical Child & Adolescent Psychology*, 43(1), 74–87.

Comer, J. S., Furr, J. M., Kerns, C. E., Miguel, E., Coxe, S., Elkins, R. M., ... & Chou, T. (2016). Internet-delivered, family-based treatment for early-onset OCD: A pilot randomized trial. *Journal of Consulting and Clinical Psychology*, 21, 1–9.

Conelea, C. A., & Freeman, J. B. (2015). What do therapists and clients do during exposures for OCD? Introduction to the special issue on theory-based exposure process. *Journal of Obsessive-Compulsive and Related Disorders*, 6, 144–146.

Coskun, M., & Zoroglu, S. (2009). Efficacy and safety of fluoxetine in preschool children with obsessive-compulsive disorder. *Journal of Child and Adolescent Psychopharmacology*, 19, 297–300.

Coskun, M., Zoroglu, S., & Ozturk, M. (2012). Phenomenology, psychiatric comorbidity and family history in referred preschool children with obsessive-compulsive disorder. *Child and Adolescent Psychiatry and Mental Health*, 6, 1–9.

Evans, D. W., Milanak, M. E., Medeiros, B., & Ross, J. L. (2002). Magical beliefs and rituals in young children. *Child Psychiatry and Human Development*, 33(1), 43–58.

Farrell, L., & Barrett, P. (2006). Obsessive-compulsive disorder across developmental trajectory: Cognitive processing of threat in children, adolescents and adults. *British Journal of Psychology*, 97(1), 95–114.

Farrell, L. J., & Barrett, P. (2007). The function of the family in childhood obsessive-compulsive disorder: family interactions and accommodation. In Storch, E.A., Geffken, G.R., & Murphy, T.K. (eds.), *Handbook of child and adolescent obsessive-compulsive disorder* (pp. 313–332). Mahwah, NJ: Lawrence Erlbaum Associates.

Farrell, L., Barrett, P., & Piacentini, J. (2006). Obsessive-compulsive disorder across the developmental trajectory: clinical correlates in children, adolescents and adults. *Behaviour Change*, 23, 103–120.

Freeman, J., & Garcia, A.M. (2009). *Family-based treatment for young children with OCD: Therapist guide*. New York: Oxford University Press.

Freeman, J., Flessner, C. A., & Garcia, A. (2011). The Children's Yale-Brown Obsessive Compulsive Scale: Reliability and validity for use among 5 to 8 year olds with obsessive-compulsive disorder. *Journal of Abnormal Child Psychology*, 39(6), 877–883.

Freeman, J., Garcia, A., Benito, K., Conelea, C., Sapyta, J., Khanna, M., ... & Franklin, M. (2012). The pediatric obsessive compulsive disorder treatment study for young children (POTS Jr): developmental considerations in the rationale, design, and methods. *Journal of Obsessive-Compulsive and Related Disorders*, 1(4), 294–300.

Freeman, J. B., Garcia, A. M., Coyne, L., Ale, C., Przeworski, A., Himle, M., ... & Leonard, H. L. (2008). Early childhood OCD: Preliminary findings from a family-based cognitive-behavioral approach. *Journal of the American Academy of Child & Adolescent Psychiatry*, 47(5), 593–602.

Freeman, J. B., Garcia, A. M., Fucci, C., Karitani, M., Miller, L., & Leonard, H. L. (2003). Family-based treatment of early-onset obsessive-compulsive disorder. *Journal of Child and Adolescent Psychopharmacology*, 13, 71–80.

Freeman, J., Sapyta, J., Garcia, A., Compton, S., Khanna, M., Flessner, C., ... & Harrison, J. (2014). Family-based treatment of early childhood obsessive-compulsive disorder: The Pediatric Obsessive-Compulsive Disorder Treatment Study for Young Children (POTS Jr)—a randomized clinical trial. *JAMA Psychiatry*, 71(6), 689–698.

Garcia, A. M., Freeman, J. B., Himle, M. B., Berman, N. C., Ogata, A. K., Ng, J., ... & Leonard, H. (2009). Phenomenology of early childhood onset obsessive compulsive disorder. *Journal of Psychopathology and Behavioral Assessment*, 31(2), 104–111.

Geller, D. A., Biederman, J., Faraone, S., Agranat, A., Cradock, K., Hagermoser, L., ... & Coffey, B. J. (2001). Developmental aspects of obsessive compulsive disorder: findings in children, adolescents, and adults. *The Journal of Nervous and Mental Disease*, 189(7), 471–477.

Geller, D. A., March, J., & AACAP (2012). Practice parameter for the assessment and treatment of children and adolescents with obsessive–compulsive disorder. *Journal of the American Academy of Child and Adolescent Psychiatry*, 51, 98–113.

Ginsburg, G. S., Burstein, M., Becker, K. D., & Drake, K. L. (2011). Treatment of obsessive compulsive disorder in young children: An intervention model and case series. *Child & Family Behavior Therapy*, 33(2), 97–122.

Iniesta-Sepúlveda, M., Rosa-Alcázar, A. I., Rosa-Alcázar, Á., & Storch, E. A. (2014). Evidence-based assessment in children and adolescents with obsessive–compulsive disorder. *Journal of Child and Family Studies*, 23(8), 1455–1470.

Johnco, C. J., & Lewin, A. B. (2016). Treatment of obsessive-compulsive disorder in very young children. In E. A. Storch & A. B. Lewin (eds.), *Clinical handbook of obsessive-compulsive and related disorders* (pp. 291–304). Switzerland: Springer International Publishing.

Kaufman, J., Birmaher, B., Brent, D., Rao, U. M. A., Flynn, C., Moreci, P., ... & Ryan, N. (1997). Schedule for affective disorders and schizophrenia for school-age children-present and lifetime version (K-SADS-PL): initial reliability and validity data. *Journal of the American Academy of Child & Adolescent Psychiatry*, 36(7), 980–988.

Kenyon, K. M., & Eaton, W. O. (2015). Age at child obsessive-compulsive disorder onset and its relation to gender, symptom severity, and family functioning. *Archives of Scientific Psychology*, 3(1), 150–158.

Labouliere, C. D., Arnold, E. B., Storch, E. A., & Lewin, A. B. (2014). Family-based cognitive-behavioral treatment for a preschooler with obsessive-compulsive disorder. *Clinical Case Studies*, 13(1), 37–51.

Lewin, A. B., & Piacentini, J. (2010). Evidence-based assessment of child obsessive compulsive disorder: Recommendations for clinical practice and treatment research. *Child & Youth Care Forum*, 39, 73–89.

Lewin, A. B., Bergman, R. L., Peris, T. S., Chang, S., McCracken, J. T., & Piacentini, J. (2010). Correlates of insight among youth with obsessive-compulsive disorder. *Journal of Child Psychology and Psychiatry*, 51(5), 603–611.

Lewin, A. B., McGuire, J. F., Murphy, T. K., & Storch, E. A. (2014b). The importance of considering parent's preferences when planning treatment for their children—the case of childhood obsessive-compulsive disorder. *Journal of Child Psychology and Psychiatry*, 55(12), 1314–1316.

Lewin, A. B., Park, J. M., Jones, A. M., Crawford, E. A., De Nadai, A. S., Menzel, J., ... & Storch, E. A. (2014a). Family-based exposure and response prevention therapy for preschool-aged children with obsessive-compulsive disorder: a pilot randomized controlled trial. *Behaviour Research and Therapy*, 56, 30–38.

Lomax, C. L., Oldfield, V. B., & Salkovskis, P. M. (2009). Clinical and treatment comparisons between adults with early- and late-onset obsessive-compulsive disorder. *Behaviour Research and Therapy*, 47, 99–104.

McGuire, J. F., Piacentini, J., Lewin, A. B., Brennan, E. A., Murphy, T. K., & Storch, E. A. (2015). A meta-analysis of cognitive behavior therapy and medication for child obsessive–compulsive disorder: moderators of treatment efficacy, response, and remission. *Depression and Anxiety*, 32(8), 580–593.

Murphy, T. K., Gerardi, D. M., & Leckman, J. F. (2014). Pediatric acute-onset neuropsychiatric syndrome. *Psychiatric Clinics of North America*, 37(3), 353–374.

Neil, N., & Sturmey, P. (2014). Assessment and treatment of obsessions and compulsions in individuals with autism spectrum disorders: A systematic review. *Review Journal of Autism and Developmental Disorders*, 1, 62–79.

Peris, T. S., & Piacentini, J. (2013). Optimizing treatment for complex cases of childhood obsessive compulsive disorder: a preliminary trial. *Journal of Clinical Child & Adolescent Psychology*, 42(1), 1–8.

Peris, T. S., Benazon, N., Langley, A., Roblek, T., & Piacentini, J. (2008). Parental attitudes, beliefs, and responses to childhood obsessive compulsive disorder: The parental attitudes and behaviors scale. *Child and Family Behavior Therapy*, 30, 199–214.

Piacentini, J. C. & Jaffer, M. (1999). *Measuring functional impairment in youngsters with OCD: Manual for the Child OCD Impact Scale (COIS)*. Los Angeles, CA: UCLA Department of Psychiatry.

Piacentini, J., Peris, T. S., Bergman, R. L., Chang, S., & Jaffer, M. (2007). Functional impairment in childhood OCD: Development and psychometrics properties of the child obsessive–compulsive impact scale-revised (COIS-R). *Journal of Clinical Child and Adolescent Psychology*, 36, 645–653.

Rapee, R. M., Kennedy, S., Ingram, M., Edwards, S., & Sweeney, L. (2005). Prevention and early intervention of anxiety disorders in inhibited preschool children. *Journal of Consulting and Clinical Psychology*, 73(3), 488–497.

Rapoport, J. L., Inoff-Germain, G., Weissman, M. M., Greenwald, S., Narrow, W. E., Jensen, P. S., ... & Canino, G. (2000). Childhood obsessive–compulsive disorder in the NIMH MECA Study: Parent versus child identification of cases. *Journal of Anxiety Disorders*, 14(6), 535–548.

Rosa-Alcázar, A. I., Iniesta-Sepúlveda, M., Storch, E. A., Rosa-Alcázar, Á., Parada-Navas, J. L., & Rodríguez, J. O. (2017). A preliminary study of cognitive-behavioral family-based treatment versus parent training for young children with obsessive-compulsive disorder. *Journal of Affective Disorders*, 208, 265–271.

Rosa-Alcázar, A. I., Sánchez-Meca, J., Rosa-Alcázar, Á., Iniesta-Sepúlveda, M., Olivares-Rodríguez, J., & Parada-Navas, J. L. (2015). Psychological treatment of obsessive-compulsive disorder in children and adolescents: A meta-analysis. *The Spanish Journal of Psychology*, 18, e20.

Rosario-Campos, M., Leckman, J. F., Mercadante, M. T., Shavitt, R. G., da Silva Prado, H., Sada, P., ... Miguel, E. C. (2001). Adults with early-onset obsessive–compulsive disorder. *The American Journal of Psychiatry*, 158, 1899–1903.

Rudy, B. M., Lewin, A. B., Geffken, G. R., Murphy, T. K., & Storch, E. A. (2014). Predictors of treatment response to intensive cognitive-behavioral therapy for pediatric obsessive-compulsive disorder. *Psychiatry Research*, 220(1), 433–440.

Rudy, B. M., Storch, E. A., & Lewin, A. B. (2015). When families won't play ball: A case example of the effect of family accommodation on anxiety symptoms and treatment. *Journal of Child and Family Studies*, 24(7), 2070–2078.

Sánchez-Meca, J., Rosa-Alcázar, A. I., Iniesta-Sepúlveda, M., & Rosa-Alcázar, Á. (2014). Differential efficacy of cognitive-behavioral therapy and pharmacological treatments for pediatric obsessive–compulsive disorder: A meta-analysis. *Journal of Anxiety Disorders*, 28(1), 31–44.

Scahill, L., Riddle, M. A., McSwiggin-Hardin, M., Ort, S. I., King, R. A., Goodman, W. K., et al. (1997). Children's Yale-Brown Obsessive–Compulsive Scale: Reliability and validity. *Journal of the American Academy of Child and Adolescent Psychiatry*, 36, 844–852.

Selles, R. R., Storch, E. A., & Lewin, A. B. (2014). Variations in symptom prevalence and clinical correlates in younger versus older youth with obsessive–compulsive disorder. *Child Psychiatry & Human Development*, 45(6), 666–674.

Silverman, W., & Albano, A. (1996). *The Anxiety Disorders Interview Schedule for Children–IV (Child and parent versions)*. San Antonio, TX: Psychological Corporation.

Skriner, L. C., Freeman, J., Garcia, A., Benito, K., Sapyta, J., & Franklin, M. (2016). Characteristics of young children with obsessive–compulsive disorder: Baseline features from the POTS Jr. sample. *Child Psychiatry & Human Development*, 47(1), 83–93.

Storch, E. A., Geffken, G. R., Merlo, L. J., Jacob, M. L., Murphy, T. K., Goodman, W. K., ... & Grabill, K. (2007a). Family accommodation in pediatric obsessive–compulsive disorder. *Journal of Clinical Child and Adolescent Psychology*, 36(2), 207–216.

Storch, E. A., Geffken, G. R., Merlo, L. J., Mann, G., Duke, D., Munson, M., ... & Goodman, W. K. (2007b). Family-based cognitive-behavioral therapy for pediatric obsessive-compulsive disorder: Comparison of intensive and weekly approaches. *Journal of the American Academy of Child & Adolescent Psychiatry*, 46(4), 469–478.

Storch, E. A., Murphy, T. K., Geffken, G. R., Bagner, D. M., Soto, O., Sajid, M., ... & Goodman, W. K. (2005). Factor analytic study of the Children's Yale–Brown Obsessive–Compulsive Scale. *Journal of Clinical Child and Adolescent Psychology*, 34(2), 312–319.

Storch, E. A., Murphy, T. K., Geffken, G. R., Soto, O., Sajid, M., Allen, P., ... & Goodman, W. K. (2004). Psychometric evaluation of the Children's Yale–Brown Obsessive-Compulsive Scale. *Psychiatry Research*, 129(1), 91–98.

Swedo, S. E., Leonard, H. L., & Rapoport, J. L. (2004). The pediatric auto-immune neuropsychiatric disorders associated with streptococcal infection (PANDAS) subgroup: separating fact from fiction. *Pediatrics*, 113(4), 907–911.

Taboas, W. R., McKay, D., Whiteside, S. P., & Storch, E. A. (2015). Parental involvement in youth anxiety treatment: Conceptual bases, controversies, and recommendations for intervention. *Journal of Anxiety Disorders*, 30, 16–18.

Waters, T. L., Barrett, P. M., & March, J. S. (2001). Cognitive-behavioral family treatment of childhood obsessive-compulsive disorder: preliminary findings. *American Journal of Psychotherapy*, 55(3), 372–387.

Wu, M. S., McGuire, J. F., Martino, C., Phares, V., Selles, R. R., & Storch, E. A. (2016). A meta-analysis of family accommodation and OCD symptom severity. *Clinical Psychology Review*, 45, 34–44.

Zohar, A. H. (1999). The epidemiology of obsessive-compulsive disorder in children and adolescents. *Child and Adolescent Psychiatric Clinics of North America*, 8, 445–460.

8 Trauma and PTSD in Preschool-Aged Children

Ann-Christin Haag, Shana Celi, and Markus A. Landolt

Trauma in children below the age of six years has been neglected for a long period of time. Over the last two decades, however, there has now been impressive development in this field. Today, there is strong evidence suggesting that not only school aged children, adolescents, and adults are affected by trauma, but that young children can also experience adverse consequences after exposure to potentially traumatic events (e.g. De Young, Haag, Kenardy, Kimble, & Landolt, 2016; Haag & Landolt, 2017; Meiser-Stedman, Smith, Yule, Glucksman, & Dalgleish, 2017).

Infants, toddlers and preschoolers are at a particularly high risk of being exposed to potentially traumatic events, such as violence, neglect or injuries (Chu & Lieberman, 2010). In fact, many young children experience more than one traumatic event and more than one type of trauma. Amongst the different types of trauma interpersonal violence represents the most frequent form of exposure (Lieberman, Chu, Van Horn, & Harris, 2011).

Moreover, exposure to trauma in early childhood is particularly harmful as such experiences can interfere with vulnerable periods of development. Researchers reason that young children are at special risk of posttraumatic maladjustment due to their rapid development of the neurobiological stress systems, their limited emotion regulation capabilities and cognitive skills, as well as their strong dependency on their caregivers (e.g. Carpenter & Stacks, 2009). Due to these factors, young children are at increased risk of suffering long-term consequences. It has been shown that, if untreated, symptoms resulting from trauma during early childhood can follow a chronic course and impact adult health outcomes (Felitti et al., 1998; Lambert, Meza, Martin, Fearey, & McLaughlin, 2017). A large epidemiological study from the United States, for example, found that one-third of adult psychiatric disorders can be attributed to traumatic experiences in childhood (Kessler et al., 2010).

This chapter is designed to give an overview of the current theoretical and empirical knowledge on trauma in early childhood. After providing the definition and epidemiological background of this subject matter, the specific traumatic reactions in young children are depicted. Diagnostic criteria, epidemiological findings, risk factors and assessment tools are presented and subsequently current evidence-based treatment methods for young traumatized children are described.

Definition of Trauma

The term "trauma" is defined in the current classification systems. According to the *Diagnostic and Statistical Manual of Mental Disorders*, 5th edition (DSM-5; American Psychiatric Association [APA], 2013), traumatic experiences in children below the age of six years include exposure to actual or threatened death, serious injury, or sexual violation. The exposure must result from one or more of the following scenarios, in which the young child either: directly experiences the traumatic event(s); witnesses, in person, the traumatic event(s) happening to others (especially to primary caregivers); learns that the traumatic event(s) happened to a parent or caregiving figure (APA, 2013).

The proposed criteria for the new version of the International Classification of Diseases (ICD-11; Maercker et al., 2013) defines trauma more generally than the DSM-5, namely as exposure to extremely threatening or horrific event(s). Traumatic experiences can include a wide range of potentially distressing events, spanning from physical and sexual violence to accidents or natural disasters. However, the validity of both definitions based on the current classification systems has been criticized for children as they do not include all potentially traumatic experiences (Cohen & Scheeringa, 2009). Especially neglect and psychological abuse do not meet the definitions of trauma along DSM or ICD.

Terr (1991) classified traumatic events according to their type. She differentiated between Type I and Type II traumas. Type I traumas consist of acute, unpredictable, and singularly occurring events, such as traffic accidents, being taken hostage, or assault. Events classified as Type II trauma, however, occur repeatedly and are sometimes foreseeable. Examples of Type II trauma include chronic sexual abuse, domestic violence, and exposure to a war zone and/or community violence (Terr, 1991). In addition to differentiating between single incidents and chronic exposure, Solomon and Heide (1999) suggested that a third type of trauma be introduced. Type III trauma was referred to as the most devastating form of trauma, as it described multiple and pervasive traumata already beginning at an early age and continuing for years. The experience of multiple and/or chronic and prolonged, developmentally adverse traumatic events, most often of an interpersonal nature (e.g., abuse, violence or neglect) beginning in early childhood was subsumed under the term of "complex trauma" (Cook, Blaustein, Spinazzola, & van der Kolk, 2003). In the same context, the notion of "adverse childhood events" (ACE) was developed in order to broaden the definition of trauma and capture cases of developmental trauma (Felitti et al., 1998).

Epidemiology of Trauma Exposure in Young Children

Epidemiological studies among young children exposed to traumatic events remain sparse. It is, however, known that preschoolers are at particularly high risk of being exposed to potentially traumatic events (PTE). Approximately one-quarter of children of a U.S. birth cohort experience a PTE before the age of four (Briggs-Gowan, Ford, Fraleigh, McCarthy, & Carter, 2010). They have a higher risk of hospitalization and death caused by PTEs when compared to children in any other age group (Grossman, 2000). Numbers are even higher amongst low-income families in which studies have reported that 72–93% of three- to five-year-old children have experienced at least one potentially traumatic event (Graham-Bermann et al., 2008; Roberts, Ferguson, & Crusto, 2013). In a mixed sample of clinically referred and non-referred children aged two to four years, approximately one in four was exposed to at least one of the following PTEs: witness to interpersonal partner violence (11.7%), sexual abuse (0.5%), physical abuse (1.9%), victim of non-family violence (0.5%), witness to death/violence (2.8%), witness the use of a weapon (1.4%), fire (0.5%), natural disaster (0.5%), animal attack (0.5%), serious fall (4.2%), burned (6.1%), poisoning (1.9%), vehicle accident (2.3%), sudden death of a loved one (5.6%), and hospitalization (17.8%; Grasso, Ford, & Briggs-Gowan, 2013).

Exposure to Childhood Maltreatment

Amongst young children, incidence rates of maltreatment, i.e., physical, psychological, and sexual abuse, as well as neglect, are very high. According to the U.S. Department of Health and Human Services, approximately 53% of abuse and neglect victims are six years of age or younger. The reports show, in fact, that the very youngest of these children are the most vulnerable to maltreatment. For example, in 2015, 27.7% of maltreatment victims were below the age of three and victimization was highest for children under 12 months (24.2 per 1,000 children). In addition, 74.8% of all child fatalities resulting from abuse and neglect were younger than three years old and the highest maltreatment death rate occurs between birth and 12 months (U.S. Department of Health & Human Services, 2017). Lastly, a study found that, in a sample of sexually abused children aged three to 14 years old, more than one-third (35.4%) of the victims were in the youngest age group of three to seven years old (McCrae, Chapman, & Christ, 2006). The findings suggest that the rate of victimization decreases as age increases, thus highlighting the particular importance of identification and treatment of trauma reactions in young children.

Exposure to Domestic and Community Violence

Witnessing and experiencing violence is a prevalent among young children. In regard to domestic violence, studies indicate that children below the age of five are more likely than older children to live in households with domestic violence. In fact, the majority of child witnesses to interpersonal violence (IPV) are younger than six years of age (Fusco & Fantuzzo, 2009). It was reported by the National Survey of Children's Exposure to Violence, that 17.2% of U.S. children aged up to five years old had been exposed to some kind of family violence or IPV over their lifetime (Hamby, Finkelhor, Turner, & Ormrod, 2011). Amongst young children (2–5 years of age) from low-income families, up to one-quarter (16.3–22.0%) experience domestic violence (Graham-Bermann et al., 2008; Roberts et al., 2013).

According to the National Survey of Children's Exposure to Violence, 9% of two- to five-year-olds in the United States have witnessed community violence in their lifetime (Finkelhor, Turner, Ormrod, Hambly, & Kracke, 2009). Additionally, a study conducted with a sample of three- to five-year-olds from low-income families in the United States showed that 18% of preschool children have been exposed to community violence (Roberts et al., 2013). Lastly, young children in clinical samples show an even higher rate of experiencing violence. One study found that 42% of three- to five-year-old children from high-crime neighborhoods witnessed at least one violent event. Twenty-one percent of the sample experienced three or more violent events, while 12% witnessed eight or more events (Linares et al., 2001). In another sample of three- to six-year-olds, referred to a hospital-based trauma clinic in the U.S., 62% witnessed violence, with high rates of IPV, and a substantial portion of these children showed patterns of polyvictimization (16%; Hagan, Sulik, & Lieberman, 2016). It is important to keep in mind that rates of exposure to violence in young children are likely underestimated due to under-reporting of physical, and especially sexual trauma (Saunders & Adams, 2014).

Exposure to the Death of a Loved One

Children between the ages of three and five from low-income families have elevated prevalence rates (18–23.5%) of experiencing the death of a loved one (Roberts et al., 2013) or of someone they know (Graham-Bermann et al., 2008).

Exposure to Accidental Injury

Young children are at particular risk for unintentional injuries. According to numbers of the U.S. Department of Health and Human Services, accidents are one of the three leading causes of death amongst one- to four-year-old children (Kochanek, Murphy, Xu, & Tejada-Vera, 2016). For children less than one year of age, two-thirds of injury-related deaths are due to suffocation. Drowning and road traffic accidents are the most common causes of deaths resulting from injury in children between the ages of one and four. Falls are the leading cause of non-fatal injury in this age group. In addition, children four years old and younger have the highest rates of burns, drowning, falls and poisoning (Borse et al., 2008). Detailed accidental PTEs experienced by children aged up to four years of a birth cohort sample were car accidents (10.3%), dog bites (3.7%) and major injuries/burns (2.0%; Briggs-Gowan et al., 2010). In the specific case of burn injuries, children below three years of age account for 80% of all pediatric burns (Schiestl, Beynon, & Balmer, 2007). In a sample from low-income families with children two to five years old, about 10% were involved in an accident or an injury (Graham-Bermann et al., 2008).

Exposure to Mass Trauma and Disaster

Due to the present-day world climate of upheaval and violence, young children are exposed to an increasingly wide variety of disasters, war, and terrorist incidents. Worldwide terrorism is escalating and modern war-fare progressively targets populated civilian locations, which impede all citizens, including children, from safe refuge (Hamiel, Wolmer, Pardo-Aviv, & Laor, 2017). Although research on terrorism (e.g. the attack of 9/11), natural disasters (e.g. Hurricane Katrina) and war (e.g. Israeli–Palestinian conflict) underlines the detrimental effect of these events on mental health of young children (Conway, Mcdonough, Mackenzie, Follett, & Sameroff, 2013; Scheeringa & Zeanah, 2008; Wolmer et al., 2015), there are only few estimates of actual exposure rates. These rates, of course, depend on the geographical location and proximity to an event. High-income countries are less prone to mass trauma than low- and middle-income countries. A review on the effects of war, terrorism and armed conflict on young children revealed that over 62% of the 35 studies were related to children suffering from the conflict in the Middle East (Slone & Mann, 2016). The review reveals a wide range of exposure rates amongst young children aged up to six: numbers ranged from 2.9% witnessing a killing of a close to relative to 95% hearing explosions, alarm sirens and living in shelters.

In light of the surging militancy of current events, trauma research will need to expand and shed light on the plight of refugees after having experienced traumatic events in their home country, during their escape and relocation. As many as 941,000 refugee children below the age of ten were living in the United States between 2009 and 2013 (Hooper, Zong, Capps, & Fix, 2016). The UN Refugee Agency reported that the number of forcibly displaced peoples in 2016 remains at a record high of 65.5 million, half of which were children (United Nations High Commissioner for Refugees, 2017).

Exposure to Life-threatening Illnesses and Invasive Medical Procedures

Regarding life-threatening illnesses amongst young children, cancer and congenital heart diseases are cited most frequently in the existing literature on childhood trauma. After accidents, cancer is the second leading cause of death in children from one to 14 years of age. In 2014, the incidence rate of all types of childhood cancer in the U.S. was 21.9 per 100,000 children aged one to four years. Children in this young age range have the highest incidence rate (U.S. Cancer Statistics Working Group, 2017).

Congenital heart diseases are the most common birth defect, and as a result, various invasive medical procedures are often necessary at a very young age. Severe and moderate congenital heart defects requiring cardiologic and surgical care occur in about 19 per 1,000 of live births (Hoffman & Kaplan, 2002). For children of all ages, some sort of invasive medical procedures are relatively common and may be experienced as traumatic, particularly when life-threatening (Marsac, Kassam-Adams, Delahanty, Widaman, & Barakat, 2014). Especially for young patients, medical treatments are often stressful and frightening and can therefore have a traumatizing effect (De Young, Kenardy, Cobham, & Kimble, 2012; Graf, Schiestl, & Landolt, 2011).

Overview of Symptoms and Disorders in Young Children Following Traumatic Events

A wide range of symptoms has been described in young children after exposure to traumatic events. Preschoolers are at risk of developing emotional and behavioral difficulties, including internalizing and externalizing behavior problems (e.g. Bakker et al., 2014; Graf et al., 2011), oppositional defiant disorder, specific phobias, separation anxiety disorder, depression, and attention-deficit/hyperactivity disorder (De Young et al., 2012; Scheeringa, Zeanah, Myers, & Putnam, 2003). Further, a loss of previously acquired developmental skills (e.g., bed-wetting and regressed verbal abilities), temper tantrums and new fears not obviously linked to the traumatic event may be observed (e.g. fear of going to the toilet alone, fear of the dark; Scheeringa et al., 2003). In addition, traumatized young children may display disrupted play activities, social withdrawal, and increased negative emotional states. Often, they have difficulties regulating emotions, and their attachment to caregivers may intensify due to an increased sense of insecurity (Goldbeck & Jensen, 2017).

The disorders following exposure to traumatic events are outlined in separate chapters of the DSM-5 (Trauma- and Stressor-Related Disorders; APA, 2013) and in the current Beta-Version of the ICD-11 (Disorders specifically associated with stress; Maercker et al., 2013). In the proposed ICD-11, there are no specific PTSD criteria for young children. In the DSM-5 however, there is a PTSD subtype specifically for children six years and younger (APA, 2013). Both classification systems describe posttraumatic stress disorder (PTSD), adjustment disorders, reactive attachment disorder, disinhibited social engagement disorder, and other specified and unspecified trauma-related disorders as possible conditions after exposure to trauma or extreme stress. While the ICD-11 proposal (Maercker et al., 2013) adds possible diagnoses of complex posttraumatic stress disorder and prolonged grief disorder, the DSM-5 additionally incorporates acute stress disorder (within the first month post-trauma), as well as PTSD with dissociative symptoms or with delayed expression (APA, 2013). Core symptoms of the new developmentally sensitive PTSD subtype for young children will be presented below.

Posttraumatic Stress Disorder

Diagnostic Classification

The DSM-IV (APA, 2000) criteria were criticized for not adequately capturing PTSD symptoms manifested in preschool children. Scheeringa and colleagues, therefore, developed an alternative PTSD algorithm (PTSD-AA; Scheeringa et al., 2003). Taking into account the limited cognitive and verbal capabilities of young children, they modified the DSM-IV PTSD criteria by making them more objective, behaviorally anchored, and developmentally sensitive. These criteria have been adopted in the Diagnostic Classification of Mental Health and Developmental Disorders of Infancy and Early Childhood, Zero to Three (2005).

The DSM-5 (APA, 2013) PTSD diagnostic criteria for preschool children include the three symptom clusters: re-experiencing, avoidance/negative alterations in cognitions and mood, and hyperarousal. Symptoms are listed in Table 8.1. Most changes with regard to the under-six years PTSD criteria have been made in the section of avoidance and negative alterations in cognitions and mood. Because these symptoms are more difficult to assess (e.g., avoidance of thoughts) or are even developmentally impossible (e.g., sense of a foreshortened future) in young children, fewer symptoms are required for diagnosis. The manifestations of specific symptoms in young children can be seen as follows:

1   Re-experiencing may manifest in posttraumatic play. Here the child vividly re-enacts the traumatic event repeatedly. Young children may also express intrusive memories by persistently drawing or speaking about the event. Importantly, in contrast to adults, the re-experiencing does not have to be distressing to the child.
2   Presenting avoidant behavior is often not easily possible for young children. For example, after an injury children may require medical check-ups, which due to adult supervision, they cannot easily circumvent. However, the child might avoid reminders about the

Table 8.1 Posttraumatic Stress Disorder in children <6 years according to DSM-5 (APA, 2013)

Symptom Cluster	Description
A Traumatic event	Exposure to actual or threatened death, serious injury or sexual violence in one (or more) of the following ways: 1. Directly experiencing the traumatic event(s) 2. Witnessing, in person, the event(s) as it occurred to others, especially primary caregivers (not witnessing in electronic media, or pictures) 3. Learning that the traumatic event(s) occurred to a caregiving figure
B Re-experiencing	One (or more) of the following intrusion symptoms: 1. Intrusive distressing memories (may not necessarily appear distressing and may be expressed as play reenactment) 2. Recurrent distressing dreams (it may not be possible to ascertain that the frightening content is related to the traumatic event) 3. Dissociative reactions (e.g. flashbacks) in which the child feels or acts as if the traumatic event(s) were recurring. Such trauma-specific reenactment may occur in play 4. Psychological distress to reminders 5. Marked physiological reactions to reminders
C Avoidance and negative alterations in cognitions and mood	One (or more): 1. Avoidance of or efforts to avoid activities, places, or physical reminders 2. Avoidance of or efforts to avoid people, conversations, or interpersonal situations that arouse recollections of the traumatic event(s) 3. Increased frequency of negative emotional states (e.g. fear, guilt, sadness, shame, confusion) 4. Diminished interest or participation in significant activities, including constriction of play 5. Socially withdrawn behavior 6. Reduction in expression of positive emotions
D Hyperarousal	Two (or more): 1. Irritable behavior and angry outbursts (including extreme temper tantrums) 2. Hypervigilance 3. Exaggerated startle response 4. Problems with concentration 5. Sleep disturbance
E Duration	More than one 1 month
F Impairment	Significant distress or impairment in relationships with parents, siblings, peers, or other caregivers or with school behavior

appointment by turning one's head away, or by forbidding the care-giver to mention the upcoming appointment in advance. Diminished interest in significant activities manifests frequently via constriction of play and participation in activities previously enjoyed. Negative alterations in mood may be manifested via social withdrawal and a decreased display of affection to family members and friends.

3   In young children, hyperarousal is marked by increased irritable beha-vior and alertness to danger, and an exacerbated startle response. Other psychophysiological dysregulation problems may present themselves in temper tantrums, sleep and feeding related issues, transient loss of developmental capacities, as well as concentration difficulties. The latter may be observed in a new and less focused play pattern (Coates & Gaensbauer, 2009; Scheeringa et al., 2003).

Some studies have compared diagnostic algorithms for PTSD in young children. They support the notion that the DSM-5 subtype for children below the age of six years and the PTSD-AA algorithm are more appro-priate than the previous DSM-IV algorithm for this age group (De Young, Kenardy, & Cobham, 2011; Gigengack, van Meijel, Alisic, & Lindauer, 2015; Meiser-Stedman, Smith, Glucksman, Yule, & Dalgleish, 2008; Scheeringa, Myers, Putnam, & Zeanah, 2012).

The proposed ICD-11 PTSD criteria include symptoms from each of the three following symptom clusters: (1) presently re-experiencing the traumatic event(s) in the form of vivid intrusive memories, flashbacks, or nightmares – these symptoms are typically accompanied by strong and overwhelming emotions, such as fear or horror, as well as strong physical sensations, similar to those experienced during the traumatic event; (2) avoidance of thoughts and memories of the event(s), or avoidance of activities, situations, or people reminiscent of the event(s); and (3) persistent perceptions of heightened cur-rent threat, experienced through hypervigilance or an enhanced startle reac-tion to stimuli, such as unexpected noises. The symptoms must persist for at least several weeks and cause significant impairment in personal, family, social, educational, occupational, or other important areas of functioning. Based on the currently available Beta-Version of ICD-11 there are no specific criteria for preschool aged children (Maercker et al., 2013).

Prevalence of PTSD

Based on the PTSD research with young children, varying prevalence rates have been reported, which appears to depend upon the methodol-ogy used. Methodological characteristics such as the investigated sample (e.g. sample size, type of trauma, etc.), the diagnostic algorithm used, and the time of assessment all seem to impact the results. It is critical that acute stress, which is often operationalized as PTSD without the time criterion, is distinguished from PTSD. Presently, there are only a few studies that reported PTSD prevalence rates according to the DSM-5 (APA, 2013). The previous criteria, PTSD-AA (Scheeringa et al., 2003), were used more frequently.

An overview of the current literature on PTSD in young children ages up to seven years is depicted in Table 8.2. To summarize briefly, after exposure to single-incident trauma (Type I) reported PTSD-AA rates for acute stress ranged between 6.5% and 29% (Meiser-Stedman et al., 2008; Stoddard et al., 2006). One study applying the DSM-5 PTSD criteria without the time criterion, found acute stress in 11.7% of children aged one to four years, approximately 19 days after accidental trauma (Haag & Landolt, 2017). PTSD prevalence rates for DSM-IV ranged between 0 and 15.7% (e.g. Ohmi et al., 2002; Scheeringa & Zeanah, 2008), while rates for PTSD-AA were found to be 7.1–50% (e.g. Meiser-Stedman et al., 2008; Scheeringa & Zeanah, 2008). Full DSM-5 PTSD prevalence rates ranged between 7.1% and 44% (e.g. Gigengack et al., 2015; Scheeringa et al., 2012). In the case of exposure to repeated trauma (Type II), DSM-IV(-TR) PTSD rates ranged from 4–44.6% (e.g. Pat-Horenczyk et al., 2017; Wolmer et al., 2015) and PTSD-AA rates from 21–69% at 0–14 months post-trauma (e.g. Kaufman-Shriqui et al., 2013; Scheeringa, Zeanah, Drell, & Larrieu, 1995). Only one study reported on young children after missile attacks with a DSM-5, and this study found a PTSD prevalence rate of 14% (Wolmer et al., 2015). Finally, there is a considerable risk for a long-term trajectory of PTSD in preschool children. It has been found that up to 50% of affected preschool children do not recover naturally, but fulfil the PTSD diagnosis for at least two years (Scheeringa, Zeanah, Myers, & Putnam, 2005).

Risk Factors of Posttraumatic Stress Symptoms

As research indicates that PTSD is clinically relevant already in early childhood, it is important to investigate which factors contribute to posttraumatic stress symptoms. The *Transactional Model of Coping with Trauma* breaks the essential factors influencing the posttraumatic adjustment into the following categories: (a) characteristics of the traumatic event, (b) the individual and (c) social environment. Factors subsumed in these categories affect both cognitive appraisal and coping behavior, and in turn influence severity of posttraumatic stress reactions (Landolt, 2012). The predictors described in this chapter are subsumed in these three categories, namely trauma-related risk factors, individual risk factors, and social and environmental risk factors.

Trauma-related Risk Factors

When discussing trauma-related risk factors, it is important to keep in mind that young children's perception of traumatic and threatening incidents may differ from that of adults. For example, it was found that in young pediatric injury patients, not only the injury, but also treatment-

Table 8.2 Prevalence of posttraumatic stress in young children after traumatic events

Author and year	Type of Trauma	N and age	Time of assessment post trauma	Diagnostic criteria and prevalence rate
Exposure to single trauma (type I)				
De Voe et al., 2006	September 11 terrorist attack	180 0–5 years	9–12 months	PTSD-AA: 17%.
De Young et al., 2011	Accidental burns	T1: 130 T2: 125 1–6 years	T1: 1 month T2: 6 months	T1: PTSD-AA: 25%, DSM-IV-TR: 5%, DSM-5: 25% T2: PTSD-AA: 10%, DSM-IV-TR: 1%; DSM-5: 10%
Gigengack et al., 2015	Accidental injuries	98 0–7 years	4–69 months M = 36.3 months	PTSD-AA: 7.1%, DSM-IV-TR: 2%, DSM-5: 7.1%
Graf et al., 2011	Accidental burns	76 12–49 months	3–48 months M = 14.8 months	PTSD-AA: 13,2%, DSM-IV-TR: 1.3%
Haag & Landolt, 2017	Accidental burns	138 1–4 years	M = 19.26 days	DSM-5: 11.7% (excluding time criterion)
Meiser-Stedman et al., 2008	Motor vehicle accidents	62 2–6 years	T1: 2–4 weeks T2: 6 months	T1: PTSD-AA: 6.5%, ASD: 1.7% T2: PTSD-AA: 10%, DSM-IV: 1.7%
Ohmi et al., 2002	Gas explosion	32 32–73 months	6 months	PTSD-AA: 25%, DSM-IV: 0%
Scheeringa et al., 2006	Accidental injuries	21 0–6 years	2 months	PTSD-AA: 14.3%, DSM-IV: 4.8%

Author and year	Type of Trauma	N and age	Time of assessment post trauma	Diagnostic criteria and prevalence rate
Scheeringa & Zeanah, 2008	Hurricane Katrina	70 3–6 years	6 months– 2.5 years	PTSD-AA: 50%, DSM-IV-TR: 15.7%
Stoddard et al., 2006	Accidental burns	52 12–48 months	within 1 month	PTSD-AA = 29%
Stoddard et al., 2017	Accidental burns	42 1–4 years	1 month	PTSD-AA: 3%, DSM-IV: 10%
Exposure to repeated trauma (type II)				
Cohen & Gadassi, 2009	Terror events	29 3.5–7.5 years	approx. 6–18 months	PTSD-AA:31%, DSM-IV: 7%
Feldman & Vengrober, 2011	Rocket attacks	232 1.5–5 years	≥ 1 month	PTSD-AA (DC: 0–3R): 37.8%
Graham-Bermann et al., 2012	Exposed to IPV	120 4–6 years	≤ 2 years	PTSD-AA: 51%, DSM-IV-TR: 17%
Kaufman-Shriqui et al., 2013	Missile attacks	167 4–6.5 years	≥ 2 months	PTSD-AA: 21%
Levendosky et al., 2002	Domestic violence	39 3–5 years	Most recent event of DV occurred within last year	PTSD-AA: 26%, DSM-IV: 3%
Pat-Horenczyk et al., 2013	Political violence (e.g. missile attacks)	262 Past sample: M = 3.00 years Continuous sample: M = 3.44 years	n/a	DSM-IV Past Sample: 15 %, DSM-IV Continuous Sample: 44.6%
Scheeringa et al., 1995	Witnessed IPV, sexual & physical abuse	12 18–48 months	0–14 months	PTSD-AA: 69%, DSM-IV: 13%
Scheeringa et al., 2001	Witnessed IPV, sexual & physical abuse	15 13–47 months	0–22 months (M = 6.6 months)	PTSD-AA: 60%, DSM-IV: 20%

Author and year	Type of Trauma	N and age	Time of assessment post trauma	Diagnostic criteria and prevalence rate
Wolmer et al., 2015	Rocket attacks	122 3–6 years	Approx. 4 weeks	DSM-IV: 4%, DSM-5: 14%
Mixed trauma samples				
Scheeringa et al., 2003	Accidental injuries, abuse, witnessed IPV, cancer	62	2–52 months (M = 11.3 months)	PTSD-AA: 26%, DSM-IV: 0%
Scheeringa et al., 2005	Same sample as in Scheeringa et al., 2003	T2: 47 T3: 35	1 and 2 years post-T1	T2: PTSD-AA: 23.4%, DSM-IV: 2.1% T3: PTSD-AA: 22.9%, DSM-IV: 11.4%
Scheeringa et al., 2012	Accidental injuries; witnessing relatives murdered, assaulted, or severely injured; domestic violence; natural disaster	284 3–6 years	36–83 months	PTSD-AA: 45%, DSM-IV: 13%, DSM-5: 44%

Note: PTSD-AA: Alternative PTSD algorithm (Scheeringa, Zeanah, Myers, & Putnam, 2003); DSM-IV: *Diagnostic and statistical manual of mental disorders*, 4th edition (APA, 1994); DSM-IV-TR: *Diagnostic and statistical manual of mental disorders*, 4th edition, text revised (APA, 2000); DSM-5: *Diagnostic and statistical manual of mental disorders*, 5th edition (APA, 2013); DC: 0–3R: Diagnostic Classification: Zero-to-Three; n/a: not applicable.

related variables (e.g. medical procedures or a temporary separation from caregivers) could have adverse effects on young children (Graf et al., 2011).

Analyzing trauma-related risk factors of PTSD in young children includes investigating type, intensity and frequency of exposure to traumatic events, as well as threat to self or others. Amongst young children (0–6 years), threat to a caregiver was one of the strongest predictors of PTSD (Scheeringa, Wright, Hunt, & Zeanah, 2006; Scheeringa & Zeanah, 1995). In the literature, PTSD rates were consistently found to be higher for traumatic events that threatened family members (e.g. family violence) compared to more distal events (e.g. accidents; Graham-Bermann et al., 2008). Furthermore, the severity of the traumatic event plays an important role in the development of PTSD symptoms in young children. For example physical factors, such as injury severity, length of hospital stay, number of medical procedures, amount of pain and elevated pulse rate are all strong risk factors for developing PTSD symptoms in the aftermath of an accidental injury (De Young, Hendrikz, Kenardy, Cobham, & Kimble, 2014; Drake et al., 2006; Graf et al., 2011; Haag & Landolt, 2017; Stoddard et al., 2006). In terms of trauma severity, it has been found that personal exposure predicted a PTSD diagnosis (Cohen & Gadassi, 2009). For example, children who were not evacuated before Hurricane Katrina developed more PTSD symptoms (Scheeringa & Zeanah, 2008) than those evacuated. In line with this, young children whose houses were destroyed in war and had to be displaced showed more PTSD symptoms than children who could stay in their homes (Laor et al., 1997).

It has been consistently found that polyvictimized young children (i.e. children exposed to multiple adverse events) are especially vulnerable to adverse psychological outcomes and that more severe exposure was associated with greater posttraumatic stress (Grasso et al., 2016; Hagan et al., 2016; Wolmer et al., 2015). In this context, some authors suggested a dose-response relationship between amount and intensity of traumatic exposure and severity of mental health outcomes, such as posttraumatic stress symptoms (e.g. Finkelhor, Ormrod, & Turner, 2009; Slone & Mann, 2016).

Individual Risk Factors

Research on the importance of age and sex for developing posttraumatic stress reactions in young children is still inconsistent. While some studies found that younger children develop PTSD more frequently (Scheeringa & Zeanah, 1995), other findings indicate that older children are more likely to develop PTSD (Feldman & Vengrober, 2011; Graham-Bermann et al., 2008). Furthermore, there are also studies that indicate no relationship between age and PTSD symptomatology (Cohen & Gadassi, 2009; Scheeringa et al., 2005).

With regard to sex, the majority of studies did not find any differences in PTSD symptoms between preschool-aged girls and boys (e.g. Cohen & Gadassi, 2009; Graham-Bermann et al., 2008; Scheeringa & Zeanah, 2008).

It is important to note, however, that pre-existing psychopathology was repeatedly found to be a predictor of PTSD. Emotional and (externalizing) behavioral difficulties were likely to predict more PTSD symptoms (De Young et al., 2014; Scheeringa et al., 2006). In addition, initial severity of PTSD after exposure to a PTE predicted a continuance of PTSD two years later (Scheeringa et al., 2005). Finally, in a single study difficult infant temperament was not found to be a predictor of PTSD symptoms in young children after witnessing violence (Bogat, DeJonghe, Levendosky, Davidson, & von Eye, 2006).

Risk Factors of the Social Environment

As young children are strongly dependent on their caregivers and attachment is crucial in early childhood (Lieberman et al., 2011), social risk factors in this age are usually related to the family. Parental posttraumatic stress has consistently been found to be a predictor of child PTSD symptoms (e.g. De Young et al., 2014; Meiser-Stedman et al., 2017; for reviews on young children in armed conflicts see Hamiel et al., 2017; Slone & Mann, 2016). Several cross-sectional and longitudinal studies confirmed the associative, predictive or mediating relationship between parental (mainly maternal) PTSD symptoms and the child's acute stress or PTSD symptoms (e.g. Bogat et al., 2006; Graf et al., 2011; Haag & Landolt, 2017; Pat-Horenczyk et al., 2017; Scheeringa & Zeanah, 2008).

Based on this strong association between child and parental PTSD, Scheeringa and Zeanah (2001) proposed a model of relational PTSD. It describes the co-occurrence of trauma symptomatology in both children and parents and the effect of each of the partners' symptomatology exacerbating the other's. One such mechanism works via restricted parenting capacities of the caregivers (e.g. unresponsiveness, overprotection, reenacting). There is recent evidence that both positive and negative parenting behaviors are linked to child PTSD (for a review see Williamson et al., 2017). Scheeringa and Zeanah (2001) depict two other effects, which might elicit the association between child and parent PTSD. First, the "moderating effect" suggests the caregiver's relationship with the child affects the link between the traumatic event and the child's PTSD. Second, the "vicarious traumatization effect" implies that the caregiver's responsiveness to the child is affected by a traumatic event, which the child did not experience. Thereby, the impacted caregiver-child relationship accounts for the effect of the traumatic event on the child's PTSD.

Another risk factor of PTSD in young children is family relationship. Lower quality of family relations and lower quality of mother-child affective communication was found to be associated with more PTSD symptoms in children (Graf et al., 2011; Milot, St-Laurent, Ethier, & Provost, 2010). In addition, lower family cohesion and adaptability were associated with more PTSD symptoms (Laor, Wolmer, & Cohen, 2001).

It must be highlighted that until present, most studies have been designed cross-sectionally, which impedes the conclusion of causality. The directionality of effects, i.e. between parental and child PTSD, therefore remains unclear, both from an empirical and a theoretical point of view.

Assessment

General Remarks

A general problem in mental health research with young children is the mode of assessment. Due to their still developing verbal capacities, primary caregivers are often the principal source of information concerning the young child. Proxy-reports can, however, be problematic. Different studies have shown that parents both under- and overestimate the child's symptoms. This may be due to reasons such as their own levels of stress (Meiser-Stedman et al., 2008; Müller, Achtergarde, & Furniss, 2011). It was found that inadequate parental reporting was most evident for the avoidance and numbing criteria (Scheeringa, Peebles, Cook, & Zeanah, 2001). It thus remains difficult to assess the child's symptomatology in an objective and valid way as standardized, and validated, objective measures of young children's PTSD symptoms are lacking. There have been attempts to develop observational measurement of children's PTSD symptoms. However, only 12% of the diagnostic criteria for children could be detected by a clinician by direct observation or interaction with the children – the remaining criteria were detectable via caregiver report only (Scheeringa et al., 2001).

Hence, questioning parents or other primary caregivers still remains the primary method to assess child PTSD. In the following section, the current instruments assessing PTSD in young children based on proxy-reports are outlined. As there is no instrument for assessing acute stress in young children, the same PTSD measures are used excluding the time criterion (e.g. Haag & Landolt, 2017).

Measures

Current instruments assessing PTSD in young children are described in the list below, including: the PTSD module of the Diagnostic Infant Preschool Assessment (Scheeringa & Haslett, 2010), the Young Child PTSD Checklist (Scheeringa, 2010), Trauma Symptom Checklist for Young Children (Briere et al., 2001) and the PTSD module of the Child Behavior Checklist (CBCL 1.5–5; Achenbach & Rescorla, 2000).

• The *Diagnostic Infant Preschool Assessment* (DIPA; Scheeringa & Haslett, 2010) can be considered as the gold-standard measure amongst current instruments. It is a semi-structured diagnostic interview conducted with a primary caregiver of children aged one to six years old and assesses various psychiatric disorders. The PTSD module (46 items) screens for exposure to potentially traumatic events, assesses symptoms commonly seen in young traumatized children and provides a measure of associated functional impairment. The interview provides both a categorical diagnosis according to DSM-5 PTSD criteria and a continuous measure of symptom severity. It also includes items on developmental specifics regarding PTSD in young children (e.g. new fears, separation anxiety). The latest version (6/30/2014) assesses both frequency and intensity ratings of the symptom items, each on a 5-point Likert scale (0–4). In two studies the DIPA has demonstrated acceptable test-retest reliability (Scheeringa & Haslett, 2010) and good inter-rater reliability (De Young et al., 2014).

- The *Young Child PTSD Checklist* (YCPC; Scheeringa, 2010) is a 42-item questionnaire assessing PTSD in one- to six-year-old children based on the report of a primary caregiver. To assess PTSD symptom frequency the instrument contains 23 items with a 5-point Likert scale (0–4). In addition, exposure to potentially traumatic events, the child's functional impairment in daily life, as well as new symptoms are assessed. A DSM-5 (APA, 2013) diagnosis can be derived from the corresponding items, as well as a continuous PTSD severity score. Two studies have looked at the psychometric properties and found acceptable to good reliability (internal consistency) for the YCPC (e.g. Haag & Landolt, 2017).

- The *Trauma Symptom Checklist for Young Children* (TSCYC; Briere et al., 2001) assesses a broader range of symptoms. The 90-item caregiver-report questionnaire assesses the frequency of PTSD and other trauma-related symptoms in children 3–12 years of age. Items are rated on a 4-point Likert scale (0–3). Raw scores are transformed into T scores and used to interpret the child's level of symptomatology. The measure also consists of seven subscales: Posttraumatic Stress-Intrusion, Posttraumatic Stress-Avoidance, Posttraumatic Stress-Arousal, Sexual Concerns, Anxiety, Depression, Dissociation, and Anger/Aggression. Combining scores of the first three subscales, a PTSD total symptom score can be formed. Studies found good psychometric properties in terms of reliability (internal consistency) and predictive validity (e.g. Briere et al., 2001; Hagan et al., 2016). The TSCYC does not assess DSM-5 PTSD criteria (APA, 2013).

- The widely used *Child Behavior Checklist 1.5–5* (CBCL; Achenbach & Rescorla, 2000) has also been used to screen for PTSD in young children. Dehon and Scheeringa (2006) used a modified CBCL-PTSD scale in a sample of traumatized preschool children (ages one to six). This subscale includes 15 items and provides a cut-off score for identifying those children at risk of PTSD. The CBCL-PTSD demonstrated adequate internal consistency (Dehon & Scheeringa, 2006). The CBCL-PTSD does not assess DSM-5 PTSD criteria (APA, 2013).

Treatment

The above sections demonstrate how preschoolers are at risk for developing both emotional and behavioral problems after being exposed to potentially traumatic events. As posttraumatic stress symptoms can take a chronic course and because they are associated with short- and long-term repercussions, it is crucial that young children receive early and effective treatment. Several treatment approaches have shown positive results when used with pre-school aged children. The following sections will focus on three well studied therapies: Trauma-Focused Cognitive Behavioral Therapy (Scheeringa, 2016), Child-Parent Psychotherapy

(Lieberman, Ippen, & Van Horn, 2015), and Parent-Child Interaction Therapy (Eyberg, Nelson, Ginn, Bhuiyan, & Boggs, 2013). Further information on these treatment approaches can be found in Landolt, Cloitre, and Schnyder (2017). Key studies evaluating the effectiveness of the above listed treatments are presented in Table 8.3.

Trauma-focused Cognitive Behavioral Therapy

Trauma-focused Cognitive Behavioral Therapy (TF-CBT) is the best studied and most effective treatment for children with posttraumatic stress disorder. TF-CBT is a method suited for children and adolescents between three and eighteen years of age and has been successful in addressing trauma-related problems such as PTSD, depression and other behavior problems (Cohen, Mannarino, & Deblinger, 2016; Kliethermes, Dreary, & Wamser-Nanney, 2017).

TF-CBT is built upon four major components, the first being stress management. This integral part of the therapy focuses on preparing the child (and parent) before being confronted with the trauma-related memories. Techniques such as age appropriate psychoeducation, affect regulation, and specific cognitive skills are introduced in order to help the child face the traumatic memories. The second core element of TF-CBT is ensuring that the exposure to the traumatic memories is done gradually. This safeguards against "flooding" and assures that the child is sufficiently equipped to deal with the traumatic content. The third pillar of TF-CBT consists of cognitive focused interventions. After a traumatic event children may have increased negative beliefs about themselves, others, and their surroundings. Such beliefs can promote negative outcomes, such as, PTSD symptoms, depression, anxiety, and aggressive tendencies. Cognitive interventions are implemented in TF-CBT in order to help the child learn to monitor destructive thoughts and emotions and aid the child in adopting more accurate beliefs. The last central mechanism that TF-CBT incorporates is caregiver involvement (Kliethermes et al., 2017).

As mentioned above, to date, TF-CBT has the strongest empirical foundation. However, thus far, only a few studies have investigated the applicability and effectiveness of TF-CBT among preschoolers. Of studies performed, Cohen and Mannarino (1996) conducted the first randomized controlled treatment study more than 20 years ago. The authors found that, in contrast to the control group, the three- to six-year-old children who received TF-CBT showed a decline in overall behavior problems, as well as in internalizing symptoms. The results of the one-year follow-up demonstrated that the intervention group showed greater improvement over time than those in the control group (Cohen & Mannarino, 1997). A further study among two- to eight-year-old children showed that children exhibited a greater knowledge of body safety skills, and their

Table 8.3 Important treatment studies of posttraumatic stress in preschool-aged children

Author & Year	Trauma	N	Age	Treatment type	Design	Findings
Cohen & Mannarino (1996)	Sexual abuse	67	3–6	Trauma-Focused Cognitive Behavioral Therapy (TF-CBT)	RCT: Intervention vs Control (Nondirective supportive therapy)	Highly significant symptomatic improvement in TF-CBT group
Deblinger, Stauffer, & Steer (2001)	Sexual abuse	44	2–8	Trauma-Focused Cognitive Behavioral Therapy (TF-CBT) in a group format	RCT: Intervention vs Control (Supportive therapy)	Children in TF-CBT group showed greater improvement in knowledge about body safety skills; Mothers in TF-CBT group showed greater reductions in intrusive thoughts and negative emotional parental reactions.
Scheeringa, Weems, Cohen, Amaya-Jackson, & Guthrie (2011)	Variety of traumatic events	64	3–6	Trauma-Focused Cognitive Behavioral Therapy (TF-CBT)	RCT: TF-CBT vs Control (Wait List Condition)	TF-CBT showed to be more effective than the wait list condition for PTSD symptoms.
Herschell et al., (2017)	Domestic violence	21	2.5–7	Parent-Child Interaction Therapy (PCIT)	Pilot Study	Improvements in child behavior and reduction in mental health symptoms of the caregivers

Study	Population	N	Age	Intervention	Design	Outcomes
Keeshin, Oxman, Schindler, Campbell (2015)	Domestic violence	8	2–5	Combination of individual and group sessions based on a portion of Parent-Child Interaction Therapy (PCIT).	Case series of 8 mothers and their children	Mothers demonstrated an increased use of positive comments and an omission of negative comments when communicating with their children
Lieberman, Ippen, & Van Horn (2006)	Domestic violence and abuse	75	3–6	Child-Parent Psychotherapy (CPP)	RCT: Intervention vs. Control (case management plus community referral for individual treatment)	Children: Reduction in behavioral problems, posttraumatic stress symptoms, negative self-representation, and increased secure attachment and cognitive function; Parents: reduction in overall PTSD symptoms, especially avoidant behavior, and parental distress

Table 8.3 (Cont.)

Author & Year	Trauma	N	Age	Treatment type	Design	Findings
Toth, Maughan, Manly, Spagnola, Cicchetti (2002)	All types of maltreatment	112	2–5	Child-Parent Psychotherapy (CPP)	RCT: Intervention vs Control (psychoeducational home visitation or community standard)	The CPP group showed a greater decline in maladaptive maternal representations and displayed a greater decrease in negative self-representations than the control groups. As compared to the control, mother–child relationship expectations of CPP children became more positive over the course of the intervention.

Note: RCT: Randomized-controlled trial

parents increased reductions in intrusive thoughts and emotional distress, after receiving TF-CBT in a group format (Deblinger, Stauffer, & Steer, 2001). Finally, a more recent study by Scheeringa and colleagues (Scheeringa, Weems, Cohen, Amaya-Jackson, & Guthrie, 2011) found that an age-adapted manualized 12-session TF-CBT protocol was effective in reducing PTSD symptoms in three- to six-year-olds after experiencing a variety of traumatic events. Taken together, there are a few studies that show that TF-CBT seems effective in treating PTSD in two- to six-year-old children. However, adaptation of the original TF-CBT protocol to younger children might be necessary. Recently, Scheeringa (2016) has published the first CBT treatment manual for preschool age.

Child-Parent Psychotherapy

Another important intervention used in the preschool age group is referred to as *Child-Parent Psychotherapy (CPP)*. This manualized therapy is designed for children from birth to five years of age after exposure to a traumatic event, such as domestic violence, who subsequently show attachment, behavioral, or emotional problems. The main objectives of CPP are: to support the parent-child relationship in order to aid the child in regaining a sense of trust and safety; to regulate affect associated with the trauma; to create a common language to describe the traumatic incident; and, to assist the parent in responding to and supporting the child in developmentally adequate ways. CPP is typically conducted as a year-long intervention with weekly 60-minute sessions with the primary caregiver, the child and the therapist. CPP may take place either in the clinic, the family's home, the child's school, or any other space the family feels secure and comfortable (Lieberman et al., 2015; Reyes, Stone, Dimmler, & Lieberman, 2017).

To date several studies have shown the effectiveness of CPP among preschoolers. Results have demonstrated that CPP significantly reduced children's behavioral problems, posttraumatic stress symptoms, negative self-representation, as well as increased secure attachment and cognitive function. When examining the parental gains of CPP the results indicate a reduction in overall PTSD symptoms, especially avoidant behavior, and parental distress (e.g. Lieberman, Ippen, & Van Horn, 2006).

Parent-Child Interaction Therapy

Parent-Child interaction therapy (PCIT) is a manualized intervention (Dyadic Parent-Child Interaction Coding System) designed for young children (ages two to seven years) and their parents (Eyberg et al., 2013). Originally, it was developed for children with disruptive behavioral issues with the aim of improving child behavior, the parent-child relationship, as well as reducing parental stress. Nowadays PCIT is a widely used intervention to treat young children with trauma-related disorders.

PCIT has a unique approach as it coaches parents during interaction with their child. The therapy is built upon two main components, namely Child-Directed Interaction (CDI) and Parent-Directed Interaction (PDI) which are consecutively applied. The focus of PCIT is to attempt a modification of interaction patterns between child and parent. The first phase of treatment (CDI) is based on attachment theory and concepts from play therapy. Through play therapy techniques and praise of positive behaviors, the parent helps the child find appropriate behaviors and new ways of reacting in multiple situations. The second phase of the therapy (PDI) focuses on discipline and limit setting. With guidance from the therapist, the parent develops helpful tools that can be implemented in a variety of settings. The 12–20 clinic-based, hourly therapy sessions take place at weekly intervals with the parent and the child (Herschell, Scudder, Schaffner, & Slagel, 2017).

Treatment effects of PCIT have been demonstrated among two- to seven-year-old children with a wide array of behavioral difficulties (for a review, see Cooley, Veldorale-Griffin, Petren, & Mullis, 2014). After exposure to potentially traumatic events, completion of PCIT was associated with improved child behavior, parenting practices, and parental mental health symptoms (Herschell et al., 2017). Taken together, PCIT is a very promising approach to treat young children with trauma-related behavioral disorders.

Outlook and Challenges

There is now a sufficient body of research demonstrating that young children are at a considerably high risk of exposure to potentially traumatic events and, subsequently, for developing PTSD and other disorders. In the long term, childhood trauma has been found to impact adult mental and physical health substantially (Felitti et al., 1998). The findings highlight the crucial role of parents, primary caregivers and family when working with traumatized children. Research also indicates that risk factors for developing and maintaining posttraumatic reactions in young children might differ from those in older children, adolescents, and adults, as the social environment has an even more central role in this young population. Because factors for developing and maintaining PTSD differ in children and adults, so do the traumatic events themselves. Likewise, it has also been shown that the manifestation of posttraumatic symptoms is different in preschoolers than in older children and adults. Therefore, the inclusion of a developmentally more suitable subtype of PTSD for young children in the DSM-5 (APA, 2013) marks an important step in adequately capturing the symptoms of young children. However, studies examining the validity of these new criteria in young children are still lacking. Another challenge for future research will be to develop standardized measures to assess PTSD in the preschool child. Finally, while there is some promising evidence regarding psychotherapeutic treatments in young children with trauma-related disorders, there is still more research to be done with regard to development and evaluation of psychotherapeutic interventions in this age group.

References

Achenbach, T. M., & Rescorla, L. A. (2000). *Manual for the ASEBA Preschool Forms and Profiles*. Burlington, VT: University of Vermont, Research Center for Children, Youth, & Families.

American Psychiatric Association (APA). (1994). *Diagnostic and statistical manual of mental disorders* (4th ed.). Washington, DC: American Psychiatric Association.

American Psychiatric Association (APA). (2000). *Diagnostic and statistical manual of mental disorders* (4th ed., text rev.). Washington, DC: American Psychiatric Association.

American Psychiatric Association (APA). (2013). *Diagnostic and statistical manual of mental disorders* (5th ed.). Arlington, VA: American Psychiatric Publishing.

Bakker, A., van der Heijden, P. G. M., van Son, M. J. M., van de Schoot, R., Vandermeulen, E., Helsen, A., & Van Loey, N. E. E. (2014). The relationship between behavioural problems in preschool children and parental distress after a paediatric burn event. *European Child & Adolescent Psychiatry*. doi:10.1007/s00787-00014-0518-y

Bogat, G. A., DeJonghe, E., Levendosky, A. A., Davidson, W. S., & von Eye, A. (2006). Trauma symptoms among infants exposed to intimate partner violence. *Child Abuse & Neglect*, 30(2), 109–125. doi:10.1016/j.chiabu.2005.09.002

Borse, N. N., Gilchrist, J., Dellinger, A. M., Rudd, R. A., Ballesteros, M. F., & Sleet, D. A. (2008). *CDC childhood injury report: patterns of unintentional injuries among 0–19 year olds in the United States, 2000–2006*. Atlanta, GA: Centers for Disease Control and Prevention, National Center for Injury Prevention and Control. Retrieved from https://www.cdc.gov/safechild/pdf/cdc-childhoodinjury.pdf

Briere, J., Johnson, K., Bissada, A., Damon, L., Crouch, J., Gil, E., ... Ernst, V. (2001). The Trauma Symptom Checklist for Young Children (TSCYC): reliability and association with abuse exposure in a multi-site study. *Child Abuse & Neglect*, 25(8), 1001–1014. doi:10.1016/S0145-2134(01)00253-00258

Briggs-Gowan, M. J., Ford, J. D., Fraleigh, L., McCarthy, K., & Carter, A. S. (2010). Prevalence of exposure to potentially traumatic events in a healthy birth cohort of very young children in the northeastern United States. *Journal of Traumatic Stress*, 23(6), 725–733. doi:10.1002/jts.20593

Carpenter, G. L., & Stacks, A. M. (2009). Developmental effects of exposure to Intimate Partner Violence in early childhood: A review of the literature. *Children and Youth Services Review*, 31(8), 831–839. doi:10.1016/j.childyouth.2009.03.005

Chu, A. T., & Lieberman, A. F. (2010). Clinical implications of traumatic stress from birth to age five. *Annual Review of Clinical Psychology*, 6, 469–494. doi:10.1146/annurev.clinpsy.121208.131204

Coates, S., & Gaensbauer, T. J. (2009). Event trauma in early childhood: symptoms, assessment, intervention. *Child and Adolescent Psychiatric Clinics of North America*, 18(3), 611–626. doi:10.1016/j.chc.2009.03.005

Cohen, E., & Gadassi, R. (2009). Effects of trauma on children, adolescents, and/ or their caregivers posttraumatic stress disorder in young children exposed to terrorism: Validation of the alternative diagnostic criteria PTSD in young children exposed to terrorism. *Journal of Child & Adolescent Trauma*, 2(4), 229–241. doi:10.1080/19361520903317295

Cohen, J. A., & Mannarino, A. P. (1996). A treatment outcome study of sexually abused preschool children: initial findings. *Journal of the American Academy of Child and Adolescent Psychiatry*, 35, 1402–1410.

Cohen, J. A., & Mannarino, A. P. (1997). A treatment study for sexually abused preschool children: Outcome during a one-year follow-up. *Journal of the American Academy of Child & Adolescent Psychiatry*, 36(9), 1228–1235. doi:10.1097/00004583-199709000-00015

Cohen, J. A., Mannarino, A. P., & Deblinger, E. (eds.) (2016). *Trauma-focused CBT for children and adolescents: Treatment applications*. New York: Guilford Press.

Cohen, J. A., & Scheeringa, M. S. (2009). Post-traumatic stress disorder diagnosis in children: challenges and promises. *Dialogues in Clinical Neuroscience*, 11(1), 91–99. Retrieved from http://www.ncbi.nlm.nih.gov/pubmed/19432391

Conway, A., Mcdonough, S. C., Mackenzie, M. J., Follett, C., & Sameroff, A. (2013). Stress-related changes in toddlers and their mothers following the attack of September 11. *American Journal of Orthopsychiatry*, 83(4), 536–544. http://doi.org/10.1111/ajop.12055

Cook, A., Blaustein, M., Spinazzola, J., & van der Kolk, B. A. (2003). *Complex trauma in children and adolescents*. National Child Traumatic Stress Network. Retrieved from http://www.nctsnet.org

Cooley, M. E., Veldorale-Griffin, A., Petren, R. E., & Mullis, A. K. (2014). Parent–child interaction therapy: A meta-analysis of child behavior outcomes and parent stress. *Journal of Family Social Work*, 17(3), 191–208. doi:10.1080/10522158.2014.888696

DeVoe, E. R., Bannon, W. M., Jr., & Klein, T. P. (2006). Post-9/11 helpseeking by New York City parents on behalf of highly exposed young children. *American Journal of Orthopsychiatry*, 76(2), 167–175.

De Young, A. C., Haag, A.C., Kenardy, J. A., Kimble, R. M., & Landolt, M. A. (2016). Coping with Accident Reactions (CARE) early intervention programme for preventing traumatic stress reactions in young injured children: Study protocol for two randomised controlled trials. *Trials*, 17(1). http://doi.org/10.1186/s13063-016-1490-2

De Young, A. C., Hendrikz, J., Kenardy, J. A., Cobham, V. E., & Kimble, R. M. (2014). Prospective evaluation of parent distress following pediatric burns and identification of risk factors for young child and parent posttraumatic stress disorder. *Journal of Child and Adolescent Psychopharmacology*, 24(1), 9–17. doi:10.1089/cap.2013.0066

De Young, A. C., Kenardy, J. A., & Cobham, V. E. (2011). Diagnosis of post-traumatic stress disorder in preschool children. *Journal of Clinical Child and Adolescent Psychology*, 40(3), 375–384. doi:10.1080/15374416.2011.563474

De Young, A. C., Kenardy, J. A., Cobham, V. E., & Kimble, R. (2012). Prevalence, comorbidity and course of trauma reactions in young burn-injured children. *Journal of Child Psychology and Psychiatry, and Allied Disciplines*, 53(1), 56–63. doi:10.1111/j.1469–7610.2011.02431.x

Deblinger, E., Stauffer, L. B., & Steer, R. A. (2001). Comparative efficacies of supportive and cognitive behavioral group therapies for young children who have been sexually abused and their nonoffending mothers. *Child Maltreatment*, 6(4), 332–343. doi:10.1177/1077559501006004006

Dehon, C., & Scheeringa, M. S. (2006). Screening for preschool posttraumatic stress disorder with the Child Behavior Checklist. *Journal of Pediatric Psychology*, 31(4), 431–435. doi:10.1093/jpepsy/jsj006

Drake, J. E., Stoddard, F. J., Murphy, J. M., Ronfeldt, H., Snidman, N., Kagan, J., ... Sheridan, R. (2006). Trauma severity influences acute stress in young burned children. *Journal of Burn Care & Research*, 27, 174–182. doi:10.1097/01. BCR.0000202618.51001.69

Eyberg, S. M., Nelson, M. M., Ginn, N. C., Bhuiyan, N., & Boggs, S. . (2013). *Dyadic Parent-Child Interaction Coding System: Comprehensive manual for research and training* (4th ed.). Gainesville: PCIT International.

Feldman, R., & Vengrober, A. (2011). Posttraumatic stress disorder in infants and young children exposed to war-related trauma. *Journal of the American Academy of Child and Adolescent Psychiatry*, 50(7), 645–658. doi:10.1016/j. jaac.2011.03.001

Felitti, V. . J., Anda, R. F., Nordenberg, D., Williamson, D. F., Spitz, A. M., Edwards, V., ... Marks, J. S. (1998). Relationship of childhood abuse and household dysfunction to many of the leading causes of death in adults. *American Journal of Preventive Medicine*, 14, 245–258.

Finkelhor, D., Ormrod, R. K., & Turner, H. A. (2009). Lifetime assessment of poly-victimization in a national sample of children and youth. *Child Abuse & Neglect*, 33(7), 403–411. doi:10.1016/j.chiabu.2008.09.012

Finkelhor, D., Turner, H., Ormrod, R., Hambly, S., & Kracke, K. (2009). *Children's exposure to violence: A comprehensive national survey*. Washington, DC: U. S. Department of Justice, Office of Justice Programs, Office of Juvenile Justice and Delinquency Prevention. Retrieved from https://www.ncjrs.gov/pdffiles1/ ojjdp/227744.pdf

Fusco, R. A., & Fantuzzo, J. W. (2009). Domestic violence crimes and children: A population-based investigation of direct sensory exposure and the nature of involvement. *Children and Youth Services Review*, 31(2), 249–256. doi:10.1016/j. childyouth.2008.07.017

Gigengack, M. R., van Meijel, E. P. M., Alisic, E., & Lindauer, R. J. L. (2015). Comparing three diagnostic algorithms of posttraumatic stress in young children exposed to accidental trauma: an exploratory study. *Child and Adolescent Psychiatry and Mental Health*, 9(1), 14. doi:10.1186/s13034–13015–0046–0047

Goldbeck, L., & Jensen, T. K. (2017). The diagnostic spectrum of trauma-related disorders in children and adolescents. In M. A. Landolt, M. Cloitre, & U. Schnyder (Eds.), *Evidence-based treatments for trauma* (pp. 3–28). Cham: Springer International Publishing AG.

Graf, A., Schiestl, C., & Landolt, M. A. (2011). Posttraumatic stress and behavior problems in infants and toddlers with burns. *Journal of Pediatric Psychology*, 36(8), 923–931. doi:10.1093/jpepsy/jsr021

Graham-Bermann, S. A., Castor, L. E., Miller, L. E., & Howell, K. H. (2012). The impact of intimate partner violence and additional traumatic events on trauma symptoms and PTSD in preschool-aged children. *Journal of Traumatic Stress, 25* (4), 393–400. doi:10.1002/jts.21724

Graham-Bermann, S. A., Howell, K., Habarth, J., Krishnan, S., Loree, A., & Bermann, E. A. (2008). Toward assessing traumatic events and stress symptoms in preschool children from low-income families. *American Journal of Orthopsychiatry, 78*(2), 220–228. doi:10.1037/a0013977

Grasso, D. J., Ford, J. D., & Briggs-Gowan, M. J. (2013). Early life trauma exposure and stress sensitivity in young children. *Journal of Pediatric Psychology, 38* (1), 94–103. doi:10.1093/jpepsy/jss101

Grasso, D. J., Petitclerc, A., Henry, D. B., McCarthy, K. J., Wakschlag, L. S., & Briggs-Gowan, M. J. (2016). Examining patterns of exposure to family violence in preschool children: A latent class approach. *Journal of Traumatic Stress, 29*(6), 491–499. doi:10.1002/jts.22147

Grossman, D. C. (2000). The history of injury control and the epidemiology of child and adolescent injuries. In R. E. Behrman (Ed.), *The future of children* (pp. 4–22). Los Altos, CA: David and Lucile Packard Foundation.

Haag, A.-C., & Landolt, M. A. (2017). Young children's acute stress after a burn injury: Disentangling the role of injury severity and parental acute stress. *Journal of Pediatric Psychology, 42*, 861–870. doi:10.1093/jpepsy/jsx059

Hagan, M. J., Sulik, M. J., & Lieberman, A. F. (2016). Traumatic life events and psychopathology in a high risk, ethnically diverse sample of young children: A person-centered approach. *Journal of Abnormal Child Psychology, 44*(5), 833–844. doi:10.1007/s10802–10015–0078–0078

Hamby, S., Finkelhor, D., Turner, H., & Ormrod, R. (2011). *Children's exposure to intimate partner violence and other family violence.* Washington, DC: U.S. Department of Justice, Office of Justice Programs, Office of Juvenile Justice and Delinquency Prevention. Retrieved from https://www.ncjrs.gov/pdffiles1/ojjdp/grants/248444.pdf

Hamiel, D., Wolmer, L., Pardo-Aviv, L., & Laor, N. (2017). Addressing the needs of preschool children in the context of disasters and terrorism: Clinical pictures and moderating factors. *Current Psychiatry Reports.* doi:10.1007/s11920–11017–0793–0797

Herschell, A. D., Scudder, A. B., Schaffner, K. F., & Slagel, L. A. (2017). Feasibility and effectiveness of parent–child interaction therapy with victims of domestic violence: A pilot study. *Journal of Child and Family Studies, 26*(1), 271–283. doi:10.1007/s10826–10016–0546-y

Hoffman, J. I. E., & Kaplan, S. (2002). The incidence of congenital heart disease. *Journal of the American College of Cardiology, 39*(12). doi:10.1016/S0735–1097(02)01886–01887

Hooper, K., Zong, J., Capps, R., & Fix, M. (2016). *Young children of refugees in the United States: Integration successes and challenges.* Washington, DC: Migration Policy Institute. Retrieved from http://www.migrationpolicy.org/research/young-children-refugees-united-states-integration-successes-and-challenges

Kaufman-Shriqui, V., Werbeloff, N., Faroy, M., Meiri, G., Shahar, D. R., Fraser, D., ... Harpaz-Rotem, I. (2013). Posttraumatic stress disorder among preschoolers exposed to ongoing missile attacks in the Gaza war. *Depression and Anxiety.* doi:10.1002/da.22121

Keeshin, B. R., Oxman, A., Schindler, S., & Campbell, K. A. (2015). A domestic violence shelter parent training program for mothers with young children. *Journal of Family Violence, 30*(4), 461–466.

Kessler, R. C., McLaughlin, K. A., Green, J. G., Gruber, M. J., Sampson, N. A., Zaslavsky, A. M., ... Williams, D. R. (2010). Childhood adversities and adult psychopathology in the WHO World Mental Health Surveys. *The British Journal of Psychiatry*, 197(5). doi:10.1192/bjp.bp.110.080499

Kliethermes, M. D., Dreary, K., & Wamser-Nanney, R. (2017). Trauma-focused cognitive behavioral therapy. In M. A. Landolt, M. Cloitre, & U. Schnyder (Eds.), *Evidence-based treatment for trauma related disorders in children and adolescents* (pp. 167–187). Switzerland: Springer International Publishing.

Kochanek, K. D., Murphy, S. L., Xu, J., & Tejada-Vera, B. (2016). Deaths: Final data for 2014. *National Vital Statistics Reports*, 65(4).

Lambert, H. K., Meza, R., Martin, P., Fearey, E., & McLaughlin, K. A. (2017). Childhood trauma as a public health issue. In M. A. Landolt, M. Cloitre, & U. Schnyder (Eds.), *Evidence-based treatments for trauma related disorders in children and adolescents* (pp. 49–66). Switzerland: Springer International Publishing Switzerland.

Landolt, M. A. (2012). *Psychotraumatologie des Kindesalters. Grundlagen, Diagnostik und Interventionen* (2nd ed.). Goettingen: Hogrefe.

Landolt, M.A., Cloitre, M., & Schnyder, U. (Eds.) (2017). *Evidence-based treatments of trauma related disorders in children and adolescents*. New York: Springer.

Laor, N., Wolmer, L., & Cohen, D. J. (2001). Mothers' functioning and children's symptoms 5 years after a SCUD missile attack. *American Journal of Psychiatry*, 158(7), 1020–1026. doi:10.1176/appi.ajp.158.7.1020

Laor, N., Wolmer, L., Mayes, L. C., Gershon, A., Weizman, R., & Cohen, D. J. (1997). Israeli preschool children under Scuds: a 30-month follow-up. *Journal of the American Academy of Child and Adolescent Psychiatry*, 36(3), 349–356. doi:10.1097/00004583-199703000-00013

Levendosky, A. A., Huth-Bocks, A. C., Semel, M. A., & Shapiro, D. L. (2002). Trauma symptoms in preschool-age children exposed to domestic violence. *Journal of Interpersonal Violence*, 17(2), 150–164.

Lieberman, A. F., Chu, A., Van Horn, P., & Harris, W. W. (2011). Trauma in early childhood: Empirical evidence and clinical implications. *Development and Psychopathology*, 23(2), 397–410. http://doi.org/10.1017/S0954579411000137

Lieberman, A. F., Ippen, C. G., & Van Horn, P. (2006). Child-parent psychotherapy: 6-month follow-up of a randomized controlled trial. *Journal of the American Academy of Child and Adolescent Psychiatry*, 45, 913–918.

Lieberman, A. F., Ippen, C. G., & Van Horn, P. (2015). *Don't hit my mommy!: A manual for child-parent psychotherapy with young children exposed to violence and other trauma* (2nd ed.). Washington: Zero to Three.

Linares, L. O., Heeren, T., Bronfman, E., Zuckerman, B., Augustyn, M., & Tronick, E. (2001). A mediational model for the impact of exposure to community violence on early child behavior problems. *Child Development*, 72(2), 639–652. doi:10.1111/1467-8624.00302

Maercker, A., Brewin, C. R., Bryant, R. A., Cloitre, M., van Ommeren, M., Jones, L. M., ... Reed, G. M. (2013). Diagnosis and classification of disorders specifically associated with stress: proposals for ICD-11. *World Psychiatry*, 12(3), 198–206. doi:10.1002/wps.20057

Marsac, M. L., Kassam-Adams, N., Delahanty, D. L., Widaman, K. F., & Barakat, L. P. (2014). Posttraumatic stress following acute medical trauma in children: A proposed model of bio-psycho-social processes during the peri-trauma period. *Clinical Child and Family Psychology Review*. doi:10.1007/s10567–10014–0174–0172

McCrae, J. S., Chapman, M. V, & Christ, S. L. (2006). Profile of children investigated for sexual abuse: Association with psychopathology symptoms and services. *American Journal of Orthopsychiatry*, 76(4), 468–481. doi:10.1037/0002–9432.76.4.468

Meiser-Stedman, R., Smith, P., Glucksman, E., Yule, W., & Dalgleish, T. (2008). The posttraumatic stress disorder diagnosis in preschool- and elementary school-age children exposed to motor vehicle accidents. *American Journal of Psychiatry*, 165, 1326–1337. doi:10.1176/appi.ajp.2008.07081282

Meiser-Stedman, R., Smith, P., Yule, W., Glucksman, E., & Dalgleish, T. (2017). Posttraumatic stress disorder in young children 3 years posttrauma: Prevalence and longitudinal predictors. *The Journal of Clinical Psychiatry*, 78(3), 334–339. doi:10.4088/JCP.15m10002

Milot, T., St-Laurent, D., Ethier, L. S., & Provost, M. A. (2010). Trauma-related symptoms in neglected preschoolers and affective quality of mother-child communication. *Child Maltreatment*, 15(4), 293–304. doi:10.1177/1077559510379153

Müller, J. M., Achtergarde, S., & Furniss, T. (2011). The influence of maternal psychopathology on ratings of child psychiatric symptoms: an SEM analysis on cross-informant agreement. *European Child & Adolescent Psychiatry*, 20(5), 241–252. doi:10.1007/s00787–00011–0168–0162

Ohmi, H., Kojima, S., Awai, Y., Kamata, S., Sasaki, K., Tanaka, Y., ... Hata, A. (2002). Post-traumatic stress disorder in pre-school aged children after a gas explosion. *European Journal of Pediatrics*, 161, 643–648. doi:10.1007/s00431–00002–1061–1062

Pat-Horenczyk, R., Cohen, S., Ziv, Y., Achituv, M., Brickman, S., Blanchard, T., & Brom, D. (2017). Stability and change in posttraumatic distress: A 7-year follow-up study of mothers and young children exposed to cumulative trauma. *Journal of Traumatic Stress*, 30(2), 115–124. doi:10.1002/jts.22177

Pat-Horenczyk, R., Ziv, Y., Asulin-Peretz, L., Achituv, M., Cohen, S., & Brom, D. (2013). Relational trauma in times of political violence: Continuous versus past traumatic stress. *Peace and Conflict: Journal of Peace Psychology*, 19(2), 125–137.

Reyes, V., Stone, B. J., Dimmler, M. H., & Lieberman, A. F. (2017). Child-parent psychotherapy: An evidence-based treatment for infant and young children. In M. A. Landolt, M. Cloitre, & U. Schnyder (Eds.), *Evidence-based treatment for trauma related disorders in children and adolescents* (pp. 321–340). Switzerland: Springer International Publishing.

Roberts, Y. H., Ferguson, M., & Crusto, C. A. (2013). Exposure to traumatic events and health-related quality of life in preschool-aged children. *Quality of Life Research*, 22(8), 2159–2168. doi:10.1007/s11136–11012–0330–0334

Saunders, B. E., & Adams, Z. W. (2014). Epidemiology of traumatic experiences in childhood. *Child and Adolescent Psychiatric Clinics of North America*, 23(2), 167–184. doi:10.1016/j.chc.2013.12.003

Scheeringa, M. S. (2010). *Young child PTSD checklist* (Version 5/). New Orleans: Tulane University.

Scheeringa, M. S. (2016). *Treating PTSD in preschoolers: A clinical guide*. New York: Guilford Press.

Scheeringa, M. S., & Haslett, N. (2010). The reliability and criterion validity of the Diagnostic Infant and Preschool Assessment: a new diagnostic instrument for young children. *Child Psychiatry and Human Development*, 41(3), 299–312. doi:10.1007/s10578–10009–0169–0162

Scheeringa, M. S., Myers, L., Putnam, F. W., & Zeanah, C. H. (2012). Diagnosing PTSD in early childhood: An empirical assessment of four approaches. *Journal of Traumatic Stress*, 25(4), 359–367. doi:10.1002/jts.21723

Scheeringa, M. S., Peebles, C. D., Cook, C. A., & Zeanah, C. H. (2001). Toward establishing procedural, criterion, and discrimant validity for PTSD in early childhood. *Journal of the American Academy of Child and Adolescent Psychiatry*, 40, 52–60.

Scheeringa, M. S., Weems, C. F., Cohen, J. A., Amaya-Jackson, L., & Guthrie, D. (2011). Trauma-focused cognitive-behavioral therapy for posttraumatic stress disorder in three-through six-year-old children: a randomized clinical trial. *Journal of Child Psychology and Psychiatry, and Allied Disciplines*, 52(8), 853–860. doi:10.1111/j.1469–7610.2010.02354.x

Scheeringa, M. S., Wright, M. J., Hunt, J. P., & Zeanah, C. H. (2006). Factors affecting the diagnosis and prediction of PTSD symptomatology in children and adolescents. *American Journal of Psychiatry*, 163, 644–651.

Scheeringa, M. S., & Zeanah, C. H. (1995). Symptom expression and trauma variables in children under 48 months of age. *Infant Mental Health Journal*, 16(4), 259–270.

Scheeringa, M. S., & Zeanah, C. H. (2001). A relational perspective on PTSD in early childhood. *Journal of Traumatic Stress*, 14, 799–815.

Scheeringa, M. S., & Zeanah, C. H. (2008). Reconsideration of harm's way: onsets and comorbidity patterns of disorders in preschool children and their caregivers following Hurricane Katrina. *Journal of Clinical Child and Adolescent Psychology: The Official Journal for the Society of Clinical Child and Adolescent Psychology, American Psychological Association, Division 53*, 37(3), 508–518. doi:10.1080/15374410802148178

Scheeringa, M. S., Zeanah, C. H., Drell, M. J., & Larrieu, J. A. (1995). Two approaches to the diagnosis of posttraumatic stress disorder in infancy and early childhood. *Journal of the American Academy of Child and Adolescent Psychiatry*, 34(2), 191–200.

Scheeringa, M. S., Zeanah, C. H., Myers, L., & Putnam, F. W. (2003). New findings on alternative criteria for PTSD in preschool children. *Journal of the American Academy of Child & Adolescent Psychiatry*, 42, 561–570. doi:10.1097/01.CHI.0000046822.95464.14

Scheeringa, M. S., Zeanah, C. H., Myers, L., & Putnam, F. W. (2005). Predictive validity in a prospective follow-up of PTSD in preschool children. *Journal of the American Academy of Child & Adolescent Psychiatry*, 44, 899–906. doi:10.1097/01.chi.0000169013.81536.71

Schiestl, C., Beynon, C., & Balmer, B. (2007). What are the differences? Treatment of burns in children compared to treatment in adults. *Osteosynthesis and Trauma Care*, 15(1), 26–28. doi:10.1055/s-2007–970069

Slone, M., & Mann, S. (2016). Effects of war, terrorism and armed conflict on young children: A systematic review. *Child Psychiatry and Human Development*, 47, 950–965. doi:10.1007/s10578–10016–0626–0627

Solomon, E. P., & Heide, K. M. (1999). Type III trauma: Toward a more effective conceptualization of psychological trauma. *International Journal of Offender*

Therapy   and   Comparative   Criminology,   43(2),   202–210.   doi:10.1177/
0306624X99432007

Stoddard, F. J., Saxe, G., Ronfeldt, H., Drake, J. E., Burns, J., Edgren, C., &
Sheridan, R. (2006). Acute stress symptoms in young children with burns.
Journal of the American Academy of Child and Adolescent Psychiatry, 45, 87–93.
doi:10.1097/01.chi.0000184934.71917.3a

Stoddard, F. J., Sorrentino, E., Drake, J. E., Murphy, J. M., Kim, A. J., Romo, S.,
. . . Sheridan, R. L. (2017). Posttraumatic stress disorder diagnosis in young
children with burns. *Journal of Burn Care Research*, 38(1), e343–e351.
doi:10.1097/bcr.0000000000000386

Terr, L. C. (1991). Childhood traumas: an outline and overview. *American Journal
of Psychiatry*, 148(1), 10–20.

Toth, S. L., Maughan, A., Manly, J. T., Spagnola, M., & Cicchetti, D. (2002). The
relative efficacy of two interventions in altering maltreated preschool children's
representational models: Implications for attachment theory. *Development and
Psychopathology*, 14(4), 877–908.

U.S. Cancer Statistics Working Group. (2017). *United States cancer statistics: 1999–
2014 incidence and mortality web-based report*. Retrieved July 27, 2017, from
http://www.cdc.gov/uscs

U.S. Department of Health & Human Services, Administration for Children and
Families, Administration on Children, Youth and Families, C. B. (2017). *Child
maltreatment 2015*. Retrieved from http://www.acf.hhs.gov/programs/cb/resea
rch-data-technology/statistics-research/child-maltreatment.

United Nations High Commissioner for Refugees. (2017). *Global trends - Forced
displacement in 2016*. Geneva: UNHCR.

Williamson, V., Creswell, C., Fearon, P., Hiller, R. M., Walker, J., & Halligan, S.
L. (2017). The role of parenting behaviors in childhood post-traumatic stress
disorder: A meta-analytic review. *Clinical Psychology Review*, 53, 1–13.
doi:10.1016/j.cpr.2017.01.005

Wolmer, L., Hamiel, D., Versano-Eisman, T., Slone, M., Margalit, N., & Laor,
N. (2015). Preschool Israeli children exposed to rocket attacks: Assessment,
risk, and resilience. *Journal of Traumatic Stress*, 28, 1–7. doi:10.1002/jts.22040

Zero to Three. (2005). *Diagnostic classification of mental health and developmental
disorders of infancy and early childhood: revised edition (DC:0–3R)*. Washington,
DC: Zero To Three Press.

9 Selective Mutism in Preschool-Aged Children

R. Lindsey Bergman and Araceli Gonzalez

Selective mutism is a childhood-onset behavioral condition characterized by a consistent absence of speech in one or more settings (e.g., at school) despite unimpaired and typical, or close to typical, speaking in other contexts (e.g., at home). Selective mutism often interferes with education and social development, as selective mutism is often associated with difficulty speaking with teachers and peers, although impairment can occur in other settings as well (Bergman, Keller, Piacentini, & Bergman, 2008). Symptoms often first appear in the preschool age, with onset typically before age five, or before the start of school. However, the extent of the severity of selective mutism and lack of speech may not become clear until the child enters the pre-school or school setting and the demands of speaking to others outside the home increase. Importantly, because many children experience emotional difficulties when starting school, a diagnosis of selective mutism cannot be made during the first month of a child starting school (APA, 2013).

Clinical Features

Although there is no clear consensus on the etiology of selective mutism, there is a growing conceptualization of selective mutism as closely related to other anxiety disorders. Consistent with this emerging conceptualization, selective mutism was re-classified from Disorders Usually First Diagnosed in Infancy, Childhood, or Adolescence to the category of Anxiety Disorders in the current edition of the DSM (DSM-5). According to DSM-5 Criteria, a diagnosis of selective mutism requires:

(a) consistent failure to speak in specific social situations in which there is an expectation for speaking (e.g., at school) despite speaking in other situations; (b) the disturbance interferes with educational or occupational achievement or with social communication; (c) the duration of the disturbance is at least 1 month (not limited to the first month of school); (d) the failure to speak is not attributable to a lack of knowledge of, or comfort with, the spoken language required in the social situation; and (e) the disturbance is not better explained by a communication disorder … and does not occur exclusively during the course of autism spectrum disorder, schizophrenia, or another psychotic disorder.

(APA, 2013, p. 195)

The child's ability to speak unimpaired in at least one setting is critical to an accurate diagnosis of selective mutism. In the large majority of cases, the setting in which the child *does* speak is the home environment. Children with selective mutism are typically able to speak freely with parents and siblings, although there may be some specific family members, usually extended family, with which the child will have limited or no speech. Families of children with selective mutism may even report that the child seems to be "overly" talkative at home. A child who persistently fails to speak entirely at home with immediate family members should be referred for further evaluation of conditions other than selective mutism.

Unique Features of Selective Mutism in Preschool-aged Children

For many children, a total absence of speech first appears in a school or other structured setting, most often with teachers or adults outside the home (Bergman et al., 2008). Prior to entering school, a child who develops selective mutism may be viewed as behaviorally inhibited or shy. Symptoms of selective mutism may first become apparent when children fail to speak to extended family members or other adults outside the home, including coaches, cashiers, and restaurant servers, although the extent of the mutism may not yet be clear. For instance, parents might report that the child failed to speak to strangers or with extended family members that the child did not see often. In these situations, it is easy for a parent to accommodate the child's anxiety in this scenario, or because this behavior is viewed as shyness due to unfamiliarity with the individual, no significant impairment is noted. However, the mutism becomes problematic in a setting such as school because the parent or siblings are no longer present to help the child communicate with others. Children with selective mutism may experience moderate or severe functional impairment in the academic setting because a failure to speak to or in front of teachers makes it difficult for the child to perform certain academic tasks (e.g., sharing a book report) and for the teacher to assess the child's educational level, learning, and readiness for school.

In some cases, there may be a complete absence of speech in a particular setting. For instance, some children will fail to speak at school or in the classroom to teachers and peers alike. In other cases, the lack of speech may depend on the context within that setting, or follow an idiosyncratic pattern. For example, in a school setting, a child may speak to peers but not to teachers or other adults. Some children may display other idiosyncrasies in their speaking patterns, such as "speaking through" peers (i.e., whispering to a peer and letting the peer communicate verbally with a teacher on their behalf), speaking with a low volume or odd voice, or using one-word phrases. In an applied sense, the label of selective mutism can generally be used to describe children who are consistently reluctant to speak or display low frequency of speech. Although some argue that children who speak inconsistently, reluctantly, or with low volume do not meet criteria for selective mutism, children with selective mutism who completely fail to speak in some situations, or to some people in some settings, often speak inconsistently or reluctantly in others.

While the presence of selective mutism is determined on the basis of speaking behavior, non-verbal social behavior can vary widely among children with selective mutism. Interestingly, even though selective mutism is categorized as an anxiety disorder, in some cases there are no visible signs of anxiety aside from the failure to speak. Some children may engage in social non-verbal behaviors, such as pulling someone by the hand or pointing to direct their attention, dancing, raising their hand in class (though often not speaking when called upon), or smiling for a photo. In many cases, however, children with selective mutism will experience difficulty or distress with nonverbal tasks like those listed above, as well as other socially-relevant tasks such as eating or writing in front of others. In some cases, difficulty with such non-verbal tasks may be prominent and can be an indication of the presence of co-morbid social anxiety disorder since selective mutism refers only to difficulties with verbal communication (i.e., speaking).

Differential Diagnoses

Because children with selective mutism fail to speak in one or more settings, this presentation can be perceived by some as a symptom of other conditions related to communication and verbal skills, social awareness and competence, anxiety, and/or oppositional behavior. As previously stated, typical or unimpaired speech in at least one setting is key in a diagnosis of selective mutism. This is essential in ruling out a communication or language disorder. Table 9.1 includes a summary of conditions for which selective mutism might be mistaken, including some overlapping clinical features and factors that may aid in differential diagnosis.

Children with selective mutism may wrongfully receive a diagnosis of autism spectrum disorder due to commonalities among the two conditions in terms of communication difficulties (i.e., lack of or limited speech) and discomfort in social interactions (Simms, 2017). In assessing a child, it is critical to note that the language deficits of a child with autism are not context-dependent, whereas the lack of speech observed in

Table 9.1 Tips for differential diagnoses; similarities and differences between selective mutism

Disorder/Condition	Potential clinical overlap with Selective Mutism	Distinguishing factors
Autism Spectrum Disorder	• Limited or no verbal communication • Poor eye contact • Limited social engagement and discomfort in social interaction	• With ASD, the communication deficits are pervasive; with SM, the lack of speaking is context-dependent (typically at school) • With SM, the child may have no difficulty with social communication and interaction with family members
Expressive or receptive language disorders	• Difficulty expressing thoughts or ideas • It may be difficult to assess the child's language abilities	• Expressive and receptive language disorders are often apparent to parents from a young age (e.g., before age 4; "late talkers") and are pervasive; with SM, the speech difficulty is context-dependent • Children with SM only do not have difficulty following with comprehension and can follow instructions
Oppositional behavior	• Seeming "refusal" to follow directions or engage in a behavior • "Defiant" behaviors may be present with only some adults	• "Defiance" in SM is often limited to the context of verbal communication when a child is expected to speak • SM is often accompanied by other anxiety symptoms (e.g., shyness in novel situations)
Social anxiety	• Shyness in novel situations • Reluctance to speak to unfamiliar individuals	• Social anxiety disorder involves difficulty with both verbal and non-verbal social behavior (e.g., gestures, taking photos, dancing, eating in front of others) • Children with social anxiety are less likely to exhibit oppositional features than children with SM who do not have social anxiety

children with selective mutism is by definition limited to certain situations and is not pervasive. Similarly, some have noted that a lack of speaking may be a severe, self-protective response to a major traumatic event (Omdal, 2007). In such cases, the criterion of speaking in at least one setting is particularly helpful in differentiating selective mutism from a traumatic stress response. For children who are immersed in second language due to immigration or relocation, one must not confuse a "silent period" in immigrant children for selective mutism (see Toppelberg et al., 2005; Toppelberg & Collins, 2010)

Clinicians might have difficulty distinguishing selective mutism from social anxiety disorder. The two disorders co-occur more often than not, and this is not surprising given the conceptual overlap between selective mutism and social anxiety disorder and the prevailing belief that social anxiety underlies selectively mute behavior in many cases (e.g., Gensthaler, Maichrowitz, Kaess, Ligges, Freitag, & Schwenck, 2016). Nevertheless, the two disorders possess distinct clinical features and one of the most successful strategies for the clinician attempting to make this differentiation is to inquire about the presence of social anxiety symptoms that do not involve speaking. For example, the presence of fear and avoidance of eating in public, having pictures taken, using public restrooms, or writing in front of others provide strong evidence for an additional diagnosis of social anxiety disorder in a child who meets criteria for selective mutism. In addition, it is helpful to know that children with social anxiety are less likely to display oppositional features than children who have selective mutism without social anxiety disorder (Diliberto & Kearney, 2016; Yeganeh, Beidel, & Turner, 2006).

Relatedly, for children with selective mutism, failure to speak is often rooted in anxiety and not in a willful desire to defy parents by not speaking. Although some studies of children with selective mutism have identified a subset of youth with oppositional features (Cohan et al., 2008; Diliberto & Kearney, 2016), in most cases of children with selective mutism, oppositional behaviors appear to be most prominent when the child is pushed to speak (Cunningham, McHolm, & Boyle, 2006) and are unlikely to be problematic outside of the context of verbal communication. On the other hand, if a child who appears to have selective mutism (failure to speak in certain situations despite speaking in other situations) also exhibits oppositional behaviors in a variety of situations, diagnoses of both selective mutism and oppositional defiant disorder may be assigned. For children whose failure to speak does not appear to follow a consistent pattern with regard to situation and targeted individuals, appears primarily motivated by instrumental gains, and occurs in the absence of any other anxiety symptoms, it is possible that oppositional defiant disorder rather than selective mutism is the correct diagnosis.

Review of the Evidence

The literature on selective mutism is relatively small compared to other anxiety disorders and emotional and behavioral disorders of childhood. Extant studies are often limited by small sample sizes and short follow-up periods, and there is a relative lack of consensus on many issues related to the epidemiology, phenomenology, natural course, and treatment of the disorder. Although many studies include preschool age children (five or younger), studies of selective mutism commonly include broader age ranges and are not limited to preschool age samples.

Epidemiology

There are few studies reporting rates of selective mutism among children and they have varied widely with respect to assessment methods and sampling strategies. Further, many studies are out of date and new research to produce current estimates is needed. Nevertheless, research shows that selective mutism is not common, though not as rare as previously thought. Prevalence estimates are under 1% in the U.S. (.50–.71; Bergman et al., 2002; Chavira, Stein, Bailey, & Stein, 2004) and ranging from .18–1.90 in international samples (Kopp & Gillberg, 1997; Kumpulainen et al., 1998). Some evidence suggests that rates of selective mutism may be higher in immigrant and bilingual children (Bradley & Sloman, 1975; Elizur & Perednik, 2003), although the reason for this is not known and requires further study of both selective mutism and second language learning (see Toppelberg et al., 2005). Mean age of onset ranges from 2.7–4.1 years (Cunningham, McHolm, Boyle, & Patel, 2004; Kristensen, 2000). While a few studies have found that the prevalence does not seem to vary markedly by sex or race/ethnicity (e.g., Bergman et al., 2002; Elizur & Perednik, 2003), several found evidence that slightly more girls than boys seem to be affected by selective mutism, with an average reported female to male ratio of approximately 2 to 1 (e.g., Cohan et al., 2008; Dummit et al., 1997; Kristensen, 2000; Kumpulainen et al., 1998). While this gender difference is consistent with gender differences in other anxiety disorders, the robustness and extent of gender difference in selective mutism is unclear given small sample sizes (Wong, 2010).

Etiology and Conceptualization

Previously, it was typically suggested that selective mutism was related to a variety of conditions including oppositionality, trauma, or family neuroses. However, current conceptualizations view the disorder as closely related to social anxiety disorder. This conceptualization is consistent with reports of extremely high comorbidity between selective mutism and social anxiety disorder, with studies reporting that 44% to 100% (Chavira et al., 2007; Dummit et al., 1997; Oerbeck et al., 2014; Vecchio & Kearney, 2005) of children with selective mutism also had social anxiety disorder. Similarly, studies have reported disproportionately high rates of interfamilial aggregation of shyness and social anxiety (approximately 30–40%; Kristensen & Torgersen, 2001) compared to control families, as well as high rates of parental taciturnity and reticence (51% and 44% in mothers and fathers, respectively; Remschmidt et al., 2001).

Growing evidence indicates that selective mutism may be best understood from a developmental psychopathology perspective as the dynamic interplay of genetic, neurological, temperament, behavioral, and social processes. In addition to the familial aggregation of shyness, anxiety, and speaking reticence noted above, two studies have found a polymorphism in the CNTNAP2 gene to be associated with selective mutism, social anxiety, and socially anxious traits (Stein et al., 2011), but also with various forms of language impairment. These genetic data provide support for the conceptualization of selective mutism as closely related to anxiety. With regard to temperament, a recent study examined the relationship between speaking behavior (i.e., spoken words in a novel situation) and behavioral inhibition in a non-clinical sample of children ages three to six and found that behavioral inhibition and social anxiety correlated with number of spoken words during an observed speech task (Muris, Hendriks, & Bot, 2016), providing empirical support for the idea that a behaviorally inhibited temperament may be a shared etiological factor among selective mutism and other anxiety disorders.

Notably, data are consistent with a conceptualization of selective mutism as a developmental variant, rather than an extreme form on a continuum (Black & Uhde, 1995), of social anxiety. From a behavioral perspective, some researchers have investigated the notion that the "non-speaking behavior" of children with selective mutism essentially should be seen as an emotion regulation strategy aimed to reduce anxiety around social interaction. Indeed, there is evidence to support that a lack of speech may be an avoidance mechanism serving to avoid or relieve anxiety. One study found that children with selective mutism experienced less physiological arousal during social interaction tasks compared to children with social anxiety disorder or no diagnosis, despite being rated by evaluators as more impaired, more anxious, and less socially effective (Young, Bunnell, & Beidel, 2012).

Because some children with selective mutism do not exhibit social anxiety with regard to non-verbal social engagement, some have questioned the link between selective mutism and social anxiety and suggested that some individuals may experience anxiety specifically related to expressive language and not to social situations more generally. In fact, some researchers have posited that selective mutism may be conceptualized as a specific phobia of speaking or expressive language (Johnson & Wintgens, 2015; Omdal & Galloway, 2008). Yet others have suggested that selective mutism has distinct but overlapping subtypes, with varying clinical presentations and different explanations for selective speech patterns (Mulligan, Hale, & Shipon-Blum, 2015). From this perspective, social anxiety may play a role in only a subset of youth with selective mutism while for others, the selective mutism may be driven by deficits in sensory processing or other emotional/behavioral difficulties (Mulligan et al., 2015).

Evidence regarding the role of speech and language processing abnormalities in selective mutism is scant and mixed. When compared to children with other anxiety disorders and non-clinical controls, some children with selective mutism appear to have language deficits, particularly as they relate to receptive language measures, including receptive vocabulary and phonemic awareness (Manassis et al., 2007). By contrast, another study examining narrative skills in children with selective mutism found that children with selective mutism displayed subtle deficits in expressive language skills, despite the average performance on assessments of cognitive and receptive language abilities (McInnes, Fung, Manassis, Fiksenbaum, & Tannock, 2004). In another study, researchers found that children with selective mutism did not exhibit deficits in visual memory, but they did show significantly poorer verbal memory than controls (Kristensen & Oerbeck, 2006). Recent studies have also examined the potential for a neural basis of selective mutism as they relate to deficient auditory processing, with particular attention to abnormalities in auditory efferent feedback pathways (e.g., middle-ear acoustic reflex) that may result in the abnormal subjective experience of their own vocalizations (see Henkin & Bar-Haim, 2015). According to this research, these auditory aberrations may interfere with one's ability to simultaneously speak and process external sounds, which may in turn lead these children to restrict or adapt speech in certain situations (Henkin & Bar-Haim, 2015).

Thus, some children with selective mutism may exhibit meaningful deficits in speech and language processing although further research is needed to clarify the nature of the deficits and this issue is poorly understood. Although some children with selective mutism may experience language delay or dysfunction and deficits in speech and language processing, it is noteworthy that among most researchers it is not suggested at this time that these problems supersede social anxiety as a major contributing factor toward nonspeaking behaviors. Furthermore, although language delay or speech disorder may be more common among children with selective mutism, the data are correlational and these problems could be a result, rather than a cause, of the disorder. Not surprisingly, the assessment of the speech and language of a child with selective mutism is quite difficult and arguably often inaccurate (some recommend deputizing the parent to do the assessment). Lastly, speech and language problems associated with selective mutism are likely to be subtle and are exclusionary criteria for the diagnosis of selective mutism when they cannot be ruled out as the cause of the lack of speech. During diagnosis, one should take careful consideration of patterns of speech, where speech and language problems are pervasive across all contexts and selective mutism is, by definition, present in only some contexts (see Table 9.1). Ultimately, however, it is important to note that many in the field believe that neurodevelopmental and language anomalies occur more frequently among children with selective mutism than among children with other anxiety related disorders.

Course and Outcomes

The research on long-term outcomes of children with selective mutism is extremely scarce. To date, only one longitudinal descriptive study has examined the naturalistic course of selective mutism and found an average duration of eight years (Remschmidt et al., 2001). An older study reported that 0.69 percent of four- to five-year-olds were completely mute in the school setting and that this rate dropped to 0.08 percent after approximately eight months. Consistent with this, another school-based study found that on average, children with selective mutism experience symptom improvement over the course of six months, although they continued to experience elevated symptoms and impairment compared to their peers without selective mutism (Bergman et al., 2002). A retrospective study indicated that children with lifetime selective mutism and social anxiety were more inhibited as infants and toddlers than children of the internalizing and healthy control groups (Gensthaler, Khalaf, et al., 2016). Importantly, however, many children with selective mutism may experience a delay in diagnosis from the onset of symptoms of one year or more (Ford, Sladeczek, Carlson, & Kratochwill, 1998).

Treatment

Psychosocial Treatment

Selective mutism has recently been categorized as an anxiety disorder, and cognitive behavioral therapy (CBT) is generally considered as an evidence-based treatment for pediatric anxiety (Wang et al., 2017). Even so, several features of selective mutism complicate the treatment and require modification to existing anxiety treatment methods as discussed below. First, the age of onset for selective mutism tends to be younger than for other anxiety disorders, and presumably, the age of the child presenting for treatment as well. Younger children such as those presenting for treatment with selective mutism, are likely less able to engage in discussion of cognitive elements of treatment and require greater parent involvement than older children. Initially, most of the established treatments for child anxiety disorders were developed and tested for children ages seven and older (e.g., Coping Cat treatment for child anxiety; Kendall, 1994). More recent transdiagnostic treatment protocols targeting younger children (e.g., Being Brave Program, Hirshfeld-Becker et al., 2010) have been developed and appear promising though, interestingly, the presence of behavioral inhibition, a characteristic associated with selective mutism, predicted poor treatment response. In addition, in light of evidence that specific anxiety treatment may be more effective than more general treatment protocols (Reynolds et al., 2012), treatments that specifically target the unique features of selective mutism seem warranted.

The second characteristic of selective mutism that contributes to the need for a unique treatment is the lack of speech that is intrinsic to the disorder. Treatment of selective mutism must proceed with the understanding that most children with selective mutism do not initially speak to the treating clinician. This presents initial challenges with communication that need to be considered and the treatment needs to include strategies for facilitating verbal communication with the therapist. Some researchers have recommended that therapists initially take a nonchalant or defocused communication approach in which the therapist does not focus too much attention directly at the child and provides praise in a neutral manner (e.g., Klein et al., 2017; Oerbeck et al., 2014). The initial lack of verbal communication with the therapist is assumed to reflect the general anxiety underlying failure to talk in situations outside the home and is addressed accordingly.

Finally, although many forms of youth anxiety disorders involve school-related impairment, unlike selective mutism, they do not typically revolve as extensively around the school environment. For this reason, treatment that integrates school participation as a central component of the intervention is necessary for the effective treatment of selective mutism. Most importantly, close rapport with school personnel that includes regular communication and support must be established to ensure the success of behavioral interventions in the school setting. Furthermore, treatment programs should include teacher education and training in the behavioral methods utilized for treatment. In most cases, specific behavioral interventions occur within the school setting, typically with the teacher's participation.

Fortunately, treatments based on child anxiety interventions but modified for the treatment of selective mutism have been developed and, not surprisingly, are most often based on behavioral principles. Indeed, recent reviews of the literature (e.g., Muris & Ollendick, 2015) indicate that behavioral treatments are by and large the recommended treatment for selective mutism. Recently, two small randomized controlled trials of treatment for selective mutism were completed (Bergman, Gonzalez, Piacentini, & Keller, 2013; Oerbeck, Stein, Wentzel-Larsen, Langsrud, & Kristensen, 2014) and support the efficacy of such interventions compared to a waitlist control. Both treatment protocols include children of approximately the same age (4–7 years old in the Bergman et al. (2013) and 3–9 years old in the Oerbeck et al. (2014); see Table 9.2), the participation of parents and school, the use of a graded hierarchy, stimulus fading procedures, contingency management, and general behavioral exposure exercises. Both interventions also include heavy school involvement and school-based exposure exercises. Generally, these and other published reports in the literature (e.g., Lang et al., 2016; Klein et al., 2017) describe treatment efforts that focus on behavioral methods that include strong elements of parent and school involvement in treatment.

Table 9.2 Treatment studies for selective mutism with N > 10* participants who received behavioral intervention

Study	N	Age Range	Mean (SD) Age (yrs)	Design	Description of intervention strategy	Treatment Length	Findings
Bergman et al. (2013)	21	4–8	5.43 (1.16)	RCT: IBTSM vs. 12-week WL	Integrated Behavior Therapy for Selective Mutism (IBTSM); graduated exposure (e.g., to verbal communication), with a focus on transfer of control from therapist to parent and teacher; large emphasis on exposures in school setting	20 sessions (24 weeks)	75% responders[a] in IBTSM vs. 0% responders in WL
Bunnell et al. (2018)	15	5–17	9.6 (3.89)	Case series[b]	All children completed shaping using the same hierarchy of successive approximations of speech. Children randomly received shaping with mobile app (iBT), shaping with other tools (tBT), or shaping with reinforcement alone (rBT)	2 sessions	93.3% completed their hierarchy, ending with five 5-minute conversations with unknown adults

Table 9.2 (Cont.)

Study	N	Age Range	Mean (SD) Age (yrs)	Design	Description of intervention strategy	Treatment Length	Findings
Klein et al., (2017)	40	5–12	6.78 (1.58)	Case series	Social-Communication Anxiety Treatment (S-CAT); shaping and graduated exposure with a focus on transfer of control from therapist to parent and teacher; see http://www.selectivem utismcenter.org/aboutus/ SelectiveMutism.Trea tment.ShiponBlum	3 in-person sessions every 3 weeks (over 9 weeks) with phone consulta-tions	Significant improvements in speaking fre-quency as mea-sured by SMQ
Oerbeck, et al. (2014)	24	3–9	6.5 (2.0) (note: n = 9 in pre-school, ages 3–5 yrs)	RCT: Home- and School-based Intervention vs. WL	Defocused communica-tion (i.e., taking direct attention off the child; see Oerbeck et al., 2014) and rewards-based beha-vioral intervention (i.e., stimulus fading).	21 sessions over 3 months	Significant group x time interaction on primary out-come measure, SSQ, favoring the intervention

RCT = randomized controlled trial; WL = Waitlist; SMQ: Selective Mutism Questionnaire; SSQ = School Speech Questionnaire

[*]Two studies, Krohn et al. (1992) and Sluckin et al. (1991) did include N > 10 (N = 20 and N = 25, respectively), but were not included in this table because both studies were based on record review and not prospective data collection using a specified intervention.

a Much or very much improved on Clinical Global Impression – Improvement Scale (CGI-I ≤ 2)

[b]Although Bunnell et al. (2018) involved randomization, all children completed the same shaping/hierarchy procedure and were randomized with respect to the support received in completing the hierarchy (mobile app, other tools, or no tools/reinforcement alone). Because all children essentially received the same intervention, we describe it here as a case series rather than randomized trial with randomization.

Table 9.2 includes a summary of selective mutism treatment studies; because many selective mutism treatment studies include small samples or single case designs, Table 9.2 includes only those studies with N > 10. For a full list of studies and summaries, see Cohan et al. (2006) and Zakszeski and DuPaul (2017).

While published reports vary on elements, such as where the treatment occurs (school, home, clinic) or how directly or initially speech is the focus, they are remarkably similar regarding most elements of treatment. For one, they include prominent psychoeducation modules to educate parents about selective mutism and to teach them how to discontinue behaviors that accommodate the lack of speech and to begin presenting opportunities for their child to speak. Second, as noted above, most published treatments successfully utilize a combination of behavioral techniques beginning with a hierarchy or rank-ordered list of situations in which the child has difficulty speaking. Then, after a period of rapport-building, the child is guided to systematically engage in speaking-related behaviors (e.g., mouthing speech, making sounds, whispering, etc.) in varied environments and individuals. Over repeated, successful attempts, the associated anxiety dissipates through the processes of autonomic habituation and inhibitory learning. Typically, the child receives positive reinforcement (rewards) following attempts to engage in speaking-related behaviors using stimulus fading, systematic desensitization, and shaping techniques. Parents tend to be quite involved in the treatment as the child practices these speaking behaviors in the therapist's office but is also given assignments to practice outside of the office with the parent as well.

The selectively mute child's lack of speech represents a somewhat unique challenge for others in the child's life, particularly parents and school personnel. Although difficulty in differentiating oppositional behavior from anxiety-related avoidance characterizes many child anxiety disorders, when failure to speak is involved, parents and others are particularly likely to attribute avoidance to oppositional motivations and to get frustrated and angry. In contrast, other reactions to nonspeaking include the tendency to accommodate the child's lack of speech and speak "for" the child with selective mutism, thus decreasing the necessity of independent communication. This tendency, along with other ways that nonspeaking may be reinforced, also needs to be addressed in the treatment of the disorder.

Parental Anxiety

As discussed above, there appears to be a heritable component to selective mutism, and therefore, children with selective mutism may have parents who have elevated levels of anxiety, particularly social anxiety. These parents may experience some discomfort when attempting to implement some of the recommendations of behavioral treatment plans. For example, since it is usually most difficult to speak at school, it is beneficial for children with selective mutism to practice attempting to speak first during playdates in their home. Therefore, parents of children with selective mutism are advised to attempt to arrange playdates with peers. For a socially anxious parent, this may elicit distress. Similarly, parents are encouraged to ask the school for help in gaining access to the empty classroom for the child to practice speaking, or to speak to the teacher in the absence of peers. Again, making requests such as these may be difficult for parents who have high levels of social anxiety themselves.

Other potentially anxiety inducing situations for the socially anxious parent of children with selective mutism are related to enduring silence when the child doesn't respond to others' speaking to him or her. It is easier, and less awkward, to respond on behalf of the child but such responding is contraindicated for treatment. If the parent of a child with selective mutism is not able to tolerate treatment recommendations due to their own anxiety, they should speak with the professional working with their child or seek professional guidance regarding their own anxiety.

Intensive Treatment

Over the last several years, programs offering intensive treatment for selective mutism have become more popular (e.g., Brave Bunch Summer Program, Florida International University, Miami, FL). These treatment programs typically offer a mix of individual and group treatment that includes a simulated classroom environment and can last a few days or more. They have the advantage of making treatment available over a relatively short period of time for families who otherwise might not be able to access appropriate treatment. However, being far away from home usually means that the environments in which the child is having difficulty are not included in the treatment. In fact, being far from home might mean that the child is not practicing new speaking behaviors in any of the environments that were previously difficult, possibly resulting in a lack of treatment generalization. In general, although it is likely that intensive treatment experiences provide benefit and symptoms reduction as has been documented (Lynas et al., in preparation), they may not provide the optimal environment for inhibitory learning experiences, a process highlighted as vital in the treatment of anxiety (Craske et al., 2008). Given the rapid increase in popularity of intensive treatment "camps" and other brief programs (e.g., a two-session Behavior Therapy program; Bunnell, Mesa, & Beidel, 2018), it will be important to establish the efficacy and lasting benefits of these programs in controlled trials.

Other Psychosocial Therapies

Parent–Child Interaction Therapy (PCIT)

In addition to the treatments described above, parent–child interaction therapy (PCIT) which was originally developed to treat externalizing problems in young children, has recently been adapted for treating internalizing disorders, including selective mutism. As discussed in Carpenter et al. (2014), the extension of PCIT to anxiety disorders, such as selective mutism, targets symptoms by attempting to alter parent–child interaction patterns associated with the maintenance of symptoms. While there are some single case reports of positive results using PCIT, the treatment has not been tested in controlled trials. This is important given that, although obvious in the case of externalizing disorders, a scientific rationale for targeting the parent–child interaction in the treatment of selective mutism is less clear. In terms of child anxiety, PCIT was first applied to the treatment of separation anxiety disorder (Pincus, Santucci, Ehrenreich, & Eyberg, 2008) with the rationale that skills learned during PCIT would help decrease difficult behaviors (e.g., tantrums, clinging) commonly exhibited by affected children during separation. In addition, it was hypothesized that the treatment would enhance warmth and security of the parent–child attachment which would then lead to easier separation. Among children with selective mutism, behavioral disturbances related to avoidance of feared situations are not routinely noted, and parent participation is usually achieved with structured and clear psychoeducation and involvement in behavioral treatment. Importantly, and as acknowledged by those conducting the treatment (Carpenter et al., 2014), when PCIT has resulted in improvement in selective mutism symptoms, it is not clear whether the behavioral component focused on exposure to feared situations was responsible for positive results.

Speech/Language Therapy

As discussed above, it is not uncommon for children with selective mutism to also have some degree of speech or language difficulty that may exacerbate speech-related anxiety or self-consciousness. Although there is no empirical data regarding the efficacy of such treatment, it is likely that combining behavioral techniques with speech or language therapy is a productive approach to treating a child with selective mutism who also has speech or language delay or difficulty. In fact, attempting to increase speech without addressing speech problems can be contraindicated because if the child begins speaking more to others who may not comprehend his or speech, she or he may become embarrassed or humiliated over not being understood, possibly resulting in heightened anxiety related to speaking.

Interestingly, even in cases without a significant contribution of speech or language dysfunction, the small supportive group setting of auxiliary speech services found in many schools may provide a beneficial environment in which to implement the graded behavioral intervention approach described earlier. When schools have speech and language services in place that can serve a child with selective mutism, it can be beneficial to seek services for the child with selective mutism regardless of whether a formal speech and language dysfunction is documented.

Psychopharmacological Treatments

Currently there are no medications that are specifically approved for the treatment of selective mutism. However, the efficacy of agents such as fluvoxamine and sertraline in the treatment of pediatric anxiety is well established (the Research Unit on Pediatric Psychopharmacology Anxiety Study Group, 2001; Walkup et al., 2008). Not surprisingly, given the central role of anxiety in the symptomatology of selective mutism, Selective Serotonin Reuptake Inhibitor (SSRI) treatment is often included in the treatment of selective mutism as well. A recent review (Manassis et al., 2016) revealed that although there is evidence for the role of SSRI medications in reducing symptoms of selective mutism, the research is hampered by suboptimal methodology with small sample sizes, inconsistent measures, and very few double-blind studies. Additional research is clearly warranted to establish parameters around dosing and to obtain information regarding tolerability and adverse occurrences. At the current time, due to frequent parental concerns about administering medication to children as young as three years old, medication is not the first option for many families. In practice, behavioral therapy, when practical and available, should be considered as the first-line intervention strategy. In treatment resistant cases, combination treatment (behavioral therapy plus medication) appears to be the strategy of choice. Please see Chapter 11, Psychopharmacological Treatment of Anxiety in Preschool-Aged Children, for more detailed information on this topic.

Future Directions

Despite a relative rise of selective mutism research in the 1990s, the selective mutism research base continues to be quite small compared to other anxiety disorders and psychological disorders of childhood, and much remains unknown. First, there is a critical need for large observational and naturalistic studies to obtain current prevalence estimates of selective mutism in a variety of settings using broad sampling and screening procedures, including school- and community-based screening and assessment of young children, especially those in preschool who are easily overlooked. Similarly, longitudinal studies would help elucidate rates of remission, risk for development of other anxiety and non-anxiety disorders and associated psychological and social sequelae. Along these lines, future research focused on identifying environmental correlates and risk factors for selective mutism would greatly contribute to our understanding of the etiology and maintenance of selective mutism. While several studies suggest a critical role of culture in the risk for selective mutism, including immigrant and bilingual status, these linkages are poorly understood, and previous studies raise more questions than they have answered.

Second, basic science research involving biological and behavioral variables would contribute to our understanding of the etiology and neurobiological correlates of selective mutism. Previous work has identified shared genetic contributions to selective mutism and social anxiety disorder, as well as a potential neurobiological mechanism (i.e., auditory neural pathways) for symptoms for some youth with selective mutism. Such studies indicate the complex and multifaceted origins of selective mutism and provide starting points for additional basic science research of selective mutism.

Finally, future research is needed to evaluate behavioral and medication treatments using greater methodological rigor. The majority of behavioral intervention studies utilized single case or non-randomized designs; of over 40 studies of behavioral interventions between 1990 and 2015, only six had a total sample size of N > 10 (see Table 9.2; Cohan et al., 2006 and Zakszeski & DuPaul, 2017), and of these, two were based on record review. To date, there have been only two randomized controlled trials evaluating the efficacy of behavioral interventions for selective mutism (see Table 9.2). While promising, both studies involved small sample sizes. Future studies involving collaboration across sites should be considered to help increase sample sizes and maximize statistical power. Additionally, extant studies utilized waitlist comparison groups and thus, the relative efficacy of different treatment modalities and the robustness of findings are unknown. In addition to larger controlled trials, future intervention studies will require longer-term follow-up assessment timeframes to evaluate the endurance of gains, and assess the role of treatment in reducing the risk for other psychological disorders. Given that selective mutism primarily involves impairment in settings outside of the home and clinical setting, school-based dissemination and implementation work may be particularly beneficial to maximize the accessibility and generalizability of selective mutism treatment.

Resources

Selective Mutism Association; selectivemutism.org: information about SM and listings of treatment professionals and support groups plus annual conference intended for professionals and families.
Selective Mutism Network; www.selectivemutismnetwork.org.

Boston University Center for Anxiety and Related Disorders; www.bu.edu/card/get-help/child-programs/child-conditions/selective-mutism.

Florida International University Center for Children and Families; https://ccf.fiu.edu/services/anxiety-and-fears/index.html.

German website focused on selective mutism with information, referrals, video clips, training information, www.selektiver-mutismus.de.

Anxiety and Depression Association of America, adaa.org Referrals to providers who have identified themselves as competent in providing anxiety treatment.

Selective Mutism Information and Research Association, www.selectivemutism.org.uk. UK based group providing information, training and resources in the UK.

References

American Psychiatric Association (2013). *Diagnostic and statistical manual of mental disorders* (5th ed.). Washington, DC: American Psychiatric Association.

Bergman, R. L., Piacentini, J., & McCracken, J. T. (2002). Prevalence and description of selective mutism in a school-based sample. *Journal of the American Academy of Child & Adolescent Psychiatry*, 41(8), 938–946. doi:10.1097/00004583 200208000-00012

Bergman, R. L., Keller, M., Piacentini, J., & Bergman, A. (2008). Development and psychometric Properties of the selective mutism questionnaire. *Journal of Clinical Child and Adolescent Psychology*, 37(2), 456–464. https://doi.org/10.1080/15374410801955805

Bergman, R. L., Gonzalez, A., Piacentini, J., Keller, M. L. (2013). Integrated Behavioral Therapy for Selective Mutism: A randomized controlled pilot study. *Behavior Research and Therapy Journal*, 51(10), 680–689. https://doi.org/10.1016/j.brat.2013.07.003

Black, B., & Uhde, T. W. (1995). Psychiatric characteristics of children with selective mutism: a pilot study. *Journal of the American Academy of Child & Adolescent Psychiatry*, 34(7), 847–856. https://doi.org/10.1097/00004583-199507000-00007

Bradley, S., & Sloman, L. (1975). Elective mutism in immigrant families. *Journal of the American Academy of Child Psychiatry*, 14(3), 510–514. https://doi.org/10.1016/S0002-7138(09)61450–61453

Bunnell, B. E., Mesa, F., Beidel, D. C. (2018). A two-session hierarchy for shaping successive approximations of speech in Selective Mutism: Pilot study of mobile apps and mechanisms of behaviour change. *Behavior Therapy*, 49(6), 966–980. https://doi.org/10.1016/j.beth.2018.02.003

Carpenter, A. L., Puliafico, A. C., Kurtz, S. M. S., Pincus, D. B., & Comer, J. S. (2014). Extending parent–child interaction therapy for early childhood internalizing problems: New advances for an overlooked population. *Clinical Child and Family Psychology Review*, 17(4), 340–356. doi: http://dx.doi.org/10.1007/s10567-014-0172-4

Chavira, D. A., Shipon-Blum, E., Hitchcock, C., Cohan, S., & Stein, M. B. (2007). Selective mutism and social anxiety disorder: All in the family? *Journal of the American Academy of Child & Adolescent Psychiatry*, 46(11), 1464–1472. doi: http://dx.doi.org/10.1097/chi.0b013e318149366a

Chavira, D. A., Stein, M. B., Bailey, K., & Stein, M. T. (2004). Child anxiety in primary care: Prevalent but untreated. *Depression and Anxiety*, 20(4), 155–164. doi:10.1002/da.20039

Cohan, S. L., Chavira, D. A., & Stein, M. B. (2006). Practitioner review: Psychosocial interventions for children with selective mutism: A critical evaluation of the literature from 1990–2005. *Journal of Child Psychology and Psychiatry*, 47(11), 1085–1097.

Cohan, S. L., Chavira, D. A., Shipon-Blum, E., Hitchcock, C., Roesch, S. C., & Stein, M. B. (2008). Refining the classification of children with selective mutism: A latent profile analysis. *Journal of Clinical Child & Adolescent Psychology*, 37(4), 770–784. http://dx.doi.org/10.1080/15374410802359759

Craske, M. G., Kircanski, K., Zelikowsky, M., Mystkowski, J., Chowdhury, N., & Baker, A. (2008). Optimizing inhibitory learning during exposure therapy. *Behaviour Research and Therapy*, 46(1), 5–27. doi: http://dx.doi.org/10.1016/j.brat.2007.10.003

Cunningham, C. E., McHolm, A. E., & Boyle, M. H. (2006). Social phobia, anxiety, oppositional behavior, social skills, and self-concept in children with specific selective mutism, generalized selective mutism, and community controls. *European Child & Adolescent Psychiatry*, 15(5), 245–255. https://doi.org/10.1007/s00787-006-0529-4

Cunningham, C. E., McHolm, A., Boyle, M. H., & Patel, S. (2004). Behavioral and emotional adjustment, family functioning, academic performance, and social relationships in children with selective mutism. *Journal of Child Psychology and Psychiatry*, 45(8), 1363–1372. doi:10.1111/j.1469-7610.2004.00327.x

Diliberto, R. A., & Kearney, C. A. (2016). Anxiety and oppositional behavior profiles among youth with selective mutism. *Journal of Communication Disorders*, 59, 16–23. https://doi.org/10.1016/j.jcomdis.2015.11.001

Dummit, E. S., Klein, R. G., Tancer, N. K., Asche, B., Martin, J., & Fairbanks, J. A. (1997). Systematic assessment of 50 children with selective mutism. *Journal of the American Academy of Child & Adolescent Psychiatry*, 36(5), 653–660. https://doi.org/10.1097/00004583-199705000-00016

Elizur, Y., & Perednik, R. (2003). Prevalence and description of selective mutism in immigrant and native families: A controlled study. *Journal of the American Academy of Child & Adolescent Psychiatry*, 42(12), 1451–1459. https://doi.org/10.1097/00004583-200312000-00012

Ford, M. A., Sladeczek, I. E., Carlson, J., & Kratochwill, T. R. (1998). Selective mutism: Phenomenological characteristics. *School Psychology Quarterly*, 13(3), 192–227. http://dx.doi.org/10.1037/h0088982

Gensthaler, A., Khalaf, S., Ligges, M., Kaess, M., Freitag, C. M., & Schwenck, C. (2016). Selective mutism and temperament: the silence and behavioral inhibition to the unfamiliar. *European Child & Adolescent Psychiatry*, 25(10), 1113–1120. https://doi.org/10.1007/s00787-016-0835-4.

Gensthaler, A., Maichrowitz, V., Kaess, M., Ligges, M., Freitag, C. M., & Schwenck, C. (2016). Selective mutism: The fraternal twin of childhood social phobia. *Psychopathology*, 49(2), 95–107. https://doi.org/10.1159/000444882.

Henkin, Y., & Bar-Haim, Y. (2015). An auditory-neuroscience perspective on the development of selective mutism. *Developmental Cognitive Neuroscience*, 12, 86–93. https://doi.org/10.1016/j.dcn.2015.01.002

Hirshfeld-Becker, D. R., Masek, B., Henin, A., Blakely, L. R., Pollock-Wurman, R. A., McQuade, J., DePetrillo, L., Briesch, J., Ollendick, T. H., Rosenbaum, J. F. and Biederman, J. (2010). Cognitive behavioral therapy for 4- to 7-year-old children with anxiety disorders: a randomized clinical trial. *Journal of Consulting and Clinical Psychology*, 78(4), 498. https://doi.org/10.1037/a0019055

Johnson, M., & Wintgens, A. (2015). Viewing selective mutism as a phobia of talking: the importance of accurate conceptualisation for effective clinical and parental management. In C.A. Essau & J.L. Allen (Eds.), *Making parenting work for children's mental health*. ACAMH Occasional Paper 33 (pp. 61–71), doi:10.13056/OP33.jLondon: Association for Child and Adolescent Mental Health.

Kendall, P. C. (1994). Treating anxiety disorders in children: Results of a randomized clinical trial. *Journal of Consulting and Clinical Psychology*, 62(1), 100–110. http://dx.doi.org/10.1037/0022-006X.62.1.100

Klein, E. R., Armstrong, S. L., Skira, K., & Gordon, J. (2017). Social Communication Anxiety Treatment (S-CAT) for children and families with selective mutism: A pilot study. *Clinical Child Psychology and Psychiatry*, 22(1), 90–108. https://doi.org/10.1177/1359104516633497

Kopp, S., & Gillberg, C. (1997). Selective Mutism: A population-based study: A research note. *Journal of Child Psychology and Psychiatry*, 38(2), 257–262. doi:10.1111/j.1469-7610.1997.tb01859.x

Kristensen, H. (2000). Selective mutism and comorbidity with developmental disorder/delay, anxiety disorder, and elimination disorder. *Journal of the American Academy of Child & Adolescent Psychiatry*, 39(2), 249–256. https://doi.org/10.1097/00004583-200002000-00026

Kristensen, H., & Oerbeck, B. (2006). Is selective mutism associated with deficits in memory span and visual memory?: An exploratory case–control study. *Depression and Anxiety*, 23(2), 71–76. doi:10.1002/da.20140

Kristensen, H., & Torgersen, S. (2001). MCMI-II personality traits and symptom traits in parents of children with selective mutism: A case-control study. *Journal of Abnormal Psychology*, 110(4), 648. http://dx.doi.org/10.1037/0021-843X.110.4.648

Krohn, D. D., Weckstein, S. M., & Wright, H. L. (1992). A study of the effectiveness of a specific treatment for elective mutism. *Journal of the American Academy of Child & Adolescent Psychiatry*, 31(4), 711–718.

Kumpulainen, K., Räsänen, E., Raaska, H., & Somppi, V. (1998). Selective mutism among second-graders in elementary school. *European Child & Adolescent Psychiatry*, 7(1), 24–29. https://doi.org/10.1007/s007870050041

Lang, C., Nir, Z., Gothelf, A., Domachevsky, S., Ginton, L., Kushnir, J., & Gothelf, D. (2016). The outcome of children with selective mutism following cognitive behavioral intervention: a follow-up study. *European Journal of Pediatrics*, 175(4), 481–487. https://doi.org/10.1007/s00431-015-2651-0

Lynas, C. M. T., Pabis, J. M., Ioffe, M., Burt, N., Holzman, J., Kurtz, S. & White, K. (2019). Adventure Camp: Intensive group treatment for selective mutism.

Manassis, K., Oerbeck, B., & Overgaard, K. R. (2016). The use of medication in selective mutism: A systematic review. *European Child & Adolescent Psychiatry*, 25(6), 571–578.

Manassis, K., Tannock, R., Garland, E. J., Minde, K., McInnes, A., & Clark, S. (2007). The sounds of silence: Language, cognition and anxiety in selective mutism. *Journal of the American Academy of Child & Adolescent Psychiatry*, 46(9), 1187–1195. doi: http://dx.doi.org/10.1097/CHI.0b013e318076b7ab

McInnes, A., Fung, D., Manassis, K., Fiksenbaum, L., & Tannock, R. (2004). Narrative skills in children with selective mutism: An exploratory study.

American Journal of Speech-Language Pathology, 13(4), 304–315. doi:10.1044/1058-0360(2004/031)

Mulligan, C. A., Hale, J. B., & Shipon-Blum, E. (2015). Selective mutism: Identification of subtypes and implications for treatment. *Journal of Education and Human Development*, 4(1), 79–96. doi:10.15640/jehd.v4n1a9

Muris, P., Hendriks, E., & Bot, S. (2016). Children of few words: relations among selective mutism, behavioral inhibition, and (social) anxiety symptoms in 3- to 6-year-olds. *Child Psychiatry & Human Development*, 47(1), 94–101. https://doi.org/10.1007/s10578-015-0547-x

Muris, P., & Ollendick, T. H. (2015). Children who are anxious in silence: A review on selective mutism, the new anxiety disorder in DSM-5. *Clinical Child and Family Psychology Review*, 18(2), 151–169. doi: http://dx.doi.org/10.1007/s10567-015-0181-y

Oerbeck, B., Stein, M. B., Wentzel-Larsen, T., Langsrud, Ø., & Kristensen, H. (2014). A randomized controlled trial of a home and school-based intervention for selective mutism defocused communication and behavioral techniques. *Child and Adolescent Mental Health*, 19(3), 192–198. Retrieved from https://search.proquest.com/docview/1611633562?accountid=14512

Omdal, H. (2007). Can adults who have recovered from selective mutism in childhood and adolescence tell us anything about the nature of the condition and/or recovery from it? *European Journal of Special Needs Education*, 22(3), 237–253.

Omdal, H., & Galloway, D. (2008), Could selective mutism be re-conceptualised as a specific phobia of expressive speech? An exploratory post-hoc study. *Child and Adolescent Mental Health*, 13: 74–81. doi:10.1111/j.1475-3588.2007.00454.x

Pincus, D. B., Santucci, L. C., Ehrenreich, J. T., & Eyberg, S. M. (2008). The implementation of modified parent-child interaction therapy for youth with separation anxiety disorder. *Cognitive and Behavioral Practice*, 15(2), 118–125.

Remschmidt, H., Poller, M., Herpertz-Dahlmann, B., Hennighausen, K., & Gutenbrunner, C. (2001). A follow-up study of 45 patients with elective mutism. *European Archives of Psychiatry and Clinical Neuroscience*, 251(6), 284–296. https://doi.org/10.1007/PL00007547

Reynolds, S., Wilson, C., Austin, J., & Hooper, L. (2012). Effects of psychotherapy for anxiety in children and adolescents: A meta-analytic review. *Clinical Psychology Review*, 32(4), 251–262. doi: http://dx.doi.org/10.1016/j.cpr.2012.01.005

Research Unit on Pediatric Psychopharmacology Anxiety Study Group (2001). Fluvoxamine for the treatment of anxiety disorders in children and adolescents. *New England Journal of Medicine*, 344(17):1279–1285

Simms, M. D. (2017). When autistic behavior suggests a disease other than classic autism. *Pediatric Clinics*, 64(1), 127–138. http://dx.doi.org/10.1016/j.pcl.2016.08.009

Sluckin, A., Foreman, N., & Herbert, M. (1991). Behavioural treatment programs and selectivity of speaking at follow-up in a sample of 25 selective mutes. *Australian Psychologist*, 26(2), 132–137.

Stein, M. B., Yang, B., Chavira, D. A., Hitchcock, C. A., Sung, S. C., Shipon-Blum, E., & Gelernter, J. (2011). A common genetic variant in the neurexin superfamily member CNTNAP2 is associated with increased risk for selective mutism and social anxiety related traits. *Biological Psychiatry*, 69(9), 825–831. doi: http://dx.doi.org/10.1016/j.biopsych.2010.11.008

Toppelberg, C. O., & Collins, B. A. (2010). Language, culture, and adaptation in immigrant children. *Child and Adolescent Psychiatric Clinics of North America*, 19(4), 697–717. https://doi.org/10.1016/j.chc.2010.07.003

Toppelberg, C. O., Tabors, P., Coggins, A., Lum, K., & Burger, C. (2005). Differential diagnosis of selective mutism in bilingual children. *Journal of the American Academy of Child & Adolescent Psychiatry*, 44(6), 592–595. doi: http://dx.doi.org/10.1097/01.chi.0000157549.87078.f8

Vecchio, J. L., & Kearney, C. A. (2005). Selective mutism in children: Comparison to youths with and without anxiety disorders. *Journal of Psychopathology and Behavioral Assessment*, 27(1), 31–37. https://doi.org/10.1007/s10862-005-3263-1

Walkup, J. T., Albano, A. M., Piacentini, J., Birmaher, B., Compton, S. N., Sherrill, J. T., … Kendall, P. C. (2008). Cognitive behavioral therapy, sertraline, or a combination in childhood anxiety. *The New England Journal of Medicine*, 359(26), 2753–2766. doi: http://dx.doi.org/10.1056/NEJMoa0804633

Wang, Z., Whiteside, S. P. H., Sim, L., Farah, W., Morrow, A. S., Alsawas, M., … & Daraz, L. (2017). Comparative effectiveness and safety of cognitive behavioral therapy and pharmacotherapy for childhood anxiety disorders: A systematic review and meta analysis. *JAMA Pediatrics*, doi:10.1001/jamapediatrics.2017.3036.

Wong, P. (2010). Selective mutism: a review of etiology, comorbidities, and treatment. *Psychiatry (Edgmont)*, 7(3), 23.

Yeganeh, R., Beidel, D. C., & Turner, S. M. (2006). Selective mutism: more than social anxiety? *Depression and Snxiety*, 23(3), 117–123. doi:10.1002/da.20139

Young, B. J., Bunnell, B. E., & Beidel, D. C. (2012). Evaluation of children with selective mutism and social phobia: A comparison of psychological and psychophysiological arousal. *Behavior Modification*, 36(4), 525–544. https://doi.org/10.1177/0145445512443980

Zakszeski, B. N., & DuPaul, G. J. (2017). Reinforce, shape, expose, and fade: A review of treatments for selective mutism (2005–2015). *School Mental Health*, 9(1), 1–15.

10 Prevention of Anxiety in Preschool-Aged Children

Brian Fisak, Lauren Persad, Julia Gallegos, and Paula Barrett

Prevention programs have been developed and evaluated to address numerous psychiatric disorders. In addition to anxiety prevention, programs have been developed to address other disorders, including depression (Stockings et al., 2016), conduct disorder (Posthumus, Raaijmakers, Maassen, van Engeland, & Matthtys 2012; Winther, Carlsson, & Vance, 2014), substance abuse (Botvin, & Griffin, 2016; Springer et al., 2004), and eating disorders (Watson et al., 2016).

For a variety of reasons, the implementation of anxiety prevention programs to young children may be a particularly effective and efficient strategy to address child anxiety. In particular, anxiety disorders are the most common of the psychiatric disorders among children, adolescents and adults (Baumeister & Härter, 2007; Polancsyzk, Salum, Sugaya, Caye, & Rohde, 2015). Onset often occurs at an early age, and symptoms in childhood tend to persist and worsen over time (Kessler et al., 2007; Cartwright-Hatton, McNicol, & Doubleday, 2006; Costello, Mustillo, Erkanli, Keeler, & Angold, 2003; Hirshfeld-Becker & Biederman, 2002). Related to this point, anxiety disorders can be diagnosed and are not uncommon in preschool-aged children (Egger & Angold, 2006; Paulus, Backes, Sander, Weber, & von Gontard, 2015). Further, anxiety disorders have a substantial, negative impact on quality of life and numerous areas of functioning (Barrett & Pahl, 2006; Langley, Bergman, McCracken, & Piacentini, 2004) and commonly precede the onset of other psychiatric disorders (Dougherty et al., 2013; Kashdan, Collins, & Elhai, 2006). Specifically, in preschool-aged children with an anxiety diagnosis, functioning can be affected by comorbid depression, sleep problems, and oppositional defiant disorder (Dougherty et al., 2013). In adolescents, social anxiety has been linked to an increase in risk-taking behaviors, and illicit drug use (Kashdan et al., 2006).

In addition, anxiety disorders are costly to society (Greenberg et al., 1999; Hoffman, Dukes, & Wittchen, 2008). For example, in a commonly cited study, Greenberg et al. (1999) estimated the economic burden resulting from anxiety disorders to be 40 billion dollars in 1990 in the United States. In a more recent study, Revicki et al. (2011) found that the cost of healthcare for patients with general anxiety disorder was significantly higher than for patients with other conditions. Overall, the early onset, persistence, and societal impact of anxiety make it a substantial public health and economic issue.

Although successful interventions have been developed to treat anxiety disorders in young children, reliance on traditional treatment approaches has certain limitations. For example, many children who receive treatment do not fully recover or experience a reoccurrence of symptoms (Compton, Burns, Egger, & Robertson, 2002; Hudson et al., 2015; Last, Perrin, Hersen, & Kazdin, 1996). Further, by the time the child enters treatment, rigid beliefs and behavioral patterns may have already developed. In contrast, prevention programs are typically implemented before the child experiences a substantial reduction in quality of life and before anxiety has a negative impact on the child or adolescent's development (Dadds, Spence, Holland, Barrett, & Laurens, 1997; Hirshfeld-Becker & Biederman, 2002). In addition, by the time anxiety disorders have developed, family members may have already accommodated, and perhaps unintentionally reinforced, the anxiety related behaviors, such as avoidance and reassurance (Norman, Silverman, & Lebowitz, 2015).

Another argument for prevention is that the approach is typically proactive, as community outreach and active recruitment are often emphasized (Beatson et al., 2014). Further, prevention programs do not always require mental health professionals for implementation, thus, potentially increasing the accessibility of services in underserved and economically disadvantaged areas (Barrett & Turner, 2001; Mrazek & Haggerty, 1994). Also, even after a child or adolescent meets diagnostic threshold for an anxiety disorder, symptoms may be overlooked or minimized, and consequently, anxiety disorders often go unidentified and untreated (Chavira, Stein, Bailey, & Stein, 2004). The proactive nature of prevention efforts may increase the early identification of at-risk children, who may otherwise go untreated.

It is noteworthy that preschool may be an ideal developmental period to implement prevention programs, as these programs are administered before the modal age of onset of most anxiety disorders, allowing a strength-based approach by working on the social and emotional competence, as well as on the increase of children's resilience. Related to this point, preschool anxiety prevention appears to be a particularly cost-effective approach to reduce the social and economic burden associated with anxiety disorders (Mihalopoulos, Vos, Pirkis, & Carter, 2011; Mihalopoulos, Vos, Rapee, Pirkis, Chatterton, Lee, & Carter, 2015).

Overall, anxiety prevention in preschool-aged children is likely to be a viable approach to reduce the incidence rate of anxiety disorders. In the following sections, the summary of the research to date in this area is provided, including a summary of the effectiveness of anxiety prevention programs and a discussion of limitations and directions for future research.

Classification of Prevention Approaches

Prevention programs can be classified based on the nature or focus of the group that receives intervention. Originally, programs were classified as primary, secondary, or tertiary (Caplan, 1964; Dozois & Dobson, 2004). In particular, primary prevention is administered regardless of risk status. Secondary prevention is intended for individuals considered to be at increased risk for developing a disorder or disease, and tertiary programs are administered to prevent the worsening, progression, or relapse of a particular disorder. A more recent classification system includes the following categories: universal, selective, and indicated (Dozois & Dobson, 2004; Gordon, 1983; Mrazek & Haggerty, 1994). Universal prevention programs are administered regardless of risk status, and considered to be applicable to all members of a specific group or population (e.g., all school-aged children). The concept of universal prevention is generally synonymous with primary prevention.

An advantage to universal prevention is that this approach has the potential to reach a large number of individuals. Further, because all members of a group are considered eligible to participate, prevention programs can be incorporated into school-based curriculums. However, a number of challenges to the implementation of universal prevention programs are noteworthy. For example, because these programs are implemented with large groups, they are often resource intensive. Further, when focused on the prevention of a specific disorder, such as anxiety, many individuals who are low risk will participate. This may lead to a floor effect and smaller effect sizes (Werner-Seidler, Perry, Calear, Newby, & Christensen, 2017). Consequently, it is probably most effective to separate participants based on risk status (e.g., high risk and low risk) when assessing program effectiveness. Further, when comparing universal programs relative to selective and indicated programs, it may be important to assess the effectiveness based on the overall number of cases of anxiety prevented over time, rather than focusing on effect size.

Selective programs are administered to subgroups in a population who are considered to have elevated risk for developing a particular disorder; however, the identified subgroup has not started to show symptoms of the problem or disorder (Mrazek & Haggerty, 1994; O'Connell, Boat, & Warner, 2009). For example, some selective programs have recruited children of parents with an anxiety disorder, as these children are at elevated risk for developing an anxiety disorder (Ginsburg, 2009). Indicated prevention focuses on individuals who have been identified, on an individual level, as being at increased risk for developing a psychiatric disorder, and the determination of risk often includes some form of screening or assessment (Mrazek & Haggerty, 1994; O'Connell et al, 2009). In general, selective and indicated programs seem to be most consistent with the concept of secondary prevention (Dozois & Dobson, 2004; Institute of Medicine, 1994).

An advantage to selective and indicated programs is that these programs may be particularly efficient and cost-effective, as most at-need children receive intervention. Further, because they focus on individuals with elevated risk, these programs tend to yield larger overall effect sizes. In addition, parents and school personnel may recognize the risk and developing difficulties in the children under their care, which may lead to increased motivation for engagement. One potential disadvantage has to do with concerns about stigma. For example, in regards to school-based programs, children and adolescents may need to be identified and either pulled out of their regular curriculum to participate or participate outside of designated school hours. Further, at-risk individuals need to be identified, which means reliance on identification of accuracy of screening measure (Bieling, McCabe, & Antony, 2004). A summary of the advantages and disadvantages of universal prevention programs, indicated prevention programs, and treatment programs is provided in Figure 10.1.

Universal Prevention Studies for Childhood Anxiety

A small number of trials have focused on universal prevention of anxiety disorders for school-aged children. Dadds and Roth (2008) conducted a universal prevention trial of a program called *Reach for Resilience*, which was a 6-session parent-based program. The program is focused on helping parents build resilience and improve coping skills in their children, and many of the strategies are consistent with cognitive-behavioral interventions. Skills addressed include building positive expectations, coping with negative emotions, building self-esteem through praise and encouragement, relaxation,

MODELS OF INTERVENTION

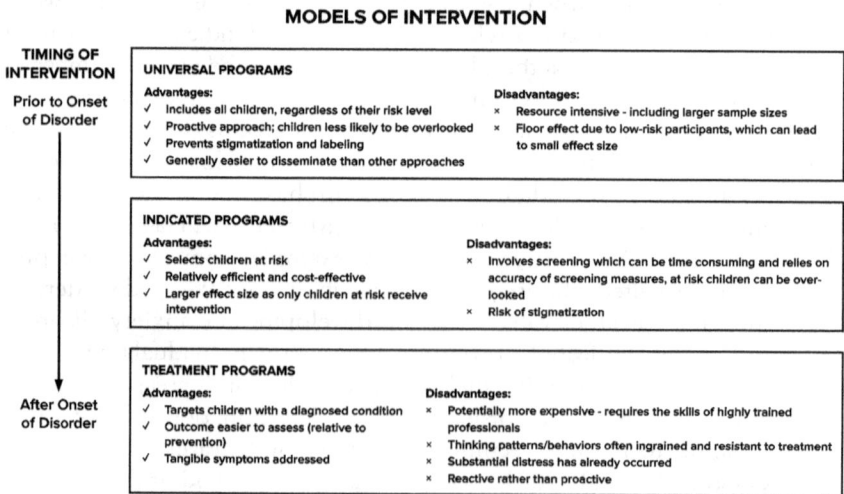

TIMING OF INTERVENTION	
Prior to Onset of Disorder	**UNIVERSAL PROGRAMS**
	Advantages: ✓ Includes all children, regardless of their risk level ✓ Proactive approach; children less likely to be overlooked ✓ Prevents stigmatization and labeling ✓ Generally easier to disseminate than other approaches — **Disadvantages:** × Resource intensive - including larger sample sizes × Floor effect due to low-risk participants, which can lead to small effect size
	INDICATED PROGRAMS
	Advantages: ✓ Selects children at risk ✓ Relatively efficient and cost-effective ✓ Larger effect size as only children at risk receive intervention — **Disadvantages:** × Involves screening which can be time consuming and relies on accuracy of screening measures, at risk children can be overlooked × Risk of stigmatization
After Onset of Disorder	**TREATMENT PROGRAMS**
	Advantages: ✓ Targets children with a diagnosed condition ✓ Outcome easier to assess (relative to prevention) ✓ Tangible symptoms addressed — **Disadvantages:** × Potentially more expensive - requires the skills of highly trained professionals × Thinking patterns/behaviors often ingrained and resistant to treatment × Substantial distress has already occurred × Reactive rather than proactive

Figure 10.1 Advantages and disadvantages of universal prevention programs, indicated prevention programs, and treatment programs

positive self-talk, problem solving, facing fears, and increasing social/friendship networks.

A matched design was used to assess outcome. Participants at specific schools were designated to receive the intervention or assigned to a control group, and assessment occurred at pre-intervention, post-intervention, and at 7-month follow-up. Overall, the authors reported challenges to interpretation of the data, which may have led to some mixed findings (Dadds & Roth, 2008). In particular, between-group differences were found at pre-intervention. Differential attrition also appeared to be a problem, parents experiencing higher levels of stress were more likely to drop out of the control condition but participants with lower levels of stress were more likely to drop out of the intervention condition. In general, based on parent-report, no between-group differences were found at post-intervention. Based on teacher-report, between-group differences were found for levels of anxiety and anger-related problems post-intervention. However, these differences were maintained only for anger-related problems at follow-up. The authors also examined the data based on risk status at pre-intervention. Based on this analysis, a higher percentage of children in the intervention group moved from high to low risk status relative to the control group.

Several studies have been conducted to examine the effectiveness of *Fun FRIENDS* (Barrett 2007a, 2007b) as a universal anxiety prevention program for preschool-aged children. In contrast to the *Reach for Resilience* Program, which was a parent-based intervention, the original universal prevention trials of the *Fun FRIENDS* intervention were predominantly child-based, with direct parent contact often limited to two sessions and parental involvement occurring for the home practice activities. The program focuses on anxiety-specific skills, along with more general resilience building and cognitive-behavioral coping skills. FRIENDS is an acronym used in the program. More specifically, "F" indicates "feelings," including affect education and strategies to cope with feelings, "R" indicates "relaxation," in which children learn relaxation strategies, "I" indicates "I can try," in which cognitive coping strategies are introduced, "E" indicates "Encourage," in which coping steps (graded exposure steps) are utilized, "N" indicates "Nurture," in which the importance of role models is discussed as well as kindness towards the community, "D" indicates "don't forget to be brave," in which continued use of the skills is discussed, and "S" indicates "Stay Happy," in which skills are reviewed. Additional skills to encourage socio-emotional learning are also included throughout the program.

Pahl and Barrett (2010) conducted the first study that evaluated the effectiveness of *Fun FRIENDS* as a universal trial, in which an intervention group and a control group were compared. Based on parent report, both groups exhibited decreases in anxiety from pre- to post-intervention. Although not statistically significant, the decrease was larger in magnitude for the intervention group from pre- to post-intervention. Comparison data was not available at 12-months, but based on within-groups comparisons, a significant decrease of anxiety symptoms was found from pre-intervention to follow-up for those receiving the program. Interestingly, in the intervention group, behavioral inhibition scores decreased over time for girls and increased over time for boys, suggesting differential gender effects for the program. Teacher report data also reported greater decreases in behavioral inhibition for the intervention group.

In a follow-up study, Anticich, Barrett, Silverman, Lacherez, & Gillies (2013) examined the effectiveness of the *Fun FRIENDS* program relative to a wait list control group and an active comparison group. The active comparison group received a program called *You Can Do It* (Ashdown & Bernard, 2012), a CBT-based social and emotional skills program. Results showed that those children receiving the *Fun FRIENDS* program exhibited the greatest improvements in behavioral inhibition, resilience, and parent-related stress at post-intervention and follow-up, and the findings were particularly salient at 12-month follow-up.

Finally, in an unpublished dissertation, Lewis (2012) examined the effectiveness of a universal intervention in a rural area of the United States, generally based on the *Fun FRIENDS* program. The author found increases in anxiety symptoms in the intervention group, whereas anxiety remained stable in the comparison group. One possible explanation for the finding is that increased awareness of anxiety symptoms in the intervention group led to higher anxiety scores at post-intervention. Further, it appears that standardized procedures recommended for the implementation of the *Fun FRIENDS* program may not have been completely followed, including intensive facilitator training and the provision of one workbook per child (see Barrett 2007a, 2007b).

Overall, a relatively small number of universal trials have focused on the prevention of anxiety in preschool-aged children. One trial was based on the *Reach for Resilience Program* and three trials were based on the *Fun FRIENDS* program. Across all studies, findings are somewhat mixed. As discussed in the previous section, one of the primary challenges to assessing universal prevention programs is that a floor effect may occur, which suppresses effect size. This may have been the case for the above mentioned studies. Due to the relatively small number of studies, it is clear that more research is needed in this area. Although follow-up data was available in a majority of the prevention trials discussed above, more research is needed to assess the long-term effectiveness of universal anxiety prevention programs, including longer-term monitoring assessment of comparison groups relative to intervention groups. As part of this evaluation, it is recommended that diagnostic status of participants is evaluated to assess the number of cases of anxiety disorders prevented over time. It is also suggested to include more protective factors measures that can evaluate variables such as resilience, social and emotional competence, optimism, social support, and self-concept, as well as measures of adherence and engagement (Dozois & Westra, 2004; Neil & Christensen, 2009)

Indicated and Selective Prevention Studies for Childhood Anxiety

A number of indicated programs, designed to prevent anxiety in pre-school-aged children, have been conducted. These programs generally recruit based on behaviorally inhibited temperament (behavioral inhibi-tion, shyness). Behaviorally inhibited temperament is utilized because this trait can be readily identified and reliably assessed at a young age (Lahat, Hong, & Fox, 2011; Paulus et al., 2015). Further, the presence of this trait seems to precede the onset of anxiety disorders, as it can be assessed as early as infancy. Based on longitudinal studies, inhibited temperament is a relatively robust risk for the eventual development of anxiety over time (Clauss & Blackford, 2012; Kampman, Viikki, Järventausta, & Leinonen, 2014). This risk appears to be particularly robust for social phobia, as children identified as inhibited have been found to be seven times more likely to develop social phobia over time (Clauss & Blackford, 2012). In addition to social phobia, inhibited temperament has also been found to be associated with increased risk for the development of panic disorder and obsessive-compulsive disorder (Kampman et al., 2014).

A series of studies by Rapee and colleagues have been conducted to assess the effectiveness of anxiety prevention programs for inhibited preschool-age children. This parent-based program is labeled the *Cool Little Kids* program (Kennedy, Rapee, & Edwards, 2009; Morgan et al., 2017; Rapee et al., 2005; Rapee et al., 2010; Rapee, 2013). In particular, Rapee et al. (2005) conducted a randomized trial to evaluate the effectiveness of a six-session version of the program. The authors found that effect sizes were relatively small on mea-sures of shyness/inhibited temperament at 12-month follow-up. In contrast, at three-year follow-up, children in the intervention group exhibited lower levels of anxiety based on the Spence Children's Anxiety Scale and fewer anxiety diagnoses, relative to children in the comparison group; however, no between-group differences were found on measures of inhibited tem-perament (Rapee et al., 2010). Finally, at 11-year follow-up, findings were mixed (Rapee, 2013). In particular, girls in the intervention group were found to exhibit fewer internalizing disorders relative to girls in the com-parison-group. Further, based on maternal report, girls in the intervention group were found to exhibit less anxiety. No between-group differences were found regarding girls' self-reported anxiety symptoms, although there was a trend toward significance, and no between-group differences were found for boys (Rapee, 2013).

In another study, Rapee and colleagues examined the effectiveness of an extended version of the *Cool Little Kids* program (Kennedy et al., 2009). In particular, two additional sessions, which were focused on parent anxiety management, were added. Behavioral inhibition was required for inclusion, and at least one parent was required to meet criteria for an anxiety disorder. At six-month follow-up, fewer children in the intervention group were absent of an anxiety disorder diagnosis (46.7%), relative to the comparison group (6.7%). In addition, lower levels of behavioral inhibition were found at post-intervention relative to the comparison group. However, parent anxiety did not seem to improve.

In a more recent study, Rapee and colleagues examined the effectiveness of an online version of the *Cool Little Kids* program (*Cool Little Kids Online*) (Morgan et al., 2017). The program consisted of eight interactive modules. Based on a randomized clinical trial, lower levels of anxiety were reported in the intervention group relative to a comparison group. However, no differences were found in overprotective parenting, which is a risk factor for child anxiety.

The above studies focused on intervention with parents and with minimal direct child involvement. In contrast, three studies have intervened directly with children. In an early study, LaFreniere and Capuano (1997) examined the effectiveness of an indicated program with inhibited preschool-aged children. A randomized clinical trial was conducted, and the intervention group received an intensive, 20-session intervention. The intervention was focused on parent-child interactions and was based on behavioral and attachment-based approaches. At the completion of the study, parents in the intervention group exhibited less over-control, and children in the intervention group exhibited greater cooperation during a parent-child interaction task. Further, based on teacher report, children in the intervention group exhibited higher levels of social competence. Although the findings were in the anticipated direction, no difference was found between the treatment and control groups for teacher ratings of anxious-withdrawn behavior.

In a more recent study, Chronis-Tuscano et al. (2015) conducted an eight-week intervention for behaviorally inhibited children called the *Turtle Program*, in which an intervention group was compared to a control group. Concurrent parent and child groups were conducted, along with a series of parent-child interaction tasks. The parent group was based on parent-child interaction (PCIT) adapted for separation anxiety (Puliafico, Comer, & Pincus, 2012). As part of the intervention, parents were coached on parent-child interaction tasks. The children's group was based on a program called *Social Facilitated Play* (see Coplan et al., 2010), which is a play-based program and focused on social skills development, including modeling and reinforcement of social skills along with exposure tasks. Significant differences in the intervention condition relative to the waitlist at intervention were found, including lower behavioral inhibition and anxiety based on parent-report, and reduced school-related anxiety based on teacher-report. Further, improvements were found in positive maternal affect.

In addition to the above mentioned studies, two open trials have been conducted on indicated anxiety prevention programs in inhibited preschool-aged children. In particular, Fox et al. (2012) conducted a pilot test of the effectiveness of the *Strengthening Early Emotional Development* (SEED) program. Sixteen children and their parents participated in this ten-session program, and parent and child groups were conducted concurrently. The children's group was play-based, addressing general social skills, relaxation, emotion regulation, peer interaction skills, and exposure. The parent group included psychoeducation, group discussions, role play, and homework. Skills addressed were basic behavioral parenting training skills, anxiety management skills to be implemented with their children, including relaxation and exposure hierarchies. The program also addressed parent anxious beliefs that may interfere with implementation of new skills. The authors found decreases in child anxiety and improvements in emotional resilience skills from pre- to post-intervention. Further, parents reported significant decreases in anxiety.

Another open trial was conducted to examine the effectiveness of an indicated program focused on inhibited/shy preschool-aged children (Fisak, 2014). The parent-based program, called the *Parent Resilience Program*, addressed on three interrelated areas. The most direct skills set targets parenting behaviors that may be related to the reduction of child anxiety, which includes decreasing modeling and overprotection, and encouraging parents to engage in exposure with their children rather than avoidance. The second area includes more general behavioral management, such as the use of special time, positive reinforcement, and limit setting. The third skills set is related to parent stress management. In relation to stress management, the program was unique in that parent mindfulness was addressed. This approach was included under the premise that improved mindfulness will lead to decreases in emotional reactivity and increases in moment-to-moment awareness, which may, in turn, increase use of more adaptive parenting strategies. Results were promising, as decreases in behavioral inhibition and anxiety scores were found from pre- to post-intervention. Parent anxiety also decreased from pre- to post-intervention.

Overall, a total of eight programs, six of which had comparison groups, focused on the prevention of anxiety in behaviorally inhibited preschool-aged children. The label "indicated" is likely the best classification for programs in which recruitment is based on inhibited/shy temperament. Outcomes at post-intervention and short-term follow-up were generally favorable. However, as with universal, there is limited long-term follow-up data (Rapee, 2013).

In addition to limited follow-up data, other challenges and directions for future research are noteworthy. One salient challenge in the use of behavioral inhibition in preschool-aged children as a risk factor for inclusion is that potential constructs overlap between behavioral inhibition/shyness and anxiety symptoms (see Rapee et al., 2005). When assessed, it appears that many behaviorally inhibited preschool-aged children already meet criteria for the diagnosis of an anxiety disorder before the intervention is implemented (see Table 10.1). This is problematic, at least in terms of classification of indicated programs, if the goal of these programs is to prevent the onset of anxiety. However, it is important to note children appear to be benefiting from these programs regardless of diagnostic status at pre-intervention. In terms of assessing the true prevention effect of these programs, one solution is to include children regardless of diagnostic status, but to separate groups based on diagnostic status at pre-intervention (e.g., Anticich et al., 2013; Dadds & Roth, 2008).

Assessing Outcome of Preschool Anxiety Prevention Programs

Defining Effectiveness

A number of challenges exist when evaluating the effectiveness of prevention programs. First, it is worthwhile to make the distinction between immediate symptom reduction (i.e., treatment effects), long-term prevention effects, and risk-factor reduction. A treatment effect occurs when an intervention group exhibits a greater symptom reduction at post-intervention, relative to a comparison group. In clinical trials, participants enter the study with clinically significant symptoms, and a greater reduction in symptoms in the treatment group is anticipated. This symptom reduction is generally expected to continue or at least be maintained over time.

Regarding prevention trials, between-group differences at post-intervention are indicative of program success, as these findings suggest that participants have benefited; however, two scenarios can lead to significant differences between intervention and comparison groups. The first scenario, a true prevention effect, would occur when the comparison group exhibits an increase in anxiety symptoms from pre- to post-intervention, whereas symptoms in the intervention group remain stable (see Figure 10.2). This scenario can be considered a true prevention effect, as cases of the targeted disorder are prevented as a result of participation in the program. Although possible, significant increases in comparison group symptoms are not likely to occur from pre- to post-intervention, as this is generally a brief time interval. A more likely scenario, scenario two, is that the intervention group exhibits greater symptom reduction from pre- to post-intervention in response to the participation in the intervention (Figure 10.3). This is best described as a treatment effect. As a treatment effect is the most likely scenario at post-intervention, this outcome does not seem to completely reflect the goal of prevention, which is generally to prevent the onset of a disorder (i.e., to decrease the incidence rate of a disorder) over time (O'Connell et al., 2009). Overall, although *immediate symptom reduction* in an intervention group is likely a marker of program success and may reduce risk over time, true prevention effects are reflected by *symptom increases* in comparison groups relative to an intervention group over time. Both longer-term follow-up and assessment of diagnostic status are ideal to assess true prevention effects.

Table 10.1 Study of prevention studies

Author(s)	Program	Design	Type	Diagnosis* Pre-Intervention	Diagnosis* Post-Intervention	Target of Intervention	Provider	Setting	Between-Groups Effect Size	Follow-up intervals
Morgan et al. (2017)	Cool Little Kids	RTC-waitlist	Targeted	69.70%	50%	Parents only	Online	Online	0.31	Post-only
Chronis-Tuscano et al. (2015)	The Turtle Program	RTC-waitlist	Targeted	78%	38.90%	Parents & children	Clinician	Clinic-based	1.71	Post-only
Rapee et al. (2005)	Cool Little Kids	RTC	Targeted	90%	50%	Parent only	Clinician	Clinic-based	0.09	12 months
Kennedy et al. (2009)	Cool Little Kids	RTC	Targeted	100%	53.30%	Parents only	Clinician	Clinic-based	0.54	Post-only
Fox et al. (2012)	SEED program	Pre-post only	Targeted	50%	37.5%	Parents & children	Doctoral Intern	Clinic-based	N/A	3 months
Rapee & Jacobs (2002)	Cool Little Kids (pilot)	Pre-post only	Targeted	Not reported	Not reported	Parents only	Graduate Student	Clinic-based	N/A	6 months
Fisak (2014)	Parent Resilience Program	Pre-post only	Targeted	Not reported	Not reported	Parents only	Clinician	School-based	N/A	Post-only

Table 10.1 (Cont.)

Author(s)	Program	Design	Type	Diagnosis* Pre-Intervention	Diagnosis* Post-Intervention	Target of Intervention	Provider	Setting	Between-Groups Effect Size	Follow-up intervals
LaFreniere & Capuano (1997)	Early Prevention program	RTC	Targeted	Not reported	Not reported	Parents & children	Graduate students	Home-based	1.03	Post-only
Anticich et al. (2013)	Fun FRIENDS	RTC	Universal	Not reported	Not reported	Parents & children	Teachers trained by lead researcher	School-based	0.39	12 months
Pahl & Barrett (2010)	Fun FRIENDS	RTC	Universal	Not reported	Not reported	Parents & children	Post-graduate Psychology students	School-based	0.10	9 weeks; 12 months
Dadds & Roth (2008)	Reach for Resilience	RTC	Universal	Not reported	14.8	Parents only	Clinician	School-based	0.47	7 months
Lewis (2012)	Early prevention program	Nonequivalent Control Group	Universal	37.5% high anxiety risk	Not reported	Parents & children	Graduate student	School-based	-0.83	3 months

Note. *Diagnosis at pre- and post-intervention includes the percentage of children diagnosed with an anxiety disorder in the intervention group. The high rate of diagnosis of anxiety in preschool-aged children may necessitate other approaches to prevent anxiety in at-risk children. For example, one possible direction is to implement intervention with the parents of inhibited children who are younger than three years of age. This may be an effective approach, as behavioral inhibition can be reliably assessed in infancy (Lahat et al., 2011). Another direction for future research is to consider the use of other inclusion criteria. For example, some prevention studies for school-aged children have recruited based on the diagnostic status of parents (Ginsburg, 2009), which would be most consistent with a selective approach to intervention.

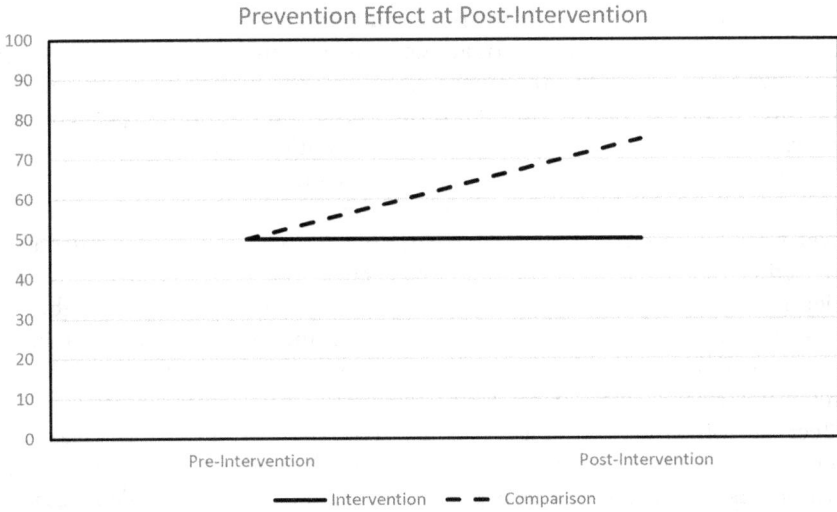

Prevention Effect at Post-Intervention

Figure 10.2 Prevention effect at post-intervention
Note. This figure depicts a hypothetical example of data in which a "true prevention effect" is present at post-intervention. Notice the stability of the intervention group, whereas the comparison group exhibits increased symptoms. True prevention effects may be unlikely at post-intervention, as symptoms would need to increase in the comparison group over a brief period of time (i.e., pre- to post-intervention).

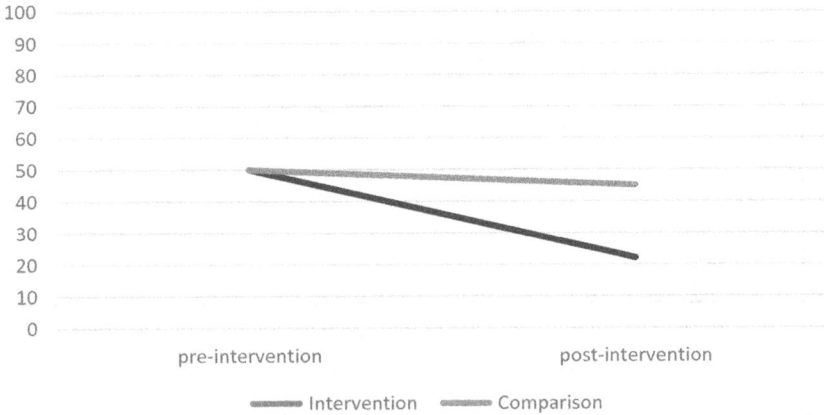

Figure 10.3 Treatment effect at post-intervention
Note. This figure depicts a hypothetical example in which a "treatment effect" has occurred at post-intervention. Notice a substantial decrease in symptoms from pre- to post-intervention in the intervention group. A smaller decrease may also occur in the comparison group, due to statistical regression and natural recovery.

Regarding long-term follow-up, a number of scenarios are possible. One such scenario is that a treatment effect is maintained at follow-up (see Figure 10.4). Again, treatment effects are of benefit to participants, but are not necessarily consistent with the true goals of prevention. Another scenario is that a long-term prevention effect occurs. In this scenario, symptoms in the intervention group either remain stable or decrease slightly, while symptoms in the comparison group increase over time (see Figure 10.5). This scenario may result in smaller effects at immediate post-intervention but larger effect sizes at follow-up, which highlights the importance of longer-term follow-up. Finally, a combined treatment and prevention effect is possible, and may be the most ideal scenario. For example, an anxiety prevention program may provide an initial treatment effect at post-intervention and an eventual prevention effect at follow-up (see Figure 10.6). The net result is a decrease in symptoms in the intervention group followed by an eventual increase in symptoms in the intervention group. This outcome would also be generally consistent with the goal of prevention programs.

It is also noteworthy that prevention programs can be evaluated based on the reduction of risk factors and the enhancement of protective factors over time. This approach is based on the assumption that the reduction of risk

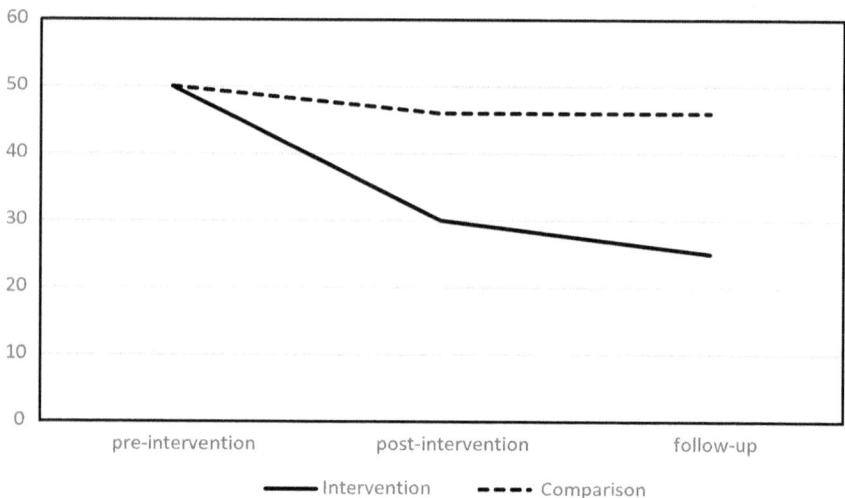

Figure 10.4 Treatment effects at post-intervention and follow-up
Note. This figure depicts a hypothetical example in which a "treatment effect" is apparent at post-intervention and at follow-up. Notice a substantial decrease in symptom from pre- to post-intervention and from post-intervention to follow-up in the intervention group. Some treatment effects can be delayed. A smaller decrease may also occur in the comparison group, due to statistical regression and/or natural recovery. This is essentially an extension of the pattern observed in Figure 10.3.

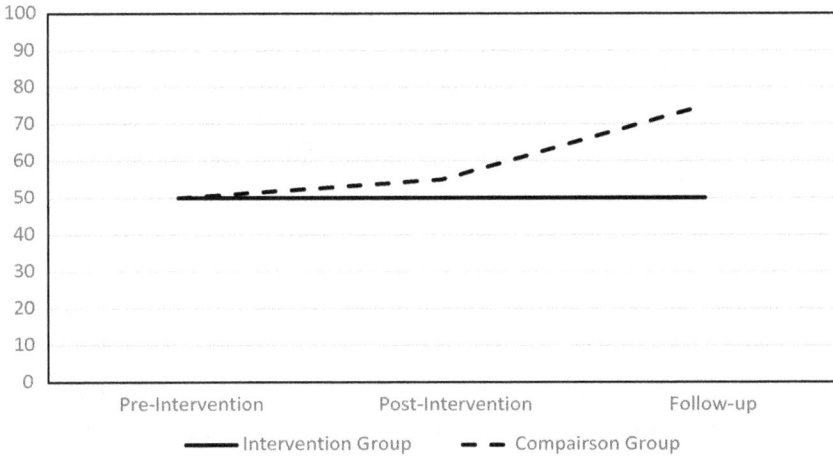

Figure 10.5 Delayed prevention effect

Note. This figure depicts a hypothetical example of a "delayed prevention effect" in which the comparison group exhibits a substantial increase in symptoms at follow-up. In contrast, the intervention group remains relatively stable. Relative to an immediate prevention-effect at post-intervention (see Figure 10.2) a delayed prevention effect may be a more likely scenario. This is because symptoms are more likely to gradually increase over time in the comparison group.

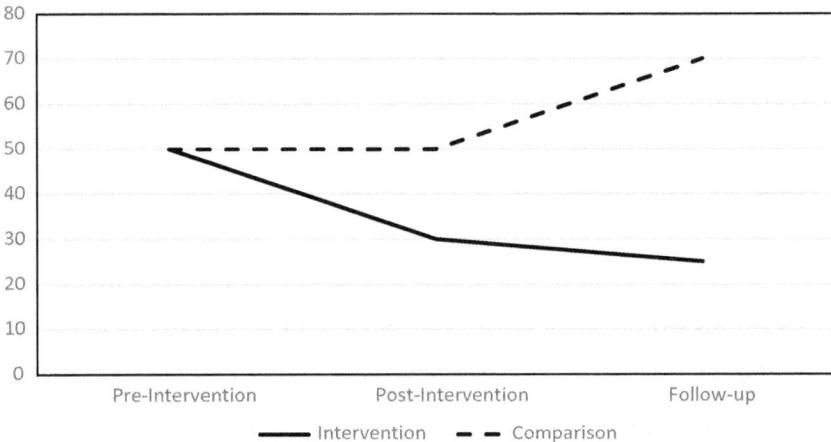

Figure 10.6 Combined treatment and prevention effects

Note. This figure depicts a hypothetical example in which treatment and prevention effects occur. The treatment effect is apparent at post-intervention and continues from post-intervention to follow-up. The prevention effect becomes most noticeable at follow-up, as symptoms in the comparison group are likely to increase gradually over time.

factors will eventually lead to a reduced probably of developing a particular disorder over time. Evidence-based risk and protective factors are usually identified, and these factors become the target of intervention and outcome evaluation. Regarding preschool anxiety, identified risk factors include inhibited temperament, parent anxiety, and parenting behaviors, including overprotection and modeling of anxiety. Protective factors include coping skills, emotional regulation, and positive self-concept, among others (O'Connell, Boat, & Warner, 2009).

The Effectiveness of Preschool Anxiety Prevention Programs

Previous reviews have been conducted to assess the effectiveness of anxiety prevention programs (e.g., Fisak, Richard, & Mann, 2011). However, effect sizes for preschool prevention programs have yet to be isolated. In response to this limitation, effect sizes were calculated for known preschool anxiety prevention programs (see Table 10.1). As a general gauge of effectiveness, between-group effect sizes were calculated at post-intervention. Based on a fixed effects model, the mean weighted effect size at post-intervention for all trials was significant, $d = -.32$, $Z = -6.56$, $p < .001$. Next effect sizes were examined separately based on intervention type. The mean weighted effect size at post-intervention was significant for indicated programs, $d = -0.40$, $Z = -4.74$, $p < .001$ and for universal programs, $d = -.28$, $Z = -4.68$, $p < .001$. Although, the difference was not statistically significant, $Q_{between} = 1.38$, $p = 0.24$, the trend towards larger effect sizes for indicated programs relative to universal programs was expected, as universal programs often yield lower effect sizes.

A common limitation of prevention trials is a lack of follow-up data, and the current dataset is no exception. Only three studies provided adequate follow-up data to calculate between-groups effect size at post-intervention (i.e., both comparison group and intervention group means at follow-up). For these three studies, between-group effect sizes were calculated at post-intervention and follow-up (operationalized as the follow-up interval closest to 12 months). The mean weighted effects sizes were significant and generally remained unchanged from post-intervention, $d = -.34$, $Z = 5.31$, $p < .001$, to follow-up, $d = -.36$, $Z = 5.17$, $p < .001$. Although these findings should be interpreted with caution due to an extremely small sample, these preliminary findings suggest that intervention gains are maintained for at least one year following intervention. Overall, the findings are promising, but more research is needed in which long-term prevention effects and the reeducation of risk factors are evaluated.

Summary and Directions for Future Research

Overall, anxiety prevention in preschool-aged children is an emerging area. To date, numerous clinical trials have been conducted and the results of these trials are generally favorable. That being said, a number of limitations and directions for future research are noteworthy. Perhaps the most salient issue is that little is known about the long-term effectiveness of preschool anxiety prevention programs, as these data are often limited. Further, one of the only studies to examine longer-term follow-up found mixed results (Rapee, 2013). Considering that one of the primary goals of anxiety prevention programs is to reduce the incidence of anxiety disorders amongst those who received the intervention, this is a substantial limitation. Although more consistent long-term follow-up in prevention trials is recommended as a solution, long-term follow-up comes with a number of challenges. One issue is attrition, which is often problematic in longitudinal studies. For example, in the comparison group, incentive to continue to participate may diminish over time. Further, Dadds and Roth (2008) found differential attrition in control groups relative to intervention groups based on level of parent stress. Another challenge has to do with the ethical management of control groups. A common approach in treatment studies is to use a waitlist control group. In particular, the waitlist group receives the intervention after participants in the treatment group complete the intervention. This approach is often adequate for the evaluation of treatment programs. However, long-term outcome is a particularly important marker of success of prevention programs, as a primary goal is to prevent the development of a disorder over an extended period of time. The waitlist control group approach limits the ability to assess the long-term effectiveness of programs, as the intervention group and the waitlist groups both have received intervention at follow-up. Consequently, with prevention programs, other options should probably be considered, including the use of active comparison studies and the use of minimal intervention groups.

Another consideration is the assessment of diagnostic status. Although not essential, the assessment of diagnostic status is an important consideration, as it allows for the assessment of incidence rates over time. However, diagnostic status was not consistently assessed in the above mentioned prevention programs. One of the challenges to the assessment of diagnostic status is that it is a resource-intensive measurement, and is particularly difficult to conduct in community-based settings.

Related to diagnostic status, in the above mentioned indicated programs, which typically recruit based on inhibited temperament, many children may have already met diagnostic criteria before the implementation of intervention. This seems to be due to the considerable overlap between behavioral inhibition and anxiety (Rapee et al., 2005). Although inhibited children with and without an anxiety diagnosis may benefit from early intervention programs, it might be beneficial to evaluate the groups separately. Further, it may be beneficial to consider other strategies. For example, perhaps it is possible to implement intervention at an even younger age, to catch children before they meet criteria for an anxiety disorder.

The target participants of the program is also an important consideration. Due to factors such as cognitive development and level of dependence on parents, higher levels of parent involvement are likely optimal for pre-school-aged children, and the above mentioned programs consistently include parents. However, considerable variation was found in terms of the level and nature of child involvement. Some programs focus almost exclusively on parents (e.g., Rapee et al., 2005; Morgan et al., 2017). Other programs emphasize parent-child interactions (Chronis-Tuscano et al., 2015), and/or include direct skills-based intervention with children (Anticich et al., 2013). Each of these approaches appears promising, and a direction for future research is to conduct active comparison studies (or studies including active comparisons) to examine the relative effectiveness of these approaches in regards to the prevention and treatment of anxiety.

Another consideration related to parent involvement has to do with the skills emphasized in programs. For example, in regards to parent-based intervention, one approach is to emphasize parenting skills to reduce child anxiety, including encouragement of exposure, decreasing reinforcement of anxiety, and decreasing modeling and overprotection. Another approach is to emphasize parent anxiety and stress reduction. In addition to direct benefits to the parents, these skills are proposed to have an indirect benefit on the child's functioning. For example, decreased parent stress and anxiety may lead to decreased stress in the parent-child relationships and decreased modeling of anxiety. At this time, it is recommended that both approaches are included. Eventually, dismantling studies are recommended to determine if both approaches are required to maximize the positive impact of intervention.

Another emerging issue relates to the specificity of the content of anxiety prevention programs. As discussed above, universal programs are administered to all children regardless of risk status. It may be practical for universal programs to provide more general resilience building skills, including problem solving and stress management, mixed with relevant anxiety and stress management skills (e.g., Barrett, 2007a; Dadds & Roth, 2008). In addition to anxiety prevention, these programs may have a more general preventative effect and appeal. Even if participants are not at particular risk for anxiety disorders they may benefit from participation.

In contrast, more anxiety-specific intervention may be ideal for indicated and selective programs, as participants are at elevated risk. In particular, these programs should include focused anxiety management skills, including exposure, relaxation, the reduction of parent overprotection and modeling, and the management of negative anxiety-related cognitions.

Setting is an important consideration when developing an anxiety prevention program. In particular, accessibility is considered an important feature of prevention. A number of the trials discussed above were conducted in clinics, which may provide a number of advantages. For example, programs that include concurrent parent and child groups and parent-child interaction tasks, may be more labor intensive and require a more controlled setting and more space. At the same time, trials conducted in clinical settings may have some disadvantages, including less accessibility and convenience for participants. Another concern relates to possible participant discomfort and reluctance to participate in a clinic-based setting. In contrast, community-based programs, including school-based programs, and internet-based programs are advantageous in that these programs may be the most conducive to dissemination and outreach efforts. A disadvantage is that these programs may be less intensive. Overall, a variety of anxiety prevention programs for preschool-aged children have been evaluated, each of which requires different resources and expertise to implement. The optimal approach may depend on the nature and needs of the community.

References

Anticich, S. J., Barrett, P. M., Silverman, W., Lacherez, P., & Gillies, R. (2013). The prevention of childhood anxiety and promotion of resilience among pre-school-aged children: A universal school based trial. *Advances in School Mental Health Promotion*, 6, 93–121. doi:10.1080/1754730X.2013.784616

Ashdown, D. M., & Bernard, M. E. (2012). Can explicit instruction in social and emotional learning skills benefit the social-emotional development, well-being, and academic achievement of young children? *Early Childhood Education Journal*, 39, 397–405. doi:10.1007/s10643-011-0481-x

Barrett, P. M. (2007a). *Fun Friends. The teaching and training manual for group leaders.* Brisbane, Australia: Fun Friends Publishing.

Barrett, P. M. (2007b). *Fun Friends. Family learning adventure: Resilience building activities for 4-, 5-, and 6-year-old children.* Brisbane, Australia: Fun Friends Publishing.

Barrett, P. M., & Pahl, K. M. (2006). School-based intervention: Examining a universal approach to anxiety management. *Australian Journal of Guidance & Counseling*, 16, 55–75. doi:10.1375/ajgc.16. 1. 55

Barrett, P., & Turner, C. (2001). Prevention of anxiety symptoms in primary school children: Preliminary results from a universal school-based trial. *British Journal of Clinical Psychology*, 40, 339–410. doi:10.1348/014466501163887

Baumeister, H., & Härter, M. (2007). Prevalence of mental disorders based on general population surveys. *Social Psychiatry and Psychiatric Epidemiology*, 42, 537–546.

Beatson, R. M., Bayer, J. K., Perry, A., Mathers, M., Hiscock, H., Wake, M., ... & Rapee, R. M. (2014). Community screening for preschool child inhibition to offer the 'Cool Little Kids' Anxiety Prevention Programme. *Infant & Child Development*, 23, 650–661. doi:10.1002/icd.1863

Bieling, P. J., McCabe, R. E., & Antony, M. M. (2004). Measurement issues in preventing anxiety and depression: Concepts and instruments. *The Prevention of Anxiety and Depression: Theory, Research, and Practice*, 330, 43–71. doi:10.1037/10722-003

Botvin, G. J., & Griffin, K. W. (2016). Prevention of substance abuse. In J. C. Norcross, G. R. VandenBos, D. K. Freedheim, R. Krishnamurthy, J. C. Norcross, G. R. VandenBos, ... R. Krishnamurthy (Eds.) , *APA handbook of clinical psychology: Applications and methods*, Vol. 3 (pp. 485–509). Washington, DC, US: American Psychological Association. doi:10.1037/14861-026

Caplan, G. (1964). *Principles of preventive psychiatry*. Oxford, England: Basic Books.

Cartwright-Hatton, S., McNicol, K., & Doubleday, E. (2006). Anxiety in a neglected population: Prevalence of anxiety disorders in pre-adolescent children. *Clinical Psychology Review*, 26, 817–833. doi:10.1016/j.cpr.2005. 12. 00doi:2

Chavira, D. A., Stein, M. B., Bailey, K., & Stein, M. T. (2004). Child anxiety in primary care: Prevalent but untreated. *Depression and Anxiety*, 20, 155–164. doi:10.1002/da.20039

Chronis-Tuscano, A., Rubin, K. H., O'Brien, K. A., Coplan, R. J., Thomas, S. R., Dougherty, L. R., ... & Womsatt, M. (2015). Preliminary evaluation of a multimodal early intervention programs for behaviorally inhibited preschoolers. *Journal of Counseling & Clinical Psychology*, 83, 534–540. doi:10.1037/a0039043

Clauss, J. A., & Blackford, J. U. (2012). Behavioral inhibition and risk for developing social anxiety disorder: A meta-analytic study. *Journal of the American Academy of Child & Adolescent Psychiatry*, 51, 1066–1075. doi:10.1016/j. jaac.2012. 08. 00doi:2

Compton, S. N., Burns, B. J., Egger, H. L., & Robertson, E. (2002). Review of the evidence base for treatment of childhood psychopathology: Internalizing disorders. *Journal of Consulting & Counseling Psychology*, 70, 1240–1266. doi:10.1037/0022-006X.70. 6. 12doi:40

Coplan, R. J., Schneider, B. H., Matheson, A., & Graham, A. (2010). 'Play skills' for shy children: Development of social skills facilitated play early intervention program for extremely inhibited preschoolers. *Infant and Child Development*, 19(3), 223–237.

Costello, E. J., Mustillo, S., Erkanli, A., Keeler, G., & Angold, A. (2003). Prevalence and development of psychiatric disorders in childhood and adolescence. *Archives of General Psychology*, 60, 837–844. doi:10.1001/archpsyc.60. 8. 83doi:7

Dadds, M. R., & Roth, J. H. (2008). Prevention of anxiety disorders: Results of a universal trial with young children. *Journal of Child & Family Studies*, 17, 320–335. doi:10.1007/s10826-007-9144-3

Dadds, M. R., Spence, S. H., Holland, D. E., Barrett, P. M., & Laurens, K. R. (1997). Prevention and early intervention for anxiety disorders: A controlled trial. *Journal of Consulting & Clinical Psychology*, 65, 627–635. doi:10.1037/0022-006X.65. 4. 62doi:7

Dougherty, L. R., Tolep, M. R., Bufferd, S. J., Olino, T. M., Dyson, M., Traditi, M. ... & Klein, D. N. (2013). Preschool anxiety disorders: Comprehensive assessment of clinical, demographic, temperamental, familial, and life stress correlates. *Journal of Clinical Child & Adolescent Psychology*, 42, 577–589. doi:10.1080/15374416.2012.759225

Dozois, D. A., & Dobson, K. S. (2004). *The prevention of anxiety and depression: Theory, research, and practice*. Washington, DC, US: American Psychological Association. doi:10.1037/10722-000

Dozois, D. A., & Westra, H. A. (2004). The nature of anxiety and depression: Implications for prevention. In D. A. Dozois, K. S. Dobson, D. A. Dozois, K. S. Dobson (Eds.), *The prevention of anxiety and depression: Theory, research, and practice* (pp. 9–41). Washington, DC, US: American Psychological Association. doi:10.1037/10722-002

Egger, H. L., & Angold, A. (2006). Common emotional and behavioral disorders in preschool children: Presentation, nosology, and epidemiology. *Journal of Child Psychology and Psychiatry*, 47(3–4), 313–337. doi:10.1111/j.1469-7610.2006.01618.x

Fisak, B. (2014). The prevention of anxiety in preschool-aged children: Development of a new program and preliminary findings. *Mental Health & Prevention*, 2, 18–25. doi:10.1016/j.mhp.2014. 07. 00doi:1

Fisak, B. J., Richard, D., & Mann, A. (2011). The prevention of child and adolescent anxiety: A meta-analytic review. *Prevention Science*, 12(3), 255–268. doi:10.1007/s11121–11011–0210–0

Fox, J. K., Warner, C. M., Lerner, A. B., Ludwig, K., Ryan, J. L., Colognori, D., & ... Brotman, L. M. (2012). Preventive intervention for anxious preschoolers and their parents: Strengthening early emotional development. *Child Psychiatry & Human Development*, 43, 544–559. doi:10.1007/s10578-012-0283-4

Ginsburg, G. S. (2009). The Child Anxiety Prevention Study: Intervention model and primary outcomes. *Journal of Consulting & Clinical Psychology*, 77, 580–587. doi:10.1037/a0014486

Gordon, R.S. (1983). An operational classification of disease prevention. *Public Health Reports*, 98, 107–109.

Greenberg, P. E., Sisitsky, T., Kessler, R. C., Finkelstein, S. N., Berndt, E. R., Davidson, J. T., & ... Fyer, A. J. (1999). The economic burden of anxiety disorders in the 1990s. *The Journal of Clinical Psychiatry*, 60, 427–435. doi:10.4088/JCP.v60n0702

Hirshfeld-Becker, D. R., & Biederman, J. (2002). Rationale and principles for early intervention with young children at risk for anxiety disorders. *Clinical Child and Family Psychology Review*, 5, 161–172. doi:10.1023/A:1019687531040

Hoffman, D. L., Dukes, E. M., & Wittchen, H. U. (2008). Human and economic burden of generalized anxiety disorder. *Depression & Anxiety*, 25, 72–90. doi:10.1002/da.20257

Hudson, J. L., Rapee, R. M., Lyneham, H. J., McLellan, L. F., Wuthrich, V. M., & Schniering, C. A. (2015). Comparing outcomes for children with different anxiety disorders following cognitive behavioral therapy. *Behavior Research & Therapy*, 72, 30–37. doi:10.1016/j.brat.2015. 06. 00doi:7

Institute of Medicine. (1994). Reducing the risks for mental disorders: Frontiers for preventive intervention research. In P. J. Mrazek & R. J. Haggerty (Eds.), *Committee on Prevention of Mental Disorders, Division of Biobehavioral Sciences and Mental Disorders*. Washington, DC: National Academy Press.

Kampman, O., Viikki, M., Järventausta, K., & Leinonen, E. (2014). Meta-analysis of anxiety disorders and temperament. *Neuropsychobiology*, 69, 175–186. doi:10.1159/000360738

Kashdan, T. B., Collins, R. L., & Elhai, J. D. (2006). Social anxiety and positive outcome expectancies on risk-taking behaviors. *Cognitive Therapy Research*, 30, 749–761. doi:10.1007/s10608-006-9017-x

Kennedy, S. J., Rapee, R. M., & Edwards, S. L. (2009). A selective intervention program for inhibited preschool-aged children of parents with an anxiety disorder: Effects on current anxiety disorders and temperament. *Journal of the American Academy of Child & Adolescent Psychiatry*, 48, 602–609. doi:10.1097/CHI.0b013e31819f6fa9

Kessler, R. C., Angermeyer, M., Anthony, J. C., De Graaf, R., Demyttenaere, K., Gasquet, I., Gluzman, S. ... & Ustun, T. B. (2007). Lifetime prevalence and age-of-onset distributions of mental disorders in the World Health Organization's World Mental Health Survey Initiative. *World Psychiatry*, 6, 168–176.

LaFreniere, P. J., & Capuano, F. (1997). Preventive intervention as means of clarifying direction of effects in socialization: Anxious-withdrawn preschoolers case . Development & Psychopathology, 9, 551–564. doi:10.1017/S0954579497001302

Lahat, A., Hong, M., & Fox, N. A. (2011). Behavioural inhibition: Is it a risk factor for anxiety? International Review of Psychiatry, 23, 248–257. doi:10.3109/09540261.2011.590468

Langley, A. K., Bergman, R. L., McCracken, J., & Piacentini, J. C. (2004). Impairment in childhood anxiety disorders: Preliminary examination of the child anxiety impact scale-parent version. Journal of Child & Adolescent Psychopharmachology, 14, 105–114. doi:10.1089/104454604773840544

Last, C. G., Perrin, S., Hersen, M., & Kazdin, A. E. (1996). A prospective study of childhood anxiety disorders. Journal of the American Academy of Child & Adolescent Psychiatry, 35, 1502–1510. doi:10.1097/00004583-199611000-00019

Lewis, K. M. (2012). An ounce of prevention: Evaluation of the Fun FRIENDS program for kindergarteners in a rural school. Dissertation Abstracts International: Section B: The Sciences and Engineering, Vol. 76(10-B)(E).

Mihalopoulos, C., Vos, T., Pirkis, J., & Carter, R. (2011). The economic analysis of prevention in mental health programs. Annual Review of Clinical Psychology, 7, 169–201. doi:10.1146/annurev-clinpsy-032210-104601

Mihalopoulos, C., Vos, T., Rapee, R. M., Pirkis, J., Chatterton, M. L., Lee, Y., & Carter, R. (2015). The population cost-effectiveness of a parenting intervention designed to prevent anxiety disorders in children. Journal of Child Psychology & Psychiatry, 56, 1026–1033. doi:10.1111/jcpp.12438

Morgan, A. J., Rapee, R. M., Salim, A., Goharpey, N., Tamir, E., McLellan, L. F., & Bayer, J. K. (2017). Internet-delivered parenting program for prevention and early intervention of anxiety problems in young children: randomized controlled trial. Journal of the American Academy of Child & Adolescent Psychiatry, 56, 417–425. doi:10.1016/j.jaac.2017. 02. 01doi:0

Mrazek, P. J., & HaggertyR. J. (1994). Reducing risks for mental disorders: Frontiers for preventative intervention research. Washington, DC, US: National Academy Press.

Neil, A.J., & Christensen, H. (2009). Efficacy and effectiveness of school-based prevention and early intervention programs for anxiety. Clinical Psychology Review, 29, 208–215. doi:10.1016/j.cpr.2009. 01. 00doi:2

Norman, K. R., Silverman, W. K., & Lebowitz, E. R. (2015). Family accommodation of child and adolescent anxiety: Mechanisms, assessment, and treatment. Journal of Child and Adolescent Psychiatric Nursing, 28, 131–140. doi:10.1111/jcap.12116

O'Connell, M. E., Boat, T., & Warner, K. E. (2009). Preventing mental, emotional, and behavioral disorders among young people: Progress and possibilities. Washington, DC: The National Academies Press; and U.S. Department of Health and Human Services, Substance Abuse and Mental Health Services Administration.

Pahl, K. M., & Barrett, P. M. (2010). Preventing anxiety and promoting social and emotional strength in preschool children: A universal evaluation of the Fun FRIENDS program. Advances in School Mental Health Promotion, 3, 14–25. doi:10.1080/1754730X.2010.9715683

Paulus, F. W., Backes, A., Sander, C. S., Weber, M., & Gontard, A. (2015). Anxiety disorders and behavioral inhibition in preschool children: A population-based study. Child Psychiatry and Human Development, 46, 150–157. doi:10.1007/s10578-014-0460-8

Posthumus, J.A., Raaijmakers, M.A.J., Maassen, G.H., van Engeland, H., & Matthtys, W. (2012). Sustained effects of the Incredible Years as a preventive intervention in preschool children with conduct problems. *Journal of Abnormal Child Psychology*, 40, 487–500. doi:10.1007/s10802-011-9580-9

Polancsyzk, G.V., Salum, G.A., Sugaya, L.S., Caye, A., & Rohde, L.A. (2015). Annual research review: A meta-analysis of the worldwide prevalence of mental disorders in children and adolescents. *Journal of Child Psychology & Psychiatry*, 56, 345–365. doi:10.1111/jcpp.12381

Puliafico, A. C., Comer, J. S., & Pincus, D. B. (2012). Adapting parent-child interaction therapy to treat anxiety disorders in young children. *Child and Adolescent Psychiatric Clinics of North America*, 21, 607–619. doi:10.1016/j. chc.2012. 05. 00doi:5

Rapee, R. M. (2013). The preventative effects of a brief, early intervention for pre-school-aged children at risk for internalising: Follow-up into middle adolescence. *Journal of Child Psychology & Psychiatry*, 54, 780–788. doi:10.1111/jcpp.12048

Rapee, R. M., & Jacobs, D. (2002). The reduction of temperamental risk for anxiety in withdrawn preschoolers: A pilot study. *Behavioural and Cognitive Psychotherapy*, 30(2), 211–216.

Rapee, R. M., Kennedy, S., Ingram, M., Edwards, S., & Sweeney, L. (2005) Prevention and early intervention of anxiety disorders in inhibited preschool children. *Journal of Consulting and Clinical Psychology*, 73, 488–497. doi:10.1037/ 0022-006X.73. 3. 48doi:8

Rapee, R. M., Kennedy, S. J., Ingram, M., Edwards, S. L., & Sweeney, L. (2010). Altering the trajectory of anxiety in at-risk young children. *The American Journal of Psychiatry*, 167, 1518–1525. doi:10.1176/appi.ajp.2010.09111619

Revicki, D. A., Travers, K., Wyrwich, K. W., Svedsater, H., Locklear, J., Mattera, M. S., ... & Montgomery, S. (2011). Humanistic and economic burden of generalized anxiety disorder in North American and Europe. *Journal of Affective Disorders*, 140, 103–112.

Springer, J. F., Sale, E., Hermann, J., Sambrano, S., Kasim, R., & Nistler, M. (2004). Characteristics of effective substance abuse prevention programs for high-risk youth. *The Journal of Primary Prevention*, 25, 171–194. doi:10.1023/B: JOPP.0000042388.63695.3f

Stockings, E. A., Degenhardt, L., Dobbins, T., Lee, Y. Y., Erskine, H. E., Whiteford, H. A., & Patton, G. (2016). Preventing depression and anxiety in young people: A review of the joint efficacy of universal, selective and indicated prevention. *Psychological Medicine*, 46, 11–26. doi:10.1017/S0033291715001725

Watson, H. J., Joyce, T., French, E., Willan, V., Kane, R. T., Tanner-Smith, E. E., & ... Egan, S. J. (2016). Prevention of eating disorders: A systematic review of randomized, controlled trials. *International Journal of Eating Disorders*, 49, 833–862. doi:10.1002/eat.22577

Werner-Seidler, A., Perry, Y., Calear, A. L., Newby, J. M., & Christensen, H. (2017). School-based depression and anxiety prevention programs for young people: A systematic review and meta-analysis. *Clinical Psychology Review*, 51, 30–47. doi:10.1016/j.cpr.2016. 10. 00doi:5

Winther, J., Carlsson, A., & Vance, A. (2014). A pilot study of a school-based prevention and early intervention program to reduce oppositional defiant disorder/conduct disorder. *Early Intervention in Psychiatry*, 8, 181–189. doi:10.1111/ eip.12050

11 Psychopharmacological Treatment of Anxiety in Preschool-Aged Children

Anuja Mehta, Jasmine Reyes, and Brian Fisak

Anxiety disorders are among the most common form of mental disorders in preschool children. In particular, based on epidemiological studies, nearly 10% of preschool children have been found to meet criteria for an anxiety disorder (Fanton & Gleason, 2009). There has been an increased awareness of the presence of anxiety symptoms in preschool-aged children, and prevalence, persistence, and level of impairment associated with anxiety in this population has led to the development of effective, evidence-based psychosocial interventions (see Chapters 6–9 of this book). Despite the effectiveness of psychosocial interventions, some children do not respond to treatment or show only partial response, and in these cases, additional treatment options may need to be considered.

The use of psychotropic medications is a possible option for severe, treatment-resistant cases, in which preschool-aged children fail to respond to evidence-based psychosocial intervention (Barterian, Rappuhn, Seif, Watson, Ham, & Carlson, 2014; Gleason et al., 2007; Fanton & Gleason, 2009; Luby, 2013). However, for several reasons, psychotropic medications should be prescribed with caution and only as a secondary treatment option. In particular, the evidence supporting the effectiveness of these medications is limited. Further, concerns exist about the tolerability, potential side effects, and impact on neurodevelopment on preschool-aged children, along with the ability of young children to metabolize psychiatric medications (Barterian et al., 2014; Gleason et al., 2007).

The Preschool Psychopharmacology Working Group (PPWG), established by the American Academy of Child and Adolescent Psychiatry (AACAP), developed practice parameters for use of medications in preschool-aged children, including guidelines for children with anxiety and related-disorders (Gleason et al., 2007). These guidelines are based on a number of factors, including common practices, the available research on the use of medications in preschool-aged children, and the research on the effectiveness and tolerability of psychiatric medications in slightly older children. Based on this available information, the PPWG developed three specific treatment algorithms relevant to anxiety and related disorders. An anxiety disorders algorithm was developed, which included the disorders typically diagnosed in preschool-aged children and found in the anxiety chapter of the DSM-5 (American Psychiatric Association, 2013). A single algorithm was used for these disorders due to the similarities in psychosocial and psychopharmacological treatment approaches. The second algorithm was developed for obsessive-compulsive disorder (OCD), and the third was developed for Post-traumatic Stress Disorder (PTSD). In addition to treatment recommendations, contraindicated medications are also discussed as part of the algorithms.

A review of the available research specific to preschool-aged children is provided below, followed by more general recommendations from the PPWG. In relation to this review, two points are particularly noteworthy. First, the available literature on the use of medications to treat anxiety in preschool children is mostly limited to case reports and case series with a few small open-label trials. Second, the use of psychotropic medications in preschool children for anxiety disorders is considered "off label," and it is recommended that this point is emphasized and discussed with caregivers when obtaining consent to treat.

Anxiety Disorders

As discussed above, the anxiety disorders algorithm includes the disorders in the anxiety chapter of the DSM-5 that are often diagnosed in preschool-aged children. Disorders in this category include specific phobias, social phobia, generalized anxiety disorder, separation anxiety disorder, and selective mutism. Relevant studies specific to this age group are discussed below followed by general recommendations from the PPWG.

Specific Phobias and Fears

Specific phobias are characterized by marked fear or anxiety about a specific object or situation (American Psychiatric Association, 2013), and three published studies have focused on specific phobias in young children. In particular, Avci, Diler, & Tamam (1998) provided a case report of a two-year-old girl, who had exhibited a severe fear of riding in cars. Ongoing symptoms included severe panic attacks, including trembling, palpitations and sweating, and she had previously failed treatments with systematic desensitization, hydroxyzine (Atarax), and alprazolam (Xanax). Following these failed trials, she was treated with fluoxetine (Prozac) 5 mg/day, and after two weeks of treatment, she demonstrated significant improvement, as she was able to ride in cars without difficulty. Fluoxetine was gradually tapered off and the symptoms did not return. In general, this case report provides some evidence that low dose fluoxetine may be safely used in young children who present with severe phobias that are unresponsive to exposure and desensitization.

Fluoxetine was also used for the treatment of feeding anxiety in two very young children. In particular, Celik, Diler, Tahiroglu, and Avci (2007) reported a case study of two 24-month-old twin girls who exhibited severe fear of eating which developed due to medical complications. After unsuccessful trials with haloperidol (Haldol) (0.5 mg/day) and behavior therapy, fluoxetine 5 mg/day was initiated. It is noteworthy that behavior therapy was continued along with fluoxetine. After two months of treatment with fluoxetine, both the children began to feed without difficulty. Fluoxetine was tapered off and discontinued at eight months of treatment and gains were maintained at follow-up.

In addition to SSRIs, buspirone (Buspar) has been used to treat feeding anxiety. Hanna, Feibusch, and Albright (1997) described a case of a four-year-old male who exhibited feeding anxiety accompanied by a refusal to eat. The authors utilized buspirone instead of SSRI to prevent gastrointestinal side effects. Buspirone was started at 2.5 mg twice daily, and after one week of treatment, the child began to use eating utensils and to eat more frequently. The progress continued when the dose was gradually increased to 5 mg twice daily.

In general, based on the limited literature for specific phobias in young children, fluoxetine may be safely used at low doses if behavioral interventions have failed. In the case of feeding anxiety, buspirone may also be considered as a possible option.

Selective Mutism

Selective Mutism (SM) is characterized by a consistent failure to speak in specific social situations, in which there is an expectation for speaking, and can lead to considerable impairment in functioning (American Psychiatric Association, 2013). Most of the psychopharmacological studies in this area are based on single case reports, in which the use of fluoxetine led to improvement in symptoms and in which the child began verbalizing (Dummit, Klein, Tancer, Asche, & Martin, 1996; Golwyn & Sevlie 1999; Harvey & Milne 1998; Wright, Cuccaro, Leonhardt, Kendall, & Anderson, 1995). The decision to initiate fluoxetine in all cases was made after the child had failed to respond to an adequate trial of psychosocial intervention. Across these studies, fluoxetine was prescribed in the range of 8 mg to 20 mg/day in the maintenance phase of the treatment. Although these studies generally found symptom improvement with fluoxetine, issues with tolerability and side effects are noteworthy. For example, Dummit et al. (1996) conducted a pilot study in the form of an open trial, examining the effectiveness of fluoxetine in the treatment of selective mutism. The authors found that two of five preschool-aged children treated with fluoxetine for SM were taken off the medication due to the side effect of behavioral disinhibition despite showing improvements, based on the Clinical Global Impressions Scale (CGI-S).

Sertraline (Zoloft) has also been used to treat SM in preschool-aged children. Carlson, Kratochwill, and Johnston (1999) reported the results of a case series of five children with SM. Two of the children were five years old, and the remaining three were school-aged. The children were treated with sertraline at a dose ranging from 50 mg to 100 mg/day. Both the preschool-aged children exhibited improvement with sertraline, as measured by the scores on Global Attainment Scaling (GAS) and Child Behavior Checklist (CBCL). Regarding notable side effects, one of the preschool child developed insomnia at 100 mg/day dose of sertraline.

Golwyn and Sevlie (1999) provided a case report using phenelzine (Nardil), a monoamine oxidase inhibitor, in a five-year-old female with SM. She had not responded to a previous 10-month trial of fluoxetine. Phenelzine was initiated at 22.5 mg/day (7.5 mg three times a day) and was gradually titrated to 30 mg/day. Her symptoms eventually improved, and she began having conversations with her babysitter, classmates, and teacher. Insomnia and slight weight gain were the only notable side effects reported.

Overall, it may be practical to consider a trial of an SSRI (either fluoxetine or sertraline), with careful monitoring for behavioral disinhibition and insomnia, for preschool-aged children who present with severe and disabling symptoms of SM and who have not responded to an adequate trial of psychosocial intervention.

PPWG Algorithm for Anxiety Disorders

Based on PPWG recommendations, a trial of fluoxetine is recommended in severe cases when psychosocial intervention has been found to be ineffective. In the case of non-response to fluoxetine, the workgroup recommends fluvoxamine as a second option. Regarding contraindicated medications, the PPWG discourages benzodiazepines, especially the persistent use of benzodiazepines. One exception to this recommendation is that benzodiazepines may be indicated in cases of severe anxiety related to medical or dental procedures. Finally, it was recommended that tricyclic antidepressants and alpha-antagonists are not used.

Obsessive Compulsive Disorder (OCD)

Obsessive-compulsive disorder, is characterized by the presence of obsessions, compulsions or both (American Psychiatric Association, 2013). Obsessions are recurrent and persistent thoughts, urges, or images that are experienced as intrusive and unwanted, and compulsions are defined as repetitive behaviors that the individual feels driven to perform in response to an obsession. Ercan, Kandulu, and Ardic (2012) conducted a series of cases studies with four preschool-aged children using fluoxetine to treat OCD. The fluoxetine dose ranged from 5 mg to 20 mg. All participants exhibited improvement based on scores on the CGI-S and

Children's Yale-Brown Obsessive Compulsive Scale (CY-BOCS); however, behavioral disinhibition occurred in three out of the four children in this study when receiving higher doses of fluoxetine. In a retrospective quasi-experimental study evaluating outcome for six preschool children with OCD, fluoxetine was prescribed ranging from 5 mg to 15 mg/day (Coskun & Zoroglu, 2009). Five out of six children showed improvements in CGI-S scores. However, one participant had to discontinue fluoxetine due to behavioral disinhibition.

Oner and Oner (2008) reported the results of a case study series in which three preschool-aged children with OCD, between the ages of four and five, were treated with sertraline 25 mg/day. Two of the three children developed behavioral disinhibition and were put on risperidone 0.5 mg/day to manage this side effect. Symptom improvement was noted for all three children, as assessed by their scores on CY-BOCS. In summary, if a very young child presents with moderate to severe OCD that has failed to respond to behavioral interventions, low dose fluoxetine or sertraline may be a viable option; however, the clinician must monitor the child for behavioral disinhibition, as this appears to be a common side effect for both medications.

PPWG Algorithm for OCD

The PPWG recommended a trial of fluoxetine, fluvoxamine, or sertraline in severe cases in which psychosocial interventions have been unsuccessful. Following nonresponse to one of the above mentioned SSRIs, it is recommended that a trial of a second SSRI from the list is conducted. Due to the potential side effects, the PPWG recommend that clomipramine is only utilized in extreme cases, as EKG changes have been reported in young children in response to clomipramine use (Gleason et al., 2007).

Post-Traumatic Stress Disorder (PTSD)

The DSM-5 has revised the criteria for PTSD in children ages six and younger to better capture PTSD in this age group using developmentally appropriate symptoms, and effective psychosocial interventions have been developed for this age group (American Psychiatric Association, 2013). Regarding psychopharmacological treatment, Harmon and Riggs (1996) reported the results of an open-label trial utilizing the clonidine (Catapres) patch for seven children between the ages of three and six years who were diagnosed with PTSD, exhibited severe symptoms, and who had not responded to at least one month of psychotherapy. In addition to the classic PTSD symptoms of hyperarousal and hypervigilance, clonidine was used to target insomnia, general anxiety, mood lability, and aggression in these children. Clonidine was started at 0.05 mg and titrated to 0.1 mg at bedtime for most children; however, one child required a higher dose of 0.05 mg twice daily and an additional 0.1 mg at bedtime. Symptom improvement was noted after three to four weeks of treatment and most of the children demonstrated reduction of target symptoms. Aside from some initial sedation, no significant side effects were reported. In general, in cases where preschool children are exhibiting severe and disruptive symptoms of PTSD and have not responded to psychotherapy, clonidine at a low dose, with careful monitoring of pulse and blood pressure, is a possibility (Harmon & Riggs, 1996). However, evidence is limited, as only one psychopharmacological study has focused on the treatment of preschool-aged children with PTSD.

PPWG Algorithm for PTSD

Due to limited evidence, the PPWG workgroup did make specific psychopharmacological recommendations for preschool-aged children with PTSD who do not respond to psychosocial interventions. However, the authors noted that the prescription of SSRIs is a relatively common practice amongst clinicians. Further, the authors indicated that the use of benzodiazepines and tricyclic antidepressants are contraindicated for this age-group.

Summary and Conclusions

Overall, there is a paucity of research examining the use of medications in preschool-aged children diagnosed with anxiety and related disorders. Further, little is known about the potential impact of long-term use of psychotropic medications, such as SSRIs, including the impact on physical and neurological development. In addition, younger children may have difficulties metabolizing psychotropic medications and may be particularly susceptible to side effects (Barterian et al., 2014; FDA, 2005; Gleason et al., 2007). For example, children are two to three times more likely to develop disinhibition and gastrointestinal side effects from taking SSRIs relative to adults (Safer & Zito, 2006), and a black box warning has been issued for the use of SSRIs in children, adolescents and young adults due to their potential for causing an increase in suicidal ideation (FDA, 2005). Based on the limited evidence and potential for adverse effects, psychosocial treatments should remain the first line intervention for anxiety disorders in preschool children. However, clinicians may encounter very young children with disabling anxiety symptoms who have not responded to psychotherapeutic interventions, and in these situations, it may be reasonable to use psychotropic medications to alleviate the burden of their symptoms. See Table 11.1 for a summary of the studies in which medication was utilized to treat preschool anxiety or related disorders.

Table 11.1 An overview of studies in which medication was used to treat preschool anxiety or a related disorder

Disorder	Study	Design	Study N	Age (in years)	Medication	Dose (mg)	Outcome	Notable Side Effects
OCD	Coskun & Zoroglu (2009)	Quasi-experimental design	6	3 to 5	Fluoxetine	5–15	Improved CGI scores	Behavioral disinhibition
	Ercan et al. (2012)	Case study series	4	2 to 5	Fluoxetine	5–20	Improved CGI and CYBOCS scores	Behavioral disinhibition
	Oner & Oner (2008)	Case study series	3	4 to 5	Sertraline	25 to 50	Improved CYBOCS scores	Behavioral disinhibition treated with Risperidone
Selective Mutism	Carlson et al. (1999)	Single case research design	2	5	Sertraline	50 to 100	Improved GAS and CBCL	Insomnia
	Dummit et al. (1996)	Quasi-experimental design	5	5	Fluoxetine	5 to 20	Improved CGI	Behavioral disinhibition
	Golwyn & Sevlie (1999)	Case study	1	4	Fluoxetine followed by Phenelzine	2–16 (Fluox), 22.5–30 (Phen)	Improved symptoms	Weight gain and insomnia treated with Clonazepam
	Harvey & Milne (1998)	Case study	1	5	Fluoxetine	2 to 4	Improved symptoms	None reported
	Wright et al. (1995)	Case study	1	4	Fluoxetine	4 to 8	Improved CBCL	None reported

PTSD	Harmon & Riggs (1996)	Quasi-experimental design	7	3 to 6	Clonidine	0.05 to 0.20	Improved	Mild sedation
Specific Phobia	Avci et al. (1998)	Case study	1	2.5	Fluoxetine	5	Improved symptoms	None reported
Feeding Anxiety	Celik et al. (2007)	Case study series	2	2	Fluoxetine	5	Improved symptoms None	None reported
	Hanna et al. (1997)	Case study	1	4	Buspirone	5 to 12.5	Improved symptoms Mild insomnia	Mild insomnia

Notes: CBCL – Child Behavior Checklist; CGI-S – Clinical Global Impressions–Severity Scale; CY-BOCS – Children's Yale-Brown Obsessive Compulsive Scale; GAS – Global Attainment Scaling.

If a medication trial is deemed appropriate for a preschool-aged child, the following points should be considered by the clinician:

1   Although specific recommendations and considerations vary by disorder, SSRIs have been successfully used to treat OCD, selective mutism, specific phobia, and feeding-related anxiety in preschool-aged children.

2   Among the SSRIs, fluoxetine appears to have the most research in terms of efficacy in the treatment of anxiety disorders and OCD in preschool-aged children. Based on the available research, sertraline is also a viable option. The PPWG also recommended fluvoxamine as a secondary option.

3   The research to treat PTSD in preschool-aged children with psychotropic medications is limited, and the PPWG did make specific recommendations with this group.

4   Medications should be started at a low dose and titrated very slowly. The child should be monitored carefully during the titration for the emergence of any side effects.

5   Behavioral disinhibition appears to be a common side effect of SSRI in preschool children. Other reported adverse effects include insomnia and gastrointestinal distress.

6   If a desirable response is achieved and has been maintained for a sufficient period of time, then the clinician should try to wean the child off the medication and monitor him/her closely.

References

American Psychiatric Association. (2013). *Diagnostic and statistical manual of mental disorders* (5th ed.). Washington, DC: APA.

Avci, A., Diler, R. S., & Tamam, L. (1998). Fluoxetine treatment in a 2.5-year-old girl. *Journal of the American Academy of Child & Adolescent Psychiatry, 37*, 901–902. doi:10.1097/00004583-199809000-00005

Barterian, J.A., Rappuhn, E., Seif, E.L., Watson, G., Ham, H., & Carlson, J.S. (2014). Current State of Evidence for Medication Treatment of Preschool Internalizing Disorders. *The Scientific World Journal, 2014*, Article ID 286085, 8 pages. doi:10.1155/2014/286085

Carlson, J. S., Kratochwill, T. R., & Johnston, H. F. (1999). Sertraline treatment of 5 children diagnosed with selective mutism: A single-case research trial. *Journal of Child and Adolescent Psychopharmacology, 9*, 293–306. doi:10.1089/cap.1999. 9. 29doi:3

Celik, G., Diler, R. S., Tahiroglu, A. Y., & Avci, A. (2007). Fluoxetine in post-traumatic eating disorder in 2-year-old twins. *Journal of Child & Adolescent Psychopharmacology, 17*, 233–236. doi:10.1089/cap.2006.0057

Coskun, M., & Zoroglu, S. (2009). Efficacy and safety of fluoxetine in preschool children with obsessive-compulsive disorder. *Journal of Child & Adolescent Psychopharmacology, 19*, 297–300. doi:10.1089/cap.2008.055

Dummit, E. I., Klein, R. G., Tancer, N. K., Asche, B., & Martin, J. (1996). Fluoxetine treatment of children with selective mutism: An open trial. *Journal of the American Academy of Child & Adolescent Psychiatry*, 35, 615–621. doi:10.1097/00004583-199605000-00016

Ercan, E. S., Kandulu, R., & Ardic, U. A. (2012). Preschool children with obsessive–compulsive disorder and fluoxetine treatment. *European Child & Adolescent Psychiatry*, 21, 169–172. doi:10.1007/s00787-012-0244-2

Fanton, J., & Gleason, M. M. (2009). Psychopharmacology and preschoolers: A critical review of current conditions. *Child & Adolescent Psychiatric Clinics of North America*, 18, 753–771. doi:10.1016/j.chc.2009. 02. 00doi:5

Food and Drug Administration (2005). Worsening depression and suicidality in patients being treated with antidepressants. Content retrieved from: https://www.fda.gov/Drugs/DrugSafety/PostmarketDrugSafetyInformationforPatientsandProviders/ucm161679.htm

Gleason, M. M., Egger, L. H., Emslie, G. J., Greenhill, L. L., Kowatch, R. A., Lieberman, A. F., … Zeanah, C. H. (2007). Psychopharmacological treatment for very young children: Contexts and guidelines. *Journal of the American Academy of Child & Adolescent Psychiatry*, 46(12), 1532–1572.

Golwyn, D. H., & Sevlie, C. P. (1999). Phenelzine treatment of selective mutism in four prepubertal children. *Journal of Child & Adolescent Psychopharmacology*, 9, 109–113. doi:10.1089/cap.1999. 9. 10doi:9

Hanna, G. L., Feibusch, E. L., & Albright, K. J. (1997). Buspirone treatment of anxiety associated with pharyngeal dysphagia in a four-year-old. *Journal of Child & Adolescent Psychopharmacology*, 7, 137–143. doi:10.1089/cap.1997. 7. 13doi:7

Harmon, R. J., & Riggs, P. D. (1996). Clonidine for posttraumatic stress disorder in preschool children. *Journal of the American Academy of Child & Adolescent Psychiatry*, 35, 1247–1249. doi:10.1097/00004583-199609000-00022

Harvey, B. H., & Milne, M. (1998). Pharmacotherapy of selective mutism: Two case studies of severe entrenched mutism responsive to adjunctive treatment with fluoxetine. *Southern African Journal of Child & Adolescent Mental Health*, 10, 59–66. doi:10.1080/16826108.1998.9632346

Luby, J. L. (2013). Treatment of anxiety and depression in the preschool period. *Journal of the American Academy of Child & Adolescent Psychiatry*, 52(4), 346–358.

Oner, O., & Oner, P. (2008). Psychopharmacology of pediatric obsessive-compulsive disorder: Three case reports. *Journal of Psychopharmacology*, 22, 809–811. doi:10.1177/0269881107083362

Safer, D. J., & Zito, J. M. (2006). Treatment-emergent adverse events from selective serotonin reuptake inhibitors by age group: Children versus adolescents. *Journal of Child & Adolescent Psychopharmacology*, 16, 159–169. doi:10.1089/cap.2006.16.159

Wright, H. H., Cuccaro, M. L., Leonhardt, T. V., Kendall, D. F., & Anderson, J. H. (1995). Case study: Fluoxetine in the multimodal treatment of a preschool child with selective mutism. *Journal of the American Academy of Child & Adolescent Psychiatry*, 34, 857–862.

Concluding Remarks

Paula Barrett and Brian Fisak

This book is the first comprehensive resource focused specifically on anxiety in preschool-aged children. The book includes up-to-date scientific information related to preschool-aged anxiety from epidemiology and nosology to assessment, treatment and prevention. The present conclusion aims to provide a conceptual summary by highlighting the main themes across the chapters.

Regarding the epidemiology and the nosology of preschool anxiety, Barrios, Leppert, and Dougherty, in Chapter 1, showed that most studies reported a prevalence of preschool anxiety from 9% to 19% (Bufferd et al., 2011, 2012; Dougherty et al., 2015; Egger et al., 2006), which is similar to what has been reported for school-aged children (Copeland, Angold, Shanahan, & Costello, 2014; Lavigne, Arend, Rosenbaum, Binns, Christoffel, & Gibbons, 1998; Wichstrøm et al., 2012; Bufferd, Dougherty, Carlson, & Klein, 2011; Bufferd, Dougherty, Carlson, Rose, & Klein, 2012). However, in comparison with the higher prevalence of anxiety observed in school-aged and adolescent girls relative to boys, no gender differences have been found in preschool anxiety (Bufferd et al., 2011, 2012).

Preschool anxiety disorders have demonstrated high comorbidity with other anxiety, mood, and behavioral disorders, and symptoms tend to be stable over time (Franz et al., 2013). Therefore, anxiety disorders in preschool-aged children are associated with substantial impairment, and risk for later psychopathology. It is important to note that prevalence rates may be partly influenced by culture and environment (Howard, Muris, Loxton, & Wege, 2017; Wang & Zhao, 2015).

Due to the high prevalence and impairment caused by preschool anxiety, age specific assessment measures have been developed. There are generally valid measures for different types of informants; however, there is still much work to be done to improve the accuracy of the measures and integrate a developmentally sensitive approach that can help differentiate normative from pathological anxiety. An important challenge for evaluating anxiety in this age group is preschoolers' limited cognitive ability and self-expression (Cartwright-Hatton, Reynolds, & Wilson, 2011; Bufferd et al., 2016). Further, as information often comes from parents, they may sometimes misunderstand the causes of their child's fear and avoidance (Najman et al., 2000; De Los Reyes, Henry, Tolan, & Wakschlag, 2009). Regarding diagnostic categories of child anxiety, most have been well established, but some other controversial categories remain, such as agoraphobia.

During the assessment process, it is crucial to distinguish normative fears from pathological fears, understanding how social environment may shape specific fears (Burnham, Hooper, & Ogorchock, 2011). Fear of dark and strangers are the most common fears of this age group (Biederman et al., 2001; Field, 2006; Kagan, 2000). The distinction between normative and pathological fears depends on the level of physiological arousal experienced by the child, their age, and the level of avoidance and functional impairment. Most importantly, fear becomes problematic when the perceived experience of fear is more intense than the reality of the threat (Flavell, Green, & Flavell, 2000; Sayfan & Lagattuta, 2009).

Given the high prevalence and negative consequences raised by anxiety in preschool children, it is crucial to understand the transactional processes that occur between various risk and protective factors. Mian and Gray, in Chapter 2, have summarized this literature explaining how the dynamic interplay between various risk and protective factors can provide a more accurate picture of the etiology of anxiety disorders. Genetic risk, inhibited temperament, anxiety symptomatology, attentional biases, and coping mechanisms have been identified as risk factors (Gregory & Eley, 2007; Kundakovic & Champagne, 2015). Specifically, behavioral inhibition/shyness may be the most robust risk factor for child anxiety and has a strong genetic influence (Kagan, Reznick & Snidman, 1988; Mian, Wainwright, Briggs-Gowan, & Carter, 2011).

At the environmental level, exposure to trauma and parenting have been well established risk factors for child anxiety (Scheeringa & Zeanah, 2008). Regarding parenting, parents' information biases may lead them to engage in an "anxious parenting style," characterized by overprotection and modeling of anxiety (Fisak & Grills-Taquechel, 2007; Möller, Nikolić, Majdandžić, & Bögels, 2016). Furthermore, parental accommodation appears to mediate the relationship between parental and child anxiety symptoms (Jones, Lebowitz, Marin, & Stark, 2015). Other parenting variables, such as insecure attachment (Brumariu & Kerns, 2010; Ollendick & Benoit, 2012) and parenting stress (Pahl, Barrett, & Gullo, 2012), have also been found to be associated with child anxiety.

To date more research has been conducted on risk factors rather than protective factors. Regarding the existing research on protective factors, there are two parental behaviors that have been found to act as protective factors: autonomy granting and encouraging appropriate challenges (Lazarus et al., 2016; Silk, Morris, Kanaya, & Steinberg, 2003). Emotion regulation and prosocial skills in children, as well as healthy parent-child relationship, also appear to serve as protective factors (Howell, Graham-Bermann, Czyz, & Lilly, 2010; Katz, Hessler, & Annest, 2007).

Spence and Muris, in Chapters 4 and 5, have provided a comprehensive review of the available assessment measures and procedures for anxiety in preschool-aged children, including various child-, parent-, and teacher-report questionnaires, behavioral observation measures, and structured clinical interviews. Assessment instruments vary in terms of focus, length and type of informant.

The assessment process is used to gather information about the emotional, cognitive, behavioral and psychological components of anxiety, as well as the risk and protective factors, in order to clarify the causal and maintaining factors of anxiety (Grills-Taquechel, Ollendick, & Fisak, 2008; Garro, 2016; McLeod, Weisz, & Wood, 2007). Through careful assessment researchers and clinicians can identify children at risk and can provide useful information for case formulation and treatment progress. Researchers and clinicians need to consider the psychometric properties of the instrument and the cultural background of the preschool-aged children (Hunsley & Mash, 2008).

One limitation in regards to the assessment of anxiety in preschool-aged children is that many existing measures have yet to be updated to reflect DSM-5 diagnostic criteria. Further, continued efforts are needed to make age-appropriate modifications of existing measures. More specifically, most measures have been developed for older children, and as a result, psychometric properties with preschoolers need to be further investigated (La Greca, Dandes, Wick, Shaw, & Stone, 1988). To tackle this challenge, some self-report questionnaires such as the *Koala Fear Questionnaire* (KFQ; Muris et al., 2003) and the *Picture Anxiety Test* (PAT; Dubi & Schneider, 2009) have been created. These measures include situations that are illustrated with pictures, in order to make the fear and anxiety items more comprehensible for young children. There are also computerized assessments that use cartoons and interviews in which puppets are used to assess the social and emotional functioning of young children (Ablow et al., 2003; Measelle, Ablow, Cowan, & Cowan, 1998; Valla, Bergeron, & Smolla, 2000).

In Chapter 6, Barrett, Games, Fisak, Stallard and Phillips start with a description of the various anxiety disorders and the available treatments. Because etiological models emphasize a complex interaction between risk factors for the development of anxiety disorders, the main approach in treatment has been to identify and target malleable risk and protective factors (Rutter, 1985).

Most of the evidence-based treatments for anxiety disorders in preschool-aged children utilized mixed protocols based on CBT, which can be adapted to treat most anxiety disorders. Earlier treatments showed positive results and were delivered as individual CBT (i.e., Kendall & Southam-Gerow, 1996), family-based CBT (i.e., Wood et al., 2006), and Group CBT, with and without a parental component (Barrett et al.,

1996). However, most of these treatments have focused on children aged eight and beyond. During the last decade, more treatments have been developed particularly for preschool children, which are also divided into parents-only-programs (i.e., *Timid to Tiger* program, Cartwright-Hatton, McNally, White, & Verduyn, 2005), or combined parent-child treatments for specific disorders (Pincus, Santucci, Ehrenreich, & Eyberg, 2008). In general, these treatments have shown positive outcomes. However, more research is needed to replicate the findings, and further adaptations are needed in order to deliver age-appropriate treatments for this age group.

The *Fun FRIENDS* program (Barrett, 2007a, 2007b) was developed and several studies have reported positive results of the program in variables such as anxiety symptoms, behavioral inhibition, emotional and behavior strengths, parenting distress and parent-children interactions (Anticich, Barrett, Silverman, Lacherez, & Gillies, 2013; Barrett, Fisak, & Cooper, 2015; Carlyle 2014; Pahl & Barrett, 2010), including a recent study that showed that the effectiveness of the program may be enhanced when parents participate in a concurrent adult resilience program (Fisak, Gallegos, Verreynne, & Barrett, 2018).

For specific disorders such as OCD, PTSD, and selective mutism, more specialized treatment protocols are available. In Chapter 7, Iniesta-Sepúlveda and Storch start by describing the unique features of OCD for this age group, including their poor insight and extreme difficulty engaging in exposure. Research has shown that CBT is the first line of treatment for pediatric OCD, and this approach has been found to be well-accepted by parents. Overall, treatment protocols for OCD include psychoeducation and parental involvement, as there is strong influence of family behaviors and attitudes on the emergence and development of OCD in childhood (Farrell & Barrett, 2007; Waters, Barrett, & March, 2001).

In Chapter 8, Haag, Celi and Landolt discuss the unique features of PTSD displayed by preschool-aged children. In particular, preschool-aged children who suffer from PTSD, often display emotional and behavioral difficulties, internalizing and externalizing symptoms. Symptom presentation may be unique in this age group, as young children have limited emotion regulation and cognitive skills and rely more on caregivers to respond to their needs (Carpenter & Stacks, 2009). There is a need to develop standardized measures to assess PTSD in these young children in order to capture the developmentally more suitable subtype of PTSD that has been described in DSM-5 (APA, 2013).

There are three well evaluated treatments for trauma and PTSD in young children: Trauma-Focused Cognitive Behavioral Therapy (TF-CBT; Scheeringa, 2016), Child-Parent Psychotherapy (Lieberman, Ippen, & Van Horn, 2015), and Parent-Child Interaction Therapy (Eyberg, Nelson, Ginn, Bhuiyan, & Boggs, 2013). These last two have been focused on preschool-aged children and positive outcomes have been reported. Although TF-CBT has the strongest empirical foundation, more research about its effectiveness is needed on preschoolers.

Research on selective mutism is limited, relative to other childhood anxiety disorders. While the presence of selective mutism is determined on the basis of speaking behavior, non-verbal social behavior can be different among children with selective mutism. It is crucial that clinicians rule out the presence of a communication or language disorder and be able to provide a differential diagnosis from social anxiety or autism (Gensthaler et al., 2016; Toppelberg & Collins, 2010). Unique features of children with selective mutism, relative to other anxiety disorders, include a younger age of onset and treatment. Consequently, they are faced with difficulty in the cognitive elements of the treatment. Communication also places a barrier between the clinician and the child, and requires the incorporation of strategies for facilitating verbal communication with the therapist. Most importantly, for this specific disorder, the strongest impairment is often shown in the school environment. Consequently, a high level of participation of school staff and of the clinician at the school setting is necessary.

Behavioral treatments are mainly the recommended treatment for selective mutism (Muris & Ollendick, 2015), and efforts have been made to deliver these treatments in an intensive format. Although it is likely that this may produce benefits on symptom reduction (Lynas et al., in preparation), it is important to consider that this will not allow inhibitory learning experiences, which are key in the treatment of anxiety (Craske et al., 2008). Alongside the treatment for selective mutism, there are also available interventions to improve the parent-child interaction (i.e., Pincus et al., 2008) and to treat any language difficulty that may be producing speech-related anxiety in the child.

In summary, there is supporting evidence for treatment programs for anxiety disorders in preschool-aged children; however, more replication studies are needed, including the examination of potential moderators of treatment effectiveness. For all treatments, the challenge is to include developmentally sensitive adaptations for young children, such as reducing and tailoring cognitive components, incorporating play contexts, and including more parent involvement. Medication needs to be used as a last resource. In Chapter 11, it is recommended that psychopharmacological interventions are only used in severe, treatment-resistant cases, and following nonresponse to evidence-based psychosocial interventions. Caution needs to be exercised, as little is known about the safety and long-term impact of psychotropic medications on neurodevelopment in preschool-aged children.

Prevention programs have been developed and evaluated to address numerous psychiatric disorders, including anxiety disorders. In Chapter 10, Fisak, Persad, Gallegos and Barrett explained that there are a number of advantages to prevention. This includes covering a large number of children, therefore being less costly, targeting children at an age where patterns of thinking and behavior are less rigid. Further, the approach is more proactive and minimizes stigma. In addition, prevention programs do not always require mental health professionals for implementation, thus, prevention has the potential to increase the accessibility of services in underserved and economically disadvantaged areas (Barrett & Turner, 2001; Mrazek & Haggerty, 1994).

Prevention programs can be classified as either universal, selective, or indicated (Dozois & Dobson, 2004; Mrazek & Haggerty, 1994). Regarding universal programs, the outcome research is promising (Barrett 2007a, 2007b; Dadds & Roth, 2008), and the *Fun FRIENDS* program the most extensively evaluated (i.e, Anticich et al., 2013). Findings on these programs are positive, but more research is needed to address the challenge of the floor effect for universal programs, and at the other levels, an accurate identification that pairs risk factors with effective screening tools is crucial. Universal interventions in schools support an ecological and sustainable approach to resilience building. Children, parents, teachers and other school staff ought to learn the same skills for long-term sustainability and mutual reinforcement of positive coping behaviors. As such, the whole community learns to speak the same language – the language of resilience (e.g., see the *FRIENDS* resilience programs).

Selective and indicated interventions have focused mostly on children with behavioral inhibition/shyness. The most extensively evaluated targeted program is the *Little Cool Kids* (Kennedy, Rapee, & Edwards, 2009; Morgan et al., 2017; Rapee, 2013), and results from outcome studies have been promising. One challenge to selective programs is distinguishing treatment from prevention, as many shy children meet criteria for anxiety disorders by the time the program is implemented.

Overall, both selective and universal programs have yielded promising result. However, regardless of the level of prevention, more research is needed. Perhaps the most salient issue is that little is known about long-term effectiveness. It is important to consider the nature of change over time, and to assess both symptom reduction and reduction of risk factors. Long-term follow-up studies are sorely needed.

Overall, this book integrates valuable information on the advances on conceptualization, assessment and treatment/prevention protocols for preschool anxiety. Across all chapters, taking account of the developmental stage of preschool children during assessment and interventions is paramount. We need to focus on a transactional approach to assess, treat, and prevent anxiety disorders, and parental involvement as a key component during treatment and accurate evaluation. Finally, through the chapters, the importance of taking into consideration cross-cultural issues has been highlighted, as cultural experiences likely impact development and maintenance of anxiety disorders in preschool-aged children.

References

Ablow, J.C., Measelle, J.R., and the MacArthur Working Group on Outcome Assessment (2003). *Manual for the Berkeley Puppet Interview: Symptomatology, social, and academic modules (BPI 1.0)*. Pittsburgh, PA: University of Pittsburgh.

American Psychiatric Association (APA). (2013). *Diagnostic and statistical manual of mental disorders* (5th ed.). Arlington, VA: American Psychiatric Association.

Anticich, S. A. J., Barrett, P. M., Silverman, W., Lacherez, P., & Gillies, R. (2013). The prevention of childhood anxiety and promotion of resilience in preschool aged population: A universal school based trial. *Advances in School Mental Health*, 6(2), 93–121. Doi: https://doi.org/10.1080/1754730X.2013.784616

Barrett, P. M. (2007a). *Fun Friends. The teaching and training manual for group leaders*. Brisbane, Australia: Fun Friends Publishing.

Barrett, P. M. (2007b). *Fun Friends. Family learning adventure: Resilience building activities for 4-, 5-, and 6-year-old children*. Brisbane, Australia: Fun Friends Publishing.

Barrett, P. M., Dadds, M. R., & Rapee, R. M. (1996). Family treatment of childhood anxiety: A controlled trial. *Journal of Consulting and Clinical Psychology*, 64, 333–342.

Barrett, P. M., Fisak, B., & Cooper, M. (2015). The treatment of anxiety in young children: Results of an open trial of the Fun FRIENDS program. *Behavior Change*, 32(4), 231–242.

Barrett, P., & Turner, C. (2001). Prevention of anxiety symptoms in primary school children: Preliminary results from a universal school-based trial. *British Journal of Clinical Psychology*, 40, 339–410. doi:10.1348/014466501163887Biederman, J., Hirshfeld-Becker, D. R., Rosenbaum, J. F., Hérot, C., Friedman, D., Snidman, N., ... Faraone, S. V. (2001). Further evidence of association between behavioral inhibition and social anxiety in children. *American Journal of Psychiatry*, 158(10), 1673–1679.

Brumariu, L. E., & Kerns, K. A. (2010). Parent-child attachment and internalizing symptoms in childhood and adolescence: A review of empirical findings and future directions. *Development and Psychopathology*, 22(1), 177–203.

Bufferd, S.J., Dougherty, L.R., Carlson, G.A., & Klein, D.N. (2011). Parent-reported mental health in preschoolers: Findings using a diagnostic interview. *Comprehensive Psychiatry*, 52, 359–369. doi:10.1016/j.comppsych.2010. 08. 00doi:6

Bufferd, S.J., Dougherty, L.R., Carlson, G.A., Rose, S., & Klein, D.N. (2012). Psychiatric disorders in preschoolers: Continuity from ages 3 to 6. *American Journal of Psychiatry*, 169, 1157–1164. doi:10.1176/appi.ajp.2012.12020268

Bufferd, S. J., Dougherty, L. R., Olino, T. M., Dyson, M. W., Carlson, G. A., & Klein, D. N. (2016). Temperament distinguishes persistent/recurrent from remitting anxiety disorders across early childhood. *Journal of Clinical Child & Adolescent Psychology*, 1–10. doi:10.1080/15374416.2016.1212362

Burnham, J.J., Hooper, L.M. & Ogorchock, H.N. (2011). Differences in the fears of elementary school children in North and South America: A cross-cultural comparison. *International Journal of Advanced Counseling*, 33, 235–251.

Carlyle, D. A. (2014). With a little help from FUN FRIENDS young children can overcome anxiety. *Community Practitioner: The Journal of the Community Practitioners & Health Visitors Association*, 87(8), 26–29.

Carpenter, G. L., & Stacks, A. M. (2009). Developmental effects of exposure to Intimate Partner Violence in early childhood: A review of the literature. *Children and Youth Services Review*, 31(8), 831–839. doi:10.1016/j.childyouth.2009.03.005

Cartwright-Hatton, S., McNally, D., White, C., & Verduyn, C. (2005). Parenting skills training: an effective intervention for internalizing symptoms in younger children? *Journal of Child and Adolescent Psychiatric Nursing*, 18(2), 45–52.

Cartwright-Hatton, S., Reynolds, S., & Wilson, C. (2011). Adult models of anxiety and their application to children and adolescents. In Silverman, W. K., & Field, A. P. (Eds.), *Anxiety disorders in children and adolescents, second edition* (pp. 129–158). New York, NY: Cambridge University Press.

Copeland, W. E., Angold, A., Shanahan, L., & Costello, E. J. (2014). Longitudinal patterns of anxiety from childhood to adulthood: The Great Smoky Mountains study. *Journal of the American Academy of Child & Adolescent Psychiatry*, 53, 21–33. doi:10.1016/j.jaac.2013. 09. 01doi:7

Craske, M. G., Kircanski, K., Zelikowsky, M., Mystkowski, J., Chowdhury, N., & Baker, A. (2008). Optimizing inhibitory learning during exposure therapy. *Behavior Research and Therapy*, 46(1), 5–27. doi:http://dx.doi.org/10.1016/j.brat. 2007.10.003Dadds, M. R., & Roth, J. H. (2008). Prevention of anxiety disorders: Results of a universal trial with young children. *Journal of Child & Family Studies*, 17, 320–335. doi:10.1007/s10826-007-9144-3

De Los Reyes, A., Henry, D., Tolan, P.,& Wakschlag, L. S. (2009). Linking informant discrepancies to observed variations in young children's disruptive behavior. *Journal of Abnormal Child Psychology*, 37, 637–652. doi:10.1007/ s10802-009-9307-3

Dougherty, L. R., Leppert, K. A., Merwin, S. M., Smith, V. C., Bufferd, S. J., & Kushner, M. R. (2015). Advances and directions in preschool mental health research. *Child Development Perspectives*, 9, 14–19. doi:10.1111/cdep.12099

Dozois, D. A., & Dobson, K. S. (2004). *The prevention of anxiety and depression: Theory, research, and practice*. Washington, DC, US: American Psychological Association. doi:10.1037/10722-000

Dubi, K., & Schneider, S. (2009). The Picture Anxiety Test (PAT): A new pictorial assessment of anxiety symptoms in young children. *Journal of Anxiety Disorders*, 23, 1148–1157.

Egger, H. L., Erkanli, A., Keeler, G., Potts, E., Walter, B. K., & Angold, A. (2006). Test-retest reliability of the Preschool Age Psychiatric Assessment (PAPA). *Journal of the American Academy of Child & Adolescent Psychiatry*, 45, 538–549. doi:10.1097/01.chi.0000205705.71194.b8

Eyberg, S. M., Nelson, M. M., Ginn, N. C., Bhuiyan, N., & Boggs, S. (2013). *Dyadic parent-child interaction coding system: Comprehensive manual for research and training* (4th ed.). Gainesville: PCIT International.

Farrell, L. J., & Barrett, P. (2007). The function of the family in childhood obsessive-compulsive disorder: family interactions and accommodation. In Storch, E. A., Geffken, G. R., & Murphy, T. K. (Eds.), *Handbook of child and adolescent obsessive-compulsive disorder* (pp. 313–332). Mahwah, NJ: Lawrence Erlbaum Associates.

Field, A. P. (2006). The behavioral inhibition system and the verbal information pathway to children's fears. *Journal of Abnormal Psychology*, 115(4), 742–752.

Fisak, B., Gallegos, J., Verreynne, M., & Barrett, P. (2018). The results of a targeted open trial of the Fun FRIENDS combined with a concurrent parent-based intervention. *Mental Health and Prevention*, 10, 35–41, doi: https://doi.org/10.1016/j.mhp. 2018.03.001

Fisak, B., & Grills-Taquechel, A. E. (2007). Parental modeling, reinforcement, and information transfer: Risk factors in the development of child anxiety? *Clinical Child and Family Psychology Review*, 10(3), 213–231. doi:10.1007/s10567-007-0020-x

Flavell, J. H., Green, F. L., & Flavell, E. R. (2000). Development of children's awareness of their own thoughts. *Journal of Cognition and Development*, 1(1), 97–112.

Franz, L., Angold, A., Copeland, W., Costello, E. J., Towe-Goodman, N., & Egger, H. (2013). Preschool anxiety disorders in pediatric primary care: prevalence and comorbidity. *Journal of the American Academy of Child & Adolescent Psychiatry*, 52, 1294–1303. doi:10.1016/j.jaac.2013. 09. 00doi:8

Garro, A. (2016). Early childhood assessment: An integrative framework. In A. Garro (Ed.), *Early childhood assessment in school and clinical child psychology* (pp. 1–24). New York, NY: Springer Science + Business Media.

Gensthaler, A., Maichrowitz, V., Kaess, M., Ligges, M., Freitag, C. M., & Schwenck, C. (2016). Selective mutism: The fraternal twin of childhood social phobia. *Psychopathology*, 49(2), 95–107. doi : https://doi.org/10.1159/000444882

Gregory, A. M., & Eley, T. C. (2007). Genetic influences on anxiety in children: What we've learned and where we're heading. *Clinical Child and Family Psychology Review*, 10(3), 199–212. doi:10.1007/s10567-007-0022-8

Grills-Taquechel, A. E., Ollendick, T. H., & Fisak, B. (2008). Reexamination of the MASC factor structure and discriminant ability in a mixed clinical outpatient sample. *Depression and Anxiety*, 25(11), 942–950.

Howard, M., Muris, P., Loxton, H., & Wege, A. (2017). Anxiety-proneness, anxiety symptoms, and the role of parental overprotection in young South African children. *Journal of Child and Family Studies*, 26(1), 262–270. doi:10.1007/s10826-016-0545-z

Howell, K. H., Graham-Bermann, S. A., Czyz, E., & Lilly, M. (2010). Assessing resilience in preschool children exposed to intimate partner violence. *Violence and Victims*, 25(2), 150–164. doi:10.1891/0886-6708.25.2doi:150

Hunsley, J., & Mash, E. J. (2008). *A guide to assessments that work*. New York: Oxford University Press.

Jones, J. D., Lebowitz, E. R., Marin, C. E., & Stark, K. D. (2015). Family accommodation mediates the association between anxiety symptoms in mothers and children. *Journal of Child and Adolescent Mental Health*, 27(1), 41–51. doi:10.2989/17280583.2015.1007866

KaganJ. (2000). Inhibited and uninhibited temperaments: Recent developments. In W. R. Crozier (Ed.), *Shyness: Development, consolidation and change* (pp. 22–29). London: Routledge.

Kagan, J., Reznick, J. S., & Snidman, N. (1988). Biological bases of childhood shyness. *Science*, 240(4849), 167–171.

Katz, L. F., Hessler, D. M., & Annest, A. (2007). Domestic violence, emotional competence, and child adjustment. *Social Development*, 16(3), 513–538. doi:10.1111/j.1467-9507.2007.00401.x

Kendall, P. C., & Southam-Gerow, M. A. (1996). Long-term follow-up of a cognitive-behavioral therapy for anxiety-disordered youth. *Journal of Consulting and Clinical Psychology*, 64(4), 724–730.

Kennedy, S. J., Rapee, R. M., & Edwards, S. L. (2009). A selective intervention program for inhibited preschool-aged children of parents with an anxiety disorder: Effects on current anxiety disorders and temperament. *Journal of the*

American Academy of Child & Adolescent Psychiatry, 48, 602–609. doi:10.1097/CHI.0b013e31819f6fa9

Kundakovic, M., & Champagne, F. A. (2015). Early-life experience, epigenetics, and the developing brain. *Neuropsychopharmacology*, 40(1), 141–153. doi:10.1038/npp.2014.140

La Greca, A. M., Dandes, S. K., Wick, P., Shaw, K., & Stone, W. L. (1988). Development of the Social Anxiety Scale for Children: Reliability and concurrent validity. *Journal of Clinical Child Psychology*, 17(1), 84–91.

Lavigne, J. V., Arend, R., Rosenbaum, D., Binns, H. J., Christoffel, K. K., & Gibbons, R. D. (1998). Psychiatric disorders with onset in the preschool years: I. Stability of diagnoses. *Journal of the American Academy of Child & Adolescent Psychiatry*, 37, 1246–1254. doi:10.1097/00004583-199812000-00007

Lazarus, R. S., Dodd, H. F., Majdandžić, M., de Vente, W., Morris, T., Byrow, Y., ... Hudson, J. L. (2016). The relationship between challenging parenting behavior and childhood anxiety disorders. *Journal of Affective Disorders*, 190, 784–791. doi:10.1016/j.jad.2015. 11. 03doi:2

Lieberman, A. F., Ippen, C. G., & Van Horn, P. (2015). *Don't hit my mommy!: A manual for child-parent psychotherapy with young children exposed to violence and other trauma* (2nd ed.). Washington: Zero to Three.

Lynas, C. M. T., Pabis, J. M., Ioffe, M., Burt, N., Holzman, J., Kurtz, S. & White, K. (2019). Adventure Camp: Intensive group treatment for selective mutism.

McLeod, B. D., Weisz, J. R., & Wood, J. J. (2007). Examining the association between parenting and childhood depression: A meta-analysis. *Clinical Psychology Review*, 27(8), 986–1003.

Measelle, J.R., Ablow, J.C., Cowan, P.A., & Cowan, C.P. (1998). Assessing young children's views of their academic, social, and emotional lives: An evaluation of the self-perception scales of the Berkeley Puppet Interview. *Child Development*, 69, 1556–1576.

Mian, N. D., Wainwright, L., Briggs-Gowan, M. J., & Carter, A. S. (2011). An ecological risk model for early childhood anxiety: The importance of early child symptoms and temperament. *Journal of Abnormal Child Psychology*, 39(4), 501–512. doi:10.1007/s10802-010-9476-0

Möller, E. L., Nikolić, M., Majdandžić, M., & Bögels, S. M. (2016). Associations between maternal and paternal parenting behaviors, anxiety and its precursors in early childhood: A meta-analysis. *Clinical Psychology Review*, 45, 17–33. doi:10.1016/j.cpr.2016. 03. 00doi:2

Morgan, A. J., Rapee, R. M., Salim, A., Goharpey, N., Tamir, E., McLellan, L. F., & Bayer, J. K. (2017). Internet-delivered parenting program for prevention and early intervention of anxiety problems in young children: randomized controlled trial. *Journal of the American Academy of Child and Adolescent Psychiatry*, 56, 417–425. doi:10.1016/j.jaac.2017. 02. 01doi:0

Mrazek, P. J., & HaggertyR. J. (1994). *Reducing risks for mental disorders: Frontiers for preventative intervention research.* Washington, DC: National Academy Press.

Muris, P., Meesters, C., Mayer, B., Bogie, N., Luijten, M., Geebelen, E., Bessems, J., & Smit, C. (2003). The Koala Fear Questionnaire: A standardized self-report scale for assessing fears and fearfulness in preschool and primary school children. *Behavior Research and Therapy*, 41, 597–617.

Muris, P., & Ollendick, T. H. (2015). Children who are anxious in silence: A review on selective mutism, the new anxiety disorder in DSM-5. *Clinical Child* and Family Psychology Review, 18(2), 151–169. doi: http://dx.doi.org/10.1007/s10567-015-0181-y

Najman, J. M., Williams, G. M., Nikles, J., Spence, S. U. E., Bor, W., OCallaghan, M., & Andersen, M. J. (2000). Mothers' mental illness and child behavior problems: Cause-effect association or observation bias? *Journal of the American Academy of Child and Adolescent Psychiatry*, 39, 592–602. doi:10.1097/00004583-200005000-00013

Ollendick, T. H., & Benoit, K. E. (2012). A parent–child interactional model of social anxiety disorder in youth. *Clinical Child and Family Psychology Review*, 15(1), 81–91. doi:10.1007/s10567-011-0108-1

Pahl, K. M., & Barrett, P. M. (2010). Preventing anxiety and promoting social and emotional strength in preschool children: A universal evaluation of the Fun FRIENDS Program. *Advances in School Mental Health Promotion*, 3(3), 14–25.

Pahl, K. M., Barrett, P. M., & Gullo, M. J. (2012). Examining potential risk factors for anxiety in early childhood. *Journal of Anxiety Disorders*, 26(2), 311–320. doi:10.1016/j.janxdis.2011. 12. 01doi:3

Pincus, D. B., Santucci, L. C., Ehrenreich, J. T., & Eyberg, S. M. (2008). The implementation of modified parent-child interaction therapy for youth with separation anxiety disorder. *Cognitive and Behavioral Practice*, 15(2), 118–125.

Rutter, M. (1985). Resilience in the face of adversity: Protective factors and resistance to psychiatric disorder. *British Journal of Psychiatry*, 147, 598–611.

Rapee, R. M. (2013). The preventative effects of a brief, early intervention for preschool-aged children at risk for internalizing: Follow-up into middle adolescence. *Journal of Child Psychology & Psychiatry*, 54, 780–788. doi:10.1111/jcpp.12048

Sayfan, L., & Lagattuta, K. H. (2009). Scaring the monster away: What children know about managing fears of real and imaginary creatures. *Child Development*, 80(6), 1756–1774. doi:10.1111/j.1467-8624.2009.01366.x

Scheeringa, M. S. (2016). *Treating PTSD in preschoolers: A clinical guide*. New York: Guilford Press.

Scheeringa, M. S., & Zeanah, C. H. (2008). Reconsideration of harm's way: Onsets and comorbidity patterns of disorders in preschool children and their caregivers following Hurricane Katrina. *Journal of Clinical Child and Adolescent Psychology*, 37(3), 508–518. doi:10.1080/15374410802148178

Silk, J. S., Morris, A. S., Kanaya, T., & Steinberg, L. (2003). Psychological control and autonomy granting: Opposite ends of a continuum or distinct constructs? *Journal of Research on Adolescence*, 13(1), 113–128. doi:10.1111/1532-7795.1301004

Toppelberg, C. O., & Collins, B. A. (2010). Language, culture, and adaptation in immigrant children. *Child and Adolescent Psychiatric Clinics of North America*, 19 (4), 697–717. doi: https://doi.org/10.1016/j.chc.2010.07.003

Valla, J.P., Bergeron, L., & Smolla, N. (2000). The Dominic-R: A pictorial interview for 6- to 11-year-old children. *Journal of the American Academy of Child and Adolescent Psychiatry*, 39, 85–93.

Wang, M., & Zhao, J. (2015). Anxiety disorder symptoms in Chinese preschool children. *Child Psychiatry & Human Development*, 46, 158–166. doi:10.1007/s10578-014-0461

Waters, T. L., Barrett, P. M., & March, J. S. (2001). Cognitive-behavioral family treatment of childhood obsessive-compulsive disorder: preliminary findings. *American Journal of Psychotherapy*, 55(3), 372–387.

Wichstrøm, L., Berg-Nielsen, T. S., Angold, A., Egger, H. L., Solheim, E., & Sveen, T. H. (2012). Prevalence of psychiatric disorders in preschoolers. *Journal of Child Psychology and Psychiatry, 53,* 695–705. doi:10.1111/j.1469-7610.2011.02514.x

Wood, J. J., Piacentini, J. C., Southam-Gerow, M., Chu, B. & Sigman, M. (2006). Family cognitive behavioral therapy for child anxiety disorders. *Journal of the American Academy of Child and Adolescent Psychiatry, 45,* 314–321.

Index

Entries in *italics* denote figures; entries in **bold** denote tables.

For Product Safety Concerns and Information please contact our EU
representative GPSR@taylorandfrancis.com
Taylor & Francis Verlag GmbH, Kaufingerstraße 24, 80331 München, Germany